DATE

Harvard Historical Studies 121

Published under the auspices
of the Department of History
from the income of the
Paul Revere Frothingham Bequest
Robert Louis Stroock Fund
Henry Warren Torrey Fund

EDWARD ROSS DICKINSON

The Politics of German Child Welfare from the Empire to the Federal Republic

HARVARD UNIVERSITY PRESS

Cambridge, Massachusetts
London, England
1996

Library of Congress Cataloging-in-Publication Data

Dickinson, Edward Ross.
    The politics of German child welfare from the empire
to the Federal Republic / Edward Ross Dickinson.
        p.   cm. — (Harvard historical studies; 121)
    Includes bibliographical references and index.
    ISBN 0-674-68862-7 (alk. paper)
        1. Child welfare—Germany—History.
    2. Child welfare—Government policy—Germany—History.
    I. Title.   II. Series: Harvard historical studies; v.121.
    HV763.D53   1996
    262.7'0943—dc20   95-38644

Contents

Preface

This book treats the history of child welfare policy in Germany between 1871 and 1961. Through a close examination of this subject, it aims to take a fresh look at two central problems in modern German and European history. First, it addresses the question of the degree of continuity and discontinuity in German history in the last third of the nineteenth century and the first half of the twentieth. Second, it reexamines the question of the relationship between the modern welfare state and modern regime forms such as democracy and fascism.

I have chosen to approach these questions through an examination of one particular field of social policy for two reasons. In the first place, the greater detail and precision this approach permits has allowed me to treat complex issues without abandoning the concrete and detailed in favor of the abstract and overgeneralized. Second, and more important, the relatively narrow focus of this study has permitted me to examine a much longer span of time than is customary for this kind of study—the entire period from 1890 to 1961 in depth, and the years 1830 to 1890 and 1961 to 1991 in much less detail. I believe this broad chronological reach gives the book a particularly useful perspective, and has permitted me to reach more accurate and more meaningful conclusions than would have been possible had I taken 1933 or 1945 as my end point or focused on any one particular period (the Empire, the Weimar Republic, the Nazi period), as is more common among historians. In particular, this book attempts to redress an imbalance imposed by historians' inevitable fascination with National Socialism, by discovering *democratic* continuities between the Empire and the Federal Republic that were every bit as important as the antidemocratic continuities between the Empire and the Third Reich, on which historians have more commonly focused.

Partly because it does cover such a broad span of time, this study does not attempt to present an exhaustive history of any one particular area of child welfare policy. The microhistory of child welfare programs is fascinating, and the interested reader can pursue it in a literature which is by now truly vast and painstakingly detailed—for example on juvenile justice; reformatory education; the organization of directed leisure activities for young people ("youth cultivation" or *Jugendpflege*); morality legislation designed to "protect" young people from pornographic or aesthetically "worthless" literary, dramatic, or film productions, ribald public amusements, and so on; day care; vocational education; school health programs; efforts to control prostitution and venereal disease; efforts to reform illegitimacy law; eugenics; employment policy and apprenticeship programs for young people; child labor law; child study and child psychology; social insurance programs (which played an important role in securing health and other benefits for children but were organizationally distinct from "child welfare"); and the history of social work methods or social work training. This study, however, examines the *politics* of child welfare policy—not the development of particular programs and institutions but the political struggle to shape those programs and to define the aims of child welfare policy generally. In much of this book I have focused on three particular institutions: public legal guardianship, correctional education, and the centralized Youth Bureau. But I have done so only because the conflicts over the development of these three institutions illustrate with particular clarity the more general themes and problems I wish to pursue. Where developments in other programs or fields illuminate a point in a particularly useful way, I have broadened my focus.

This is not entirely standard practice for a historian, and it has entailed a regrettable sacrifice of detail (and in some cases of narrative continuity). I believe, however, that it also gives this book analytical depth and precision. In particular, it is one of the arguments of this book that the development of social policy most influenced politics at the level of the state precisely through the political conflicts that it unleashed—and *not* through the structure and methods of particular welfare programs or the (democratic, authoritarian, emancipatory, or genocidal) logic inherent in their daily operations, the language used by those active in them, or the assumptions on which they were founded.

There are, of course, a number of further limitations imposed by the approach I have chosen. First, the whole question of the accuracy of policy-makers' perceptions of social reality, and of the effectiveness of particular programs, is not addressed. Quite aside from the difficulties of figuring out what was "really" going on among working-class youth, an account of the social history of youth is beyond the scope of this study. As for the effectiveness of social policy, in some cases (such as that of infant welfare) it is virtually self-evident from crude statistics, while in most others (correctional education, juvenile justice, political or religious indoctrination) it would be almost impossible to reach any meaningful conclusions. In any case, the question is not one that is particularly relevant to the topic at hand; unfortunately, and as always, what mattered politically was what policymakers chose to believe, not what was really happening.

Second, this study concentrates—though by no means exclusively—on Prussia. In many cases, of course, it deals with national policies and national debates; in other policy areas, however, the states had a free hand, and child welfare policy in some parts of Germany (particularly in the southern states of Baden, Württemberg, and Bavaria, but to some extent also in the Hanseatic cities of Hamburg, Bremen, and Lübeck) differed considerably from policy in Prussia. The same can be said, though to a far lesser degree, of the states of the Federal Republic of Germany after 1949. Where it seemed important, I have briefly discussed different state policies, institutional structures, and regional cultures, and I hope that the attentive reader will come away with some feel for the nature of regional differences in policy. More than that is, again, simply beyond the scope of this book; and I believe that, in their grand outlines, different state policies represent for the most part variations on the common themes which are the focus of this study.

Third, I decided to leave out of this study the history of child welfare programs in the German Democratic Republic after 1945–1949, for two reasons. On the one hand, it was difficult or impossible in the period during which I completed my research (1988) to gain access to the papers of East German government agencies. On the other hand, I believe that the break made in child welfare policy in the late 1940s and the extraordinary social, political, and cultural transformation brought about by the communist regime in the 1950s was sufficiently profound to more or less remove the subsequent development from the framework I am analyzing here.

I should add, finally, that the published literature and archival records on the development of child welfare programs in Germany are vast. I cannot pretend to have exhausted them; my research has of necessity been selective in places. I hope I have identified and adequately pursued the critical issues. Because comparative analysis is the best corrective for this problem, I have tried in the notes to draw the reader's attention to the literature on child welfare policy in other countries; and this book is meant to be read in the context of that literature. A subsequent work on child welfare policy in the United States, Germany, and Italy will pursue a comparative perspective more systematically.

Acknowledgments

I am grateful to a number of people and organizations for helping me to complete this book. They are in no way responsible for its faults; but without their help it would never have been written.

First, I owe thanks to Gerald D. Feldman of the University of California at Berkeley, whose assistance to me went far beyond the duty of a dissertation supervisor. I could not have completed this study without his help and advice. Margaret L. Anderson, also of the University of California at Berkeley, was kind enough to subject the first draft of this study to a careful reading, and I have tried to profit from her cogent and insightful criticisms. James Leiby, of U.C. Berkeley's School of Social Work, took the time to read my dissertation and to attempt to broaden my perspective.

My research was supported by several institutions. The German Academic Exchange Service supported two trips to the Federal Republic of Germany, in 1987–88 and in 1989; I am most grateful to them for their financial support and for their patience and flexibility. The International Research and Exchanges Board (IREX), with funds provided by the National Endowment for the Humanities and the United States Information Agency, also supported the research for this book; none of these organizations is responsible for the views expressed. IREX supported my stay in the German Democratic Republic in 1988; again, I owe the IREX staff special thanks for their patient assistance. Two shorter trips in 1987 and 1989 were funded by U.C. Berkeley Humanities Graduate Research Grants; and two further trips in 1991 and 1992 were funded in part by the Internal Grants Committee of Victoria University of Wellington, New Zealand.

I am especially grateful to Wolfgang Strecker, director of the Archive of the Deutscher Caritasverband in Freiburg im Breisgau, and to Hans-Joseph Wollasch, director of the DCV's library. They made my stay not only productive but also a pleasure. I owe thanks as well to the Sozialdienst Katholischer Frauen for allowing me to use its archives, which are in the care of the Archiv des Deutschen Caritasverbandes. I am also particularly grateful to Helmut Talazko, director of the archive of the Diakonisches Werk der Evangelischen Kirche in Deutschland, in Berlin-Dahlem. I worked also in the Bundesarchiv Koblenz, the Geheimes Staatsarchiv Preussischer Kulturbesitz in Dahlem, the Historisches Archiv der Stadt Köln, the Nordrhein-Westfälisches Haupstaatsarchiv Düsseldorf, the Landesarchiv Berlin, the Evangelisches Zentralarchiv in Berlin, the Niederrheinisches Hauptstaatsarchiv Hannover, the archive of the Institut für Gemeinwohl at the Metallgesellschaft AG in Frankfurt am Main, the library of the Deutscher Verein für öffentliche und private Fürsorge in Frankfurt, the Zentrales Staatsarchiv Potsdam, the Zentrales Staatsarchiv Merseburg, the Stadtarchiv Berlin, the Staatsarchiv Potsdam, the Hauptstaatsarchiv Dresden, the Staatsbibliothek Preussischer Kulturbesitz in West Berlin, and the Staatsbibliothek in East Berlin; each of these institutions not only allowed me to use its holdings but also accommodated my special requests and sometimes erratic work habits. The Studentenwerk Freiburg was particularly helpful in solving logistical problems, as were the Ministerium fur Fach- und Hochschulwesen and the Humboldt-Universität in East Berlin.

I must thank also a number of my colleagues and friends for their generous help: Carole Adams, Patricia Bancik, my brother Ben Dickinson, Gudrun Egloff, Nicoletta F. Gullace, Young-Sun Hong, Sabrina Klein, Elliot Y. Neaman, Jessica A. Ogden, Erna Hellerstein Olafson, Troy Paddock, Horst Pietschmann, Alessandra M. Rauti, James J. Sheehan, Richard Wetzel, Bernd and Gela Teichgräber, and Ronald V. Yanosky.

Thanks also to my parents, of whom I am so proud, and who have stood by me in this as in all things.

Abbreviations

ADB	Archiv Deutscher Berufsvormünder (Organization of Professional Legal Guardians)
ADCV	Archiv des Deutschen Caritasverbandes, Freiburg
ADW	Archiv des Diakonischen Werkes der Evangelischen Kirche in Deutschland, Berlin-Dahlem
AFET	Allgemeiner Fürsorgeerziehungstag (General Conference of Correctional Education)
AGJJ	Arbeitsgemeinschaft für Jugendwohlfahrt und Jugendpflege (Working Group for Child Welfare and Youth Cultivation)
AIGM	Archiv des Instituts für Gemeinwohl, Metallgesellschaft AG, Frankfurt
ALR	Allgemeines Landrecht (Prussian Law Code)
ARSO	Arbeitsgemeinschaft sozialpolitischer Organisationen (Working Group of Social Policy Organizations)
BAK	Bundesarchiv Koblenz
BDF	Bund Deutscher Frauenvereine (Federation of German Women's Associations)
BGB	Bürgerliches Gesetzbuch (Code of Civil Law)
BJP	Bundesjugendplan (National Youth Plan)
BJR	Bundesjugendring (National Youth Council)
BSHG	Bundessozialhilfegesetz (Federal Social Services Law)
CAW	Centralstelle für Arbeiterwohlfahrtseinrichtungen, later ZVW (Central Bureau for Organizations for Workers' Welfare)
CDU	Christlich-Demokratische Union (Christian Democratic Union)

CSU	Christlich-Soziale Union (Christian Social Union)
CVWAC	Centralverein für das Wohl der arbeitenden Classen (Central Association for the Welfare of the Working Classes)
DCV	Deutscher Caritasverband (National Caritas Association) (until 1921 Caritasverband für das katholische Deutschland)
DDP	Deutsche Demokratische Partei (German Democratic party)
DGT	Deutscher Gemeindetag (National Association of Local Government)
DNVP	Deutschnationale Volkspartei (German National People's party)
DST	Deutscher Städtetag (National Municipal League)
DVAW	Deutscher Verein für Armenpflege und Wohltätigkeit (National Association for Poor Relief and Charities)
DVöpF	Deutscher Verein für öffentliche und private Fürsorge (National Association for Public and Private Welfare) (until 1919 DVAW)
DZJ	Deutsche Zentrale für Jugendfürsorge (National Center for Child Welfare) (from 1923 Deutsche Zentrale für freie Jugendwohlfahrt [National Center for Private Child Welfare])
EB	*Erziehungsberatung* (pedagogical counseling)
EFB	Evangelischer Frauenbund (Protestant Women's League)
EGBGB	Einführungsgesetz zum Bürgerlichen Gesetzbuch (Law for the Introduction of the Code of Civil Law)
EREV	Evangelischer Reichserziehungsverein (Protestant National Educational Association)
EZA	Evangelisches Zentralarchiv, Berlin
FAD	Freiwillige Arbeitsdienst (voluntary work service)
FAZ	Frauenarbeitszentrale (Women's Labor Center)
FDP	Freie Demokratische Partei (Independent Democratic party)
FEH	Freiwillige Erziehungshilfe (voluntary educational assistance)
FpVO	Fürsorgepflichtverordnung (Emergency Decree on Welfare Services)
GSAPKB	Geheimes Staatsarchiv preussischer Kulturbesitz, Dahlem
GSR	Gesellschaft für Soziale Reform (Society for Social Reform)
HASK	Historisches Archiv der Stadt Köln
HAV	Hauptamt für Volkswohlfahrt (Central Office for National Welfare of the NSDAP)
HJ	Hitlerjugend (Hitler Youth)
IKV	Internationale kriminalistische Vereinigung (International Criminological Association)
JGH	Jugendgerichtshilfe (juvenile court assistance)
JWA	Jugendwohlfahrtsausschuss (Child Welfare Committee)
JWG	Jugendwohlfahrtsgesetz (Child Welfare Act of 1961)

KAVH	Kaiserin-Auguste-Viktoria-Haus zur Bekämpfung der Säuglings-sterblichkeit im Deutschen Reich (Empress Auguste-Viktoria Institute for Combating Infant Mortality in the German Empire)
KDF	Katholischer Deutscher Frauenbund (National Catholic Women's Federation) (earlier Katholischer Frauenverband)
KFV	Katholischer Fürsorgeverein für Mädchen, Frauen und Kinder (Catholic Welfare Association for Girls, Women, and Children)
KJHG	Kinder- und Jugendhilfegesetz (Children and Young People's Welfare Act of 1991)
KP	*Kommunalpolitische Blätter: Zeitschrift für Gemeindepolitik und Gemeindesozialismus*
KMFV	Katholische Männerfürsorgeverein (Catholic Men's Welfare Association)
KPD	Kommunistische Partei Deutschlands (German Communist Party)
KRV	Kinderrettungsverein (Berlin) (Child-Saving Association)
LAB	Landesarchiv Berlin
Nachrichtendienst	*Nachrichtendienst des Deutschen Vereins für öffentliche und private Fürsorge*
NRWHSAD	Nordrhein-Westfälisches Hauptstaatsarchiv, Düsseldorf
NSDAP	Nationalsozialistische Deutsche Arbeiterpartei (National Socialist German Workers' Party)
NSF	Nationalsozialistische Frauenschaft (National Socialist Women's Organization)
NSHSAH	Niedersächsisches Hauptstaatsarchiv, Hannover
NSV	Nationalsozialistische Volkswohlfahrt (National Socialist People's Welfare)
Rep.	*Repositur* (papers or collection)
RJGG	Reichsjugendgerichtsgesetz (National Juvenile Justice Act of 1922)
RJWG	Reichsgesetz für Jugendwohlfahrt (National Child Welfare Act of 1922)
RStGB	Reichsstrafgesetzbuch (National Code of Criminal Law)
SA	Sturmabteilung (storm troops of NSDAP)
SAB	Stadtarchiv Berlin
SAD	Haupstaatsarchiv Dresden
SAP	Staatsarchiv Potsdam
SKF	Sozialdienst Katholischer Frauen (Catholic Women's Social Service) (earlier KFV)
SLW	Seraphisches Liebeswerk
SPD	Sozialdemokratische Partei Deutschlands (Social Democratic party of Germany)

USPD	Unabhängige Sozialdemokratische Partei Deutschlands (Independent Social Democratic Party of Germany)
Zentralblatt	*Zentralblatt für Vormundschaftswesen, Jugendgerichte, und Fürsorgeerziehung*
ZSAM	Zentrales Staatsarchiv Merseburg
ZSAP	Zentrales Staatsarchiv Potsdam
ZVW	Zentralstelle für Volkswohlfahrt (Center for Popular Welfare)

The Politics of German Child Welfare
from the Empire to the Federal Republic

Society, Politics, and Modern Social Policy

Since the late 1970s there has been a tremendous flowering of historical study of the welfare state. There is now an imposing body of literature on the origins and development of social policy in Europe, North America, Australia, and New Zealand, informed by a broad and nuanced spectrum of theoretical orientations. Particularly in the late 1970s and early 1980s, historians using the concept of social control studied in great detail the ways in which social policy served the needs of employers for the creation of a disciplined labor force, or, more broadly, sought to contain and control all those who posed a threat to middle-class norms of behavior and to the stability and efficiency of the capitalist social order in general. These included the dissolute and disrespectful poor, vagrants and vagabonds, beggars, the *Lumpenproletariat* generally, the mentally ill, single mothers or families in which the husband was not the sole breadwinner, criminals, prostitutes, rowdy or delinquent youth, alcoholics, and so forth.[1] This critical assessment was further refined by historians working with paradigms developed by the Frankfurt school or by French poststructuralists, who saw in welfare policy one aspect of the universal process of social rationalization, bureaucratization, and professionalization, of intensifying social discipline, of the medicalization of social problems and the growing power of scientific experts such as doctors and psychologists.[2]

Particularly since the late 1980s, feminist historians have explored in detail the ways in which ideas about men's and women's nature and appropriate social roles have shaped the aims and forms of social policy and social work, both by imposing limitations and by creating opportunities for women's activism, and the ways in which social policy has helped to reinforce or (more infrequently) undermine patriarchal social relations. An almost equally extensive literature, again largely feminist, has examined the relationships between social reformers and social workers on the one hand and the targets of policy on the other. In particular, much of this work has argued that a great deal of social policy grew not out of the grand social control ambitions of middle-class male experts but out of a distinctive set of values—above all nurture, responsibility, morality, self-sacrifice, and social harmony—embedded in nineteenth- and early twentieth-century women's culture and feminism; and that the relationship between social workers (usually women) and their clients (also usually women) was often an interactive one, in which clients sometimes elicited intervention and always sought to negotiate its terms and forms.[3] Since the 1980s comparative study of welfare policy by political scientists has given us an increasingly refined knowledge of the grand "strategic" social and political origins of welfare policy, and particularly of the ways in which differing social configurations gave rise to different policy structures.[4] Finally, a developing literature has described the growth of social policy as a progressive socialization of risk driven by the application of statistical and actuarial principles to social problems.

There are a number of important questions, however, which this recent literature has seldom addressed—questions which were often central to the earlier literature. In particular, with some important exceptions, the relationship between welfare policy and regime form has more or less dropped from sight. In the "social control" literature the formal political constitution and political ideas appear almost irrelevant, since social policy is seen as essentially a tool or an expression of the informal *social* power of a particular class or group. Comparative studies of welfare policy focus on explaining different policy structures in different countries but rarely ask why the welfare states—in all Western countries—are democratic or question the extent to which they *are* substantively democratic or the precise *sense(s)* in which they are. Similarly, with important exceptions, the feminist literature on social policy does not address the matter of the formal constitution of political power in Western societies, focusing instead on the politics of gender relations.[5] Histories of particular organizations have tended to treat the broader political context largely as a given.

The question of the relationship between state structure and social policy is, of course, one that must inevitably occur to the historian of Germany, a country that has played a pioneering role in the development of social policy and that also experienced four changes of regime in the century between 1850 and 1950. Indeed, the greatest exception to the current neglect of this issue is the recent literature on the German welfare state. Curiously, however, the literature on the development of social welfare in Germany has focused on the relationship of social policy to fascism and to eugenic and racist mass murder.[6] The relationship between welfare policy and *democracy* is rarely an important theme. Fifty years after the collapse of

National Socialism and the establishment of a stable democratic welfare state in West Germany, this approach has clearly become somewhat problematic. This is not to say that social policy in the period before 1933 did not contribute to the construction of a racist and fascist alternative to democracy, much less that the Holocaust is passé. The Holocaust in all its complexity remains the single most important event of modern history, the one thing that *must* be understood. But we can no longer understand it adequately—much less come to grips with its contemporary significance and relevance—by studying German history as if it ended in 1945. And the history of social policy in Germany and elsewhere is more than merely part of the prehistory of fascism. It *is* that; but it is also part of the prehistory of the democratic welfare state. We must place social policy—and the Nazi period—in the context of a continuing social, political, and cultural development.

Finally, and as an important corollary, the question of the relationship between welfare policy, fascism, and democracy is a particularly timely one. For, not only in Germany but throughout the West, both social policy and democratic institutions are apparently slipping into a crisis more profound than any since the 1930s; and at no time since 1945 has fascism—or at any rate its historical echo—been more popular and politically significant than it is today.

This study, then, attempts to "bring the state back in" (to borrow a phrase)[7] by examining in detail the politics and the political implications of one particular field of welfare policy, in one particular country, between the 1890s and the 1950s. Child welfare is an especially fruitful field of investigation for a number of reasons. It was often a leading sector in the development of welfare policy generally. Because intervention for the protection and disciplining of children involved abridging parental rights, child welfare raised the issue of the relationship between state and society with exceptional clarity, and was the field in which conflicts over the philosophical foundations and the grand aims of social policy were often most explicitly formulated. And ideas about child welfare policy were almost always explicitly political in their content, almost always quite consciously related to particular political convictions and ideals. Pedagogy is always rooted in an explicit or implicit ideal of the kind of people and thus the kind of society it aims to create. Child welfare policy is therefore always "about" politics, whether domestic or international, and usually both. This is by no means to assert that the people who made child welfare policy were unfeeling Machiavellians. Many of them were genuine humanitarians, involved in child welfare policy for the children's sake; many were motivated by the ethical imperatives of human or class solidarity; even more believed that they served in Jesus' cause. But the question of what social and political order would best serve the interests of children, the will of God, or the common needs of humanity, or at least of a particular social class, was always foremost in their minds. Germany, finally, is an exceptionally promising case for this kind of study precisely because its political history has been so tumultuous, making it possible to examine the ways in which welfare policy has "fit" into various kinds of regimes.

Industrialization, the Middle Classes, and the State: The Complexity of Social Reform

In order to accomplish the aim of this study, it is necessary first of all to abandon generalizations about "the" middle class and "its" ideology. These generalizations are certainly not meaningless: the fact that the middle classes dominated German society between 1860 and 1960 ruled out certain policy outcomes, since the various social groups that made up those classes shared some fundamental interests (for example, the legal institution of private property) and a certain cultural heritage (such as the culture of respectability). But the history of child welfare policy in Germany makes clear the limitations of what those generalizations can tell us. It is impossible for the historian of politics to speak of a single, unitary middle class as an agent in the making of social policy because the political struggles in which child welfare policy was forged were very often struggles *within* a middle class that was divided against itself in fundamental ways.

The response of the dominant classes to the process of industrialization and modernization was necessarily ambivalent. On the one hand, social, political, and cultural mobilization posed an existential threat to their social power and cultural hegemony. The movement of masses of people into industrial cities shattered the networks of dependency which had tied them to rural nobility or small-town bourgeoisie; removed them from the cultural complex of towns or villages, with their traditions, corporate social institutions, and local cultures; and often isolated individuals from their families, networks of patronage and dependency, and the Christian churches. All these ties were replaced by very different structures: the commercialization of the economy and the growing power of the market; wage labor in a fluid labor market; the awakening of class consciousness; growing participation in formal political processes; the commercialization of cultural consumption and the emergence of "mass" culture; secularization; and social mobility and new professional commitments in new kinds of economic units. These trends weakened older forms of social and cultural dominance, such as the power of the landholder, the personal authority of the employer, the authority of the priest, the habits and patterns of deference. At the same time, the emergence of mass political movements such as socialism, anti-Semitism, and political Catholicism, and of new economic organizations such as peasant populist parties, agrarian pressure groups, the trade unions, and employers' organizations, threatened the political power of the traditional elite.

On the other hand, the process of mobilization benefited the dominant social groups as much as it threatened them. Economic growth profited above all those with the capital to participate in it as investors and entrepreneurs. At the same time, the process of political mobilization gave the state, with which the dominant social classes identified, a new internal cohesion and legitimacy; and it expanded opportunities for the state to champion—both at home and abroad—the economic interests of what were called in Germany the "state-bearing" classes. Nationalism, after all, benefited the ruling classes at least as often as it did radical movements. More to the point, the dominant classes were themselves transformed by the process of mobilization. Economic change created new groups within these dominant classes whose social status and livelihood derived from their position in the new industrial economy—not merely industrialists, bankers, and entrepreneurial middlemen but also officials in the expanding bureaucracies of state and municipal government, teachers in the growing educational establishment, white-collar employees and technical specialists, managerial staff in commercial and industrial concerns, journalists, and so on. The nationalization of culture and the increasing fluidity of the economy gave the dominant classes a much higher degree of cohesion, whether political, cultural, social, or economic. The new media presented not only a threat to cultural hegemony but also the opportunity to create a much more pervasive and more easily politicized and manipulated *new* hegemony. And perhaps most important of all, the social mobilization of the dominant classes themselves brought about a massive proliferation of voluntary organizations—cultural, political, economic, charitable, and professional. These constituted the new informal government of society and the informal self-government of the dominant classes; they gave, or attempted to give, order and structure to a society which had burst the bonds of its inherited social constitution. Never entirely autonomous of the organs of the state, by the beginning of the twentieth century these organizations formed an increasingly dense web, and their influence was ever more pervasive.

As Jacques Donzelot has pointed out in the case of France, therefore, there were two fundamentally divergent middle-class responses to the social transformation brought about by industrialization; and these became the bases of two broad strategies of bourgeois social reform, two approaches to the problem of governing a mobilized society. One was socially and culturally conservative, familialist and hierarchical, repressive and authoritarian, traditionalist, backward-looking. It sought to re-create social harmony and social stability in a society in turmoil by reimposing the social and cultural patterns of preindustrial society: face-to-face social relations of authority and dependence; the culture of deference, Christian faith, and morality; the cohesion and power of the extended family and the power of (biological or metaphorical) fathers. This was to be accomplished through mechanisms of coercive intervention where natural dependence had broken down and through the orchestrated revival of traditional Christian culture, with its emphasis on humility, obedience, and self-restraint. Rejecting the formation of mass bureaucracies, the fluidity of social relations, the active participation of the masses in political and social life, and the flexibility of administrative "norms" (Donzelot's term), the champions of this strategy remained loyal to the ideal of adjudication, of a society structured by clear-cut legal "standards" enforced by judges and founded on the socializing function of the private family—and one in which the masses of the population were essentially passive. The fundamental character of this reform strategy is best summed up by the word its adherents used to characterize the bygone golden age of social order: it was "patriarchalist."

There was, however, a second middle-class response to social change, an optimistic, socially and culturally progressive one. Rather than seeking a return to a static social order, it sought to *direct* the energies released by modernization—to achieve social harmony, political stability, and national power through the ordering and management of the processes of social, political, cultural, and economic mobilization. Its proponents assumed that by creating modern institutions and flexible administrative agencies and rules appropriate to a mass society, they could shape a dynamic, powerful national society in which individuals liberated from the constraints of the preindustrial social order would be constructively integrated into the economy and polity. Deference and passivity would be replaced by committed participation and the pursuit of opportunity, and personal relations of dependence would be replaced by the constraints and incentives of institutions designed to structure mass society according to its own principles. Political and economic participation would foster not rebellion and chaos but stability and power. The place of Christian morality as the foundation of social order would be taken by scientific realism, nationalism, and intelligent self-interest. I characterize this strategy as social-managerial and progressive (see Chapter 1). Many, but not all, of its advocates were social-liberals; and many more were—in the sense that they were fascinated with military and economic power as a source of national well-being—imperialists.

To some extent these reform strategies reflected the divergent experience and social place of different groups within the middle classes. The champions of the first were often priests, judges, committed Christians of the old bourgeoisie; those of the second might be managers, professionals, and municipal administrators of the so-called new middle class. For the most part, however, the sociological and intellectual distinctions between these two strategies were not so clear. Most middle-class people are, after all, both threatened and inspired by the ongoing social revolution they experience.

Moreover, while intellectual systems are generally coherent and consistent, consciousness rarely is; it is quite common for one person to subscribe simultaneously to two contradictory perspectives. Finally, these two systems were also not entirely contradictory. Coercive patriarchalist and managerial or social-liberal policies could often be combined as parts of a carrot-and-stick sociopolitical strategy, as complementary responses to "deviant" and "normal" targets of social policy, or in the form of attempts at authoritarian political and social mobilization.

Despite this pattern of overlap and of unclear distinctions, however, there were fundamental tensions between the two middle-class responses to the formation of industrial society. As Donzelot has pointed out, in the early twentieth century these tensions developed, not only in France but throughout the West, into a "general confrontation." In this period the divergence of intellectual commitments and social perspectives which gave rise to these two strategies condensed into a bitter conflict between two opposing middle-class cultures—one scientific and implicitly materialist, the other religious and romantic; one committed to the state and to bureaucratic administrative power and accepting of the forms of mass society, the other committed to the power of the autonomous social organizations of the dominant classes or of the preindustrial social order and to face-to-face personal relations; one championing participation, the other authority; one committed to scientific rationalism, innovation, dynamism, and motion, the other to revealed truth, tradition, and stasis.

This cultural and political confrontation was further complicated, however, by the existence of a more libertarian tradition, institutionally anchored in the judiciary, which was hostile to the interventionist aims of both patriarchalist and social-managerial reformers. As we will see, this native hostility of the judiciary (and of jurists and lawyers generally) both to the administrative application of "norms" to society and to the curtailment of individual rights through an aggressive enforcement of legal "standards" has historically been decisive in the evolution of child welfare policy. It has both limited its impact and driven forward the evolution of its forms. Furthermore, a very different but equally important role was played by the medical profession. In the development of child welfare policy and programs, doctors were often the group most committed to public intervention; but their professional ambitions and intellectual commitments brought them into conflict not only with jurists and Christians but also with social workers and social reformers.

In addition to these intellectual and professional divisions, moreover, the middle classes were also divided internally along gender lines. The German women's movements can often be identified more or less closely with one or the other of the great social reform currents. Protestant and Catholic women's organizations, for example, were closely tied to the churches and in most respects socially conservative, while the small secular women's groups were closer to left-liberal and progressive groups. But one purpose of all the women's organizations was to define and champion women's interests and concerns specifically, as distinct from men's interests and concerns; and the ways in which they did so were of critical importance for the formulation of social policy, for the development of the profession of social work, and in the political process of policy-making. At times women reformers found themselves opposing, on the basis of their particular interests and values, even groups of men with whom they otherwise had a great deal in common politically and intellectually. More often the development of policy has been guided by the existence of a distinct set of "women's" values and issues (which united women across ideological, religious, and social divides) and of distinct and frequently pioneering women's welfare organizations.

Most decisive of all in the development of child welfare policy in Germany, finally, has been the division of the German middle classes along religious lines—the confessional rift within German Christianity and the peculiar place in German society of the Catholic subculture and the powerful social, political, and religious institutions rooted in it. German Catholicism was committed both to Christian moralism and to the rights of parents and of the church under natural law; it was fundamentally alienated from the German state by the *Kulturkampf* of the 1870s and by its own hostility to the totalizing claims of nationalism; it was socially conservative but little susceptible to imperialist and authoritarian statist enthusiasms; and it was consistently more flexible in its methods than was German Protestantism. As we will see, it played an increasingly central role in debates over the methods and political organization of child welfare policy. By the 1950s Catholic social and political thought (championed by Christian Democracy) achieved outright dominance in social policy.

In addition to these divisions within the middle class, the development of child welfare policy in modern Germany has orbited relentlessly around the problem of the political and social abyss separating middle-class reformers of all stripes from the working-class people who were the targets of their efforts. By replacing the social power of the dominant classes—whether exercised "privately" and personally or by institutions whose authority was traditional and often more or less informal—with the public exercise of administrative and legal power, child welfare policy, like all social policy, exposed the power of those classes to public critique and political response by the organizations of the lower classes. Indeed, the creation of public agencies of social discipline made it distinctly possible, in the context of political mobilization and democratization, that the dominant classes would actually lose control over these organs of the government of society. German Social Democracy was slow to develop its own conceptions of social policy and concrete commitments regarding the structure of the state before the transition to socialism. By the 1920s, however, it had become an important player in the struggle to shape the political organization of child welfare policy, and it played a decisive role in the period after 1945. And the *potential* threat of organized socialism has always been central to the calculations of middle-class reformers and administrators of all stripes, shaping their thinking and their agendas in the most fundamental ways.

Even aside from the political role of socialism, finally, the dissolution of the direct connections between social power, economic power, and cultural authority made working-class resistance to public programs particularly tenacious. As middle-class people complained, it was often possible for the targets of intervention to disappear in the anonymity of a large city. The solidarity of urban and rural subcultures in the face of intervention by alien agencies and elites, too, sometimes heightened the effectiveness of personal resistance. What is more, middle-class social reformers often believed that social policy could not be effective unless it met with a certain degree of understanding and cooperation among the working classes. The passive and active resistance of the latter therefore had an important impact not merely on the success or failure of particular programs but on the policy-making process as well. Again, political and individual resistance not only limited the impact of policy but also forced its evolution forward, either toward intensifying coercion or toward cooperation, persuasion, and consensus building.

Perhaps the most fundamental problem of modern German political life has been that of creating a viable relationship between the state and this mobilized and divided society, a state structure appropriate to the new social constitution created by industrialization. The determination of the dominant classes to maintain their hold over the state and society, the need to create an effective and efficient industrial social order, and the clear necessity of generating a new degree of consent and a new legitimacy for the state and its policies among a politically enfranchised population all made an expansion of the state's direct role in the government of society unavoidable. While the outcome may have resembled a one-way street in its grand institutional pattern, the presence of all these different interests—"patriarchalist," social-liberal, progressive, juristic, medical, socialist, Protestant, Catholic, feminist—meant that the process by which the modern social-interventionist state and social policy were made more often resembled a demolition derby. The problem of constructing an organization of social policy which could direct the lives and gain the consent of the lower classes while at the same time reconciling competing ideological commitments within the dominant classes was, in retrospect, a desperately complicated one. Whereas the emergence, growth, and gross outlines of public social policy reflected the grand imperatives imposed by the social transformation

of industrialization, this study will show that the specific *political* potentials of the development of social policy were determined precisely by the
dynamics of the political conflicts between and among these various
groups.

The discussion of the origins of fascism in the literature on German history
has revolved around the relative importance and role of premodern cultural, institutional, and social survivals and of capitalist and democratic
modernity, with some scholars seeing fascism as the product of the survival
of archaic ("feudal" or "premodern") social groups and values into the
modern age, and others seeing it as a product of the peculiar nature of capitalist modernization in Germany.[8] In this study I argue that the origins of
both fascism and democracy lie neither in modernity nor in archaism, neither
in a deficit nor in an excess of progress. Both modern, social-managerial
strategies and antimodern, patriarchalist strategies could be built either
into a fascist solution to the problem of creating a viable industrial social
order, or into a *democratic* solution. And the crucial problem for the construction of social policy has been the political necessity of accommodating
both approaches. To use a geologic metaphor, these regime structures re-
semble landscapes made up largely of the same fundamental blocks of terrain (some more recent, some more ancient in origin), organized into very
different relationships with one another. The nature and shape of those
blocks of social, intellectual, and cultural terrain made various modern regime structures possible, but they did not dictate their creation.

    It was, therefore, not the imperatives but the *choices* inherent in reform
cultures, social thought, and social policies which made them contributors
to the establishment of fascism or of democracy. Political culture, political
context, and political choice determined the political consequences of social
change.

    For this reason the reader will find neither "good guys" nor "bad guys"
in these pages. This book tries to do justice to the complexity and flexibility
of ideas, institutions, and people, to their potential for both good and evil.

CHAPTER ONE

The Inception of Modern Child Welfare Policy, 1840–1895

Christian and Liberal Social Reform in the Early Nineteenth Century

The basic terms and patterns of modern child welfare policy in Germany grew out of the middle-class response to the social transformation of the early nineteenth century—the gradual disintegration of the corporate social order of closed rural communities; of guilds with their hierarchy of master, journeyman, and apprentice; of parish and small town, of the relationship of lord and peasant, under the impact of industrial capitalism, population growth, and migration. The central term in the middle-class analysis of this transformation was *Verwahrlosung*. Literally, *Verwahrlosung* means "without protection," and it described the condition of people who were deprived of the support of traditional institutions and social networks—paupers, the vagabond poor, beggars, orphans, and above all urban proletarians, who were isolated from their rural communities by migration, from the churches by their failure to penetrate the new industrial cities, from their families by factory labor. *Verwahrlosung*, however, also described a spiritual state, an inward condition of disorder that is best translated by the English term "wayward." For in nineteenth-century theory the function of social institutions was not only to meet people's material needs but also to give them moral and spiritual guidance, to protect them from their own natural, sinful natures through the imposition of obedience to rational authority and moral law. Their isolation from authoritative social institutions was therefore believed to allow the development in "wayward" people of a "disposition toward the bad," "bad tendencies," "immorality," and "depravity."[1] In the eyes of middle-class people, in fact, poverty was not primarily a *cause* but a *consequence* of spiritual waywardness, since deficient self-discipline and dissolution made it impossible for the wayward to live an orderly, productive life.

Not coincidentally, crime, which middle-class observers regarded as above all a moral rather than a "social" phenomenon, was for them a more meaningful symptom of social collapse than were poverty and mortality. And the most serious of all symptoms of waywardness was the political movement of the lower class—their revolt against authority and social order. Yet, it was not only the poor who were wayward: on the contrary, most middle-class reformers—in the 1840s and throughout the century—believed that the social and political crisis of their age was above all a product of the unrestrained pursuit of personal gain by the *wealthy,* their heartless exploitation of the laboring classes, their materialism and greed, their corruption of the legal and political systems.

There were two divergent responses to social transformation and the problem of waywardness. Although the Protestant response was more aggressive, conservative Christians of both faiths regarded the social transformation of the early nineteenth century as symptomatic of a deeper spiritual crisis induced by rationalism, materialism, the faith in man's capacity to shape his own life, and liberal legislation emancipating the individual from the norms and institutions of traditional society. The Christian social reform impulse in this period was therefore fundamentally an impulse toward religious revival. It included the distribution of tracts and Bibles, the founding of "urban missions" and Bible study groups, temperance agitation and a campaign for the prohibition of work on Sundays, evangelization among seamen and prisoners, organizations for the "rescue" of prostitutes, and so on. And the many Christian charitable enterprises that proliferated after about 1830 pursued not merely the amelioration of suffering but also the salvation of the soul—by imposing orderly, moral behavior through the threat of withholding benefits, by protecting those they helped from temptation (for example, by erecting hostels for seamen or for reformed prostitutes), or by winning direct personal influence over the poor through charitable "visiting."

In conservative Christian thought (Catholic and Protestant), the family was the foundation of the social order, the key institution of Christian society. On the one hand, it was through its relationship with its father that the child learned willing obedience to legitimate, loving authority, and thereby learned to understand the authority of God. On the other hand, it was also in the family that the child learned to love others and gained the capacity for self-sacrifice and ethical self-restraint, above all through the example of the mother. Both these pedagogical functions of the family were essential to social order. If individuals were incapable of recognizing and obeying authority and of curbing their own egoistic desires, society would dissolve into a war of all against all. Much of the Christian social reform movement, therefore, was focused on the family and children, above all on the effort to develop a self-consciously Christian family life, since, as the pedagogical theorist Ludwig Völter pointed out, "religion is the support of families, as of states; where it is lacking, there also household happiness and household discipline will be lacking. . . . Disunity, domestic strife, marital infidelity, the lust for entertainment outside the home, dissipation, play, drunkenness, impoverishment, and need will win the upper hand."[2]

Christian, and particularly Protestant, reformers also concentrated their efforts on the "rescue" of children whose families had already "failed," leaving them "wayward." If these children could be brought up to be pious and obedient adults, the most threatening human by-products of the social crisis—criminals, prostitutes, socialists—would disappear. The "House of Salvation," or *Rettungshaus,* therefore became one of the central institutions of the Christian social reform movement. The first such *Rettungshäuser* were established by anti-Enlightenment pietist circles in southern and central Germany in the 1820s; but the methods and theory of the *Rettungshäuser* were systematized by Johann Hinrich Wichern, whose "Rauhes Haus," founded in Hamburg in 1833, was the most influential of these early Houses of Salvation. The *Rettungshaus* as envisioned by Wichern reproduced the structure of the preindustrial patriarchal family. Each was under the direction of a "house father" and was staffed by lay "brothers," and the spiritual reformation of the child was accomplished by the enforcement of strict obedience, by constant admonition and moral instruction, by the example of Christian life provided by the staff, and by the beneficial influence of supervised agricultural and artisanal labor.

Through tireless agitation in Protestant reform circles and through the publication of one of the earliest charity journals in Germany, the *Fliegende Blätter aus dem Rauhen Haus,* Wichern forged a coherent *Rettungshaus* movement; by 1847 there were sixty-four *Rettungshäuser* in Germany.[3] And by that date Wichern's efforts had become the focal point for Protestant social reform activity—which also included, in the field of child welfare, the Protestant Education Associations (*Erziehungsvereine*) and Child-Saving Associations; the Protestant day schools *(Kinderbewahranstalten);* Theodor Fliedner's great school for Protestant deaconesses and day school teachers at Kaiserswerth (1835); and the Protestant youth organizations for journeymen and young workers, the Evangelische Jünglingsvereine (founded in 1834). In 1848, at the urging of Wichern, this reform movement was given institutional focus with the formation by the Protestant church of the Centralausschuss für Innere Mission (Central Committee for Domestic Missions, or Inner Mission). Thereafter, Protestant charitable activity entered a new phase of expansion. By 1868, for example, there were 355 *Rettungshäuser* in Germany.[4] And the development of the Catholic charities—partly in defensive response to Protestant activity—was almost equally impressive; these included the Society of Saint Vincent de Paul, the

Good Shepherdesses (Gute Hirtinnen, who cared for wayward girls) and Sisters of Mercy (Barmherzigen Schwestern), the formation of young men's associations under Adolf Kolping (from 1846), and a growing number of Catholic equivalents to the Houses of Salvation—43 by 1850, 141 by 1860.[5] Both confessions also founded a growing number of institutions for the care of retarded children (9 by 1860, 15 in the 1860s, 8 in the 1870s, 13 in the 1880s).[6]

These conservative Christian reform efforts were paralleled by a very different social reform movement among liberals. In contrast to their conservative counterparts, liberal reformers believed that the process of social change was an essentially positive one of social and material progress and spiritual liberation, and they saw the upheaval of the 1840s more often as a transitional stage than a fundamental crisis. For them social reform was a means of preserving the fundamentals of the liberal social order rather than of counteracting them. Indeed, the Central Association for the Welfare of the Working Classes (Centralverein für das Wohl der arbeitenden Classen, or CVWAC), the most important organizational expression of the liberal reform movement, was founded in 1844 in part by industrial entrepreneurs from the Rhineland, who sought to extend the achievements of the infant industrial economy and protect it from the danger of social revolution by ameliorating the lot of the working classes. Rather than placing the problem of morality and the individual will at the heart of their theory of social order, they focused on the imperatives and opportunities with which people were confronted by the institutions within which they lived. They sought to devise institutional innovations and global solutions that would equalize opportunity, and above all to teach the values that underlay the new commercial-capitalist social order. Their goal was to provide the working poor with the skills and the organizational and material resources that would allow them to hold their own in the emerging new society— what they called "help toward self-help" (Hilfe zur Selbsthilfe). Their ideal for the working classes was thus not dependence and deference but self-help and initiative; not restoration and static harmony but progress and the harmony born of dynamic growth.

While Christian reform tended to find expression in paternalistic forms such as charity associations and the Rettungshaus, liberal reformers focused on consumers' and producers' cooperatives; health insurance, pension, and burial funds; savings banks; schools for factory children and apprentices and adult education groups (Bildungsvereine); or housing reform and public health and hygiene programs.

As we will see in later chapters, the fundamental philosophical tensions between these two traditions would trouble German social reform throughout the nineteenth and twentieth centuries. In practice, however, these two reform impulses were not always very distinct. Most German liberals were practicing Protestants, and shared many of the assumptions of their more conservative counterparts. The terms of liberal social analysis, particularly regarding the family, were often secularized versions of conservative Christian views—with paternal rationality, for example, standing in for the divine authority and moral law, or ignorance for sinfulness. The two groups often worked together as a single "humanitarian" party. Wichern, for example, was a longtime member of the CVWAC, where he agitated particularly for prison reform.

Finally, though for different reasons, both reform currents shared an aversion to state intervention. For liberals, state intervention would only slow progress and sabotage the resolution of the social problem by restricting the initiative of the individual citizen, either by oppressive regulations or by fostering dependence and passivity. For conservative Christians, state intervention was at best irrelevant, since they believed that the state could not by nature address the deeper *spiritual* causes of social crisis. The state could only support the efforts of Christian individuals to gain spiritual influence over the "wayward" by prohibiting vice or distributing subsidies. Given this anti-interventionist consensus, state action in the field of child welfare was limited, before the 1870s, to a smattering of (largely unenforced) child labor laws, subsidies to private charities, and some regulation of foster care. The creation of the public school system was the greatest child welfare measure of this period. In fact, particularly in Prussia, economic liberalization was fundamentally conceived of as the heart of a reasonable social policy.

The 1870s: From Restraint to Intervention

By the 1870s, as the industrial economy began to boom, middle-class observers were increasingly alarmed by the condition of German youth. In particular, conservative Christians, of both confessions and in very different regions, remarked on the growing restlessness and immorality of young people. In a report published in February 1876, for example, the Royal Consistorium of the Province of Prussia deplored the "sad relations between domestics and their employers, apprentices . . . and masters, workers and employers"; the decline of "deference, gratitude, and filial piety"; rising "work-shyness," obstinacy, unreliability, gluttony, drinking, and "sexual intemperance"; the labor shortage on the land (the product of the selfishness of young people who went to the city to make good); the obsession with dress and appearance among females; and "feverish chasing after money, concern only for this life, a blasé attitude, and open confession of atheism" among the young.[7] In the same year the Catholic Anton Kohler condemned the youth of Baden for "their disobedience, their lack of love, their stubbornness, their ingratitude," their "sassy, inconsiderate manner," their "nonsense and pretentiousness"; for tearing families asunder to move to the city; for the "mockery and scorn" they heaped on relatives and teachers; for desecrating "holy places and sacred objects," spending too much time in taverns, and singing "shameless songs." The youth of his day, he complained, "resist laws, constitution, and institutions out of sheer wantonness," and he asked, "What separates such a generation, that wants not to obey but rather to command, that wants not to listen but to rule, from open revolt against spiritual and secular authority, from disturbing the public order and security?"[8]

Critics sought the causes of the decline of young people's morality in virtually every aspect of the process of social transformation. As the Consistorium complained in its report, child labor in factories, and the greed and ignorance of parents who encouraged it, meant "that the children are already at an early age removed from the parental household and an orderly upbringing." The claims of the factory on fathers and mothers had the same effect. But "to this must be added also the dominant materialism of the *Zeitgeist*" with its many consequences—peep shows, newspapers, outrageous theater pieces, display windows full of "certain pictures," and "the false revolutionary teachings and agitation of the social democrats."[9] Kohler was even more sweeping. Nationalism and national culture, he argued, undermine the basis of traditional morality, for "where . . . local customs fall, there fall with them also moral and political limits which had resisted the corrupt currents of our times." Even worse was the impact of capitalism: "The great majority today," he believed, "prays to the golden calf, and bends its knee before money!" Witness "stock swindles, usury, industrial empire-building . . . materialism, egoism, liberalism, and the lust for emancipation." The result would be like the "Paris Commune and the bloody years of the French Revolution," for "once mankind has lost the guiding star of faith, it sinks back into barbarism."[10]

Part of the middle-class response to this growing sense of unease about youth was simply the expansion of initiatives that had their origin in the 1830s and 1840s, such as religious organizations for girls and boys, day schools, evangelization, school savings plans, and so forth. Among liberal reformers, efforts to improve young people's relation to their work gave rise in the 1870s to a movement for "boys' craftsmanship" *(Knabenhandarbeit)* and "home craftsmanship" *(Hausfleiss)* and growing attention to vocational education and apprenticeship. By the middle of the 1870s, however, numbers of bourgeois social reformers were convinced that private and local efforts alone were insufficient to order industrial society. As Anton Kohler wrote, the Child-Saving Associations were of course "praiseworthy institutions," but they lacked the authority to combat the growing and willful social disorder. Arguing that "extraordinary conditions require extraordinary measures," he suggested that public authorities would have to take a hand in disciplining youth by creating a "Morals Authority" with jurisdiction over young people.[11]

Such proposals in the field of child welfare reform reflected and were reinforced by important changes in social reform thinking generally. By the 1870s the crisis of pauperism, vagabondage, and hunger which had characterized the 1840s had given way to the gradual emergence of a distinct factory working class. Addressing the permanent structural problems of class society seemed to growing numbers of Germans to demand solutions other than religious revivalism or self-help programs. Bismarck captured this new understanding with characteristic economy: not only was the "belief in the harmony of interests . . . historically bankrupt," he said; it was also clear that "only the state can resolve the social question."[12] The emergence of the socialist movement in the 1860s, the Paris Commune of 1871, and the formation of the Social Democratic party in 1875 eroded liberal resistance to state intervention, while the great industrial and financial crash of 1873 helped to discredit liberal economic and social theory. Finally, the unification of Germany under Prussian auspices encouraged at least the Protestant bourgeoisie to see the state as an ally of the most vital and creative forces in national life. Indeed, the project of social reform became in many reformers' minds a part of the drive to consolidate the unification of Germany. The economist Gustav Schönberg, for example, argued for social reform as a necessary "internal founding of the Empire," the social equivalent to the political creation of the German national state.[13] Within the Catholic community, by contrast, private charitable activity was seen as a weapon in the defensive struggle against that same state.

Intellectually this shift was reflected among liberal Protestant reformers by the emergence in the 1860s of what came to be called the historical school of economics. Rejecting exclusive reliance on the free market, its representatives argued that the state must intervene to shape economic and social life according to its own principles—justice, the common good, and its own survival imperative. At the same time, they moved toward abandoning the legal formalism of the socially neutral *Rechtsstaat* and toward an acceptance of targeted administrative (rather than general and legislative) state intervention. By 1871 the economist Albert Schaeffle was able to formulate a coherent program for a pragmatic and social-managerial state policy aimed at positive social justice:

The proper ordering of social life cannot be achieved entirely through formal . . . legal articles. Also required are the careful observation and supervision of social developments, rapid and energetic intervention, action according to the circumstances for the good, quick decisions in brief consultation, in part discovery and application of the right rule in concrete situations, and for all these the appropriate apparatus of watchful, battle-ready administrative organs [of the state] familiar with particular [local] conditions and accustomed to immediate ordering intervention.[14]

In terms of organization these reformers' drift away from classical liberalism led in 1872 to the creation, by dissidents within the CVWAC, of the Social Policy Association (Verein für Sozialpolitik), which came to play an important role in establishing the social scientific legitimation for social policy reforms. It was soon supported by the National Association for Poor Relief and Charities (Deutscher Verein für Armenpflege und Wohltätigkeit, or DVAW), a forum for discussion among practitioners in the private charities and especially in municipal poor relief agencies, which was established in 1880. A similar intellectual shift in favor of positive public social policy was accomplished at the end of the 1860s within Catholic circles by Bishop Emmanuel Ketteler and Catholic social activists in the Rhineland. Among conservative Protestants, the rapid organizational consolidation of the Inner Mission and the changing social context had a certain sobering effect, so that in 1878 the organization's statutes were revised to reflect the shift from missionary to "social" work.

These intellectual developments made possible the introduction of national health, accident, and old age insurance programs between 1883 and 1889; and they also provided the underpinning for an impressive expansion of social policy at the local level—including, for example, urban services such as transportation, lighting, sewage, gas, and electricity.

The growth of public child welfare policy in the 1870s reflected, and in some respects anticipated, this shift from restraint to intervention. Of particular importance were debates in Prussia over two important pieces of legislation, the Legal Guardianship Code of 1875 and the Law on Correctional Education of 1878. These debates reveal the tenacity of liberal conceptions of the relationship between the state and society in the 1870s. Yet, at the same time, the discussion of these laws laid the intellectual foundations for the abandonment of those liberal commitments over the next two decades.

The Prussian Legal Guardianship Code and the Law on Correctional Education

Under the Prussian Allgemeines Landrecht (ALR) of 1794, each illegitimate or fatherless child was given a legal guardian, ideally a relative such as the maternal grandfather, who was appointed by the Guardianship Court to take the place of the child's father—or to see to it that the father fulfilled his obligation to support his illegitimate child. Under the ALR, the Guardianship Court exercised strict supervision over the legal guardian; its task was to invest and administer the child's inheritance, see that the legal guardian did his job conscientiously, and apply all the various rules contained in the hundreds of paragraphs of the ALR that treated legal guardianship.

This system was increasingly criticized during the middle decades of the nineteenth century. The growth of the German population and its geographic mobility made it difficult for both the courts and the guardians themselves to perform their functions effectively. Guardians, who were not paid, often saw their office as a burden and neglected their duties. Many did not have the necessary time or legal competence to secure their wards' rights; and those who did frequently shunned contact with their mostly lower-class wards. The long delays involved in finding guardians and bringing paternity suits in any case gave fathers ample time to disappear. And since most single mothers also did not have the time, the knowledge of the law, or the resources (psychological or material) to file claim against the father for child support, mothers and their children made up a disproportionate number of those living in poverty. The infant mortality rate among illegitimate children was accordingly almost twice that of children born to married women, and bastards grew up to be disproportionately represented among unskilled and casual laborers, as well as criminals, vagrants, prostitutes, and the like.

By 1870 some observers were arguing that only the state had the resources to help these people: R. Zelle, for example, suggested establishing a public Guardianship Bureau in each local self-governing community *(Gemeinde)*, which would take on all wards who owned no substantial property.[15] The reform introduced by the Legal Guardianship Code, or Vormundschaftsordnung, of 1875 was, however, clearly a part of the great outpouring of liberal legislation of the first decade after national unification (and of the effort to integrate the large areas annexed by Prussia in 1866). Advocates of the new law believed that under the ALR the guardian had "been reduced to absolute dependency on the guardianship judge and has ceased to be that which he is called upon to be"—namely, an independent, authoritative surrogate father. Instead he stood "in the same relationship to the judge as a servant to his master," and naturally he avoided the office or, once appointed, shirked his duties.[16] The new law aimed to give the individual guardian autonomy and responsibility, and thus enlist his own interests and energies. Indeed, the Inner Mission even demanded that the guardian be given the paternal right of corporal punishment.

At the insistence of the Inner Mission, however, the Prussian parliament amended the bill, establishing what was called the Community Orphans' Council *(Gemeindewaisenrat)* in each town or county. The *Gemeindewaisenrat* was to consist either of a single individual or, if local government so decided, of several representatives of the charities and schools, local doctors and notables, and so on, and would assist the Guardianship Court and the guardians in performing their duties. As the Inner Mission argued, "In legal guardianship all the actually existing moral forces must be given the influence that they in fact have, and should have, in [public] life, and . . . therefore not only the state, but rather also society must be given consideration in full, and a vital organism must be created."[17] The new law thus allowed the creation of an intermediary institution between the state and civil society, a hybrid public-private agency. In doing so it tendentially undermined both the liberal principle of the separation of state and civil society and the patriarchal conservative model of social order, in which the family and other social authorities remain independent of the state, autonomous bearers of the moralizing principles of love and authority.

The Prussian Law on Compulsory Correctional Education of 1878 revealed this tendency in a more unequivocal fashion. The law was a response to problems created by the National Code of Criminal Law (Reichsstrafgesetzbuch, or RStGB) of 1871, which neither allowed criminal prosecution of children under twelve years of age nor provided for their transfer to foster families or reformatories for wayward children. Many involved in the administration of criminal justice found the lack of any means of contending with child offenders extremely frustrating. One parliamentary advocate of reform claimed, for example, that it was a "major factor . . . which has contributed to the raising of lawbreakers and the growing numbers of crimes." In 1876, therefore, an amendment to the RStGB was passed by the national parliament, allowing the individual states to adopt laws providing for the placement of child offenders in reformatories. The new Prussian law allowed the Guardianship Courts to place a child convicted of a crime in a *Rettungshaus* or foster family if this step was "necessary in order to prevent further moral waywardness."[18]

That the law established the right of the state to intervene in the internal affairs of the family was not itself revolutionary. The Prussian Allgemeines Landrecht (ALR), for example, had allowed the institutionalization of children who were mistreated, starved, or turned to the bad by their parents. What the law did do was establish entirely new grounds for doing so: the commission of a crime by the child rather than by the parents. Whereas prior to 1876 only parents guilty of actual abuse could be deprived of their children, the state laws passed thereafter allowed the invasion or annulment of private parental rights in response to the failure of the family to socialize its children appropriately.

Resistance to this step in the Prussian parliament was very strong. Catholics, persecuted by the Prussian state since 1870, regarded it as *an extremely dangerous prerogative in the hands of the administrative authorities.* Liberals insisted that correctional education was "an oppressive and unhealthy state of things," and that "we must try to avoid wherever possible such a serious assault on the rights of the parents . . . except in the utmost need." One even saw the law as proof that "social democratic ideas have already penetrated fairly far into government circles." Others, finally, viewed the state as essentially a "cold and heartless" police regime incapable of providing for the spiritual rescue of wayward youngsters, a task that could be accomplished only by "a heart that glows with love for children."[19]

But while some viewed the law as potentially too far-reaching, others criticized it precisely for its restraint. Baron von Manteuffel, for example, regretted that the law "confines itself to . . . those [children] who have actually come into conflict with the criminal law, and does not extend to those perhaps just as much in need of betterment, just as much in need of another guiding hand than that of their nearest relatives."[20] In other words, state intervention should be triggered not just by the objective fact of criminality but by the subjective determination of a particular child's internal condition. The state would thus not merely be a police agency enforcing laws; it would actively intervene to secure a precise social result.

Correctional Education, 1878–1892: From Liberalism to the Organic State

Within a few years, as the liberal optimism of the 1870s gave way to class fear and cultural pessimism, this proposal would become increasingly popular. By 1881, 3,364 children had been committed under the new law—a boon to the *Rettungshäuser,* which had suffered declining enrollments for a decade. By the mid-1880s many institutions were being expanded and new ones founded to accommodate the flood of charges. Yet the number of commitments soon dropped off, and by 1898, only 30,722 of the 40,626 places in private reformatories in Prussia were filled.[21] More important, as the sense of social crisis created by industrialization intensified, the law of 1878 rapidly came to seem insufficient. The optimistic liberal belief that a harmonious society of independent producers would evolve from economic freedom and industrial development was bankrupt, as Albert Ohly told the DVAW conference in 1884. It was time to face up to this fact and to create public institutions which would counteract the social pathologies created by liberal reforms such as freedom of movement and of economic activity. "If we . . . simply 'let things be' as we have been doing," he said, "then the danger to the state and the community which arises from . . . the waywardness of children will gain such dimensions . . . that finally even the harshest coercive measures will not be sufficient, and we will have to spend the greatest part of public revenues on police organizations, workhouses, prisons, and penitentiaries." It was therefore necessary that the state be able to take over the socialization of neglected, abused, and morally endangered children *"before* [they] entered onto a career of crime."[22]

In 1886 the state of Baden passed a law allowing placement in a reformatory or foster family if a child's "behavior"—not necessarily criminal activity—"indicates that the authority of the parents . . . and the disciplinary power of the schools is not sufficient to prevent [his or her] complete moral ruin";[23] and a number of other states passed similar laws by 1890. The decisive development in the evolution of correctional education came with the publication of a draft of the new national Code of Civil Law (Bürgerliches Gesetzbuch, or BGB) in 1888. To the dismay of reformers, this draft represented a retreat even from the position of the Prussian law of 1878, since it did not provide for the commitment to correctional education even of children who had committed a crime.[24]

The prospect that this provision might become national law galvanized reform circles' discussion of correctional education. The DVAW discussed the bill critically in 1889 and 1890.[25] More important, in 1892 the German chapter of the International Criminological Society (Internationale kriminalistische Vereinigung, or IKV) published a report produced by a committee of prominent jurists under the direction of Hugo Appelius.[26] Abandoning the moralistic tone and anecdotal argumentation of his predecessors in the 1870s, Appelius adopted a pragmatic and social scientific style, using statistics to prove that "the development of juvenile delinquency is now a danger to society." People between the ages of twelve and eighteen, he pointed out, had committed only 30,719 crimes in 1882, but 40,905 already in 1890. Juvenile delinquency was rising faster than adult criminality: minors had committed 8.9 percent of crimes in 1885 but 10.7 percent in 1890. The state, Appelius argued, had to prevent this deterioration rather than merely punish crimes once they were committed.[27] In this Appelius was merely echoing the arguments of the leading penal reformers of the day, most notably of Franz von Liszt, who was also a member of the IKV commission. But Appelius held that this argument was particularly valid in the case of young offenders. The child at birth, he said, was essentially a savage, without ethical capacities, and governed entirely by asocial, selfish drives. The capacity to contain "the egotistical, but natural desires" (and so to avoid criminal acts) was the product of a long process of education. Yet many parents could not give their children a proper upbringing of this kind (or did not want to, or were prevented from doing so by the conditions of modern life), and to punish such children for their crimes was therefore a grave injustice. It was also ineffective as a form of crime prevention, since unthinking children would neither be deterred by the threat of punishment nor adequately resocialized while serving brief jail sentences for minor crimes. Indeed, Appelius held that these arguments were valid not only for children under twelve, but also for those up to age eighteen.[28]

Appelius therefore argued that delinquents under eighteen should be liable for commitment to correctional education. But he also held that the state should intervene in *all* cases where "domestic education proves insufficient"—not only where children committed crimes but also where they showed recognizable signs of waywardness. Indeed, he believed that correctional education was appropriate even where the child was merely "endangered" by its living conditions—for example, where the family was impoverished, or where "father *and* mother work outside the house all day."[29] In other words, any child who was not part of what middle-class observers would consider a proper family—in which the husband earned a family wage and the mother was a housewife—would be a candidate for correctional education.

Appelius justified this massive intervention in the private sphere, again, on the purely pragmatic grounds that the existing legal stipulations and the 1888 draft of the BGB simply did not meet the "crying needs of public law" and the "inescapable demands of our time"; neither they nor the ALR "measure[d] up to all the requirements of the present social structure of the Empire." In other words, the ideal of a society of autonomous family units, governing themselves under private law, was no longer an appropriate guide to the task of ordering the new industrial society. Criminal law should not be "satisfied with the hopeless quest for an ideal of abstract justice"; rather, it "must be aware that it is called upon above all to champion society against the criminal element on the basis of concrete reality."[30] The justice system must be reshaped to function as an arm of social policy, responding to social phenomena (in this case crime) not according to abstract principles held to be valid in each and every instance but flexibly, according to the specific characteristics of each case and the individual needs of those involved, and with an overall social goal in view.

Behind this program, obviously, lay a conception of the relationship between family and society very different from those posited by nineteenth-century liberalism and conservatism. Whereas these saw the family as an autonomous, closed social sphere and as the source of the ethical values on which the social and political order were founded, Appelius adopted an essentially natural scientific model of society, in which the family was the fundamental "cell" of an organic, unitary social body, and therefore subject to the rules and necessarily serving the ends of that body—a model common in social theory at the time. Appelius stated this view with remarkable clarity and force: "The interests of the state are more important than those of the individual, and where the two collide the latter must therefore yield. We wish to intervene in the family only where this is necessary in the interests of legal security; only where the family does not fulfill that [task] which it must accomplish for the state, where it does not raise the next generation as the state requires, so that they do not fall into criminal ways."[31]

But Appelius's tendential erasure of the boundaries between society and the state cut both ways. Arguing that the state would have to rely on volunteers to oversee children placed in foster families, he remarked:

> We too often make the old mistake of regarding the state as something foreign, something antagonistic to us; and yet, we are all members of the one great whole, which we all make up. Everyone who acts as even a tiny cog in the great machine acts on behalf of all of society, the well-being of which in turn benefits the individual. The more the state recruits its citizens, within the limits of their capacities, to help solve the common tasks, the more the sense of belonging together, the sense of solidarity with the interests of the state, will become and remain lively.[32]

If the state had to be more active in society, the citizen had to become more active in the state. The implications of this notion obviously paralleled those of the Inner Mission's proposal for the administration of legal guardianship.

The atmosphere of social crisis prevailing in the early 1890s was fertile ground for Appelius's ideas. The Prussian Ministry of the Interior, for instance, produced a position paper in 1892 which supported the extension of correctional education to children who were wayward but not delinquent; such a step was necessary to counteract not only juvenile delinquency but also the "ever growing participation by wayward, ill-mannered, or poorly raised youths wherever there are disturbances of the peace, resistance to state authority, social democratic movements, revolts, and disorders."[33] By 1893 the commission working on the BGB bowed to pressure from Baden, Prussia, and other state governments, and altered the draft of 1888 accordingly.[34]

An article in the *Rettungshausbote* in 1896, titled "Social Principles," illustrates with unusual clarity the transformation achieved during the 1880s and 1890s. The "time has come," the editors wrote, "when people seek to limit rights and power within the family for the good of society. To many it will sound dangerous . . ., [they will] say: 'That is socialism in matters of education!' But . . . we hold this kind of socialism to be a great blessing."[35]

Legal Guardianship, 1875–1896

Like the correctional education law, the Prussian Guardianship Code of 1875 came in for sharp criticism almost immediately after its passage. The Orphans' Councils proved no more effective than the Guardianship Courts at supervising guardians, and service on them was no more welcomed than legal guardianship. Guardians were not inspired by their new autonomy to devote more time and energy to the care of their wards. The Inner Mission reported in 1880 that a large proportion of the young people serving sentences for theft or prostitution still "fell into moral decay through neglect of legal guardianship."[36]

By the mid-1890s, however, the decisive innovative response to the failure of the system of individual legal guardianship had already been achieved in Leipzig, a rapidly growing industrial city in Saxony. Between 1880 and 1900 Max Taube, the chief doctor of the city's Foster Children's Bureau, developed the institution of public or "professional" legal guardianship *(Berufsvormundschaft)*, which would prove critical to the entire future development of public child welfare policy in Germany.

Taube faced a daunting problem. The maternity clinics built in Leipzig in the late nineteenth century brought a steady flood of single mothers to the city, tremendously increasing the number of children whom the Foster Children's Bureau had to supervise. Many of them did not stay in the city itself, but moved with their mothers back to the countryside or into the growing suburbs, in either case far from the reach of Taube and his one paid assistant. The frequency with which single mothers moved even within the city made it difficult to check regularly on their children's health. Moreover, Taube's agency had jurisdiction only over those children who were in *paid* foster care, whereas in fact the great majority of illegitimate babies were in the *unpaid* care of relatives and neighbors.

Taube therefore undertook a gradual expansion of the groups of children under supervision. From 1883 anyone who took a child into paid foster care was required to register with the poor relief authorities, and to bring their charges to be examined by the municipal doctor every six months. In 1884 Taube began a steady expansion in the number of paid "visitors," or social workers, in his bureau: by 1913 there were thirty-six.[37] In 1891 Taube's supervision was extended to all illegitimate children not living with their mothers, whether in paid or unpaid foster care. In later years the Foster Children's Bureau kept a register of foster mothers, offered premiums for breast-feeding, and coordinated its efforts with the police residents' registry and local midwives.

These administrative steps were accompanied by an important analytical shift. Taube's initial analysis of the problem of illegitimacy was quite conservative: the problem, he believed, was that in industrial society girls were removed or allowed to escape from the protective and controlling realm of family life too early. "The main cause of the moral decline of our times," he wrote, "is to be found in the unconstrained life and the too-early independence of the female sex." His solution was therefore to re-create the "concept of female virtue," as well as to teach "the young man what dangers for honor and body he exposes himself to" through premarital sex.[38] As for infant mortality, he believed, it was the product of ignorance and slovenliness, or even infanticidal intent, on the part of mothers and foster mothers, and would be eliminated by close supervision. Yet the expansion of the system and Taube's rudimentary statistical studies of his "clientele" soon began to reveal that both single mothers and foster parents were for the most part competent and well-meaning. The critical problem was that only a tiny proportion of illegitimate fathers actually paid the child support they were legally required to give their children, so that single mothers—whose wages were usually absurdly low—simply could not pay foster care fees regularly. Taube accordingly launched a blistering attack on the fathers of illegitimate children. Illegitimacy and the high rate of mortality among illegitimate infants were the products not of the growing economic freedom and the slovenliness or evil purpose of *women,* but rather of the predatory pleasure seeking and consequent irresponsibility and heartlessness of *men.*

In 1901 Taube achieved the administrative reform that, in light of this analysis, was the logical culmination of his efforts: the director of the Foster Children's Bureau—still Taube himself—was made legal guardian for all illegitimate children born in Leipzig and all children supported by the local poor relief agency, effective at birth rather than by court appointment. This system, he argued, had manifold advantages. The public authority of the new public guardianship agency; its official connections to other governmental agencies such as the police or ·the district attorney's office; the resources and sources of information which it could tap through ties with the poor relief agency, the local registry of inhabitants, municipal clinics, and so on; and the benefits of having a paid staff: all these advantages allowed Taube's public legal guardianship to care for its wards far more effectively than could the individual legal guardian, and in particular would make it much more successful in forcing illegitimate fathers to pay child support. Securing child support payments would ensure stable foster care; and relieving the poor relief system of some of its most stubborn and expensive cases would more than compensate for the administrative costs of public legal guardianship.

The effects of this system were, in Taube's eyes, immediately apparent. Whereas infant mortality in Leipzig in 1870–1880 had been 21 percent for legitimate and 29.6 percent for illegitimate children, in 1881–1890 it was 19.9 and 24.5 percent, respectively. As the system expanded, its apparent success was more impressive still: between 1900 and 1914, while the infant mortality rate for legitimate children in Leipzig fell by 7 percent, that for illegitimate children fell by 14 percent.[39]

By the turn of the century, then, Taube had created a mature institution in Leipzig which was constructed according to principles very different from those which had guided either liberal or Christian social reform. Rejecting moral regeneration, individual responsibility, social authority, and private legal relationships as means of imposing social order, public legal guardianship sought to resolve the problem of illegitimacy through administrative efficiency, public authority, professionalization, and scientific medical knowledge. Taube's system represented a conscious abandonment of the attempt to regenerate patriarchal social relations by reintegrating the illegitimate child into an imagined system of "normal" patriarchal social relationships. Instead, the new system embraced Zelle's and Schaeffle's suggestions of 1870, creating a thoroughly modern, rational, bureaucratic mass institution for the care of a specific disadvantaged social group. Accepting the terms imposed by modern industrial society, Taube sought to order that society according to modern "industrial" principles.

Integration and Efficiency: The Writings of Franz Pagel

In the course of the late 1890s the Berlin schoolteacher Franz Pagel formulated and popularized the principles implicit in Taube's program. Pagel acted as moving spirit and chief theorist for a group of Berlin teachers and officials who formed the Voluntary Educational Council for Graduating Orphans (Freiwillige Erziehungsbeirat für schulentlassene Waisen), the practical work of which was essentially organizing systematic career counseling and employment services for all fatherless (orphaned or illegitimate) children graduating from the public schools.

Pagel's seminal essay of 1896, like Appelius's of 1892, was informed by a socially and politically conservative perspective. Like Appelius in the case of wayward children, Pagel argued that the "principle of self-preservation" demanded society care for fatherless children, lest they fall "into the ranks of those wild hordes . . . who wait in the shadows of houses and trees in the finest quarters of town for the harmless pedestrian and, in the dark of night, threaten the life and property of the peaceful citizen." Whereas their fathers had fought and bled for the Reich in 1870, today, while the emperor and his advisers

> work themselves to the bone for peace, the general welfare, and the cause of civilization . . ., a great mass numbering in the millions doesn't want to join in. Filled with dark hatred, they rebel against all who stand out owing to wealth, office, or rank, indeed against the entire social order . . . an army of failed existences of all kinds is trying by all means to spread explosives among the masses, hoping that one day it will be enough to turn the stately edifice of culture, which all of mankind has labored upon for . . . thousands of years, into a giant heap of rubble by the crude force of violence.[40]

Yet, unlike conservatives, who regarded socialism as an expression of spiritual corruption and of selfish, immoral rebellion, Pagel readily conceded that the industrial social order produced genuine suffering and injustice. The ruling classes, he argued, must recognize the real needs and problems to which the socialist movement was a response; he urged them to "let the sorrows and dreams of the poor and helpless work upon your hearts in all their power, upon a heart glowing with the holy fire of the love of your fellow man, the love of humanity!" To resolve the social question it would then be necessary only to translate this "holy fire" into effective action through the application of scientific principles to the task of social reform. The ruling classes, he said, must "take a careful look at the evil! *Investigate its causes* without prejudice and think, with a noble, good, and helpful attitude, of *appropriate means for a successful cure . . .*! Work in the great field of popular welfare has been crowned with success only when it has undertaken a *careful analysis of the situation of the economic and social groups* that it seeks to help, and *exactly suited* the chosen treatment to the *particular condition of the social body.*"[41]

Specifically, Pagel argued that rather than "wanting to stem the tide of the advancement of human civilization," social reform must make the worker "qualified to fill the position which a new time has made for him." What was needed was not the revitalization of the ethical essence, much less the substance, of an imagined traditional social order. Rather, the working classes had to be integrated smoothly into the workings of the modern economy through appropriate training and rewarding employment. Industrial society, in other words, was not doomed to tear itself apart: it bore within itself the means by which it could be healed and stabilized. Social order did not have to be created through the repression of the forces of disorder and modernity or through the reimposition of a religious and deferential cultural pattern; social reform did not have to reverse the direction of social development. On the contrary, he believed that reform must not oppose progress but direct and smooth it, must not demand sacrifice from individuals but rather enlist their own creative energies and interests by offering incentives and channels for their integration into the new social order. Participation ought not to be denied but directed. Echoing Appelius's organic conception of society, in which the energies of each must be mobilized for the good of all, Pagel argued that "the state is an organic whole, a social organism. . . . In it there is a rich articulation and unbreakable interdependence of the individual parts. . . . Each part is important for the whole, just as in a clock even the smallest wheel cannot be missing." And since unemployment, poverty, idleness, and crime were harmful not merely to the individual but also to society as a whole, society should seek to secure its own stability and progress by facilitating the healthy development of every individual: "If society . . . ensures the natural development of the physical and mental powers of its members, then it creates factors which create and transmit value, which will serve the personal well-being of the individual and the well-being of the nation."[42]

Central to Pagel's argument, then, in addition to the fundamentally conservative concern for social order was also an essentially imperialist concern with industrial efficiency, national wealth, and national power. Indeed,

Pagel's arguments were less moralistic than economistic. About 10 percent of children graduating from the public schools, he wrote, were fatherless and therefore would have particular difficulty finding their proper place in economic life. This was a personal tragedy, of course, but also a national disaster, since "the development of the individual's physical and intellectual powers to the greatest possible perfection is also a profit in the industrial and economic sense." He calculated that the poor training and low wages of young workers—850,000 of them—was costing the nation 121 million marks in "lost" wages annually. And the poor integration of these young people into economy and society cost the state further millions for prisons, reformatories, workhouses, and poor relief.[43]

Pagel set out to make his own contribution to resolving this problem through the Voluntary Educational Council. The council's volunteer "advisers" *(Pfleger)* offered fatherless children graduating from school career counseling and help in finding work, and then later personal counseling and support. Ideally boys were to be found apprenticeships which would lead them into well-paid skilled jobs, while girls would be found positions as domestic servants in order to train them for the task of making stable, happy homes, to which their husbands would gladly return at the end of a day of satisfying work.

More important than the practical efforts of the council, however, was Pagel's remarkable success in spreading his ideas regarding child welfare generally. He won the financial and moral backing of the Prussian ministries of the interior and culture, and finally the explicit blessing of the Kaiser himself, for a speaking tour in 1897 in which he encouraged the formation of analogues to the Voluntary Educational Council in other cities. His enthusiastic, optimistic message seems to have struck a resonant note: he was greeted in a number of cities by packed lecture halls and enthusiastic audiences. By 1899 there were plans to establish similar associations in "twenty-five or thirty" other cities.[44] The journal Pagel edited, *Die Jugend-fürsorge,* also served as a crystallization point for reform thought and remained the most influential one in the field until 1909.

As an active member of Berlin's bourgeois charitable community, Pagel had serious misgivings about state action. State intervention, he felt, could not have the same ethical meaning and human significance that voluntary social action did. His ideal was that the council's adviser should, as Paul Felisch, later director of the Voluntary Council put it, "as far as possible . . . replace the father."[45] Such a relationship would, Pagel believed, be impossible if the adviser were the agent of a state bureaucracy. And yet Pagel's program clearly implied the creation of a grand network of institutions that would achieve the integration of working-class youth into society and economy—a task that only the state, with its financial and legal resources, could master. In fact, already in 1895 Pagel looked forward to the day when "the state and the municipal authorities see themselves in the position to take over the ideal, in part even the material care for working adolescent youth . . . say, until age 16 or 18."[46]

Progressive Child Welfare Reform

The proposals of Appelius and Taube, while they originated in different institutional and legal frameworks, both converged on precisely the same aim as that implied in Pagel's program: the establishment of a system of public guardianship over all children not being raised in "proper" families, and even over children whose families were merely poor. Appelius, starting from the criminal law and the problem of juvenile delinquency, argued for the placement of these children in foster homes under public supervision. Taube, starting from the law of public guardianship, eventually extended his authority over all children living in single-parent families and all children being supported by the public poor relief system. These two proposals were fundamentally in competition with each other, and in fact the tension between them runs through the history of German child welfare right down to the 1960s.

Yet, although the methods differed, in an important sense the aim in each case was fundamentally the same. While they shared much of the conservative Christian critique of industrial society, these reformers had abandoned the goal of spiritually regenerating the patriarchal premodern social order; and they had also discarded the liberal hope of creating a society that would govern itself through the formal legal relationships defined by private law, or through voluntary or individual initiative. Accepting the industrial order, they sought to use its principles—organization, bureaucracy, technical expertise—to create public institutions which would compensate for what they understood to be the destructive and destabilizing aspects of industrialization.

In truth, of course, the patriarchal, familial social order had always cast off marginal people (and specifically marginal children); but under the particular conditions of the late nineteenth century this was increasingly unacceptable. The creation of a new pattern of industrial labor and a new working class, the process of urbanization, the development of the commercial capitalist economy, and the introduction of mass suffrage—in short, the economic and political mobilization of the population—had transformed the "moral" problems of patriarchal society into the "social crisis" of industrial society. It was less an objective decay of social conditions than rising standards for participation, productivity, health, and political and personal behavior that provided the impetus for social reform.

Whereas Taube argued, for example, that the system of individual legal guardianship was failing because of the nature of the society being created by industrialization (the anonymity of great cities, the mobility of the population, the disintegration of "patriarchal" families), in fact the increasing concern with guardianship over lower-class illegitimates was probably not so much a product of social change as a result of the rising standards that middle-class people applied to working-class socialization in a society in which the lower classes were increasingly important to national political and economic life. In 1910 the Austrian professor E. Mischler remarked that legal guardianship had traditionally been a functioning institution only among the upper classes, so that replacing individual with public guardianship amounted to an extension of legal guardianship to the masses.[47] Similarly, the fact that there was a disproportionate number of urban children in correctional education did not concern reformers, since they believed that city life "corrupted" youth; but in fact, urban children were often committed for offenses that were considered unimportant, or dealt with informally, in rural areas.[48]

I have chosen to use the label "progressive" for the ideas that motivated these reformers. The term is preferable to that more commonly used in the literature, "social-liberal," because progressive reformers were often not liberals at all. Classical liberal social thought they rejected explicitly, often using the dismissive and pejorative term "Manchesterism." But social-liberalism proper (as advocated, for example, by Lujo Brentano) was only one part of the broader spectrum of progressive, modernizing reform; and most progressives (a standard example is Gustav Schmoller) were more statist and paternalist than the more liberal wing of the reform movement. Furthermore, the term is meant to suggest the remarkable parallels between the ideas and backgrounds of German reformers and the American Progressives of the same period. In particular, like American Progressivism, the German child welfare reform movement of these decades was immensely complex and difficult to define, including as it did Catholic, Protestant, and secular reformers, centralizers and local administrators, activists and academics, politicians, bureaucrats, private citizens, and so on. And, like American Progressivism, it never achieved the same degree of influence within the mainstream political parties that the New Liberalism or *solidarisme* did in Britain or France, relying instead on the persuasive power of autonomous reform associations.

Appelius's thinking perhaps best reveals the conceptual transition that these progressive reformers accomplished in the 1890s. On the one hand, Appelius adopted much of the pedagogical model and the socially conservative program of the Protestant pioneers of correctional education. As he put it, correctional education must impose on wayward children "discipline not dissimilar to the most strict paternal discipline."[49] Removed from its chaotic, amoral milieu and placed in this patriarchal setting, the wayward child could be given an upbringing which would anchor in its psyche the beliefs, values, personality traits, and living habits of traditional society. The aim of correctional education (as of the *Rettungshaus*) was to make an end run, as it were, around the freedom and anarchy produced by social change.

Appelius's arguments regarding the reform of juvenile justice make the issues at stake here particularly clear. In arguing that it made no sense to punish young criminals, Appelius was essentially admitting that there were young people who did not share the values which underlay the law. The law, for these children, was not (or, in Appelius's analysis, was no longer) a moral sanction; punishment was ineffective because they did not share the ethical view which made it meaningful. The problem of juvenile delinquency was thus potentially, like socialism, a problem of the legitimation of existing authority.

Yet within the context of the system of public childhood socialization as envisioned by Appelius, this project of cultural restoration took on a very different meaning than it had in Wichern's vision of moral revitalization. Wichern saw the *Rettungshaus* as part of a cultural and religious rebirth which would heal society and, by galvanizing and regenerating its religious foundations, restore the patriarchal social order. His ideal was of a society essentially in stasis, a kind of crystalline social fabric of repeating familial units, each perfect unto itself, arranged in a concentric hierarchy of functionally and morphologically identical structures of authority and obedience, each determined by the identical (sinful) nature of the individual human beings making it up, and the whole maintained by universal ethical laws like the axes of rotation of a crystal lattice. In contrast, Appelius saw society as a dynamic organism which was constantly in flux and which must be constantly regulated by public institutions, the relationships between its parts or organs continuously monitored and adjusted, since the life of the whole depended on the functioning of each part. Indeed, Appelius's avowed aim was precisely to destroy patriarchal privilege, to break open the family unit and subject its internal workings to continuous supervision and correction by the state and by the social organism as a whole. He clearly assumed that the malfunction of the patriarchal family—its production of criminal children—under the conditions of industrial capitalism could not be eliminated through cultural revitalization. His goal was not to heal this malfunction but to compensate for it through state action, revoking the legal privilege of paternal authority which isolated it from the public realm. His intention was to save patriarchy by destroying it.

Max Taube, working with children who were already outcasts from the patriarchal social order, could make the argument for this kind of social management with a great deal more clarity. Taube's hope was to stabilize the families (that is, the foster families) of his wards. But his ambition was less to reconstruct a more familylike social niche for the illegitimate child than to build an effective social bureaucracy, with the power to supervise directly those caring for the child and to intervene at will in their decisions.

His intention, even more openly than Appelius's, was to penetrate effectively into the life of the lower classes and reshape it through the use of administrative public power. Whereas the Legal Guardianship Code of 1875 had appealed to the authority, wisdom, and initiative of the individual legal guardian, or to the vital energies and independent institutions of civil society, Taube appealed to a very different authority: that of the doctor—the wielder of scientific, hygienic knowledge—and, behind him, that of the state. His program involved a frontal assault on male privilege; and while Appelius clearly assumed that the volunteers who would supervise the correctional education of children in foster families would be middle class, Taube argued that paid social workers recruited from the working class would be more knowledgeable and effective—and less resented—than middle-class "ladies."[50]

Pagel articulated most clearly the social ideal that motivated these reformers. They envisioned a society of competent, active, committed, productive workers and citizens—"useful members of human society," as child welfare advocates often put it. They also envisioned a society in which harmony, efficiency, and industrial power were guaranteed by the influence of a bureaucracy which could intervene wherever private relationships failed to secure the effective social integration of individuals—a society, in other words, whose resources and workings were "managed," like those of a corporation, by a social bureaucracy that could intervene wherever necessary to ensure efficiency and quality. It was also one in which the distinction between the state and civil society was blurred: the social bureaucracy was envisioned not merely as a protective police agency but as an integral part of the orderly functioning of ("private" or civil) society. And whereas Appelius's managerial institutions were intended to remove children forcibly from a social milieu which placed them in moral danger, Pagel intended to integrate them into their industrial-capitalist social context in such a manner that they were not endangered but rather served and nurtured by it.

Indeed, despite Pagel's interventionism and his ties to the conservative society of official Berlin, his program was essentially optimistic, and derived in part from the tradition of liberal social reform. His goal was not simply to repress the forces of modernity and revolution but to create economic efficiency, social harmony, political stability, and national power through integration and participation. If the proper skills could be imparted to the individual worker and citizen, he argued, the process of mobilization itself would be the source of social order. The material well-being and psychological satisfaction created by adequate training, skilled work, and a stable and pleasant domestic life would stabilize industrial society.

In all this Pagel's program clearly belongs to that social-liberal and proto-corporatist current of social reform in the 1890s which would be given institutional expression in the foundation, in 1901, of the Society for Social

Reform (Gesellschaft für Soziale Reform, or GSR). The GSR argued for the abandonment of paternalism in social reform and for the construction of institutions which would integrate the working classes into the social and political order not as passive recipients of aid or orders but as active, educated, willing, and competent participants. The society's chairman, the former Prussian minister of commerce Baron von Berlepsch, even argued for the legal recognition of the socialist trade unions, suggesting that reform could not bring about social peace unless the "equal rights of the worker are . . . recognized [and] guaranteed. . . . The social development of our times demands justice, not good deeds."[51] In a sense, then, this progressive program adapted the liberal social reform tradition to the fundamentally conservative environment of the Empire, and in doing so, as we will see in Chapter 3, laid the foundation for a massive expansion of public welfare programs after the turn of the century.

CHAPTER TWO

Competing Reform Conceptions in the 1890s

Youth and Progressive Reform in the 1890s

By the early 1890s social and cultural authority and cohesion appeared to many middle-class observers to be disintegrating completely under the impact of economic and social change. Various developments gave rise to a widespread perception among middle-class Germans that the preservation of social and political stability demanded the imposition of alternatives to prevailing social and economic patterns, philosophies, and policies. These developments included the growing recruitment of women and young people into the factory labor force and changes in working-class family life; the rapid growth of the Social Democratic party and unions after the abandonment of the Anti-Socialist Laws in 1890 and the long-term decline of the conservative and liberal parties; strikes and lockouts; the decline of traditional patterns of deference in an increasingly stratified, divided, urban, and anonymous society; the rise of technical culture and commercial values within the new white-collar middle class; the growing power and extraordinary wealth of the industrial "plutocracy"; the growing concentration of economic activity and cartelization of industry; the proliferation of voices in the burgeoning mass press; and the flourishing of non-"respectable" mass entertainments as discretionary spending rose and a distinctive urban working-class and lower-middle-class culture was elaborated and consolidated.

The result was an extraordinary outpouring of reform energies. This was perhaps best reflected in the founding of numerous new social reform, agitational, and women's organizations, including, for example, the German Catholic People's Association (Volksverein für das katholische Deutschland, founded in 1890); Caritas, the association of Catholic charities (Deutscher Caritasverband, or DCV, 1897); the Protestant-Social Congress

(Evangelisch-Soziale Kongress, 1890) and the Independent Religious-Social Conference (Freie kirchlich-soziale Kongress, 1896); the semiofficial Prussian Central Bureau for Organizations for Worker Welfare (Centralstelle für Arbeiterwohlfahrtseinrichtungen, or CAW, 1890), a coordinating body for public and private welfare organizations; the Institut für Gemeinwohl (1890) in Frankfurt; central associations of most of the Christian youth groups; and the Federation of German Women's Associations (Bund Deutscher Frauenvereine, or BDF, 1894), the Catholic Women's Association (Katholischer Frauenverband, formed in 1903 and after 1921 called Katholischer Deutscher Frauenbund, or KDF), and the Protestant Women's League and Protestant Women's Auxiliary (Deutsch-Evangelischer Frauenbund, or EFB, and Hilfswerk evangelischer Frauen, both 1899). The Patriotic Women's Leagues also expanded rapidly, reaching 1,380 local chapters with 395,054 members in 1897.[1] In these years, finally, the SPD also became increasingly active in welfare policy, as it gained a foothold in municipal assemblies. This national organizational activity was paralleled in many areas by similar activity at the local level; indeed, while the great reform associations had some success in securing further social legislation at the national and state levels, social reform generally found a more congenial home in the municipalities in this period.

This proliferation of reform organizations fostered a much broader public discussion of social problems and social policy, effectively removing welfare policy from the exclusive realm of high politics. It was this broader public interest that brought about, in the years around the turn of the century, a wave of legislative activity in the field of correctional education (1900 in Prussia), child labor law (in the Industrial Code of 1891 and in a major law of 1903), social insurance (extended in 1903, 1908, and 1911), protective legislation for women workers (1891, 1908), and countless local initiatives.

A sense of impending social and political crisis and a rejection of materialism and modernity fueled much of this reform activity; but a growing segment of the social reform community was motivated by a fundamentally optimistic progressive (and often an explicitly social-liberal) perspective. While there was increasing concern about a wide range of social problems, a number of social reformers in the 1890s did not regard them as evidence of a fundamentally faulty economic and spiritual development. The municipal administrators who predominated within the Association for Poor Relief and Charities (DVAW), for example, were often quite positive in their estimation of the implications of social change. Many of them in fact believed that it was social *progress,* rather than decay and degeneration, that made social reform seem necessary by heightening contrasts and creating rising expectations. The DVAW's chairman, Emil Muensterberg, remarked in a speech to the organization's fifteenth anniversary conference in 1895: "The perspective that is most sharply apparent is not that today we suddenly have such shocking conditions that they cannot be borne any longer; but steam, electricity, the telegraph—all these have suddenly given us the need to illuminate all [social] conditions with a bright light."[2]

This more optimistic perspective led such people, like the liberal reformers in the early nineteenth century, to devise institutional mechanisms of social integration and conflict resolution which accepted, indeed were based on and exploited, the principles of the industrial-capitalist social order: public housing, recreational and educational institutions, public health and hygiene programs, urban planning, social work agencies, and so on. At the same time, by the turn of the century many more social-liberal reformers were moving toward a conception of social order in which economic interest groups would carry out their conflicts as independent and equal partners bound by a set of rules and institutions designed to channel conflict, facilitate compromise, and limit social and economic upheaval—institutions such as collective bargaining and industrial arbitration. They argued that if unions could achieve a tolerable standard of living for their members, social tensions would be defused and demand would generate economic growth. Imperialism, finally, played an important role in the thinking of many progressive reformers, who argued that an aggressive colonial and commercial policy were essential for growth.

The organizational home of many of these reformers was the Society for Social Reform (Gesellschaft für soziale Reform), founded in 1901 as a more activist alternative to the Association for Social Policy. The first chairman was Baron von Berlepsch, who had been the Prussian minister of commerce during the relatively liberal and social reforming period of the "New Course" from 1890 to 1894; many of its members were close to Friedrich Naumann and his left-liberal, imperialist National Social movement.

For a number of reasons the problem of working-class youth became a particularly important focus for social reform in the 1890s. The concentration of young migrants in industrial cities and the "outstanding role" of "half-grown punks" (as one observer put it) at socialist meetings and demonstrations helped to associate working youth with the threat of social and political revolution in the minds of many.[3] At the same time, the consolidation in the great industrial cities of a coherent subculture of working-class youth reinforced earlier fears that the new generation of workers was losing contact with the values of civilized life—notions of sexual morality and the family, the work ethic, religiosity, respect for authority and property, and so on. Alarming statistics on juvenile delinquency in particular seemed to confirm this fear. Middle-class observers believed that the freedom and autonomy young workers were enjoying as a result of expanding opportunities for unskilled factory work undermined paternal authority, the power of employers to shape their young workers' "character" through personal contact during long apprenticeships, and young people's own understanding of the value of a disciplined and orderly life. Factory work also exposed them to the influence of older socialist colleagues. And, finally, young people were becoming accustomed to turning to spectacular and immoral amusements for relief from the monotony of "machinelike" labor, for relatively good wages and the absence of supervision made them particularly vulnerable to these "seductions" of city life.[4] The influence of music halls and dance halls, the cinema, late-night cafés, cheap mass-produced literature (whether weekly satirical journals or the serialized adventure literature of the period), and sport and gambling was believed to be particularly regrettable in the case of "impressionable" young people. While the focus of concern in this period was on male youth, an apparent increase of prostitution and general immorality and the independence of girls who worked in factories seemed to threaten young women as well.

Yet if working-class youth appeared to be a danger to civilization, they were also its best hope. For if bad education made barbarians and socialists of workers' children, then good education could just as easily make them civilized and orderly. As we shall see, the hope of preventing criminality by better socializing working-class youth played a major role in child welfare reform in the 1890s. But the hope of creating a more orderly and less threatening society through improved socialization was also expressed in explicitly political terms. "We will not succeed in converting those who have become Social Democrats," the conservative official and publicist Carl von Massow wrote; "but over the youth . . . we can exercise influence, if we wish, and thereby cut off the Social Democrats' recruitment."[5] In short, as a common axiom and battle cry of the day ran, "He who has the youth has the future."

The initiatives of Pagel, Taube, and Appelius were among the most theoretically mature reforms in the field of child welfare, but they were by no means the best known or the most institutionally well developed. Much more in the public eye and much more widespread, for example, was the massive effort to integrate youth into the imperial political and cultural order through religious and patriotic indoctrination in associations and clubs designed to cultivate morally healthy social life and recreation—an effort that came to be known as *Jugendpflege,* the "care" or "cultivation" of youth. The older religious youth groups remained the largest, but in the 1890s, as reformers concluded that only a small proportion of young people were interested in religious matters, gymnastics groups, sports clubs, the Boy Scouts, and other nonreligious associations proliferated rapidly. In 1875 there may have been 50,000 boys and girls (in about equal numbers) in *Jugendpflege* groups; by 1900 there were probably around 750,000.[6] At the same time, a growing number of communities established vocational schools offering young people opportunities for self-improvement in the form of night and weekend classes giving instruction in business, crafts, agriculture, and industrial arts, and to a lesser extent training in homemaking skills for girls. Usually this vocational training was combined with "citizenship education" *(staatsbürgerliche Erziehung),* which mixed the patriotic teaching of history, politics, and religion with simple instruction regarding the rights of citizens and the workings of government. In 1882 there were 623 of these schools in Prussia (the state with the lowest proportion of students); by 1897 there were 1,425. Saxony, Baden, Hessen, and several smaller German states had adopted mandatory vocational schooling by 1900.[7] In a related development, by 1899 some 2,000 teachers in 861 schools in 605 towns were offering industrial arts courses.[8]

Finally, a complete list of the most important child welfare initiatives of the 1890s would have to include initiatives such as the introduction of school breakfast and lunch programs and in-school medical services; special schools for handicapped or "difficult" children; Railway Station Missions for the "rescue" of wandering youth; shelters for abused, "endangered," or "fallen" girls; day care centers and preschools for the protection of the very young; cultural institutions such as public libraries and school libraries; temperance clubs, school savings plans, and an aggressive offensive against work on Sundays as forms of protection against immorality; stricter laws against child abuse (passed in 1901); orphanages and Educational Associations or Child Saving Associations; the continued expansion of care for mentally and physically handicapped children; and the mounting campaign for stricter child labor laws, which bore fruit in national legislation in 1903.

The Resistance to Progressive Reform

As this list suggests, the more liberal progressive response was by no means the only response to the "crisis" of the 1890s. The progressive affirmation of the fundamental principles of industrial society—bureaucracy, social administration, science, professionalism, social mobilization, and participation—was not universally accepted. More conservative people were far less sanguine in their assessment of the prospects for creating an orderly, healthy, "modern" social order. Although they were by no means blind to structural social problems, conservative reformers tended—as had those of the 1830s and 1840s—to believe that industrial society was destroying the underpinnings of social order by denying the spiritual foundations of social harmony. They bitterly decried the spread of philosophical "naturalism" and the decline of religiosity, the disintegration of the patriarchal family, the decline of respect for authority and morality. While the materialism and goal-rationality of capitalist culture undermined the sense of social and personal responsibility among both rich and poor, they held, the amoral selfishness of capitalist entrepreneurs was destroying the social institutions—in particular the family—in which those ethical norms were learned and made sense. Technical, materialistic capitalist society, grown too predatory and amoral, was destabilizing itself.

The Christian clergy played the leading role in articulating this conservative critique of industrial capitalism. Equally important in the 1890s, however, were parallel criticisms launched by the rapidly expanding women's movement. This alliance of women and the clergy for a "moral regeneration of the German people on a Christian foundation," for a "reform of human society in the spirit of Christianity," was of course clearest in the case of the Christian women's groups, which were founded with the assistance of the DCV and the Inner Mission and conceived of themselves largely as social service organizations.[9] But the dominant "maternalist" current within the moderate feminist mainstream of the bourgeois women's movement also represented in part a secularization of Christian critiques of capitalism. Individualism, materialism, rationalism, aggression, instrumental logic, and the struggle for power and wealth were interpreted as "masculine" principles. A revaluation of the feminine qualities of nurture, self-sacrifice, ethical commitment, and harmony had to be achieved, these women believed, as a corrective to the excessively predatory character of modern industrial capitalist society, which seemed to be on the verge of ripping itself apart in class and political conflict and cultural decay.[10] It was on this basis—that woman's "cultural mission" *(Kulturaufgabe)* of restoring harmony and ethical content to modern civilization and social relations demanded greater influence for women in public affairs—that most German feminists, particularly from the 1890s on, demanded that women be granted full civil and political rights. But charity and social work were seen as particularly appropriate expressions of the universal "motherliness" *(Mütterlichkeit)* of woman, her nurturing spirit, her capacity for ethical, self-sacrificing love, and they therefore became the most important sphere of activity for women's organizations, particularly the Christian women's groups.

A good example of the Christian critique of industrial society is an article published by Wilhelm Baur in 1891, in which social tension was interpreted as the expression of a "falling away from God." After the unification of Germany, he wrote, "we lived through years of national happiness"; but the serenity of those years was destroyed by the "chase after profit and pleasure" among the rich and the "wicked growth of grumbling discontent" among the workers.

> We have in our country firm institutions, but they are . . . terribly threatened by the forces of rebellion. . . . Insofar as these deny God, they deny the way of life derived from God's Word. They do not seek to end human injustice in society through any ideal pleasing to God. The new order which they praise . . . springs from the uncontrolled instinct of vulgar, earthly nature. . . . It is merely the organized and brutal expression of the naturalistic and emancipatory spirit at work in all classes of society. The siblings of socialism are all the other expressions of the same spirit: a science that is blind to God's revelation; an art

which brings to view not the beautiful, as prophet of a higher world above im-
perfect reality, but the downright ugly, if only it be real; a literature the often
brilliantly written products of which reveal already in their first pages the inevitable bacillus of adultery; an economic life whose virtue is satisfied with a
narrow escape from prison; [hedonistic] pleasures which degenerate from
crazed orgy into suicidal pessimism.[11]

In an article of the same year, Pastor Friedrich von Bodelschwingh outlined
the obvious solution to these problems: the family "must be [re]built on the
foundation of the Christian worldview."[12]

Whereas conservative Protestant reformers of the 1840s had hoped for a
spiritual revival, in the 1890s many proposed simply to reimpose, by law
and often by brute force, "patriarchal" relations within the family, the
workplace, and society at large. For this reason I have chosen to call this
current in reform thought *restorationist* reform. It was paralleled in national politics by the resignation of Chancellor Leopold von Caprivi in
1894 and of the Prussian minister of commerce, Baron Hans von Berlepsch,
in 1896; by talk among court circles of a coup d'état; and by government
attempts to secure the introduction of a number of measures intended to
contain or even crush social democracy—most notably the so-called Penitentiaries Bill (Zuchthausvorlage) and the Sedition Bill, and attempts to
pass an antiunion "law for the protection of labor." The "Lex Heinze" introduced in the national parliament in 1892 sought to gain control of the
urban underclass and of popular culture by introducing strict censorship as
well as harsh sentences for habitual criminals. And in labor law, the Industrial Code of 1891 introduced "protective" limitations on mothers' and indeed all women's industrial labor in an effort to impose patriarchal norms
on working-class families. All through the 1890s some social critics argued
that mothers should be banned from the factories entirely.

Restorationist reformers also viewed the problem of youth in highly
moralistic and punitive terms, a tendency well documented by Detlev
Peukert. Progressives saw socialist gains among young workers as a lamen-
table but understandable product of the experience of proletarian life and
labor; representatives of the more conservative view, though they condemned capitalism as exploitative and amoral, were less charitable. Peukert
quotes, for example, Ernst Floessel's complaint that

disobedience toward the parents expands into disobedience toward the employer, further toward the authorities, toward society itself. The so hotly de-
sired and so boundlessly arrogated freedom of our working youth consists
therein, that they . . . seek fame and honor in freedom and wildness, in disloy-
alty and betrayal, in uncaring selfishness and unbounded pleasure-seeking, and
thus discard all shame and all respect for the good order of society. Thus, big
industry raises up a host of young workers . . . who lend a willing ear . . . to the
mad teachings of the seducers of the people.[13]

Floessel commented with particular disapproval specifically on the habits of young workers' gangs, including singing dirty songs, public drinking, noisy and disorderly public outings (for example, while walking home from work), and open defiance of written or unwritten moral codes. The proper response to this rebelliousness, many suggested, was coercion. The conservative journal *Reichsbote* suggested that since "a great part of the social danger lies in the lack of discipline of the young workers," mandatory savings, corporal punishment at home, and an occasional "healthy smack from a policeman" were in order.[14] There was considerable support for judicial beatings for young offenders. Revisions of the Industrial Code in 1891 and 1897 not only allowed governments to require that young workers' wages be paid directly to their parents but also gave employers and foremen the right to beat their "apprentices," or young workers. And in 1899 conservative parliamentarians in Prussia even suggested revoking young people's freedom of movement in order to prevent them from leaving their families in the morally, physically, and politically "healthy" countryside to migrate to the corrupt and socialist cities—and, incidentally, to combat the rural labor shortage as well.[15]

Debate in the 1890s

The relationship between progressive and restorationist reformers in the 1890s was complex. While some conservatives were simply political, social, and cultural reactionaries, others were clearly part of the broader social reform movement, seeking what they considered to be modern solutions to modern social problems. The common commitment of social reformers to Christian bourgeois culture and particularly to the patriarchal, single-earner family, their shared perception of the "social question" as a collapse of patriarchal power, and the common aim of restoring order and elite control over society ensured a certain unity and overlap of social and social reform thought within the middle class. Moreover, some liberals remained committed in the 1890s to a more "Manchesterian" or laissez-faire approach to social change; they resisted both coercive restorationist and compensatory, social-managerial progressive proposals. Similarly, some conservative Christians, particularly Catholics, rejected progressive social management but also doubted the efficacy of brute force in the socialization of children. In the Prussian debate of 1899, for example, the Center party deputy Florian Hoheisel argued that since the root of disorderliness among young people was the collapse of religion, simple force would not suffice to restore good behavior. "We don't want [more] beatings," he objected; "we want to raise the child . . . on the basis of Christianity."[16] But while Catholics more often stressed the need for a *positive* response to social problems and the threat of socialist revolution, many conservative Protestants were also skeptical of mere repression. An article in the Protestant *Rettungshausbote* in 1896, for example, denounced as "moral philistines" those who recommended more beatings and better locks as a solution to social problems.[17]

Despite conceptual overlaps and confusing coalitions, however, the aims and methods of managerial progressive and restorationist reformers were sufficiently different, and their positions sufficiently clear, to lead to genuine conflicts in the 1890s. In 1897 Paul Felisch, the chairman of the Voluntary Educational Council in Berlin, summed up the progressive belief that restorationist measures would be futile: "One may lament the passing of patriarchal conditions, but no one can bring them back for us. The wheel of history cannot be rolled backwards, social development cannot be stopped."[18] At the other extreme, Wilhelm Baur found the very prospect of social reform itself suspect. Even the modern organizational forms and the mobilization of middle-class activism central to the Christian charities seemed to pose a threat to the culture of traditional society, to that form of private life in which authentic spiritual life flourished. "It might become necessary," he warned in 1891, "to protect the home, the insularity and warmth of family life, from the Inner Mission . . . and its instrumentalization of Christian personalities for the common good."[19] Baur also warned against allowing Christianity to become "one-sidedly feminine"—clearly a slap at the reform alliance of pastors and women, and at declining church attendance among men.

The case of vocational education illustrates the complexity and even confusion of these debates in the 1890s. Conservatives hoped to use these schools in the intensifying drive to indoctrinate working youth, to reduce the "damage" done by "premature" independence, and to inoculate youth against socialist influence. As the National Liberal deputy Albert Ernst somewhat euphemistically put it to the Prussian parliament in 1899, citizenship education had a crucial corrective political function, since, "when the German Empire was created and every German citizen was given the right to vote, the state should have taken care that in the schools the necessary instruction was given concerning the rights and duties of German citizenship." And yet the vocational school was primarily intended to offer young people opportunities to develop technical skills. "We have reached a cultural level," Ernst remarked, "upon which we can look with some pride. But, gentlemen, if we wish to progress with the times and not let ourselves be outstripped by our neighbors, then it is not enough that only the best in our society progress; rather, we must also see to it that the populace as a whole progresses."[20] By integrating young workers into the industrial labor force at higher skill levels, the vocational schools would secure two aims: on the one hand, that of giving them a better standard of living and the

moral stability of a proper calling *(Beruf)*; and, on the other, that of preserving and expanding national power by facilitating industrial growth.

But in the eyes of conservatives, of course, it was precisely this economic
transformation which had created the political and cultural problem of
youth in the first place; and many genuine conservatives believed that urban
industrial-capitalist life was unnatural and harmful, and could not be made
otherwise. Nor did conservative thinkers necessarily see educational opportunity as a good thing: as Martin Hennig, director of the Rauhes Haus in
Hamburg, wrote in 1900, "Expanded knowledge is a dangerous means to
the bad in the hands of the mass of the people, if it does not rest on the
basis of religious and moral education."[21]

Moreover, the political indoctrination pursued by the vocational schools
was not always merely reactionary in spirit. On the contrary, the progressive assumption that bourgeois society could make peace with modernity
through strategies of management and integration could be applied to the
political realm as well as to the social. Carl von Massow argued, for example, that "the working man often knows nothing of his rights. If
working youth were made familiar with the laws and also with the protection which they give the people, social democracy would not have such an
easy time spreading its mad teachings. Here one can say again: . . . We
cannot go back, so—forward!"[22] Paul Scheven made a similar point in
1898: "The government of the modern state no longer relies simply upon
the activity of its officials and the passivity of its inhabitants, but rather
upon the cheerful collaboration of all citizens. The age of the police state, in
which people only commanded or obeyed, is irretrievably past. Consultation and cooperative action are the order of the day." He listed not only
voting in parliamentary elections but also jury trials, the industrial courts
of arbitration, the municipalities, the self-governing health insurance agencies, and associational life as offering "each and every one the opportunity
to engage his energy for the public interest."[23]

In other words, progressive reform, in blurring the distinction between
state and civil society, tended toward a political ideal of active participation
rather than passive obedience. This was not a message calculated to please
conservatives, who rejected not only political democracy but the entire optimistic assessment of the potentials of modernity, the affirmation of economic change, state intervention in social relations, and the political and
social mobilization which lay at the heart of progressive reform.

At the same time, even programs as innocuous as training in housekeeping for girls, which was introduced in many vocational schools, could
seem even to less conservative activists to be a threat to traditional patterns
of individual responsibility. At the 1893 conference of the semigovern-
mental CAW, for example, one Headmaster Reddersen (an advocate of
the extension of correctional education to the "not yet" criminal) warned
that making such courses general might keep the "better mothers" from

teaching their children, and so weaken the daughters' bond with the family. One should "resort to this radical measure" only where it was necessary "in order that everything not be lost," in cities with large populations of working mothers. Speaking of child welfare generally, he drew his colleagues' attention

> to the fact that we must not fail, in our chase after new institutions . . ., to weigh carefully whether the hoped-for gain is not canceled by an equally great loss, or whether we are not chasing out one evil with another, one bad spirit with another. All institutions which are created to meet the gross failures and harms which occur in the performance of the basic tasks of child rearing must be regarded strictly as emergency measures. Overhasty, even if well-meaning, efforts to create such institutions obviously lure parents into giving up their natural duty toward their children. . . . If we want to support the maintenance and promotion of family spirit and domestic virtues, then we must try to prevent parents from becoming even more accustomed to needlessly shifting the care of their children onto other people's shoulders. . . . Where proper foresight and insight are lacking, the ethical bonds which connect parents and their children can easily be loosened even more, and that would be a further, hardly concealed step toward socialism.[24]

Reddersen's comments drew a chorus of approval.

Three years later, in a discussion of school lunch programs at the conference of the DVAW, the debate was livelier; but again the critics of reform outnumbered its supporters. The main speaker, City Councillor Cuno of Königsberg, took the position that children should be given breakfast in school only if that was necessary in order for them to be able to concentrate. He rejected the demand, made by Social Democrats, that all children be served a common meal in school. If a family could not feed its children properly, then it should petition for assistance from the poor relief authorities; otherwise, argued his colleague Victor Böhmert, one might "weaken the parents' sense of responsibility and loosen family ties."[25] To Hermann Abraham, who represented a private organization providing meals in Berlin schools, this position seemed "absolutely incomprehensible." "However one may judge the worthiness and need of the parents," he protested, "nowhere should children suffer, even if unwillingness to work or lack of thrift cause insufficient nourishment." Not only was it inhuman to allow children to go hungry, but also a poorly nourished child could all too easily fall victim to "bad impulses" toward theft and social envy, and hunger could "even often become the driving force behind excesses and the wellspring of a life of crime."[26] Nevertheless, the assembly favored Cuno's formulation, rejecting the notion that the schools should be used as a field on which to fight social problems.

Finally, the issue of committing merely wayward children to correctional education sparked a lively and very confused debate. Criticism of the idea came from diverse quarters. Cuno warned in 1899 that even the existing law, which allowed commitment where parents "misuse[d] the right to raise their children," was so vague that it could "give a foothold to a modern Inquisition" in which bringing up a child according to the beliefs of a particular political party or religious confession would constitute "misuse."[27] Many predicted, too, that the suggested reform could have a disastrous effect on popular morality by undermining parents' sense of responsibility. The Prussian Ministry of the Interior, for example, argued that "as long as one cannot prevent imprudent and bad parents from bringing children into the world, one should make them aware by every possible means that they are responsible to society for the children's respectable upbringing."[28] Such fears were particularly common in more conservative Catholic circles, owing to their special concern for the autonomy of the family and the church and to their experience with state repression. At the third annual conference of the DCV, leading figures in Catholic reform (Lorenz Werthmann, its director, and Franz Brandts, a major figure in Catholic politics and charities in the Rhineland) vigorously argued that only "theorists" worried about state socialism. But the organization's official spiritual counselor warned against the "leaning toward the socialist conception of the state which this measure documents." Not only was there the danger that children might be committed on religious or political grounds, but also it would be extremely difficult to limit the number of commitments on *social* grounds, since, "in the big cities, what children are *not* endangered?"[29] The socialization of children, he insisted, was the business of family and the church, and not of the state; he therefore favored a more effective organization of private charity rather than a revision of the law.

Protestants were less fearful; in fact, the Prussian General Synod itself asked the government to work for the extension of correctional education.[30] Nevertheless, there were still many Protestants who preferred private action to that of the state. Martin Hennig, for example, warned that "he who expects everything from the state will feel the state's might," and claimed that the proper response to the "youth problem" would therefore be to organize a national network of private educational associations.[31] Of course, Wichern himself had believed that the trust necessary for real spiritual influence would be destroyed among children and their families if the *Rettungshaus* became a "penal institution" serving the state.[32] The Christian project of religious revitalization, in other words, was not necessarily compatible with that of social management.

The Bürgerliches Gesetzbuch of 1897–1900

The strength of all these objections was such that in the debate over the passage of the new Code of Civil Law (Bürgerliches Gesetzbuch, or BGB) between 1896 and 1899, progressives were forced to mount a desperate lobbying campaign merely to avoid seeing all legal basis for their proposed child welfare programs abolished. The BGB did produce some substantial gains for supporters of correctional education: the maximum age of commitment was raised from sixteen to eighteen, and children could now be held until the age of twenty-one rather than only eighteen. But these concessions were more than balanced by the fact that the Reichstag's commission for revising the draft of the BGB passed by a slight majority a petition, presented by the Catholic Center party, which proposed simply striking from the draft the stipulation that a child could be committed to correctional education even if the parents were not to blame for its waywardness.[33] Without such a clause, of course, the passage of the national code would have invalidated the state laws passed in the late 1880s, such as Baden's.

Legal guardianship reform fared no better. The 1888 draft of the BGB virtually reproduced the provisions of the Prussian Vormundschaftsordnung of 1875, arguing that individual guardianship was "the most natural and appropriate form," since it reproduced the "natural" pattern of independent paternal authority.[34] Rather than permitting public guardianship, the committee preferred instead the simple expedient of allowing *women* to be legal guardians: this would, it believed, secure a sufficient supply of guardians, and women would also, because of their native "motherliness," be *better* guardians.[35] Since the new code did nothing to improve the position of single mothers under private law, progressives such as Taube saw its passage as a disaster.

In the face of these threats, progressive reform circles and state and municipal governments just managed to save their initiatives. At the last minute clauses were inserted into the Law for the Introduction of the Code of Civil Law (Einführungsgesetz zum Bürgerlichen Gesetzbuch, or EGBGB) which allowed state laws regarding correctional education and public guardianship to stand—although in the case of correctional education these laws had to stipulate that commitment was allowed only where it could be shown to be "absolutely necessary for the prevention of the complete moral ruin of the child," a condition that appeared to rule out, among other things, commitment of children who were simply poor.[36]

Progressive reformers thus snatched from the jaws of defeat if not a victory at least the chance of a rematch. In the decade after 1900, however, in the context of growing prosperity and optimism, they hastened to exploit the narrow window of opportunity left open by the EGBGB.

CHAPTER THREE

Expansion and Consolidation, 1900–1914

The Expansion of Correctional Education and the Juvenile Courts

In the decade after the passage of the BGB the opportunities salvaged in the EGBGB were exploited by a growing movement of child welfare reform entrenched in social organizations and state and local bureaucracies. The years between 1900 and 1910 saw an explosive, exuberant growth of both private and public welfare activity, informed by the ideas which men like Appelius and Pagel had worked out in the preceding decade and by an extraordinary spirit of optimism and urgency. By 1910 the organizational forms of modern child welfare had taken definitive shape in numerous local and experimental initiatives, and reformers were poised to take legislative steps to impose them nationally.

In the field of correctional education the passage of the BGB created a flurry of advocacy at the state level, as child welfare reformers scurried to ensure that their governments would take advantage of the loophole created by the EGBGB. By the time the Prussian government presented a bill to parliament, in 1899, these groups had ensured that the passage of the new law was a foregone conclusion. Paragraph 1 of the law, passed on July 2, 1900, allowed commitment of children up to age eighteen to correctional education not only if they were abused or had committed a crime but also simply "in order to prevent complete moral ruin."[1] These provisions immensely expanded the number of children eligible for correctional education, and indeed altered the character of the institution fundamentally—a change reflected in the Prussian parliament's decision to call it *Fürsorgeerziehung* (welfare education) rather than *Zwangserziehung* (forcible education).

The new law inspired a tremendously enthusiastic response among middle-class reformers. For the *Rettungshäuser* it meant a flood of new inmates and public subsidies. And private charities hoped that the government's explicit instructions to local authorities to rely on private organizations in locating potential cases of waywardness would galvanize public interest in their work. The director of the Rauhes Haus, Martin Hennig, noted approvingly that it was "a unique characteristic of this law that it has adopted in quite unusually high degree the idea of the mobilization of the free energies" of civil society.[2] More important, the program of the new law appealed to the tradition of moral regeneration, since many Christians hoped that the threat of losing their children would frighten working-class parents into greater respectability. Thus, the conservative Carl von Massow, in a pamphlet that was widely distributed in reform circles, called the law "one of the greatest social acts, if not the greatest of all those which the history of states and peoples records"; Pastor Gustav von Rohden called it "one of the great social and moral acts of our time"; and the Child Protection Commission of the Federation of German Women's Associations (Bund Deutscher Frauenvereine, or BDF) called it and the child labor law of 1903 "the most important innovations in social policy."[3] But the law also appealed to the more managerial, progressive reform current. The idea of managing crime, of preventing children from becoming wayward and criminal by resocializing rather than punishing them, paralleled the progressive program of making society more efficient and just rather than merely enforcing its laws.

The enthusiastic efforts of private organizations helped to produce an explosive expansion of correctional education. In the first year the total number of children committed was 7,787, compared to 1,402 committed under the law of 1878 in 1900.[4] That number fell to 6,470 in 1903–04, but then rose steadily to 7,995 in 1908–09. Indeed, while the Prussian government had estimated in 1900 that the total number of children in correctional education would eventually double under the new law, from some 10,000 to some 20,000, in fact by 1914 there were 55,229 children in correctional education in Prussia.[5] Rates of institutionalization varied greatly from state to state (for example, about 4 per 10,000 minors in the general population in Prussia, and 2 per 10,000 in Bavaria under a law of 1902), but everywhere the expansion after 1900 was substantial.[6]

The reform of correctional education also imparted a new momentum to efforts to revise criminal procedure for minors—the other item on the agenda set forward by Appelius and the International Criminological Association (Internationale Kriminalistische Vereinigung, or IKV) in 1892. Reform in this area was also inspired, however, by the example of the creation of juvenile courts in the United States after 1899 and the imminence of a re-

form of the Code of Criminal Law after mid-decade. Meetings of the
Conference of German Jurists (Deutscher Juristentag) in 1904 and 1905
adopted a clear call for reform, as did a meeting of the German section of
the IKV in 1906; and by 1908 the idea of juvenile law reform had broad
support among middle-class reformers.

Their central concern was that the application of criminal law to minors
should have as its aim not primarily abstract justice and punishment but
rather reintegration of the child into society through education. The arguments of reformers in the 1900s in favor of *"Erziehung statt Strafe"* (education, not punishment) for young offenders were much the same as those
advanced by Appelius: punishing children with prison terms was, they held,
both unjust and ineffective. They proposed setting up juvenile courts, and
providing each with a special organization, the "juvenile court assistance"
(*Jugendgerichtshilfe,* or JGH), to advise the judge from a pedagogical, psychiatric, and social—rather than a merely legal—perspective. The JGH
advisers might include psychiatrists, volunteer social workers, and self-
appointed "experts" of social standing; they would investigate the child's
family life, milieu, development, and mental state in order to orient the
judge as to the meaning and origins of the crime; "stand by" the child and
testify during the trial; and provide a volunteer probation officer if the child
were given a conditional sentence.

The fundamental hostility of reformers to certain aspects of established
legal procedure led to serious conflicts with more conservative jurists and
prevented the adoption of legislation. At the local level, however, judicial
officials pushed ahead despite the failure to secure new legislation, through
the simple expedient (proposed in 1905 by Paul Köhne, a Guardianship
Court judge in Berlin) of combining the offices of criminal judge and
Guardianship Court judge in a single person. The first such juvenile court
was created in Frankfurt am Main in 1908, with that city's private Verein
Kinderschutz (an offshoot of the Centrale für private Fürsorge, of which
Wilhelm Polligkeit was director) providing juvenile court assistance and assuming the duties of probation officer. Thereafter the idea spread with what
one supporter called "elemental force": by the beginning of 1909 there
were some 70 juvenile courts, and by 1913 there were 556.[7]

The Roots of Infant Health Policy

The reform of correctional education and the formation of the juvenile
courts obviously grew out of that sense of social crisis discussed in Chapter
2. By the middle of the 1900s, however, an important change of emphasis
within the child welfare movement was taking place, as attention shifted
gradually from issues of social order, cultural hegemony, and political legitimacy toward the central themes of Pagel's essay of 1895: economic

efficiency, the integration of the working class into the industrial social order, and national power. This shift was reflected above all in the rapid expansion after 1905 of programs for the control of infant mortality.

Several developments were critical in bringing about this shift. In the first place, by the 1900s Germany was caught up in an unprecedented and sustained industrial boom. By 1905 the Great Depression of 1873–1895 was ten years in the past, and the "second" industrial revolution—the emergence of the new chemical and electromechanical industries, the rationalization of factory production, and the triumph of management over entrepreneurship—was transforming the industrial landscape. Overall industrial production more than doubled between 1890 and 1910, and the value of foreign trade also doubled in these two decades.[8] The factory system, already familiar by 1890, was consolidated by a wave of industrial concentration. Whereas establishments of over fifty workers employed 26.2 percent of all workers in 1882, by 1907 the total was 47.7 percent.[9] The population of Germany poured westward into the urban industrial areas: while Prussia's five easternmost provinces lost 646,000 inhabitants between 1890 and 1900, Berlin gained 142,000, and Westphalia and the Rhineland 411,000. In 1882, 35 percent of the work force was employed in industry, mining, and construction; by 1907, 42.8 percent.[10]

Despite these massive social and economic changes and the rapid growth of socialism and the trade unions, there were some indications that the more confrontational period of class politics might be on the wane. Real wages, for example, rose slowly but steadily.[11] The controversy over revisionism and the publication in 1899 of Eduard Bernstein's *Evolutionary Socialism* suggested that democratic socialism might abandon the more threatening aspects of revolutionary ideology. What is more, as socialists slowly broke into municipal government, it became apparent that they were often willing and eager to support or initiate many pragmatic progressive reform measures against conservative and liberal opposition, particularly in public health. And though urban growth before 1900 had indeed created frightening urban problems (including the cholera epidemic of 1892 in Hamburg), by the middle of the 1900s it was clear that government intervention could resolve at least some of them. Early successes in combating disease and in lowering mortality rates generally were particularly important in this respect, but improvements in services such as lighting, transportation, sanitation, and police protection also had an impact.

Whereas rapid social change in the 1890s had inspired a sense of impending social and political catastrophe, after 1900 the mood of many reformers was becoming more optimistic, as the outlines of a powerful, potentially stable industrial social order emerged. It was increasingly plausible to argue, as Pagel had a decade earlier, that social stability was the product not of stasis and hierarchy but of progress and change, and social harmony the result of economic growth and participation rather than of a culture of passivity and deference. By 1909 the district court judge J. F. Landsberg could argue that while industrialization had created severe social tensions, "that must not be allowed to mislead us into seeking a cure in the inhibition of industrial development. On the contrary: the forces which have brought about the danger by their emergence must also bring forth the remedy."[12] Moreover, a growing number of child welfare reformers began to consider not merely stability but growth, dynamism, and power as the goal of their efforts. In the context of the adoption of a crass Darwinistic model of international relations, chauvinistic economic nationalism, the national government's aggressive imperialist *Weltpolitik,* and the rising threat of war, industrial growth came to be a reassuring expression of national vitality. Frieda Duensing, director of the National Center for Child Welfare, remarked in 1907 that "our victories on the world market speak of the health and strength of our people."[13] Indeed, by 1910 Germany was clearly the second greatest industrial power on earth, after the United States.

In this context the issue of infant mortality became increasingly central to social reform discourse—both because of the perceived need for an expanding pool of military recruits and because of the nascent labor shortage created by industrial growth. The problem of infant mortality was a daunting one. Average infant mortality in the German Empire was 20.7 percent in 1901—among European nations lower only than rates in Russia, Romania, and Austria-Hungary. Poor people were simply unable to provide a healthy environment for infants; mortality among infant children of senior civil servants was 11 percent in 1901, that for the children of unskilled workers was 20 percent, and for children of recipients of poor relief 36.37 percent.[14]

These figures were not new; in Prussia, for example, infant mortality had peaked in 1871–1875 at 22.4 percent. The infant mortality rate had been a central concern for the growing number of doctors involved in public health in the 1870s, and the Imperial Health Bureau (Reichsgesundheitsamt) had studied the problem as early as 1875–1877.[15] It was not until the end of the 1890s, however, that infant mortality became a high priority. The Central Bureau for Organizations for Workers' Welfare (CAW) held a major conference on the subject in 1899.[16] After 1901 the government published separate statistics for infant mortality. In 1904 a Society to Combat Infant Mortality (Gesellschaft zur Bekämpfung der Säuglingssterblichkeit) was created in Berlin, which established a system of veterinary inspection for the dairies that supplied Berlin with milk and undertook a publicity campaign in favor of breast-feeding. This organization's success (by 1907 it was distributing sterile milk to 3,642 women) helped move the city council of Berlin to budget 80,000 marks in 1905 to establish four "infant welfare stations" *(Säuglingsfürsorgestellen)* to provide free medical consultation, sterile milk, and other services. At the end of 1904 the empress officially directed the Patriotic Women's League (Vaterländische Frauenvereine)—of which she was patron—to assist the authorities in their efforts to reduce infant mortality.[17] A conference of the DVAW on the subject in 1905 offered a broad range of practical policy proposals and focused attention on the issue. In 1906 a national center for infant health, the Empress Auguste-Victoria House for Combating Infant Mortality (Kaiserin Auguste-Viktoria Haus, or KAVH), was founded as a coordinating center for these efforts (though the center did not open until 1909). By 1908 the campaign against infant mortality was, as one organizer put it, a kind of "popular movement."[18]

The advance of medical knowledge and the development of a coherent understanding of the causes of infant death played an important role in inspiring this "discovery" of infant mortality by discrediting Malthusian fears and the view that children who died in infancy were simply "weak" (and therefore, for the good of the "race," *should* be allowed to die). Moreover, because infant mortality was declining more rapidly in many other areas of Europe, a growing number of observers found it "shameful" (so said the keynote speakers at the conferences of 1899 and 1905) that Germany's infant mortality rate was second only to those of its less advanced eastern neighbors.[19] Concern over the growth of women's employment in industry and the possible effects of this trend on birthrates and infant health also grew as the industrial boom drew women into the factories. Finally, the government's support for infant health campaigns was motivated in part by a desire to create a respectable conservative alternative to the demands of the radical feminist League for the Protection of Motherhood (Bund für Mutterschutz), founded in 1904–5. Those demands included, for example, expanded legal rights for illegitimate children and single mothers, sex education in the schools, and public maternity benefits for all mothers.[20]

But the most important motivation for controlling infant mortality and morbidity derived from the prevailing imperialist mood of the 1900s. As the director of the KAVH, Arthur Keller, remarked in 1909, few people were outraged by the simple fact that so many infants died.

> But that significantly fewer infants die in neighboring countries, that their birthrate, that their population growth is significantly greater, that moves people to pay attention, and *so protection of infants becomes a national cause, care for the individual becomes care for the nation.* . . . This shows that this [concern] has less to do with protection of the child than protection of the nation. People speak much less of nationalistic motivations than of children's rights and our ethical duties, but the former are, even if not spoken loudly, considerably more attractive.[21]

Max Seiffert's essay of 1906 "On the Cultural and Social Significance of Child Mortality" summed up the progressive perspective on infant welfare in detail. Infants, Seiffert pointed out, represented a considerable investment on the part of the parents and of society. Fertile parents were a form of fixed capital investment, of productive machinery, which had been created at considerable cost to society over a period of generations; reproduction represented an "investment" of productive energies as well, since it cost parents energy, time, and money, and removed women from the work force. This sacrifice was in vain if the infant died. Finally, the death of an infant destroyed the potential productivity of that particular child, representing a "diminution of the living raw material from which the future bearers and protectors of our cultural assets are drawn." In fact, assuming that every infant was worth at least 100 marks, Seiffert calculated that in 1900, with 440,992 infant deaths, total lost investment was 44,099,200 marks—a conservative estimate, since middle-class and upper-class children received better, more expensive care, and were therefore worth 200 and 300 marks each, respectively.[22]

Moreover, as another study of 1906 pointed out, there were further costs, since "mortality grows only on the soil of heightened morbidity, which impairs the constitution of the survivors."[23] Not only did families and the state have to bear the costs of medical treatment of sick infants, but since children whose constitutions were damaged by childhood disease and privation grew up with below-optimum resistance to disease, society also had to bear the costs of treating them for the rest of their lives. And these costs were nothing compared to the loss of productivity caused by the lost workdays and shortened working lives of sickly adults.

All this inefficiency, Seiffert argued, had a cumulative effect. The strain of repeated pregnancy and childbirth weakened women, with the result that they gave birth to sickly infants. Having a large family might also force the woman to go out to work rather than stay home and breast-feed her newborn, yet again increasing the likelihood of its early demise or constitutional weakness—and of conception. A vicious circle of weakness, infant death, and renewed pregnancy was thus created, perpetuating reproductive inefficiency and creating generations of costly weaklings. This pattern was "the deepest root of physical, economic, and moral proletarianization." It trapped families in poverty generation after generation and brutalized them emotionally and spiritually, creating fatalism and passivity. This "moral proletarianization" was "inseparably bound up in iron complementarity with economic proletarianization." The whole process thus created a "serious social danger."[24]

But again, whereas the social threat presented by the poor had been central to Pagel's analysis, Seiffert's was informed above all by imperialist and eugenic concerns for the quantity and quality of population as the foundation of national power. His central fear was that the direct and indirect costs of high infant mortality and morbidity weakened the nation "in the physical and economic battle for existence among the peoples of the earth."[25] A speech delivered by the doctor and infant health advocate Arthur Schlossmann to an assembly of notables in the industrial Rhineland in 1906 summed up this analysis of the significance of high infant mortality rates:

> In an age in which military strength is the foundation for the political position of a state relative to other states, every addition to the population must be most welcome *because it increases our influence in the concert of nations.* And here in Düsseldorf, in the center of west German industry, I need not explain in detail what it means if we have 500,000 more people every year, if every year 500,000 new workers mature who can be welcome helpers in production for the world market and who are at the same time consumers for all that is produced. Population growth means heightened consumption and heightened consumption means heightened profits. Population growth is one of the most important factors by which we have developed from the poor agrarian people of the past into the rich industrial nation of our days.
>
> But we want to grow not only quantitatively but also qualitatively. Just as the world market is, in the long term, open only to the best producers, so only a people whose individual members . . . are physically in top form can keep its place, economically and politically, in the sun. The unrelenting drive of our times demands a resistant, healthy population.[26]

Such pronouncements were not unique to the field of infant health; on the contrary, there was a growing tendency among child welfare advocates to regard children, and indeed the population at large, explicitly as a resource for the state, which had to be managed and exploited in a rational manner. In 1907, for example, the feminist Helene Simon referred to young people entering the labor force as "the most valuable and also the most expensive annual harvest."[27] Heinz Potthoff remarked in 1909, in an article titled "The Profitability of Child Welfare," that "the human being is not only the subject but also the most important object of social economics."[28] And a retired minister named Hentig wrote in the same year that if a child can be kept alive and healthy to the age of fourteen, educated, and trained for a career, then everything he or she produces "represents a profit" on investment.[29]

The growing popularity of these ideas created, as in the case of correctional education and juvenile courts, a rapid and impressive wave of institutional development. Whereas there were four sterile milk distribution centers in Germany in 1900, between 1901 and 1910 fifty-eight more were established. There were seventy-eight infant day care centers *(Krippen)* in 1900, 148 in 1910. There were nineteen infants' homes *(Säuglingsheime)* and infant health clinics in 1900, 101 by 1910. The backbone of the new programs, however, was formed by the infant welfare stations created after the pattern established in Berlin: four existed in 1900; 251 were established in the next ten years.[30] The stations were usually created and staffed by bourgeois women's organizations (particularly the Patriotic Women's Leagues) though usually placed under the authority of the municipality and directed by a doctor. Not included in these figures were public supervision of foster children, which spread rapidly after a conference of the DVAW once again warmly recommended the system in 1902; provision of free medical treatment for indigent mothers and children; increased nonmandatory services by health insurance agencies; birthing clinics and postnatal clinics; support for private associations that offered maternal advice or paid premiums to women who agreed to breast-feed; and so on.

The Pattern of Expansion: The State and "Private" Social Reform

In each of these fields—correctional education, juvenile justice, infant health—the rapid expansion of child welfare programs was accomplished by a "movement" or campaign in which governmental and private efforts were closely coordinated. In most cases the distinction is virtually meaningless; the great flowering of "private" child welfare organizations in this period was in fact a semiofficial campaign to activate the ruling class—whether inside or outside of government—in support of the social reform agenda. Paul Weindling has quite rightly referred to these private organizations as "intermediary stages in the shift . . . to state intervention."[31]

In the field of correctional education, advocates of expanding the system launched a drive aimed at creating such associations in as many towns as possible; but it was the initiative of government officials acting in semiprivate roles which was most effective in translating the enthusiasm sparked by the new law into practical action. Across Prussia, administrative and judicial officials worked hand in hand with private persons, often calling the initial organizational meetings, to found a large number of private and semiprivate associations and coalitions of charity organizations *(Zentralen)*. A similar process occurred in Bavaria after the passage of its new correctional education law in 1902.[32] The makeup of the leadership of these *Zentralen* suggests the extent to which they were the product of the mobilization of a single social elite both within and outside government. The paying members of the Danzig Child Welfare Association, for example, included the highest officials of the provincial Protestant church and a number of lower clergy, the highest officials of the provincial administration and several lesser bureaucrats in the provincial and city governments, the mayor and four city councillors, *Landräte* (heads of local county administration), the directors of local schools and of the provincial school administration, the judicial elite of city and province, and a host of lesser judicial officials, several lawyers, and a cross-section of the economic leadership, including bank directors, factory owners, apothecaries, and so forth.[33] Also active in many such organizations were the wives of officials and judges—who also were often prominent within the Patriotic Women's Leagues, which did much of the practical work of child welfare. Teachers frequently formed the core working staff of such organizations.

The interpenetration of "public" and "private" efforts was even greater in the case of the juvenile courts. The system of juvenile court assistance involved an even more active role for the private groups, and closer association with the supporting state institution, than did commitment of children to correctional education. Just as important, however, the governments of the several states played an even more active part in enlisting private aid than they had in the case of correctional education. The Prussian and Hessian justice ministries, for example, issued decrees warmly recommending the system to district courts and private charities in 1909. The Bavarian government went the furthest: in 1908 it directed local administrations to create child welfare associations to take on the functions of juvenile court assistance wherever such did not already exist.[34] Quite apart from these government decrees, moreover, the courts themselves often took the initiative in summoning up private juvenile court assistance. The organizations which emerged to assist the guardianship court judges, then, were in fact only very nominally "private" associations. The Child Protection Association of Krefeld, for example, though it took the legal form of a private association, consisted of the Orphans' Councillor, the city's public guardian for illegitimate children, the local district attorney, the juvenile court judge, and four members elected by the city council. The more aptly named Committee of Lennep included the mayor, the Catholic and Protestant pastors, the directors of the Catholic and Protestant schools, one social worker from the city's Orphans' Council, and four members elected by the town assembly.[35]

The pattern was continued, finally, in the infant welfare campaign. At the national level, the "private" KAVH was in fact an appendage of the Prussian government's health bureaucracy. It acted as a semiofficial clearinghouse passing information and directives from the imperial health authorities to "private" organizations at the local level. Those local organizations, of course, were again only nominally private. In January 1907 a position paper of the Imperial Health Bureau was circulated to the state governments, which responded in the following year with a series of decrees directing local authorities to take steps to encourage or initiate the development of infant health programs in the municipalities and counties.[36] A good example of the result was the development of the Verein für Säuglingsfürsorge im Regierungsbezirk Düsseldorf in the Rhineland, a model organization which would be critically important in the future development of child welfare programs (and social work generally). The organization was conceived at a meeting of regional medical and administrative authorities and charity leaders called by the head of the district administration in December 1906 and officially founded at a larger meeting of industrialists, administrative and judicial authorities, and the "socially concerned" elite in February 1907. Cooperating closely with and in some degree coextensive with the administration of the district, the organization was in fact a semi-public welfare agency.[37]

Cooperation at the local level was equally close. A good example is the Saxon district of Schwarzenburg, where, in response to a directive of the state Ministry of the Interior in the spring of 1907, the head of the local administration *(Amtshauptmann)* called together the district doctor and the district veterinarian, the local mayor, a private doctor named Mönch, and the director and owner of a factory in the district (presumably its largest employer) to create a "committee or association" which would institute voluntary supervision of local infants by Dr. Mönch and, as his assistants, "those ladies who . . ., by virtue of the position of their husbands, will have influence over the mothers."[38] Finally, even the individual institutions established by infant health reformers often reproduced the same pattern. Of the 101 existing maternal advice centers in Germany in 1907, twenty-eight were municipally owned, thirty-one were owned wholly by private associations, and forty-two were operated privately but funded at least in part by local governments.[39]

The Science of Social Management

As the institutional consolidation of child welfare progressed, child welfare practitioners increasingly turned to an "objective" language of natural science and to medical knowledge to guide, and to legitimate, their day-to-day activities. By 1910 scientific models and language were clearly becoming increasingly central to progressive child welfare reform, transforming its potential and dynamics, and the influence specifically of doctors and of medical metaphors was growing.

This transition is perhaps most strikingly revealed in shifting interpretations of the causes of waywardness. Abandoning the Christian understanding of the nature of waywardness, a growing number of child welfare practitioners adopted an interpretation drawn directly from the contemporary development of psychiatric "science." Where Christians saw moral derailment resulting from the pathological freedom of modern life as the cause of delinquency, prostitution, and rowdiness, psychiatry posited simply "degeneration," and particularly the existence of organic brain defects. In the early 1900s psychiatric models usually amounted to a secularization of Christian moralistic interpretations; the view that the lower classes were degenerate and defective was little more than a variant of the older belief that they were dissolute and immoral. Clemens Neisser, for example, remarked in 1906 that the inmates of reformatories were recruited from the same social class *(Volksschicht)* as most criminals, the mentally ill, and "all those who are in any way socially or morally deviant."[40] Paul Köhne similarly restated traditional cultural critiques in neurological terms, writing of the "excessive demands placed on the nervous system of modern youth" by the variety and velocity of urban life, and of the resulting growth in the incidence of "hysteria, neurasthenia, and psychopathic constitution" among young people.[41]

This superficial adoption of scientific rhetoric could imply a profound pessimism: obviously, it was impossible to achieve the moral reformation of someone who suffered from a brain defect. But the use of natural-scientific metaphors (which is all that psychiatric "science" really amounted to) could also imply a rejection of the pessimism of conservative cultural criticism, since it suggested that an effective scientific "cure" for the problems of modernity could be constructed. Köhne held that it would "be a stupid and futile beginning to seek . . . to hold back the tide of our economic life or steer it onto another path. Our task is rather to harness all intellectual and moral forces in order to find new ways and expedients which make it possible despite more difficult conditions of life to retain and strengthen the physical and moral health of youth."[42] And in 1901 Franz von Liszt voiced the hope that in the case of the excess of vital energies in which crime was rooted (as in the case of other "social phenomena"), men would, "once the causes have been recognized, be able to direct it according to our will, like the course of rivers and electric power."[43] This was obviously a perspective more congenial to the progressive reform project than the cultural pessimism of Christian moralist social theorists.

There were, moreover, important practical incentives for practitioners to adopt psychiatric models. The spread of psychiatric theories of waywardness greatly strengthened reformers' arguments for the "preventive" use of correctional education. The moralistic pathos and subjective style of Christian discourse left it open to challenge; but psychiatry as the "science" of waywardness could claim to be able to identify in a child's behavior the early "symptoms" of a defined and predictable "organic" moral degeneration or faulty development. The transformation of waywardness from a moral judgment into a medical diagnosis promised to offer judges and child welfare agencies a much more universally legitimate and authoritative basis for making the decision to remove children from their families. And it helped to legitimate the entire system of surveillance by private associations and public agencies which was designed to transform correctional education into a system of *preventive* management, rather than merely of corrective intervention.

The adoption of scientific models was even more rapid in juvenile justice reform than in correctional education. The program of the juvenile court in fact represented a striking abandonment of standards of justice and due process in favor of a "social scientific," managerial-administrative approach. Reformers hoped that JGH would transform the court into a kind of social work agency for delinquents, in which judicial measures were guided by knowledge not merely of the character of the crimes committed but by the insights of experts in child psychology and social work. In the context of this system of informal expert consultation there was little room for the formal rules of criminal procedure. Instead, reformers adopted a medicalized terminology and agitated in favor of a formal role for nonjudicial experts. Reservations were expressed particularly about allowing a formal defense, especially in the presence of the defendant, since this might heighten the young offender's sense that he or she was being wronged. Thekla Friedländer declared at a 1909 conference, for example, that in many cases legal "defense is downright pernicious," while Max Taube suggested that all young offenders be examined by a psychiatrist; a third speaker at the same conference suggested that "the doctor's voice must then be decisive in the judge's decision." Wilhelm Polligkeit, finally, explained at the same meeting that while the old formal trial "was like a dramatic performance in which the young person could incorrectly feel himself the hero," trial by the juvenile court resembled more closely "an operation in a clinic."[44]

In the case of infant health, of course, this process of medicalization was fastest and most widespread. It was the discovery that the greatest proportion of infant deaths were produced by gastrointestinal diseases that gave infant health campaigners a viable strategy for combating infant mortality. Given the problems of hygiene in lower-class housing, they concluded that the most important factor determining mortality was whether infants were breast-fed or not. Persuading mothers to breast-feed was also, of course, the cheapest method of approaching the problem. The infant health campaigners therefore made doing so their primary goal, enlisting the aid of doctors, midwives, infant welfare stations, and foster care systems.

The growing role of medical men in these three fields was of course merely part of a broader development. In fact, in the first decades of the twentieth century the medical profession was gradually expanding its role across the whole spectrum of child welfare reform, gaining footholds also in the schools through the introduction of in-school medical services from the beginning of the 1890s, in the special schools for "slow" children, and in institutions for the care of mentally and physically handicapped children.

The Two Faces of Progressive Reform

The expansion of public child welfare programs after the turn of the century starkly reveals the two potentials or poles of progressive reform—one authoritarian and repressive, the other incipiently democratic and integrative. As a number of scholars have pointed out, these two faces of progressive reform, though divergent and often (as we shall see) even contradictory, were also complementary in the sense that both were implicit in the progressive social ideal and in the project of social management. For those who seemed willing and able to become productive, well-adjusted members of society, progressive reforms offered assistance, support, and opportunities. For those who seemed unwilling to be integrated into the ideal organic society, welfare programs were less benign. Rising standards of health and vocational competence meant that some children and young people gained substantial benefits from vocational training, from child support payments brought in by a professional legal guardian, or from infant welfare programs; but they also meant that other young people faced repression, stigmatization, and institutional confinement.

Correctional education is the most striking example of this double-edged quality of progressive reform. In response to rising expectations for the socialization and behavior of young people, correctional education laws in the various German states established progressively more extensive and vague grounds for removing children from their families. For some, undoubtedly, removal from the family represented a blessing. For others—and in fact, as we will see in Chapter 4, probably for the great majority—it was a bitter hardship. Touted by reformers as a form of "welfare," a just and appropriate response to children's misbehavior, correctional education was actually a far more severe penalty than the short prison sentences that a system inspired by the "sterner" doctrine of free will and individual responsibility had imposed. Moreover, although some hoped that the "discovery" that organic brain and nervous defects were at the root of much waywardness would lead to more lenient and effective treatment of delinquents, it also threatened the young victims with permanent stigmatization and exclusion. As Detlev Peukert and others have pointed out, the project of classifying people according to scientific categories of "normalcy" and "deviance" could lead directly to the punitive isolation, and eventually the murder, of those labeled "deviants"—particularly in fiscal emergencies, when the issue of the costs and benefits of therapeutic approaches became critical. The adoption of scientific models, in other words, was itself a precondition of and an important step in the development of a racist and, ultimately, potentially homicidal social language.[45] In fact, the vaulting ambition of reformers sometimes took on quite sinister overtones even in the first decade of the twentieth century—as in the case of one judge who argued that a final solution to the "Gypsy problem" could be achieved in one generation by the simple expedient of committing all children of Sinti and Roma parents to correctional education.[46] Such scientific language could easily be turned against welfare policy, too: by 1913 there was growing discussion, particularly among academic "race hygienists," of the economic costs and racial dangers of supporting "inferior" *(minderwertig)* people and allowing the survival of the unfit through welfare and public health programs. Jens Paulsen, in an article of 1914, even went so far as to deplore the "tyranny of the weak" in Germany.[47]

Equally ominous, of course, were the procedural innovations and underlying aims of the juvenile courts, which amounted to a de facto abrogation of the civil rights of minors accused of even the most trivial crimes. It was the universal assumption of reformers that young people brought before the juvenile courts were guilty as charged. Deprived of the opportunity to prove otherwise in a public trial, and often excluded from the courtroom during their own defense, young people faced the distasteful prospect of being placed on probation, or even in a reformatory, for an indefinite period. *"Erziehung statt Strafe,"* in other words, often meant in practice a refinement and expansion of control, supervision, and repression.

At the same time, as many recent students of health and welfare programs have pointed out, there was an authoritarian potential inherent in the nature and social organization of scientific and particularly medical "knowledge." Medical language in this period was becoming increasingly the privileged property of experts; and the possession of scientific "truth" often allowed these experts to sacrifice the freedom of their clients in the name of effective policy and "correct" decisions. The desire to shape social relations according to the insights and rationality of "objective" science easily led to professional empire building, the expansion of professionals' competence and authority into ever larger areas of social and individual life. And "expert" knowledge in fact often produced an impatience with resistance which easily degenerated into vindictive, punitive prejudice.

In the case of infant welfare, for example, reformers were probably correct in assuming that in the short term the best way to reduce infant deaths was to persuade new mothers to breast-feed. As Ann Taylor Allen has pointed out, however, this strategy almost inevitably "placed responsibility for infant mortality chiefly on mothers."[48] In fact, there was a powerfully moralistic, misogynist current among infant health reformers, a tendency to blame mothers for causing the deaths of their children through ignorance, selfishness, and reckless, willful irrationality. Heinrich Finkelstein, a speaker at the 1905 conference of the DVAW, argued that 85 to 90 percent of women could breast-feed their infants if they "seriously wanted to," and that most of those who did not did so for "completely trivial reasons," a view seconded even by the Imperial Health Bureau in 1908.[49] Many reformers—particularly professional medical men—revealed by their harsh and judgmental tone the misogyny latent in the project of managing reproduction and in the relationship between mothers and doctors. The growing importance of eugenic thought in this period, and the "organic" conception of society, also led many doctors to assume that their primary responsibility was not to the patient but to society at large—and to seek to exercise and expand their power accordingly. Women often appeared in their eyes merely as potential obstacles to healthy reproduction, essentially passive machines that had to be made to function properly. As one Stuttgart doctor argued at the 1899 conference of the CAW, "We must have the courage to draw the proper conclusion from the principle which the opponents of the radical women's movement rightly . . . stress, that 'woman belongs at home'!" and prohibit all factory work by married women.[50] And often doctors' instructions regarding household hygiene flew in the face of the material realities of proletarian life.

It should be obvious from these examples that doctors in particular were susceptible to the adoption of autocratic and moralistic attitudes. But nonmedical administrators, while they less frequently adopted punitive or misogynistic perspectives, were often deeply paternalistic. Public guardians and their assistants, for example, often believed that one of their primary functions was to police the behavior and child rearing practices of mothers. Public guardians sometimes freely admitted that they blackmailed single mothers into accepting their choice of foster family by threatening to refuse to pay any other family.[51] Some even argued for the transfer of the right of primary care (*Personensorgerecht*, which included the right to determine with whom the child would live) from single mothers to public legal guardians.[52]

Again, however, this was not the only pattern of "scientific" reform. For "scientific" approaches (particularly social scientific, as opposed to medical, approaches) also opened the way to a structural analysis of social problems and social behavior; and this, in turn, drove even paternalist welfare advocates unavoidably toward the project of expanding choices rather than of limiting them—of assisting and of offering incentives for behavior which conformed with the aims of policy, enlisting the active cooperation and the interests of the targets of policy. In particular, the discovery of the social origins of delinquency and mortality led to an increasing concern with preventive rather than corrective intervention. By 1913 Deputy Fritz Schepp of the Progressive People's party could call in the Prussian House of Representatives for improved career advising, more effective housing policy, better day care provision, more determined enforcement of the Child Labor Law of 1903, improved programs for the control of alcoholism, and controls over the film industry as measures of "child welfare."[53] Blaming individuals (for example, ignorant, self-indulgent, or negligent mothers) was attractive because it was cheaper than such comprehensive reforms and conformed better to the prejudices regarding working-class and poor people often harbored by middle-class reformers; but it was not, in fact, the dominant tendency among social reformers.

In the case of correctional education and juvenile justice, for example, attention began to shift toward the social rather than the moral origins of waywardness soon after the passage of the Prussian law. Some, particularly those who worked in reformatories, and doctors for whom the commitment to treating the physical illnesses of individuals created a bias against social analysis, became obsessively concerned with organic brain defects and racial degeneration as causes of criminality (a subject to which we shall return in Chapter 4). But the expansion of these systems confronted a growing number of government agencies and charity workers for the first time with the background and milieu of working-class and poor children. The result was a growing sense of the need for *prevention* rather than merely *intervention*. The Berlin Child-Saving Association (Kinderrettungsverein, or KRV), for example, which was founded by the Berlin branch of the Inner Mission in 1901 in response to the correctional education law of that year, soon concluded that one cause of waywardness and delinquency was the poverty of illegitimate children. Its director, Pastor Pfeiffer, therefore established himself as a "professional guardian" in order to secure child support or poor relief payments to their mothers.[54]

Similarly, although the issue of breast-feeding tended to dominate their strategy, most infant welfare activists were acutely aware of the *social* origins of infant mortality. It was clear to them that circumstances quite beyond the control of working-class mothers—such as unsanitary housing, lack of clean water, lack of money for medical care, the necessity for women to work to help support their families, or simply malnutrition—contributed both to the high rate of bottle-feeding and to high infant mortality. In 1903 Dr. Adolph Würtz argued in the *Deutsche Vierteljahrsschrift für öffentliche Gesundheitspflege* (National Public Health Quarterly) for improvements in public sanitation, in public housing policy, in the purity of water supplies, in the public health insurance system, and in working conditions for women; for the provision of free public hospitals and clinics; for closer regulation of prostitution; for public supervision of foster care; for national regulation of the milk industry; for further expansion of maternity leave; for laws requiring firms employing women to provide day care facilities (under municipal oversight) and regular feeding breaks; and for dress reform as ways of combatting infant mortality.[55] At the 1905 conference of the DVAW, while Finkelstein berated mothers for not breast-feeding, his two co-speakers—a Dr. Brugger and Marie Baum—called not only for breast-feeding propaganda but also for financial support for mothers. The resolution adopted by that conference pointed out first of all that infant mortality was the product of the "poor economic position of that portion of the population most heavily affected," and that the most effective means of fighting the problem was therefore to improve the economic prospects of the poor.

Most infant welfare stations in fact offered a variety of services, including free medical care, sterile milk at cost or free, day care, nutritional advice, and—most important—premiums for mothers who breast-fed. It was these material benefits that enticed working-class women to the stations, where their children's health could be monitored. Infant health advocates also supported improved prenatal care by the poor relief agencies, improved training for midwives, postnatal clinics and shelters, day care centers and feeding breaks in large factories, and improved day care services. Improvements in pre- and postnatal social insurance coverage for mothers were secured in 1903 and 1908, and again under the new Imperial Insurance Code of 1911.

Finally, one should not exaggerate the punitive and moralistic aspect of propaganda for breast-feeding. The aim of such propaganda was in fact to spread beneficial scientific knowledge of infant care throughout the population at large. The literature and advice given to mothers included information on nutrition, cleanliness, and simple prophylaxis; directions for sterilizing milk; simple precautionary tips; signs of illness to look for; and, of course, information on where to seek assistance—as well as arguments for breast-feeding and attempts at moral blackmail. As the Prussian medical official Eduard Dietrich commented, the first assumption of welfare policy generally must be "that all measures for the improvement of the commonweal achieve their full effect only if they meet with the necessary understanding among the populace, if the broad masses of the people are sufficiently informed as to the efficacy and the intentions of the action. . . . Therefore [we] must above all attempt to inform the populace."[56]

In this effort at education or "enlightenment," the infant welfare campaign conformed to the general pattern of progressive reform. While claiming for themselves a special role and authority as technicians, specialists, and social managers, progressives fundamentally perceived that the growing economic, social, and political mobilization of their society created a dynamic of growing popular participation—and they embraced it. They sought to use both the principle and the fact of widening participation as a tool with which to achieve social integration, political stabilization, and national power. As the chief justice of Dresden's district court wrote in 1909:

The modern state needs . . . the gathering of all national energies for its existence and . . . vital development. . . . Just as the constitutional state and the municipal administration depend upon the input and contributions of all social groups, just as the calling of jurors in the courts has become a need and an axiom . . .[,] just as our whole social legislation rests on the shoulders of society at large, so must the general acceptance of public responsibility for the rearing of the younger generation be rooted in the feelings and in the cooperation of the entire people.[57]

This notion was at the root, of course, of the subjection of private life and private relationships to public—and private professional, for example, medical—controls and surveillance, for it meant that people were a valuable resource for the state. But it also implied a participatory and potentially democratic structuring of public life. This ideal of participation, of the organic republic of productive workers and active citizens, was central to Pagel's vision of peaceful social integration; to the mobilization of "private" welfare in the child welfare campaigns; to much of "citizenship education"; and to propaganda in favor of breast-feeding. The aim was to *guide* participation but also to empower people to create a better life for themselves. In the case of infant welfare, again, women seem to have responded enthusiastically: in their first eight months Berlin's infant welfare stations gave 37,348 medical consultations, distributed 90,159 liters of sterile milk, and paid cash premiums to 1,813 women, all on a voluntary basis. In 1906, 12,441 children were brought to the stations; in 1908, 18,114. Nurses and volunteers conducted 20,677 house visits in 1906 and 34,388 in 1908.[58]

Where moralistic paternalism was combined with professional arrogance, "scientific" reform could become punitive and authoritarian. And the very ideal of participation and social harmony, combined with the goal of social management, turned those who could not or would not participate constructively into a "problem" to be tackled by expert bureaucracies wielding extensive legal powers and often discriminatory "scientific" theories. For this reason, historians have rightly pointed to important continuities between scientific reform in the early twentieth century and the social policy of National Socialism. We will return to this connection in later chapters. But at least as frequent was the ideal not of *imposing* but of *eliciting* compliance, of using scientific knowledge not to enforce exclusion but to secure inclusion; and progressive reform was connected not only to authoritarian medical enthusiasm and eugenics but also to left-liberalism, mainstream feminism, reformist socialism, and even radical feminist sex reform (for example, in the Bund für Mutterschutz).

In fact, at least in larger cities, Social Democratic city councillors played an important role in the expansion of child welfare programs. As we will see in Chapter 4, Social Democrats bitterly rejected and criticized correctional education as a particularly crass case of class oppression. But in the municipalities, and to a lesser extent in the party hierarchy itself, they helped to develop and particularly to realize the progressive reform program. The SPD had devoted little attention to social welfare before the turn of the century, regarding welfare programs as mere palliatives at best, and as cold-blooded manipulation at worst. The growth of Social Democratic representation on city councils after about 1890, however, confronted Social Democratic municipal politicians with the opportunity to use public funds to achieve concrete improvements in the quality of life of their constituents; and the growing influence of revisionism within the party encouraged the pursuit of such gains. As early as 1901 and 1902, the party's program for municipal politics supported the creation of public day care institutions. And while Social Democrats rejected the imperialist motivations of the bourgeois infant health advocates, the party strongly supported the development of public infant health programs, pre- and postnatal care, and so on. Despite the party's official rejection of private charity, in fact, Social Democratic city councillors even voted regularly to subsidize semiprivate infant health institutions such as the *Säuglingsfürsorgestellen*. The party's 1906 conference in Mannheim, and the associated conference of Social Democratic women, was an important turning point; each passed a unanimous resolution deploring the "mistreatment, waywardness, and exploitation" of proletarian children, and encouraged party members to take systematic action against these problems.[59] Social Democratic city councillors also supported the creation of special juvenile courts.

Particularly important for the early development of Social Democratic interest in child welfare was the passage in 1903 of legislation prohibiting the economic exploitation of children (though agricultural and domestic labor were excluded). The 1904 party conference officially directed party organs to pursue the strict enforcement of this law, for example, by bringing cases to the attention of the factory inspectors. This task was taken up with particular vigor by Social Democratic women, who (partly for legal reasons) were given little role in the public affairs of the party. After 1904 they began to form Child Protection Commissions (*Kinderschutzkommissionen*) in each electoral district—a step encouraged by the 1906 party conference on the grounds that the care of children was woman's "natural" sphere of action. These commissions sought to educate parents regarding the ill effects of child labor, to negotiate with or warn employers and parents, or, where necessary, to notify the Factory Inspection Bureaus (*Gewerbeaufsichtsämter*). In 1909, after the passage of a new national Association Law allowing women membership in political organizations (1908), the party and Social Democratic unions took a direct hand in creating such commissions. By 1911 there were commissions in 135 localities, making this one of the largest organizations involved in child welfare work. By now some of these local commissions were beginning to extend their activities to include, for example, distributing money or goods to needy families, petitioning for commitment to correctional education, seeking appointment as volunteer probation officers, assisting in juvenile court, and organizing daytime outings for working-class children.[60]

Again, the convergence of interests between Social Democrats and bourgeois reformers should not be exaggerated: Social Democrats denounced correctional education and rejected the imperialist argumentation of progressives. Nevertheless, there was a great deal on which they could agree. And in a sense the development of Social Democratic child welfare policy was an example of the functioning of precisely that dynamic of mobilization and integration posited by progressive reform: working people, particularly through their political representatives, contributed in their own interest to the improvement of public health, the spread of sound principles of hygiene and child rearing, and so on. There were parallel developments in other fields, for example, workers' participation in the administration of the health insurance funds created in 1883, or in the industrial courts of arbitration *(Gewerbegerichte)* created in 1890 and introduced in all larger cities by legislation in 1901. Undoubtedly, the implications of this development were conservative, since it contributed to the stabilization of the existing social order. Social insurance programs also contributed—and were often intended to contribute—to the construction of divisions within the working classes between the respectable, insured workers and casual laborers, or between white-collar and blue-collar workers covered under different schemes. Indeed, the observations of Social Democratic women of the *Kinderschutzkommissionen* on the child rearing practices of the poor, and their efforts to enlighten them regarding the proper treatment of children and the dangers of sending them out to earn, to teach them hygienic principles, and even to force them by threats of legal action to behave "responsibly," sometimes strikingly resembled those of bourgeois child welfare advocates. Nevertheless, the conservatism of this strategy of integration clearly had very different political implications than did the authoritarian expertism discussed previously. It could extend, for example, even to the recognition of the socialist trade unions as a method of allaying the radicalism of workers. And it was part of a broad trend toward integration and cooperation which resulted in the electoral alliance between left-liberals and the SPD in 1912, and eventually in the gradual crystallization of a coalition for political reform, the "Weimar Coalition" of 1918–19.

In fact, the creation of a system of public child welfare was accomplished, after 1910, by people who spoke not of moral *duties* but of social *rights;* and it grew not out of institutions such as correctional education and the juvenile courts but out of the development of infant welfare programs. The remainder of this chapter deals with that process.

Public Legal Guardianship and the Youth Bureau, 1905–1910

In some cities, at least, infant welfare programs achieved considerable successes. In Berlin as a whole, infant mortality dropped between 1904 and 1910 from 19.7 to 14.9 percent. At the other end of the country, in Freiburg im Breisgau in southern Baden, infant mortality sank from 25.3 percent in 1900 to 17.3 percent in 1905 and 11.0 percent in 1910.[61] Yet the impact of the infant health campaign on *national* rates was apparently not as great. The national rate fell fairly smoothly, from 22.1 percent in 1891–1895 to 19.9 percent in 1901–1905 and 16.4 percent in 1911–1914.[62] The discrepancy reflected the unevenness of provision for infant health: the infant welfare stations required sizable subsidies for providing sterile milk or breast-feeding premiums and for machinery and buildings, and systems of foster care supervision necessitated the hiring of doctors and paid social workers—all expenses that were beyond the means of most small cities and rural counties. The infant health movement therefore became increasingly preoccupied with the search for an adequate fiscal and legal foundation for public intervention.

In that search they increasingly focused their attention on the problem of illegitimate children. In 1905 mortality among legitimate infants was 19.4 percent, among illegitimate 32.6 percent. Bastards also made up a disproportionately large part of the "wayward" and criminal population: in Prussia in 1904, for example, 17.5 percent of children committed to correctional education were illegitimate, though only 7.3 percent of births were. In 1905, 9.2 percent of penitentiary inmates were illegitimate, although only 4 percent of the adult population was.[63] Studies undertaken by Othmar Spann (later a major philosopher of corporatism and a key intellectual figure in Austro-Fascism) in Frankfurt am Main found that only 36.8 percent of illegitimate males whose mothers remained unmarried were fit for active military service when they were inducted at age twenty, compared to some 53 percent of legitimate male youths. The illegitimate population was less qualified professionally as well: the Frankfurt studies found that 22 percent of adult bastards were employed as unskilled workers, compared to 12 percent of the legitimate population.[64] And yet infant welfare programs often did not reach these children, since their mothers were too poor, too busy, or too mobile to seek regular help. Hugo Neumann found in 1911 that only about one quarter of Berlin's illegitimate infants had any contact at all with the city's infant welfare stations.[65]

But if illegitimate children were more endangered, they also offered reformers a unique opportunity, since the EGBGB allowed the transfer of legal guardianship to public agencies. As Taube had pointed out, this step would allow infant welfare programs to become effectively self-funding, since child support payments secured by the public guardian unburdened the local poor relief funds. Beginning around 1900, state governments—the Prussian Ministry of the Interior, for example, in a circular of July 13, 1900—began to urge local authorities to adopt systems similar to that in Leipzig.[66] Between 1904 and 1909 Othmar Spann's studies of illegitimacy in Frankfurt am Main helped to place public guardianship on a firm "scientific" basis. The DVAW recommended the system at its 1907 conference. Thereafter, public legal guardianship spread rapidly, with strong support in municipal assemblies not only from left-liberals but also from Social Democrats, moderate conservatives, and reform-minded Catholics. State law allowed public legal guardianship in Bavaria after 1908 and in Baden and Württemberg after 1912 and 1914, respectively. Hamburg established automatic public legal guardianship over all illegitimate children in 1910, as did Bremen in 1909 and Lübeck in 1912.[67] Where public guardianship was not allowed, as in Prussia and Hessen, multiple appointive guardianship and public guardianship over children supported by the poor relief agencies spread rapidly, with enthusiastic encouragement from the Prussian government. By 1911 Franz Recke was already celebrating the "triumphal procession" of public guardianship throughout all of Germany.[68] According to a list compiled by the Prussian Ministry of the Interior in 1918, 12 Prussian communities adopted public legal guardianship between 1900 and 1905, 69 between 1906 and 1910, and 168 between 1911 and 1913. By 1913 there were some 127,000 children under public guardianship in Germany in over three hundred towns.[69] By 1912 there were already suggestions that the system be made mandatory for all large communities.[70]

The spread of legal guardianship precipitated a rapid process of administrative centralization of municipal child welfare programs. Since legal guardianship extended from birth until age twenty-one and involved general and undefined responsibility for the child's development, the public legal guardian dealt of necessity with all the problems of his wards in all stages of life from infant health care to career guidance. He therefore became involved wherever his wards had contact with public or private agencies. For this simple reason, the organization of professional legal guardians noted in 1909, "professional guardianship shows a tendency to become the central organ of all public and private child welfare."[71]

Between 1908 and 1910, then, public legal guardianship came into focus as the critical element of a comprehensive child welfare policy. The decisive breakthrough came in the wake of two separate developments in 1910. First, in that year the cities of Hamburg and Mainz established the first public child welfare agencies in which virtually all municipal and several state programs were centralized. Hamburg's Public Child Welfare Authority in particular would provide a model for the structure and methods of child welfare agencies in other cities, as well as an informal center for propaganda for the creation of such agencies, for the next thirty years. And second, the DVAW conference of 1910 was devoted largely to the question of the organization of child welfare. The keynote presentation by Mayor Georg Schmidt of Mainz won endorsement of the proposal to create centralized, independent municipal child welfare agencies (later referred to simply as Youth Bureaus, or *Jugendämter*)—a concept proposed first in 1908 by Konrad Agahd, an advocate of child labor law, and similar to proposals for the centralization of the public health system made by Social

Democrats, also in 1910.[72] Johannes Petersen, the director of Hamburg's Public Child Welfare Authority, summed up the social-managerial ambition underlying the concept of the Youth Bureau for the conference, pointing out:

> Whoever examines child welfare work carefully will often have the impression that it works largely by chance. How do we gain access to the children we want to serve? Mostly only because one child or another by coincidence comes into contact with an agency or with a philanthropist, and then one discovers suddenly that there are abuses. But the organs of child welfare should work *systematically;* chance work must disappear. . . . The organizations of child welfare must quite systematically build a net of agents . . . fine enough so that no case, so to speak, slips through its mesh, so that *every* case of waywardness and endangerment of any kind must become known.[73]

The Organization of Progressive Reform

Simultaneously with the emergence of the program of local centralization of child welfare in the Youth Bureau, progressive reform at the national level was achieving a new degree of organizational maturity. By 1910 there were several national, secular, progressive child welfare organizations—many growing out of Pagel's Voluntary Educational Council—which paralleled and increasingly competed with the older Inner Mission (founded in 1848) and the Caritasverband (1896–97). The new associations often combined representatives of public and private organizations, and their conferences, which served propaganda purposes as well as organizational ones, were well attended by the representatives of public authorities. The Voluntary Educational Council itself changed its name in 1901 to the National Central Association for Child Welfare and launched a short-lived effort to create a network of local chapters and regional associations. In 1907 it united with the Berlin Center for Child Welfare, which it had founded in 1904, to form the National Center for Child Welfare (Deutsche Zentrale für Jugendfürsorge, or DZJ). Under its capable new director, the feminist lawyer Frieda Duensing, the DZJ became a central organization and motor for the theoretical elaboration and practical propagation of progressive child welfare reforms.

Meanwhile, a number of important specialist organizations were emerging as well. In 1906 the General Conference of Correctional Education (Allgemeiner Fürsorgeerziehungstag, or AFET) emerged from informal groupings of private Christian and public provincial reformatories. The AFET immediately took on a leadership role within correctional education as a forum for the discussion of methods and problems of correctional education, and as a lobbying group for private institutions. Also in 1906 public legal guardians from around Germany formed the Organization of Professional Legal Guardians (Archiv Deutscher Berufsvormünder, or ADB), under the directorship of Christian Jasper Klumker, who held the first German chair in social work in Frankfurt am Main. After 1909 occasional National Conferences of Juvenile Courts (Deutsche Jugendgerichtstage) were held, although no permanent organization emerged until 1917. In 1909 a National Association for the Protection of Infants was formed, and state groups were set up between 1906 (Baden) and 1910 (Prussia). In 1913, finally, the National Society for Child Protection, committed to preventing child abuse, was founded. In close association with both the DZJ and the DVAW, these groups rapidly assumed a leading role both as lobbyists for progressive child welfare reform and as forums for the articulation of the principles of secular, modernist, "scientific" social work. After 1909 they had their own jointly supported journal in the *Zentralblatt für Vormundschaftswesen, Jugendgerichte, und Fürsorgeerziehung.*

This organizational activity reflected and helped to consolidate the influence of a rapidly growing army of professionals, employed by public and private agencies, who were involved in child welfare programs. This group was very diverse, including pastors in the Christian churches; doctors employed by the municipalities or in private practice; judges, assessors, and lawyers interested or active in juvenile justice; ministerial officials in state and national governments; public statisticians, criminologists, and psychiatrists (particularly in public service); prison pastors and penal administrators; police officials and public prosecutors; poor relief officials; and others. But all of these people made child welfare their business (sometimes quite literally), and many had a direct material or professional interest in the expansion and consolidation of public or private child welfare programs. They formed an increasingly vociferous, well-organized, and influential lobby.

By 1910 the organizational and propagandistic efforts of these groups were clearly securing the triumph of the progressive reform agenda over conservative and liberal resistance to state intervention not only in practice but also in theory. The contrast between the 1896 conference of the DVAW on school lunch programs and that held by the Center for Popular Welfare (Zentralstelle für Volkswohlfahrt, or ZVW, earlier CAW) on the same subject in 1909 illustrates this transition well. Whereas the DVAW had agreed that school lunch programs must be strictly limited to cases in which nourishment was required to enable a child to concentrate during school hours, thirteen years later the ZVW took a more activist view. The main speaker, Max Rubner, pointed out that about one third of schoolchildren were undernourished or even malnourished, and that maladies such as rickets, scoliosis, and lung disease compromised "the military strength and the economic performance of the nation," burdened the health insurance funds, and shortened working lives. And Konrad Agahd, the Berlin teacher who played a central role in the passage of expanded restrictions on child labor in 1903, warned that the time was coming "when we will see the necessity of these measures in the declining number of bayonets." Whereas in 1896 the humanitarian arguments of Hermann Abraham had been rejected, in 1909 the assembly agreed that, just as in England and France, "the danger of physical decline . . . [and] of the lessening of the productivity of the nation" must be countered by adopting the "radical step" of using public funds to feed schoolchildren.[74]

"The Right of the Child to Education"

The institutional expansion of public child welfare was supported by and helped to fuel the consolidation of the intellectual foundations of the progressive child welfare reform program in a series of important articles and speeches between 1908 and 1912. Of particular significance was Othmar Spann's "Extension of Social Policy through Public Legal Guardianship" (1912), in which he set forth the definitive statement of the social-managerial aims of progressive child welfare policy by arguing that public legal guardianship was simply one branch of general "social policy" *(Sozialpolitik)*. This term referred at that time to social insurance programs rather than to poor relief or welfare programs *(Wohlfahrtspflege)*, and by using it Spann implied the existence of a right to aid, and the aim of social integration and stabilization rather than individual "emergency" assistance. Public legal guardianship, he held, had world-historical significance and a certain inevitability, since it was merely one expression of that epochal change in the nature of the state which had begun with Fichte and the historical school of economics and which had achieved a "refinement of the idea of the state, the belief in the *moral essence* of social life." A social order which had "constituted itself in all too individualistic, even anarchic [form] must now organize itself ever more coherently and strictly on the basis of higher solidarity. This transformation is a historical necessity." In sharp contrast to the liberalism of the preceding century, he argued, "a more universalistic perspective . . . has come to dominate, one which cannot hesitate to make the whole responsible for the disadvantaging of particular social groups, and to set the idea of solidarity and justice in the place of freedom and competition."[75] Public guardianship was destined to become the institutional expression of this higher solidarity by drawing together all the disparate, unconnected institutions of child welfare into a systematic branch of social policy for children and the family, paralleling the social insurance programs intended to meet the specific needs of workers.

Yet while Spann justified this "mission" of public legal guardianship in terms of solidarity and justice, the aim of social policy for him, as for most progressives, was unmistakably the welfare of the social "body" as a whole. By helping an entire social group who "by virtue of their position in the system of economy and social relations are at a disadvantage and in need," public guardianship would go beyond mere aid to individuals: "It is not the individuals themselves who are helped, but rather they are assisted in carrying out their social functions and activities. Not the person, but rather the bearer of an activity of interest to society, the fulfiller of a social task or function is assisted."[76] Again, it was the "organic" conception of the state and society, rather than the heritage of liberal individualism, which was dominant in Spann's conception of social integration and social justice.

If Spann's article summed up the general claims and overall goals of social-liberal child welfare policy as a part of social policy generally, an article of the same year by Paul Felisch staked out the specific claims of child welfare policy in particular. Titled "A National Child Welfare Law" (and building on ideas first presented before the ADB in 1909), Felisch's article called for a grand codification of all laws and regulations relating to young people. This goal was, of course, patently unrealistic, and was never seriously considered a policy option. Nevertheless, his justification of such a comprehensive youth code summed up and consolidated the growing perception of the uniqueness of children and of the necessity of establishing distinct institutions—a distinct branch of *Sozialpolitik*—for their welfare. The essential aim of these institutions must always be "the transformation of natural man into a bearer of culture"—and thus of education or socialization *(Erziehung).*[77] Felisch's decisive formulation of this demand that policy toward youth be governed by a specific set of principles and a specific goal marked and completed the consensus among progressives that child welfare programs must be institutionally autonomous—a step resisted since the 1890s by some municipal poor relief administrators.

These two fundamental themes—the conception of the place of the individual in society and the idea that children had particular needs which it was the duty and interest of society to fulfill—came together in the years between 1908 and 1912 in a program and a slogan that would be fundamental to child welfare policy for the rest of the century: the "right of the child to education." This concept had in fact been worked out by Wilhelm Polligkeit, of the pioneering Institut für Gemeinwohl in Frankfurt, in an important essay of 1908 titled simply "The Right of the Child to Education." Polligkeit's essay elaborated the implications of the organic conception of state and society with ferocious clarity. "The adherents of the view that the rights of parents over their children constitute an inviolable . . . right," Polligkeit wrote, "completely misunderstand the relationship of the family . . . to the state." The family, he insisted, was not an autonomous realm in which the ethical foundations of society were nurtured in privacy, in isolation from politics and the state; rather, it performed a practical function *for* the state:

> Schaeffle has called the social organism of the family the simplest vital element of the social body, and compared its relationship to society and the state to the relationship between an organic cell and the complete organism of a living thing. . . . Just as the cell fulfills certain tasks . . . for this living thing, upon which the health and growth of the whole organism depend, so certain tasks fall to the family as the foundation unit of the social body, of which the most important is the increase, maintenance, and reproduction of the individual members of the social body. The family serves not only the physical-organic but also the intellectual-moral regeneration, development, maintenance, and replenishing of the . . . social body.[78]

Society had a rightful interest, he continued, in the proper functioning of the family, and should have the right to intervene to correct its "pathological degeneration." In fact, Polligkeit argued, such intervention was becoming increasingly necessary. Social, economic, and political development was continually heightening the needs of children, raising the level and expanding the variety of skills they had to master to become competent adults and citizens. Meanwhile, the erosion of family life by industrialization made the family less and less effective in socializing children. The old patriarchal private family could no longer fulfill its essential function; the state must therefore step in to socialize the young.

To justify this intervention, Polligkeit construed an implicit legal right of the child to education which corresponded logically to the parents' duty, under the BGB, to educate their children—a legal right for which the child could claim the state's protection. "The oft-raised objection that intervening in parental rights is a disruptive limitation of personal freedom," in other words, was a secondary question: "In this matter one should pay more attention to securing the child's enjoyment of its rights than to worries about expanding the powers of the state at the expense of the personal freedom of the parents."[79] Concretely, Polligkeit proposed a "minimum level of education" which the state must secure for any child, and which must include not only the ability to earn one's own living but also the capacity for "activity as a citizen of the state" and "insight into the legal order of the state" (and the capacity and will to avoid conflict with the law).[80]

In Polligkeit's work the "right of the child" was used to justify intervention by the courts into a family's child rearing, in the form of correctional education. By 1912, however, Johannes Petersen, director of Hamburg's public child welfare agency, had developed this concept of the right of the child to education into a theoretical justification for creating a comprehensive public child welfare system—in short, for the Youth Bureau. The child, Petersen warned, "requires education even simply in the interests of society itself, the stability of which would be endangered if even only a noticeable proportion of her members grew up without education," and this implied the necessity of "the construction of a comprehensive child welfare policy which aims at mass effect." Happily, he observed, "Manchesterism in the field of education" had been increasingly abandoned. But it was still necessary to create a unitary system of child welfare; for the "yawning gap between the private law right of the child to education and the realization of this right in public law absolutely must be filled; the systematic, planned organization of child welfare programs is necessary." Only the centralized Youth Bureau, equipped with sufficient financial resources and adequate "capacities, rights, and powers," would be able to secure the rights of all children.[81]

By the following year Karl Flesch was already arguing in the Prussian parliament that the creation of a unified public child welfare system should be made mandatory for all local governments: "We are dealing with institutions which . . . should not, following the whims of chance, be present here and there and not present elsewhere, but rather institutions which, like the public schools . . . *must* be present."[82] In fact, by 1912 advocates of *public* responsibility for child welfare were not simply arguing that the child had to be protected where the family failed to socialize it adequately; some began to suggest that *no* family alone was equal to the task of socializing children in and for a modern industrial society. The complexity of industrial society and the demands it placed on the individual were such that the family, even where it functioned "normally," was not always capable of preparing young people to be productive workers and competent citizens. A public "socializing agency" such as the Youth Bureau had to be prepared to act as a *complement* to any and all families rather than replacing only those families that "failed" or broke down. Polligkeit argued as early as 1905 that "our present system of socialization is no longer equal to the conditions of the age," and Petersen suggested that "in a civilized society [*Kulturstaat*] the demands placed on the independent members of the community have . . . become so high that no family is in a position to offer the child . . . all that which it needs."[83]

The modern reader is struck by what appears to be a curious blindness in all of these works to the distinction between the rights of the child and the needs of the state, and between the good of the child and the good of the state or of society. In fact, the conflation of the two was typical of reform discourse in this period and grew quite naturally out of liberal theory. The two justifications of state policy, and the social-liberal and organismic-statist conceptions of society which underlay them, seem contradictory to modern eyes; but in fact the connection between them was quite logical and natural. These reformers were arguing, after all, for an expansion of the *powers* and prerogatives of the state precisely in the interests of securing the *rights* of the child. What is more, of course, liberal social and political theory had held from its inception that freedom and the safeguarding of individual rights would create a wealthier, more stable society—and, by no means less important, a more powerful nation. The two—individual rights and national power, right and might—were not separable in liberal theory, though historically, particularly in Germany, they had often been separated in liberal practice.

In fact, the social-liberal and imperialist discourses have historically been inextricably interrelated. Their affinity has been particularly well documented in the German case, and the imperialist, democratic, and social reforming program developed by social-liberals such as Friedrich Naumann and Max Weber is well known. There were close ties between the social-liberal imperialist leadership and that of child welfare reform in Germany: Christian Jasper Klumker, for example, ran in the 1903 campaign for parliament as a member of the Nationalsoziale Verein organized by Naumann (himself a pastor and one-time volunteer in Wichern's Rauhes Haus). Frieda Duensing, too, the first director of the DZJ, was a Naumann supporter.[84] But this phenomenon was not unique to Germany; liberal imperialists such as Edward Grey and Richard Haldane in England are analogous characters, as are many of the American Progressives.

The reasons for this relationship are clear. It was rooted in a long tradition of political and social thought in Germany, in which rights were viewed as the logical consequence of duties, and vice versa.[85] But again, the social-liberal reform discourse also clearly appealed to the liberal nationalist tradition of progress and development, of the release of individual energy and individual initiative in the interests of the commonweal and of national power. In the "social" incarnation of liberalism as it emerged in the 1890s and 1900s, the state was to take a positive role in ensuring that *all* citizens' energies were released and harnessed. The goal of social-liberal reform, as of progressive reform more broadly, was precisely to achieve harmony between individual and national interests. Progressives intended to establish a social system in which the individual's pursuit of his or her own aims, far from creating anarchy, conflict, and paralysis, was the glue of social cohesion and the source of vitality and power. Nor, as Polligkeit's definition of the "minimum" education indicates, was this strategy limited to the sphere of economics: the goal of the *political* mobilization of young people, pursued for example in the "citizenship education" of

the vocational schools, clearly echoed the liberal ideal of political participation and active citizenship. While there was some tension between the
two sides of the social-liberal argument, then, in fact the combination of
imperialist and social-liberal beliefs which characterized arguments for
the expansion of child welfare programs after 1910 was a natural and logical one.

At the moment of its formulation before the First World War, the language of social rights formed an important part of the language of the liberal left and was associated with the drive for greater democracy and social
justice. In fact, the formulation of the idea of the "right of the child" in the
field of child welfare was not an isolated phenomenon but rather was part
of a more general development within the field of social welfare. Between
the turn of the century and the war, reformers within the DVAW and other
social reform groups argued with increasing urgency that the system of
poor relief—which provided only minimum subsistence to recipients while
entailing the loss of civil rights (such as the right to vote or hold office)—
was obsolete and no longer served the needs of a modern society, that it did
not work and did not conform to the principles and values according to
which a modern society had to be constructed. The system of poor relief, or
Armenfürsorge, reformers argued, must be transformed into a system of
soziale Fürsorge, or "social welfare." In such a system public assistance
would be a right, and its goal would be not merely to keep the poor alive
but to pave the way for the effective reintegration of the citizen into society;
a punitive and moralizing view of the poor would thus be replaced by a social analysis of the problem of poverty, and the poor treated not as subjects
but as citizens. Within the DVAW, Klumker and Polligkeit played important
roles in this transition.

As we shall see, however, this complex and unclear relationship in progressive thought between individual rights—in this case particularly the
rights of children—and the good of society or the nation, and the tendency
to look on the interventionist state as the guarantor of rights, would prove
fateful, for it made progressives susceptible to the attractions of ideas that
were anything but democratic. Both the language of social defense—people
in society at large have a "right" to be protected from the consequences of
irresponsible or ineffective child rearing—and the language of social
rights—children have "rights" which must be secured even against the
wishes of their parents—were used by fascists, and by progressives drawn
to fascism, to justify virtually unlimited state intervention, up to and including mass murder. The language of social rights, in other words, was
just as ambiguous in its political potentials as was the other central theme
in secular social reform in this period: the language of "scientific" social reform.

In the first decade and a half of the century, however, the expansion of public welfare programs at the local level which these ideas fueled was looked on with deep skepticism not by champions of individual rights but rather by the defenders of the charities, of the poor relief system, and of traditional understandings of the problem of poverty. By 1910 conflicts between these defenders of the status quo and progressive reformers was reaching a critical severity, just as were conflicts between the champions of the conservative constitution and of political democratization. Nowhere were the debates over policy and institutional forms more intense than in the field of child welfare. We turn to them in Chapter 4.

CHAPTER FOUR

The Struggle over Child Welfare Policy, 1910–1914

The Complexity of the Struggle: Cultural Crisis and Divergent Strategies of Social Reform

By 1910 public child welfare programs had expanded immensely, and progressive ideas and institutional forms had reached a new level of coherence and maturity. Their advocates stood poised to create a centralized, uniform child welfare bureaucracy. But of course the conception of child welfare reform sketched out in the critical statements of 1908–1912—modernist, imperialist, "scientific," and bureaucratic—was by no means shared by the entire social reform community, much less by society at large. The expansion of child welfare programs and the refinement and clarification of the progressive program had, by 1910, in fact begun to bring the broader reform movement up against its own internal contradictions—and the objections of its targets. The conflicts generated by this process exploded in the immediate prewar years into a complicated, interrelated set of struggles over the shape and powers of public child welfare. By the beginning of the Great War, these struggles had begun to transform child welfare policy in ways that would be critical in determining its development for the rest of the century.

The debate over child welfare in the 1910s cannot be understood except in the context of the generalized cultural upheaval of the decade prior to the Great War. For while the logic of progressive reform brought about the steady drift of a large fraction of the reform community away from the religious and voluntarist foundations of nineteenth-century reform and toward materialist scientific analysis, professionalization, and social-liberal reform strategies, at the same time other developments were encouraging more conservative reformers to move in the opposite direction, toward cultural fundamentalism and repressive responses to social change. Faced with what appeared to be the disintegration of the cultural fabric of Christian society, the culturally conservative middle classes responded increasingly after 1900 with an aggressive organizational and intellectual offensive.

We have seen the roots of this conservative reaction in the 1890s. In the 1910s, however, conservatives were increasingly on the defensive, and increasingly frightened and embittered. In the field of child welfare this was reflected in a growing concern over the solidification of the subculture of urban working-class youth and over the growth of the socialist youth movement, and in the increasing intemperance of verbal attacks on these youths. The *Deutsche Tageszeitung* published an article in 1910 under the title "The Savagery of the Youth," which was typical of the tone of these denunciations:

> Whoever has observed the half-grown young men between school and military service in the alleys of our big cities—how they slouch around with their hands in their pockets and jostle every quiet citizen, how they have a butt stuck in their mouths, how their mouths overflow with filthy language and insults— senses their crudeness. Before, looking like a hoodlum was shameful; now it seems, among a part of big-city youth, to have become a matter of pride. . . . These rude punks . . . seem to have respect for nothing. . . . Boys who . . . do not shrink from any hooliganism, impudence, or coarseness cannot be handled gently.[1]

Around 1912 such images of troublesome, provocative, lazy, disorderly urban youth were systematized by Pastor Clemens Schultz of Hamburg into a negative social type, under the pejorative name *Halbstarke* (roughly, "punk"); the term thereafter became a focus for those who believed that, as *Der Tag* put it in 1910, "we need healthy coercion for our youth."[2]

As in the 1890s, however, these concerns about youth were merely one part of a much larger critique of modern culture. In 1905 the *Fliegende Blätter* of the Inner Mission denounced the "current of rebelliousness in the entire spirit" of modernity.[3] The development of the mass media, photographic reproduction, and popular literature, as well as changing patterns in gender relations (the development of "relationships" among the young, for example) and mass entertainments such as public bathing, amusement parks, and the cinema, seemed to be creating a crisis of sexual morality and public decency. And because conservative Christians believed that sexual self-restraint was a school and precondition of self-restraint in all areas of human life, including politics, these two crises seemed to be intimately linked. The eroticization of advertising and art and the lessening formality of relations between the sexes were viewed as fostering in the masses a tendency toward pleasure-seeking egoism and thus also toward revolt against legitimate authority; both were seen as consequences of philosophical naturalism and materialism. And the youth movement, the women's movement, and particularly the feminist sex reform movement—centered on the Bund für Mutterschutz—seemed to give ideological and organizational form to these threats.

As I have suggested in the case of legal guardianship and of correctional education, rising standards for lower-class political and technical competence and social behavior were at least as instrumental as any objective deterioration of popular morality in creating this sense of crisis. In some rural areas where it was traditional to "test" a prospective bride's fertility before marriage, for example, pastors were struggling in this period to impose "respectable" standards for the first time, rather than to "reimpose" what had never existed. Nevertheless, the offensive against licentiousness was cast in terms of decline and in a language of righteous indignation. This stance was encouraged by the growing sense of political crisis created by the fact that the Social Democratic party had become, by 1912, the largest faction in the national parliament and was steadily gaining ground in municipal governments; and it was paralleled in national politics by renewed discussions within the government of a coup d'état in 1912, the announcement of a "freeze" or pause in social reform legislation, and the creation of a reactionary, antisocialist "Cartel of the Productive Estates" outside it in 1913.

The growing attraction of appeals for repressive measures to combat this "crisis" made progressive reform strategies, which were rooted in a nonmoralistic, materialist analysis of social change, increasingly suspect in the eyes of conservative Christians. As culturally conservative Christians confronted with modern mass culture clarified and deepened their commitment to cultural "fundamentals," growing numbers of those who had drifted into the reform alliance without stopping to examine first principles discovered that there was, in fact, a deep cultural divide between themselves and many of their more secular, social-liberal colleagues. This trend was encouraged by the growing importance of reform coalitions of left-liberals and Social Democrats at the municipal level, and by the electoral alliance between the left-liberal Progressive People's party and the SPD in the national elections of 1912. Ties between sex reform feminists and the left-liberal leadership (Friedrich Naumann, for example, was a member of the Bund für Mutterschutz) only exacerbated the problem.

As in the nineteenth century, the divisions within bourgeois reform were not always apparent to those involved in policy debates over particular child welfare programs. Bourgeois reformers of all stripes continued to cooperate against jurists and recalcitrant children; both religious and "scientific" reform traditions were broad enough to accommodate either authoritarian repressive or more liberal integrationist tendencies; and because the logic of the issues involved cut across ideological and political divisions, individuals found themselves involved in shifting, contradictory alliances. Nevertheless, by 1914 the reform community seemed to be polarizing into two divergent intellectual systems—the one Christian, anti-industrial,

moralist, patriarchal and authoritarian, voluntarist, and middle-class populist; and the other secular, modern, materialist, incipiently consensual,
statist and centralist, and managerial. These conflicts were complicated,
moreover, by fractures running along gender and confessional lines, which I
will examine later in this chapter.

An excellent example of this divergence is the response to the decline in
the birthrate. By the beginning of the twentieth century the emergence of a
new pattern of working-class family life—characterized on the one hand by
earlier marriage and pregnancy, and on the other by limitation of number of children through increased use of birth control by older women—
brought about an overall decline in the number of children born to each
adult woman.[4] This phenomenon received relatively little attention before
about 1908, although it had been discussed since the 1890s: it was not an
issue, for example, at the major conferences on infant welfare in 1899 and
1905. After 1905, however, the decline accelerated, and by 1908 it began to
translate, despite falling infant mortality, into a decrease in the annual population gain. In the last three or four years before the war, concern with the
problem became, in the words of Arthur Schlossmann, "monomaniacal,"
particularly within government circles.[5] Pessimists—such as Jean Bornträger,
an official in the Prussian Ministry of the Interior who published an important study in 1912—saw in this phenomenon a sign of moral decline and
a "turning away from religion and the old respectable opinions and customs." Selfishness, materialist desire for the good things in life, and lust
were leading irreligious, rationalist, and often socialist and/or—in the case
of mothers—feminist urban parents to limit the number of their offspring.
The pessimists' proposed solutions were therefore primarily repressive: the
introduction of stronger measures against couples living together out of
wedlock *(wilde Ehen)* and against trade in contraceptive devices; prohibition of the dissemination of information about or in favor of family planning; the testing of teachers regarding their views on the subject; censorship
of "trashy" or indecent literature and theater; and a national campaign
against materialism, socialism, and feminism and for regaining religious
and moral influence over youth.[6] In Prussia, for example, bills that would
have banned the sale of contraceptives were introduced in 1910, 1913, and
1914, and a bill against "trashy" literature was in the works in 1914.

In contrast to such views, which predominated within the government of
Prussia and the Empire, the leadership and most supporters of infant health
reform were more optimistic. They argued that limiting family size, if accompanied by a sufficient decline in infant mortality, was beneficial, since it
increased the efficiency of reproduction. Arthur Schlossmann, for example,
welcomed the decline of the birthrate in 1914 "from a national-economic
standpoint" because "the same population growth is achieved with a lower
birthrate."[7] Moreover, they viewed the decrease in the birthrate as a product

of social change, not of moral decline: universal schooling and the prohibition of child labor meant that children began to contribute to the family income later than ever before, while universal military service removed sons from the family work force earlier; and urban families had to buy what their ancestors in the nineteenth century had produced themselves—food, clothing, furniture, and so on. Their favored response was therefore state intervention to reduce the burdens of raising children. Schlossmann, for example, proposed an "obligatory insurance which would ensure rising income with rising number of children" and a special tax on single men and childless couples, the proceeds of which would go to families with many children. Others suggested school lunches, "maternity insurance," free education, and other incentives to childbearing.

A similar conflict emerged over vocational schooling and "youth cultivation" or organized leisure activities for young people *(Jugendpflege)*. By the 1910s *Jugendpflege*, or the private organization of young people's leisure time (which I discussed briefly in the context of the 1890s), had expanded tremendously. In 1910 membership in the various religious, sports, and social clubs totaled somewhere around 1.5 million young people. Yet all these organizations together never managed to encompass more than a maximum of some 20 percent of all youth, and they seldom reached those about whom middle-class reformers were most concerned—proletarian youth. As one organizer remarked in 1918, *Jugendpflege* remained "work for the maintenance and moral reinforcement of the middle class."[8] After 1904, moreover, socialist youth groups, while still very small in numbers, were expanding rapidly.

By 1907, therefore, the Prussian government was searching for means of gaining greater political influence over working-class youth. In 1908 the new national Law of Associations ruled out membership in political associations for young people; this measure was used to contain the socialist youth movement, and by early 1914 the Prussian Ministry of the Interior was planning to have socialist trade unions also declared "political" associations.[9] To complement these purely repressive measures, in 1910 the ministries of war and of culture suggested that control over vocational education should be transferred from the competence of the economic ministries (trade, finance, and agriculture) to their own; attendance would be made mandatory for all working youth, and the curriculum would be changed to include more physical education and political indoctrination. Industrial development, the minister of war warned, was causing a steady decline in the percentage of new draftees who were fit for active duty. This development, combined with the declining birthrate, meant that it was "not impossible that . . . we will be faced, already in the course of the twentieth century, with a shortage of recruits." Moreover, since a growing number of draftees were affected by social-democratic ideas, he felt himself "duty bound, in the interests of the reliability of the army, to press for the elimination of existing evils" in the area of youth socialization.[10] As the Ministry of Culture argued, the task of the vocational schools had changed in the context of the growth of socialism; it had become "necessary . . . not merely to transmit a certain measure of knowledge, not merely to serve the general needs of practical life and prepare [the student] . . . for the particular demands of a career in . . . industry, but rather systematically . . . to rally the youth around the cause of duty, patriotism, and fear of God."[11]

But the ministries of trade and industry, of finance, and of agriculture rejected these proposals. Drawing their arguments from the work of Georg Kerschensteiner, director of Munich's continuation schools, they held that these changes would actually reduce the schools' influence, since without the "material incentive" of purely vocational training, students would lose interest in instruction.[12] Obligatory attendance at political lectures and athletic practice would create resistance and antipathy among the students.[13] So far from being merely indoctrination, the goal of "citizenship education" was political competence: the schools must "introduce [students] to an understanding of the foundations and the structure of our state" and give them the capacity to critique the "whisperings of their colleagues and the inflammatory speeches of agitators." In this process purely technical education was superior to religious instruction, since an understanding of his profession and the economy would give the student an appreciation of the interdependence of all citizens.[14] Abandoning vocational training in favor of political indoctrination was a fundamental error, since the most dangerous young workers were precisely those who had no skills and thus no social standing and no stake in society; to make skilled workers of these people would be the most effective means of stabilizing the political situation. Finally, the technical training offered by the vocational schools was becoming an ever greater economic necessity. "The industrial development of the whole country," Minister of Finance August Lentze wrote, "depends in large degree upon the predominantly technical character of the vocational schools."[15]

In the end, a compromise solution was adopted: authority over the vocational schools remained in the hands of the ministries of trade and agriculture, but that over *Jugendpflege* was transferred to the Ministry of Culture, which budgeted 1 million marks for that purpose (up from 200,000 in 1910).[16] But government efforts to create a mass patriotic youth movement (the semiofficial Young Germany League) and to guide *Jugendpflege* groups by training "youth cultivators" failed in the face of indifference among young people and the passive resistance of established religious youth groups, which regarded these efforts as an attempt by the state, as the 1912 Conference of Catholic Bishops put it, to "steal the wind out of the sails of religious *Jugendpflege*."[17] The costs of this conflict were high: the resistance of the Catholic church, along with that of employers, brought about the defeat of the minister of trade's proposal that all communities over ten thousand inhabitants be obliged to institute vocational schools.[18]

While the contrast between repressive and managerial reform strategies is clearly dominant in the case of vocational education and *Jugendpflege*, a number of other conflicts figured in the policy debate of the immediate prewar years—conflicts which cut across this deep division and made that debate tremendously complex and confusing, even to those engaged in it.

The development of a cadre of child welfare "experts" committed to scientific standards, therapeutic models, and flexible, "individualizing" administrative decision making was the source of growing friction between child welfare reformers and the more conservative legal establishment, which remained committed to principles of legality, to due process, and, more fundamentally, to law and adjudication rather than administrative discretion and social-managerial expertise as the basic ordering principle of society. The resistance of individual judges to wholesale commitments to correctional education generated immense frustration at the local level, while the objections of the higher judiciary severely hampered reformers' efforts to resolve the problems created by the system through a revision of the law. A similar conflict plagued public legal guardianship, since the desire of reformers (and municipalities) to free the public legal guardian from the supervision of the Guardianship Court estranged the jurists; and juvenile justice reformers, as we have seen, sought to reduce the power of judges drastically. Johannes Trüper, editor of the *Zeitschrift für Kinderforschung* (Journal of Child Study), regarded the central role of the judiciary in the correctional education system as a "relic of the age of absolutism."[19] One high judicial official summed up the growing alienation between reformers and the legal community in 1912 by referring to the "war against the judges" being waged by child welfare reformers.[20] Again, such debates could severely hamper reform efforts: the reform of juvenile justice, for example, bogged down in parliament in a debate over whether "justice" or "socialization" should be the goal of the juvenile courts. The bill was finally abandoned at the close of the legislative session in 1913.

Even more important, the tension between the Prussian government and the religious *Jugendpflege* organizations was symptomatic of a much more general problem. For the rapid expansion of state and municipal child welfare programs and the professionalization which they encouraged quickly created friction between those attached to the voluntarist traditions of private charity and those who argued for professionalization and the mobilization of expertise and scientific knowledge by the state. The transition from private to state action was not smooth, despite the connections between public and private organizations. This conflict emerged most clearly within the infant health movement, where medical professionals employed as doctors or administrators in infant welfare programs soon found themselves at odds with the women's charitable organizations—which still did most of the practical work of infant welfare programs, provided thousands of volunteers, and believed fiercely in the ethical and social value of individual, voluntary social action. Health officials such as Taube and Dietrich argued with growing urgency for better training for the women involved in infant welfare work, and for the replacement of volunteers by trained, professional, and more obedient social workers; by 1910 Arthur Schlossmann was denouncing the "crass dilettantism" and the "pushiness" of volunteers in infant welfare work.[21] Again, this conflict exacted a high price; in 1908 in Bavaria, for example, a bill providing for compulsory medical examinations for infants in districts with high infant mortality was defeated by conservative Catholics. While liberals and the government argued that the "preservation of newborns is without doubt an essential determinant of the labor power and the military power of a nation," Catholics favored local "private" efforts supported by municipal subsidies, and denounced compulsory health inspection as an assault on personal liberty.[22]

Inextricably related to this rejection of law, bureaucracy, and scientific expertise in favor of mobilization and self-help was the mounting tension between the commitment of the intellectual and administrative leadership of child welfare reform to technical knowledge and scientific rationality, and the religious and ethical motivations central to the charities and much of the middle-class social reform movement. This conflict ran through the debate in every area of policy. The preference of some of the Prussian ministries for technical education as opposed to religious and political indoctrination in the vocational schools is an example of this conflict. But it was probably clearest, again, in the case of infant health programs. In a 1908 article in the *Journal of Infant Welfare*, for example, a Dr. Wichura explained the frustratingly slow pace of progress in reducing infant mortality as partly a product of the fact that "in school and church the creation of children in marriage is represented as something which is in principle and uniformly good, even holy, although it can only be such if the progeny has good conditions of existence." He added that "biblical aphorisms" such as "be fruitful and multiply are only too likely to dull or repress the parents' sense of responsibility."[23] Marie Liedtki's angry reply in the following issue indicates the alienation such outbursts created:

> Only through Christianity did we come to understand the value and the dignity of *every* human being, and the sense of responsibility grew up together with this understanding and answered the question, "Am I my brother's keeper?" with a resounding "Yes!" . . . If the representatives of Christianity, instead of recommending an *artificial* limitation of the number of children, see the dominion of the spirit over the senses and the taming of the instincts as the goal of socialization, they thus show that they have a higher estimate of human dig-

nity than many representatives of a new morality. . . . That indolence, stu-
pidity, and laziness are a product of religious education is an assertion which
truly is suited to break the bridges which have been built, despite all differences in worldview, by active humanitarianism.[24]

There were similar conflicts, moreover, in the field of correctional education between "scientific" psychiatry and the religious pedagogy of the *Rettungshaus* movement. At the first meeting of the AFET in 1906, for example, the psychiatrist Clemens Neisser lectured his audience on the need
to recognize that a third or a half of their charges were "psychopathic" and
that only a psychiatrist was competent to deal with them.[25] By 1910 the
Rettungshausbote was speaking of a nascent "War of the Psychiatrists
against the Pedagogues," and a Protestant reformatory director at that
year's conference of the AFET pointedly thanked psychiatrists "for partici-
pating so eagerly in our work—on the condition, however, that a contradiction of worldviews is not present. If . . . anyone bases himself squarely on a
materialist point of view and says, 'There is no afterlife, there is . . . no
God, there is no free will, but rather human beings are no more than a
product of heredity and the milieu in which they live,' then, gentlemen . . .,
we must declare war on the psychiatrists."[26]

There was often an explicitly confessional undertone to these conflicts,
since it was the Catholic church and the Catholic charities which most vehemently resisted statism and science in child welfare policy. It was Catholic organizations, for example, which were most skeptical regarding the
state direction of *Jugendpflege*. Similarly, in the case of infant welfare—as
the example of Bavaria, discussed earlier, suggests—Catholic organizations
resisted the intrusion of state and municipal bureaucracies, defending the
autonomy and vitality of civil society. Meanwhile, many Protestant experts
regarded Catholicism with ill-disguised hostility: Johannes Trüper, for example, criticized the "medieval monkishness" and "false teachings [*Irr-
lehren*]" of Catholic institutions for the mentally ill.[27]

At the same time, there was also often an important element of gender
conflict in the debates over child welfare as well. Women's organizations
formed the backbone of the private charities, and secular feminist groups
had developed both the theory and the fundamental forms of modern social work in the course of the 1890s and early 1900s. They adhered to a
"maternalist"—and often explicitly Christian—conception of welfare and
charity work, one that focused on the alleged special spiritual qualities and
individualizing, caring talents ("motherliness," or *Mütterlichkeit*) and the
moral and cultural mission *(Kulturaufgabe)* of women and the bridging of
social divisions through personal service, rather than on science and social
efficiency. Even where men (particularly pastors) were the formal directors
and spokesmen of private religious charitable organizations, it was usually
bourgeois women who performed the practical and administrative work.

This was particularly true of infant health programs, but women also played an important role as investigators and caseworkers in correctional education and juvenile justice, especially where girls were involved. A similar division existed in secular organizations. There were feminist women who were important figures in progressive reform circles—Frieda Duensing, for example, who helped to train a whole cadre of "Miss Doctors" *(Fräulein Doktor)* at the DZJ, or Alice Salomon, one of the founders of social work training and the social work profession. And women did much of the practical and pioneering work in setting up and operating secular welfare organizations. But the leadership of progressive, scientific reform was nevertheless overwhelmingly male, partly because German universities were only just being opened to women in this period (in Prussia, for example, in 1908). There was thus an undercurrent of tension between Christian women of the Patriotic Women's League, for example, and the male administrators and doctors appointed by municipal and provincial governments to rationalize and centralize child welfare programs, as well as between secular feminists and the doctors and officials who dominated the progressive child welfare movement.

Guardianship, Socialization, and the Women's Movements

These tensions were particularly evident in the debate over legal guardianship. The nonconfessional women's movement in particular was not at all opposed to public legal guardianship. Since women's organizations were deeply involved in welfare and charitable activities, they were familiar with the failings of guardians, and mainstream feminist organizations were among the first important groups to agitate for the introduction of public legal guardianship. The 1906 conference of the Federation of German Women's Associations (Bund Deutscher Frauenvereine, or BDF) even submitted a petition to the various state governments urging this step.[28] But guardianship was one of the first public offices women were allowed to hold, and the secular women's movement was reluctant to give up this strategically important foothold to male professionals. Equally important, the traditions of the bourgeois women's movement, whether liberal or Christian, were deeply personalist. Women's organizations—like the charities generally, and indeed like many social scientists and pedagogues—argued that the formation of character and of lasting moral, social, professional, and religious commitments and the inculcation of a capacity for responsible membership in society could be accomplished only in an intimate personal relationship between two people organically linked by the ethical and spiritual bond of love, and by profound, prerational understanding and empathy—relationships like those found in the family. Only in such a relationship, they held, would the educator have the legitimate authority and the pupil the unconditional trust which would allow the transmission of fundamental ethical and spiritual values. And only such a relationship could give the educator the intimate knowledge of the pupil which would allow him or her to nurture, support, and appropriately direct or "train" (as one trains the growth of a plant) the developing individuality of the child—rather than crushing, stifling, and warping it with arbitrary and insensitive demands. Thus, Paul Natorp, one of the great theorists of "social pedagogy" *(Sozialpädagogik)* after 1900, wrote, "The capacity for community . . . arises only in the soil of a close and intimate direct relationship between one person and another, on the basis of which alone every further and indirect human community . . . can be securely built."[29] Sister von Tiele-Winkler, speaking to a training session for women legal guardians in 1917, put the same notion in more religious terms: it was not enough to watch over the outward development of the child, arrange its living situation, advise, or admonish; for "socialization . . . does not deal with outward processes, but with the child's soul." The legal guardian must give a ward *love.* "Oh," she lamented, "how many a poor child slumbers like Snow White in the sleep of death and awaits the kiss of love!"[30]

The very idea that a *public* agency—a creature of law and bureaucratic routine—could assume the intimate, deeply ethical human task of socializing children seemed to these people simply impossible. Indeed, some critics objected that such a measure "carries . . . the stamp of the socialization of child rearing and family life itself."[31] The ideal of the BGB and of many child welfare activists was precisely that legal guardianship should establish a "familylike" relationship; the guardian would be a surrogate father. One Dortmund city councillor, for example, told the DVAW at its 1907 conference that the "legal guardian should replace mother and father . . . for the child without family."[32] Obviously, the public guardian could not create this sort of relationship with each of his hundreds or even thousands of wards. For this reason a great number of middle-class reformers agreed with the speaker at the 1907 conference of the DVAW who objected that "the most natural form is individual legal guardianship, which cannot be replaced by public legal guardianship in its essential nature and end, to care for the *individual person.*"[33]

It was precisely the "mass effect" which secular modernist progressives saw as the unique and necessary benefit of public guardianship, then, that other reformers saw as its great drawback. Isolated from his wards by their sheer numbers and locked away in his office, critics warned, the public legal guardian was in danger of becoming a soulless, heartless bureaucrat, a "paper-pusher," falling into a routine or "schematism" *(Schematismus)* which could never accommodate the human complexities of his wards' lives and needs. Becoming ineffective because he could have no real—that is, personal and moral—influence on his wards, the legal guardian would necessarily become abusive because he would expect and demand that they all, despite the unique individuality of each, respond to the same established procedures.

As we have seen in Chapter 2, there was an important *political* content to these arguments. For the charitable activities of many bourgeois organizations were posited on the belief that only the creation of personal ties through selfless service could resolve the social tensions built into the operations of the soulless, uncaring economy which men had created. Such self-sacrificing kindness was suited, a speaker at the Christian-Social Women's Group in Berlin in 1913 pointed out, "to build a bridge between the different . . . classes."[34] Social peace, in other words, would be achieved not through social management by professionals, but only through personal commitment and personal contact with—female—volunteers.

The women's movement sought in the years after 1900 to offer an alternative to the technocratic and bureaucratic solution of public guardianship by recruiting women as legal guardians, that is, by mobilizing a particular segment of civil society to meet the social problem of illegitimacy. Where individual guardianship could be made to function well, then, women's organizations argued that it should not be abandoned. In the eyes of most German feminists, women were uniquely suited by their nature to the task of revitalizing individual guardianship. After all, the creation and maintenance of intimate family relationships and the nurture and rearing of children were the "natural" task of women. Both feminists and patriarchalists, however, also held that women were by nature uncomfortable with formal legal procedures and the personal confrontations involved in legal guardianship. Rather than supporting simple individual guardianship, therefore, feminists argued for the creation of what they called "organized individual guardianship." In this system, women would be recruited as guardians by a private association, which would establish a central bureau to train the women and to take any necessary legal action. Lawyers employed by the association would advise the guardian in all legal matters, prepare the child's claim against the father, and facilitate all the guardian's interactions with the courts or with municipal agencies. The women would therefore be free to perform that part of their duties for which they were uniquely qualified: personal care for the child and its mother.

Some supporters of public legal guardianship were more or less sympathetic to these ideas; but they doubted that private associations could recruit sufficient numbers of good guardians. "It's lovely," Taube told the ADB in 1911, "when a female guardian leads a child by the hand through life; but give me some examples." A Guardianship Court judge from Stettin agreed: "The ladies are invaluable," he remarked, "but where I needed ten or twenty, I found only one."[35] In fact, the oldest and largest of the nonreligious "organized guardianship" groups, the Alliance for Female Guardianship in Berlin, reported in 1911 that after five years of recruiting, it still had only 305 guardians and 581 wards. In contrast, two years after its introduction the public legal guardianship of Berlin had 8,814 wards.[36]

Yet the most committed proponents of public legal guardianship explicitly defended the bureaucratic element in that institution. According to the BGB, they pointed out, it was the *mother*'s right and duty to care for her child; legally the guardian was merely her "adviser" *(Beistand)*. And whatever the law might stipulate, in reality there was almost never a close "familial" relationship between legal guardians and their wards. The real task of the legal guardian, Klumker argued, was not "socialization" but rather "choice of socializers" and "supervision of socialization," since it was really the foster family or the mother that reared the child.[37] As for the child's individuality, Petersen held that "far and away the greatest percentage of wards are . . . average people" whose "little idiosyncrasies" would be apparent only to the primary care giver in any case.[38] In fact, enthusiasts held that an advanced division of labor, public authority, and the refined pedagogical insight developed through experience with hundreds of wards would far *better* enable the public guardian—and assisting jurists and doctors—to take the "individuality" of his or her wards into account. The public guardian's staff of paid or volunteer social workers would provide whatever loving individual care the legal guardian should and could give his ward. Oblivious to the ideal of love and sympathy fundamental to critics' views, supporters of public guardianship stubbornly clung to a strictly pragmatic, managerial notion of socialization, viewing "individualization" merely as a question of understanding what the child needed and supplying it. In 1914 Klumker even pointed out that while for some "the ideal of individualization appears as a goal of education," others were more concerned with accomplishing "the adjustment of the coming generation to the existing economic and social conditions"—for example, through vocational training or career guidance.[39]

In practice, most cities preferred some sort of compromise between individual and public legal guardianship. In Leipzig and other major Saxon cities, universal, automatic legal guardianship was in fact instituted. In most areas, however, the child was passed on to an individual guardian as soon as the father was making regular child support payments, or when it reached a certain "safe" age (Dortmund, Hamburg); or the Guardianship Court decided whether to appoint the municipal public guardian or an individual (Strasbourg); or "dual" guardianship was established, with the public guardian responsible for the child's material well-being and an individual guardian appointed to see to its spiritual welfare.

Much more important, however, was the creation in these years of the subaltern profession of social work. Some feminists argued that women, like men, would take a greater interest in the children under their care if they were autonomous and personally responsible; but in fact both mainstream feminist and patriarchal theory tended to view women as unsuited for independent public action. Those who favored individual guardianship for women over the dependent role of social worker in the apparatus of a public agency were therefore at a distinct rhetorical disadvantage: if the main object of involving women in child welfare was to tap their "motherly" and nurturing nature, then it made instinctive sense to many that there should be a stern, authoritative, rational "father" to take care of the traditionally "male" tasks involved in guardianship: securing the child's rights, providing for it, choosing its profession. Thus, the rhetoric of "motherliness," the feminist vision of the general cultural mission of woman as champion of warmth and nurture in a competitive and selfish society, militated *against* responsibility and emancipation through welfare work, and *for* an ideal of service.

It was in this form that municipalities most often recognized the necessity of involving women in the care of children. As child welfare agencies expanded, women came to dominate paid social work in the new Youth Bureaus. Leipzig's public legal guardianship, for example, employed a staff of over one hundred trained women social workers to oversee the wards' upbringing; and a survey of forty-five major cities in 1913 counted 682 trained women social workers in paid employment.[40] This "marriage" of feminine nurture and fatherly public authority became increasingly entrenched in the rhetoric of the social work profession and in the curricula of the schools, which had begun as early as 1893 to train women for social work (the first recognized school was founded in 1905 by the Inner Mission; Alice Salomon founded a second in Berlin in 1908, and by 1914 there were fourteen such schools in Germany). It is important to remember that the forms of social work were not simply imposed on women, and neither did women play a passive role in the organization of social work. On the contrary, the first training in social work was begun by feminist women, and the ideal of feminist theorists of social work was always that of the autonomous, skilled professional social worker. What is more, the ideology of "motherliness" *did* permit women to create social work as a specifically female profession, in a long and stubborn battle against the male administrators and volunteer visitors who dominated the old poor relief system (in 1907, for example, Berlin had four thousand male and forty female visitors). Nevertheless, the expansion of the profession was in a sense a pyrrhic victory for feminists, since women social workers were virtually excluded from responsible administrative positions.[41]

Public Legal Guardianship, the Youth Bureau, and the Charities

But if the terms of the feminist critique of public guardianship left it vulnerable to cooptation, the same was not true of the other major organized group which opposed public legal guardianship—the Catholic church and

Catholic charities. Like nonreligious women's organizations, Catholics did not initially oppose public legal guardianship. The 1905 conference of the Deutscher Caritasverband (the national Catholic conference of charities, or DCV), under the influence of Catholic municipal reformers, endorsed public guardianship on both ethical and economic grounds; and Catholic women's groups in particular supported the institution, at least for infants.[42] By 1910, however, the rapid expansion of public legal guardianship in the municipalities was creating growing concern among the Catholic leadership. In 1905 the DCV qualified its resolution with the condition that "the religious education of the wards be guaranteed through collaboration with the responsible church agencies." By 1909 the annual National Conference of German Catholics (Katholikentag) issued a resolution suggesting that the form of dual guardianship was preferable to simple public guardianship.[43] And in 1911–12 the growing misgivings of Catholic organizers about the attitude of public legal guardians toward religious education erupted into a bitter legal battle in Berlin.

Under a Berlin statute of 1912, all illegitimate children were placed under the guardianship of a municipal official—who happened to be a Protestant. The private multiple guardianship established by the Berlin branch of the DCV for the illegitimate children of the city's small Catholic minority was thereby effectively deprived of wards; it therefore challenged the system in the courts. In its suit the DCV-Berlin pointed out that the law required that the Guardianship Court "take the ward's confession into account" in appointing a guardian, and that there be "special grounds" for the appointment of a guardian of a different confession. The city argued that the material advantages of public legal guardianship were sufficient "special grounds" to justify the appointment of a Protestant municipal guardian for Catholic children, while the DCV-Berlin insisted that its own multiple guardianship was just as effective as the city's.[44] The DCV eventually won its case on appeal, but not before Catholics were thoroughly alarmed by their opponents' rhetoric and attitudes. Klumker, for example, argued that the physical well-being of illegitimate children must be the first priority of public policy and religious education a secondary consideration—a position which naturally infuriated devout Catholics, for whom religious education was the paramount focus of all child rearing. A questionnaire sent out by the government of Berlin to forty-six other Prussian cities found that Protestant municipal public guardians were routinely appointed for Catholic wards.[45]

By 1913 the tone of the struggle between secular municipal experts and Catholics had led even the first conference of the Educational Office of the Protestant Inner Mission (Evangelische Erziehungsamt der Inneren Mission) to pass a resolution to the effect that "only the Gospel decisively recognizes the worth of the individual person, and only it can give, under the condition of belief, the awareness of true forgiveness for our sins, and powerful impetus to the development of our moral powers. . . . The real program of this new conference might be: unconditional preservation of the spiritual influence over all child welfare."[46]

The response among Catholics was much more decisive. Dr. Bernhard Wuermeling, director of the DCV-Berlin, argued that mass legal guardianship could not possibly provide the individual care and attention necessary for the shaping of individual character and personal morality. "The legal guardian," he told the Prussian House of Representatives, "should replace the departed head of the family and, as far as possible, take the place of the father." A public legal guardian, a mere "gear in the machine" of city government, could never perform this function. Wuermeling insisted, moreover, that a religious upbringing was "no less important than good health care and securing the legal rights of the child," particularly for the prevention of waywardness. Not only was it unlikely that a municipal official (much less one of the wrong confession) could secure the child a proper religious education, said Wuermeling, but often public guardians *would* not do so. In big cities, he suggested, "left-liberal and Social Democratic" administrators rejected religious education, since they regarded confessional concerns as "unmodern and backward." Because they cared only for the smooth and uncomplicated operation of their bureaucratic apparatus, they would furthermore leave little room for the "collaboration of private charity in the religious-moral care of the child." Thus, for Wuermeling, the battle over legal guardianship was part of the general struggle to preserve the "religious-moral powers in popular life," the "religious-moral foundations of the state," and the "precious heritage of . . . ideals and religious values" against "modern 'free' thought" and socialists who sought "deliberately to kill, rather than nurture, the seeds of love for religious-moral values and the fatherland."[47]

The DCV moved quickly in 1912 and 1913 to establish Catholic unity on the position developed by Wuermeling. The annual Catholic conference of 1912 warned "the Catholic people of Germany and the authorities involved . . . of the dangers which the new movement for public guardianship by the local governments . . . brings with it . . . for the religious-moral education of its wards on the basis of their faith." The conference suggested that preference should be given to "organized" individual guardianship or, failing that, private multiple legal guardianship created by private associations. As a last resort, public legal guardianship was acceptable only if there were guardians of *each* confession, or if individual Christian co-guardians were appointed.[48]

The reputed fiscal benefits of public legal guardianship, however, were sufficiently attractive to municipal governments that Catholic resistance did not appreciably slow its spread (see Chapter 3). Under these circumstances, the Catholic charities concluded that only a concerted effort to organize political resistance and effective competition by private associations could guarantee that confessional interests would be protected against the secularism and empire building of municipal social bureaucracies. By the outbreak of the war, therefore, the issue of legal guardianship had converged with that of the proper relationship between private charity and public welfare.

Prior to the 1890s most Catholic welfare work had been performed by the Catholic religious orders, in cooperation with the parish priesthood and the church hierarchy. The early 1900s, however, saw the emergence of a new kind of Catholic charitable organization—bureaucratic in structure, geographically extensive rather than strictly local, often working closely with local government, and intended to address the needs and problems of (Catholic) society at large, rather than only to express the religiosity of its members. But though the secular organizations created in the 1900s were in a sense organs of state policy, the new Catholic organizations were conceived, at least in part, as a private Catholic counterweight to public programs. Despite their small beginnings in the 1890s, by the outbreak of the war the unity of the Catholic welfare organizations and their effectiveness in recruiting middle-class volunteers were unrivaled. The DCV played a crucial role in galvanizing this effort. The organization had its roots in the late 1880s, in efforts to stem what its founders saw as a religious offensive by the Protestant Inner Mission and a steady drift of youth away from the church. The DCV was formed by an assembly of Catholic notables in Freiburg in 1895, and headed by Lorenz Werthmann. Despite often stormy relations with the Catholic charities and very slow growth (by 1914 the DCV had established regional chapters in only one third of the German dioceses), by 1910 the organization was playing an important leadership and coordinating role.[49]

The development of Catholic organizations was extremely rapid after about 1905. The most important was unquestionably the Catholic Welfare Association for Girls, Women, and Children (Katholische Fürsorgeverein für Mädchen, Frauen und Kinder, or KFV, now the Sozialdienst katholischer Frauen).[50] The KFV was founded in Dortmund in 1899–1900 by Catholic women who, since the mid-1890s, had been visiting young women in prison, in the venereal disease wards of local hospitals, and in the offices of the morals police who controlled prostitution—often at the behest of the Prussian minister of the interior or local authorities. The organization rapidly spread to other cities and into work for the welfare of women and children generally, and changed its name accordingly. In 1903 a central headquarters was founded in Dortmund, under the leadership of the extraordinarily capable Agnes Neuhaus; thereafter the organization spread rapidly, playing an important part in—and drawing its strength from—the

Catholic women's movement. By 1913 the KFV had some eighty local chapters throughout the Rhineland and northwest Germany, thirty-three shelters for women and children (with 1,200 beds), and between five and six thousand new cases each year.[51] In 1912 the organization was strong enough to assist in the creation of a parallel Catholic welfare association for men and boys to complement the work of the KFV, the Catholic Men's Welfare Association (Katholische Männerfürsorgeverein, or KMFV), which had seventeen local chapters by 1913.[52]

Where these two groups did not establish branches, the older Catholic charities, such as the societies of St. Vincent and St. Elizabeth, were often galvanized by their influence and became more involved in child welfare activity; outside the Northwest, where the KFV and the KMFV were concentrated, local branches of the DCV played a similar role. In Bavaria the Catholic church after 1910 organized a remarkably unified and extensive system of quasi-private child welfare associations in each parish and diocese, which paralleled that created by the state. In response to this blossoming of Catholic child welfare activity, a national Association for Catholic Charitable Educational Activity (Vereinigung für katholische caritative Erziehungstätigkeit) was formed in 1908–9; its journal, *Jugendwohl*, soon became the center of the intellectual life of Catholic child welfare.

Neuhaus's association worked very closely with public authorities; indeed, at the DCV's 1905 conference in Dortmund, she argued that the local chapters could survive and flourish only by establishing a close working relationship with public agencies.[53] Yet the KFV was the most effective champion of "organized" individual guardianship—much more successful, for example, than the Berlin Alliance. And, despite all collaboration, it was essentially in competition with the growing public child welfare agencies. Its goals remained essentially religious. Neuhaus insisted—in the face of charges of worldliness from conservative Catholic circles—that her goal was "to lead our fellow creatures and ourselves to God," and that "we want above all to protect and preserve for our young people that which is our and their most precious possession: the living Catholic faith."[54] In fact, as public programs expanded, the KFV and the DCV increasingly regarded it as their task to combat creeping secularism. Lorenz Werthmann, for example, argued in 1910 that the emergence of the Youth Bureau made autonomous Catholic organizations all the more indispensable, and Neuhaus urged the creation of a seamless national network of Catholic child welfare organizations.[55]

Although the relationship between Catholics and the state was particularly problematic, it was only a specific instance of a much more general problem. By the 1910s, the founding of a growing number of private child welfare organizations was leading to what many observers decried as "fragmentation," producing inefficiency in the form of top-heavy welfare associations and redundant services. The annual report of Breslau's Center for Child Welfare listed 111 corporate members in 1908, and Frankfurt had over 200 associations in 1900.[56] This concern soon led to a process of vertical integration, the formation of numerous regional and national organizations *(Verbände)* uniting local associations *(Vereine)*. At the same time, there was horizontal integration at the local level, as private child welfare centers *(Zentralen)* were formed.[57]

Municipal governments found it easier to work with such *Zentralen,* and therefore encouraged their formation. They also often heavily subsidized private organizations, which could relieve the city of considerable expense by providing volunteer social workers or reducing the municipal agencies' caseloads. But both the more thoroughgoing organization of private charities and the growth of public child welfare programs made the issue of the proper relationship between the two an increasingly pressing one. And even where religious tensions played no role, there were deep philosophical divisions between advocates of public and of private child welfare.

Frieda Duensing, director of the National Center for Child Welfare and of the Berlin Alliance for Female Legal Guardianship, summed up the fundamentally liberal and voluntarist views of the majority of middle-class reformers in a speech before the DVAW conference of 1910, at which the idea of the Youth Bureau was endorsed. Duensing conceded that ultimate responsibility for child welfare lay with the state, since it involved the nation's military and economic security. But, she continued, the social and spiritual costs of allowing the Youth Bureau to shoulder aside private charities would be far too high. For the activity of bureaucracies regulated by laws was devoid of ethical value. In fact, it threatened the ethical life, the essential vitality, of the nation. The resources of the nation, she argued, are not limited to the state; indeed, the state

is only its outward form, the totality of its compulsory and obligatory relations. The essential, the nation in its natural, voluntary life, is *civil society.* . . . The child welfare activity of the state is really only, so to speak, the activity of a machine, and voluntary self-sacrifice for common goals is the ethically superior form of action; state action is, it is true, necessary for the accomplishment of mass tasks, but alongside it the voluntary work of the people must proceed if the life of the nation is not to become completely ossified. . . . Self-help, that is the life principle, that is the symptom of the health of society.[58]

If freedom and spontaneity were crushed by a proliferation of laws, institutions, and regulations, society would lose its vital creativity.

In particular, many child welfare advocates feared that expanding state intervention would disrupt and hollow out family life. Paul Natorp, for example, warned in 1910 that the modern, industrial, scientific age displayed a "tendency of development which threatens irretrievably to destroy all *individuality* and therefore also the form of organization which until now gave this individuality its surest protection: the close, intimate association of the family, based essentially upon *personal* relations." Reformers must be careful to preserve this "native soil of all human community," and with it the ethical and psychological foundations of social order.[59]

The question for most reformers, then, was not whether public should replace private welfare work, but rather how to preserve the vitality and ethical energies of voluntary social action despite the expansion of public intervention which most people believed was necessitated by social change. Some proposed that public agencies should merely provide organizational and financial resources for the charities, delegating practical work to them—an idea rejected, of course, by municipal administrators. Petersen suggested in contrast that the "voluntary" element in social work should be preserved simply by persuading those private persons interested in child welfare to offer their services to the municipal welfare agencies, while others proposed that public agencies should refer cases requiring more individual attention to private organizations.[60] But supporters of the charities saw either alternative as tantamount to reducing private charity to a "drudge" or "serving maid" for public agencies.[61] They preferred the metaphor of marriage: the "female" charities would represent the ethical and spiritual values, while the "male" government would be the provider and represent authority.[62] The precise practical meaning of this metaphor, however, was the subject of much disagreement.

In practice, therefore, the program of the defenders of the charities often amounted simply to creating a private counterweight to public agencies that was powerful enough to prevent the latter from establishing a monopoly over child welfare work—very much as the Catholic charities were doing. Frieda Duensing stated this plan explicitly before the DVAW in 1910, arguing for the creation of a grand unified national organization of private charity to secure the interests and influence of private activity.[63] But whatever its chances of success, as Agnes Neuhaus pointed out, this scheme clearly implied an essentially "adversarial relationship" between private and public activity when what seemed necessary was "trusting cooperation."[64] Nevertheless, it proved impossible between 1910 and 1914 to arrive at any better solution. And as public programs expanded, tension between public and private organizations continued to rise.

By the outbreak of the war, then, the progressive centralization of public and private child welfare alike seemed to be creating a growing ambivalence within the social reform community—and a growing potential for polarization between those who embraced the benefits of public action and those who focused on the dangers they saw arising from it. By the eve of the war, the relative unity created by common concerns about the problem of youth, which had fueled the expansion of child welfare for over a decade, was clearly breaking down over the issue of the state's role in child welfare.

The Crisis in Correctional Education: Resistance and Rebellion

This division, however, was not the only conflict created by the growing intervention of the state in child welfare. Perhaps equally important in these years was the intensifying conflict between public child welfare programs and their targets, particularly in the field of correctional education. In the years just before the war, correctional education too was clearly drifting toward political crisis. And because the problems of correctional education raised fundamental issues of cultural and social authority, these two conflicts were becoming increasingly intertwined.

The system of correctional education established by the Prussian law of 1900 was plagued from the very beginning by a seemingly endless series of unfavorable and contradictory judicial decisions. Faced with a flood of children, the provincial authorities, which bore two thirds of the costs of correctional education under the new law, immediately appealed a large number of commitments on the grounds that local governments were requesting them merely in order to escape the burden of paying for foster care for children whose own families had endangered or abused them (as paragraph 1666 of the BGB stipulated)—costs which were borne by the locally funded poor relief system. In 1901 the Kammergericht (the highest Prussian civil court) ruled in the provinces' favor, holding that correctional education was justified only where "special pedagogical measures" were necessary. The number of commitments of merely "endangered" (that is, not yet obviously "wayward") children immediately fell off—from 33.2 percent of commitments in 1901 to 17.5 percent in 1908.[65] The municipalities, however, thereupon appealed to the Supreme Administrative Court (Oberverwaltungsgericht), which duly found in their favor, ruling that the "artificial need" created by removing children to foster care under paragraph 1666 did not qualify a child for poor relief. Such removal, it held, was an "educational" measure—and in Prussia, as in most of the German states, the poor relief system was not legally responsible for the costs of education. Thus, while many children could not be committed to correctional education owing to the Kammergericht's decision, the Oberverwaltungsgericht's ruling meant that funds were also not available to remove those children to a foster family. Since there was no single supreme court in Prussia, the situation could not be resolved by appeal. Yet the government, urged by parliament in 1903 to solve the problem by legislative action, argued that it was still too early to conclude that the law was a failure.[66]

The results were extremely frustrating to child welfare advocates. Clarifying decisions by the Kammergericht gradually brought the number of commitments back up after 1902. But the Guardianship Courts continued to refuse to commit younger, merely "morally endangered" children. Only 170 of the 6,650 children committed in 1905–6, for example, were under age six; about 30 percent were aged six to twelve, 55 percent were twelve to sixteen, and 13 percent were seventeen or eighteen.[67]

In the eyes of those who ran the reformatories, the advanced age of children in the institutions lay at the root of a problem that was, by the middle of the decade, coming to dominate all discussion of correctional education: the deepening unpopularity of the law and the growing resistance and rebelliousness of the children in the reformatories. Not surprisingly, parents often pulled every possible string in order to avoid losing their children, whom they loved and who also often made an important contribution to the family income. They appealed commitments, attempted to pressure local notables, sought allies in positions of authority. In one celebrated case of 1908–1910, a mother "kidnapped" her child from the foster family in which it had been placed and kept it hidden for two years.[68]

But much more disturbing for practitioners was the rebelliousness of the children themselves. In one instance in 1905, four inmates of an institution near Cologne trampled their overseer, beat him with boards, and stabbed him with his own saber in order to secure their transfer from correctional education to prison.[69] Much more common was simple flight: in fact, of the 38,600 children in correctional education in 1908, 3,879 ran away in the course of the year. And the proportion of children in correctional education who were at large at the end of each fiscal year was rising slowly but steadily, from 2.3 percent in 1904 to 3.5 percent in 1911.[70] But those involved in correctional education pointed out that such figures merely reflected a much more generalized oppositional attitude which made it extremely difficult to "correct" the flaws in children's socialization—what Wilhelm Backhausen in 1912 called "the collective resistance of the children."[71] By 1910 there was a semitechnical term for children who offered this kind of passive, internal resistance to institutional (re)education—as well as violent forms. They were referred to as "difficult" to educate, or "incorrigible," or "ineducable" (schwererziehbar or unerziehbar).

This resistance was a natural response to incarceration. It was heightened, however, by the peculiar character of the reformatories. While Christian institutions were dominated by what one critic called an "ascetic-methodistic spirit," the methods and structure of public institutions were conceived, and often staffed, largely by penal officials and retired military men. Many amounted to gigantic children's prisons, in which life was boring, stifling, oppressive, and loveless. Children in reformatories usually slept in large common halls; they were allowed few or no personal posses-sions, and often wore uniforms; the windows were frequently barred, the grounds fenced; food, clothing, beds, tools, and staff were of poor quality or in short supply. Although about 50 percent of children in correctional education were placed in foster homes rather than reformatories, condi-tions there were often not much better. Many foster families treated their charges as cheap labor, attempting to extract the maximum of work from them at minimum expense.

But the fundamental problem of correctional education was not rooted in these practical difficulties; it was a product of the cultural chasm sepa-rating middle-class reformers from lower-class children. For one thing, the norms applied by middle-class social workers were different from those prevalent within working-class communities. As one Catholic observer re-marked in 1925, "Children of the lower classes are often held 'wayward' by the members of the upper who are, in the judgment of their families and members of their class, in no way such."[72] Nor did children always view life in their own families as social workers did. As the Catholic reformatory director Wilhelm Rhiel admitted in comments before the AFET in 1912, much of the resistance *within* the reformatories was grounded in "bitter-ness," since many of the children were "very fond of their homes and par-ents" and—wrongly—believed that they had "suffered an injustice" in being removed from them.[73] Working-class children also had pressing family responsibilities: in one case in 1911, for example, a single mother persuaded her son to escape from the reformatory so that his wages might allow her to "eat her fill again."[74] Moreover, since the vast majority of chil-dren in correctional education came from urban working-class and poor families, the law on correctional education was perceived widely as a par-ticularly crass case of class justice, and was resented accordingly.[75] Finally, working-class children apparently resented the fact that most reformatory administrators, because of their antiurban and anti-industrial bias, gave their charges no useful vocational training beyond gardening or farming skills for boys and housekeeping skills for girls. The same prejudice often led officials to place urban children with farm families. In any case, the stigma that attached to having been in correctional education made it more difficult for ex-inmates to find employment after their release.

But, worst of all, the pedagogy adopted in the reformatories was simply inappropriate for the children kept in them. Reformatory staff usually took an uncompromisingly moralistic view of their charges: Rhiel, for example, held that many reformatory inmates "have no abhorrence of the bad, in-deed they wish it."[76] Conservative Christian theory maintained that by forcing the child to obey authority and habituating it to a moral way of life, the foundations for morality and for an autonomous ethical sense would be laid. The reformatories therefore sought first of all to impose a strict code of discipline and unquestioning obedience to the authority of the staff. The model was that of the patriarchal, consciously Christian family, in which authority, earned by exemplary behavior, exercised in a spirit of love and understanding, and guided by faith, shaped the child's character. Work—the development of habits of industry and disciplined labor—played an important part in this process; and so did the constant teaching of Christian dogma, Christian religious and moral precepts, and Christian practice.

But many of the working-class children who were committed to correctional education were not responsive to these methods. By 1900 middle-class observers had, after all, been complaining for thirty years or more about the decline of respect and religiosity among working-class youth. As Günter Dehn, a pastor who organized a youth club in the suburb of Moabit in Berlin, wrote in 1913, in proletarian society "religion has been discarded like a worn-out shirt." Moreover, their experience in their own families and communities did not give working-class children a strong sense of the necessity and righteousness of authority. Dehn reported, for example, that working youth "really have no respect for anything at all. Whence should they get it? They have outgrown the schools, they are too good for the church, they lead their mothers and fathers around by the nose, in the factory only fear makes them obedient—in Berlin-Moabit everyone is a free citizen and does whatever he pleases."[77] Rhiel expressed the puzzlement of Christian educators faced with such children. "Often," he wrote in 1912, the educator "stands . . . helpless before the pupil, before this total lack of religious and moral foundation."[78] Many working-class children were no doubt equally nonplussed by the behavior and demands of their educators.

Yet the confrontation fostered by this misunderstanding was seen by those educators as a stubborn refusal to bow to legitimate authority and to face up to one's own sins and weakness—as the unreasoning revolt of anarchic egoism against the moral order of the universe. This view—and the Christian idea that the sinner must recognize his or her wrongdoing and accept punishment—gave rise to an apparently increasing resort to corporal punishment as a disciplinary method in the reformatories. As one speaker told the first conference of the AFET, "Refusal to obey and lack of respect for authority must, if earnest fatherly reminders of God's fourth commandment do not bear fruit, be punished with the necessary severity, until the stubborn will is broken."[79] Psychiatrists, who were beginning to gain influence, at least in public reformatories, did not do much better. Otto Mönkemöller, for example, though he argued that beatings must be a last resort and that they must be supervised by doctors, held that "physical pain is the only thing which some persons respect; and if beatings do not make people better, they do make them more cautious."[80] For many conservatives, finally, a less intellectualized understanding of the efficacy of beatings sufficed: as Baron von Manteuffel remarked before the Prussian House of

Lords in 1900, "It is self-evident that in the reformatories the brats will receive beatings."[81]

In this climate of opinion, frustration sometimes gave way to veritable orgies of violence. Karl Krohne argued in a position paper for the Prussian Ministry of Justice in 1910 that the mass of "deeply wayward elements" committed under the new law (those "who had strayed onto the path of crime, run wild in the big city") "posed special problems for correctional education; they were an element until then unknown to most educators, who had no understanding of the fact that they were the product of their social surroundings. . . . The pedagogically unschooled officers of the reformatories believed that they had to break, with violence, corporal punishment, prisonlike lock-ups, and other, worse coercive measures, the evil will which they suspected everywhere. Crass excesses . . . were the result."[82]

Popular outrage over such "excesses" finally broke in early 1911, when a revolt in an institution in Mieltschin, in east Prussia, sparked a scandal. In court it was discovered that in Mieltschin at least one child was beaten with a stick or whip each day; that children received up to one hundred blows for minor infractions; that the other children had to watch, and outsiders were invited as spectators; that children were locked in dark basements; that they were chained in such a manner that they were unable to lie down or stand; that in one case a boy was tied to a tree, beaten unconscious, revived, and beaten again.[83] This and a rash of lesser scandals—reported in spectacular detail by the mass press—convinced much of the general public that the system of correctional education was bankrupt.

The Social Democrats were especially active in condemning correctional education; indeed, after about 1908 concern with this issue came to dominate Social Democratic thinking about child welfare. The Social Democrats of course feared that the law was sometimes used for political purposes (and not without reason). More important, however, they held that it was fundamentally misguided and ineffective. They denounced the harsh methods used in the reformatories. Karl Zielke, for example, referred to corporal punishment as "a barbarity." In January 1913 the socialist deputy Arthur Stadthagen told the Reichstag that in the reformatories "the humanity is beaten out of the good elements."[84] The monotonous, often physically exhausting work reformatory inmates were forced to perform (usually without pay), critics held, "literally kills the spirit" and achieved the opposite of educating children for a life of responsible and steady labor.[85] They argued that "mass child rearing" and "herd methods" in barrackslike buildings were bound to crush individuality and self-reliance, and they denounced the exploitation of children placed in foster families.[86] They demanded the abolition of most corporal punishments, the institution of proper vocational training, the transfer of control over placement from provincial and state agencies to the municipalities, and adequate training of reformatory staff. And they argued that it was industrial capitalism, which forced working-class mothers out of the home to seek work or to take on sweated work at home, that was the cause of widespread waywardness, and that the proper response was not incarceration but universal day care and a comprehensive public child welfare policy, particularly through school health services, school lunch programs, and the like—a view that was in fact shared by many middle-class progressives.[87]

While Social Democrats were most vehement in their attacks on the re-formatories, bourgeois "experts" too were increasingly alarmed by the de-velopment of correctional education. Johannes Trüper, editor of an early journal of child psychology and a critic of the dominance of the "bureau-cratism and . . . police spirit" of the Prussian law, spoke angrily after Mieltschin of the "complete fiasco of correctional education."[88] By 1911 the *Rettungshausbote* protested that "all the liberal papers unanimously cry, 'Away with this scandal.'"[89] In fact, even in government circles correc-tional education was being regarded with growing skepticism; in 1911, for example, a privy councillor *(vortragender Rat)* in the Ministry of Justice an-nounced that "correctional education is a fiasco!"[90]

The irony of this situation is obvious. Correctional education had been adopted as a public, political means of maintaining the patriarchal social order and the culture of deference which underpinned it. Policymakers had taken in stride or overlooked the immediate paradox of this measure—the fact the it undermined the same patriarchal power it was meant to re-place or bolster. By the 1910s, however, it was becoming apparent that by politicizing the functions of private patriarchal social authority, correc-tional education had exposed it to public critique and organized political resistance.

Divergent Responses: Punishment or Self-Government?

One response to the problem of "incorrigibility" was reflected in the growing popularity of the belief, propagated by psychiatrists, that children who made trouble in the reformatories suffered from brain defects which made them in fact "ineducable" *(unerziehbar)*, and that the answer lay in intensified repression and coercion. This response was popular among re-formatory staff, probably because it was comforting; and it was legitimated by a psychiatric "science" so primitive that almost any statistic or diagnosis dressed up in the proper jargon sounded plausible. Adalbert Gregor, who published early psychiatric studies of children in reformatories, posited, for example, the existence of an inherited organic brain defect called "lack of discipline." Estimates of the proportion of reformatory inmates who were "psychopathic," or at least "hereditarily tainted" *(erblich belastet),* ranged from one quarter to three quarters (though the Prussian government itself, in 1906, found only 9 or 10 percent to be "abnormal," an estimate which incensed psychiatrists and eugenicists).[91]

Child welfare practitioners increasingly insisted that these "difficult," defective children were making it impossible for them to socialize properly those children who were normal, merely endangered, or only mildly wayward. The "bad" elements were not only "ineducable" but were also disrupting the resocialization of the "good." Some therefore suggested simply abandoning the project of resocializing older children. The Saxon correctional education law of 1908 in fact included a clause to the effect that children over sixteen years of age "should be committed to correctional education only if there is the well-founded prospect that it will achieve betterment."[92] But Christian educators balked at the idea of declaring some people "irredeemable." As Hans Uellner argued, "Christian optimism is unbounded."[93] And of course older, more "corrupt" children were precisely the ones who were most in need of "saving," and who posed the greatest threat to society. More popular, therefore, were proposals for the refinement of coercive methods—the creation of special institutions for "abnormal" children, or of special "punishment sections" where, as Uellner suggested, "the pedagogical perspective can yield for a time" while the children were held in cells and put to work at "mechanical repair work" under "military supervision."[94] The AFET conference of 1910 suggested legislation allowing for the indefinite incarceration in special institutions of "ineducable" children.[95]

More popular than such plans, however, was the program of circumventing the whole problem by introducing reforms which would bring children into reformatories at a younger age (and thus presumably less corrupted). Late in 1911 Deputy Adolf Schmedding of the Catholic Center party presented a petition to the Prussian parliament requesting that the government introduce a bill revising the Law on Correctional Education. The law would be amended so as to require that *all* children removed from their families by the courts would be placed in correctional education, thus resolving the conflict between the Kammergericht and the Oberverwaltungsgericht.[96] Despite the resistance of the Ministry of the Interior, which insisted that "it cannot be the goal of the Law . . . to bring every minor whose education is endangered, who is neglected or wayward, into correctional education,"[97] Schmedding's petition was passed unanimously by a committee of the Prussian House of Representatives, and the government at last relented and presented a bill to the parliament in early 1914. It was passed on March 26, 1914.

But this intensification of intervention and repression was not the only response to the crisis of correctional education. Other child welfare advocates became increasingly convinced in the 1900s that *less* confrontational and coercive methods must be found.

For one thing, of course, in a very real sense public legal guardianship and the Youth Bureau were an *alternative* to correctional education, one that avoided coercive intervention in favor of prevention. Christian Jasper

Klumker, for example, argued that, unlike guardianship, "criminal law treatment" of the problem of delinquency could never be prophylaxis; it was merely treatment of "those already fallen ill, to use a medical metaphor."[98] In addition to its appeal as a foundation for the Youth Bureau, then, public legal guardianship became increasingly attractive in the years before the war precisely because, as the troubles of correctional education and juvenile justice intensified, child welfare reform shifted more and more toward preventive solutions.

A second alternative to correctional education was "protective supervision" *(Schutzaufsicht)* by volunteer social workers, who were assigned by the court to keep tabs on the young offender, assist in finding him or her a respectable job (not, for example, in a bar, café, or nightclub), attempt to change his or her recreational habits by encouraging membership in a sporting or religious youth group, and so on—a system based on the concept of probation developed in Massachusetts. Protective supervision promised to antagonize parents less; it also kept children in their own homes and out of the reformatories. Already by 1910 it constituted an important alternative to correctional education in some places: the number of children committed to correctional education by the Berlin juvenile court, for example, fell by 30 percent from 1909 to 1910 after the court established a stable working relationship with city agencies and private associations which provided social workers for protective supervision.[99]

Some child welfare advocates argued at the same time for the reform of correctional education itself—for improvements in the system of government supervision and inspection of the reformatories, for the introduction of a system of appeals by reformatory inmates to an outside agency, for limitations on corporal punishment (which were in fact introduced, for girls over age fourteen, in Prussia), for better vocational training, and particularly for increased efforts to gain the goodwill and cooperation of parents and to reconstruct children's families sufficiently that they would no longer be "endangered" in them and could be returned to their parents' custody after a year or two in a reformatory.

Much more important than such administrative changes, however, was the development of an alternative to authoritarian Christian and psychiatric models of waywardness and accordingly of an alternative pedagogy. As the extension of social services made practitioners more familiar with the lower-class social milieu, and as Social Democratic criticism of correctional education mounted, a growing number of child welfare activists abandoned moralistic theories in favor of a more social and psychological perspective. J. F. Landsberg pointed out that proletarian youths were more likely to come into conflict with the law because working-class children were released from the discipline of the schools much earlier than bourgeois children, and because the social order of capitalism denied them the luxuries which the latter could take for granted. They were also more likely to outrage judges and reformatory staff because they were more accustomed to fighting back verbally and physically.[100] Klumker was one of many who expressed a growing skepticism regarding the conclusions of psychiatry, pointing out that many "normal" children were *also* "difficult," while most of the 50 percent who were deemed "abnormal" could nevertheless be turned into "something useful" to society. Rather than simply giving up on these children, he suggested, practitioners should "find and test new methods."[101]

Such assessments encouraged the development of a pedagogy very different from that of conservative Christians. A growing number of child welfare advocates were in fact concluding by about 1910 that the stubborn resistance of children in correctional education was evidence neither of organic brain defects nor of rebellion against God; instead it was a perfectly natural aspect of the process of growing up, of developing an autonomous will and an independent individuality. As such, it was not to be crushed but rather merely directed toward constructive ends, toward healthy independence. These conclusions were reinforced by progressive educational experiments in the United States, such as W. R. George's "Junior Republic." But reformers could also draw on native traditions. Wilhelm Backhausen, for example, who replaced the more conservative Wilhelm Seiffert as chairman of the AFET in 1911, quite consciously "rediscovered" Johannes Wichern's commitment to freedom in the work of the *Rettungshäuser* (see Chapter 1).[102] The new correctional pedagogy paralleled, in many respects, Georg Kerschensteiner's program for vocational schools. Some students of the problem of child abuse and neglect—for example, Frieda Duensing—strongly advocated a less authoritarian pedagogy.[103] And some Social Democrats had long demanded the development of a pedagogy based on freedom and self-government, one that would heighten rather than destroy correctional pupils' "strength of will," "self-respect," and "belief in . . . justice."[104]

This change of perspective brought about a revolution in pedagogy in the years just before the war, at least among a small circle of pedagogical reformers. They implicitly rejected the idea that society should be a static hierarchical structure in which each individual is contained and moralized by passive obedience to authority. By breaking the will of delinquent youth and enforcing unconditional discipline, a Pastor Knaut told the AFET in 1912, "one will raise dependent, weak-willed people;" whereas, by contrast, if one directs that drive "into the correct paths, it will serve the education of happy, free, independent persons."[105] Only such autonomous persons would be capable of positive moral action and moral responsibility: "If I educate my pupil for mere *passive* discipline," wrote Friedrich Wilhelm Förster in 1914, "then my pupil will always be undisciplined in *action*."[106] The decay of the social and political authorities which ordered traditional society and the social and economic complexity peculiar to modern life made the creation of such dependent, passive people increasingly dangerous and inappropriate. Förster, for example, noted that a psychiatrist had discovered "that many people contract nervous disorders because their upbringing has not prepared them for self-direction, while . . . modern life demands most of precisely this capacity,"[107] while Gertrud Bäumer, head of the BDF from 1910, suggested that the conditions of the modern age were such that "the power of the independent conscience" was more important than mere "obedience."[108]

The pedagogical reformers in fact held that traditional methods were simply no longer effective precisely because modern youth—and indeed modern people generally—were no longer responsive to authority. "Our present pedagogy," wrote Friedrich Zimmer in 1910, "is no longer appropriate. An earlier age could accomplish something with the enforcement of authority because that age believed in authorities and believed them willingly. Children called their parents 'Sir,' and unconditional obedience to the parents was something self-evident. That is no longer so. There is no feeling for authority anymore, and pedagogy can rely on it no more than can the social and political authorities."[109] The effect of trying to impose authority on modern individuals, therefore, would be not obedience but rebellion. Knaut told the AFET in 1912 that if one suppressed children's natural tendency toward collective activity, one would merely "encourage secret plots and unhealthy cliques."[110] An effective modern pedagogy would have to harness the energies latent in youth itself for the educational project. Rather than denying responsibility to the born leaders among children in an institution—the "key boys" and "key girls," a term taken from American practice—the educator must involve them in the task of bringing order to the mass of his pupils through the creation of offices to which they could be elected or by delegating tasks to them. The "pedagogy of self-government . . . alone," Förster concluded, was "capable of rescuing the authority of the educator from its modern crisis" while also preventing the emergence of a "blind and unordered dictatorship of the mass over the individual." He declared:

> Precisely *that* authority which seeks to lead and to be fruitful, which seeks to heighten and organize vitality, must, in the interests of its own leadership function . . ., permit a high degree of self-direction and initiative on the part of those led. . . . The richer and stronger the élan of the forces which we have to lead, the more effectively also our directives share that vitality . . .; the absolutist principle, by contrast, is by its nature incapable of injecting into the vital forces themselves a higher plastic principle, an organizational tendency; that can be accomplished only through practice, responsibility, and enthusiastic collaboration of the children in the area of order. Leadership deserves its name only when strong and independent forces are released to which direction can

be given; mere repressive discipline is the opposite of leadership, a failure to lead, an assassination of life.[111]

In practical terms, "self-direction" and "self-government" in the reformatories probably most often meant merely a relaxation of asceticism and military discipline, allowing inmates some responsibility for carrying out assigned tasks or enforcing predetermined rules. Nevertheless, the significance of these ideas should be apparent. The new pedagogical model precisely paralleled the participatory ideal developed in circles close to the Society for Social Reform and by reformers such as Franz Pagel and Georg Kerschensteiner. Indeed, it was clearly intended to create the new people who would make up the dynamic, harmonious society envisioned by progressives. The "pedagogical reform movement," Gertrud Bäumer wrote, arose from the "sense that a new age demands new *people*."[112]

By 1914, then, there were several divergent responses to the crisis of correctional education—just as there were divergent responses to the crisis of conservative political and social authority in German society at large. Conservative practitioners continued, despite revolts and vehement criticism, to rely on brute force and authority to crush godless rebellion. Psychiatry veered toward the scientific refinement of repression, and toward discrimination and exclusion. And the new social-liberal pedagogy drifted rapidly toward an ideal of self-government, of participation and responsibility as integrative forces. This triad eerily parallels the development of German politics in the years immediately before the war. On the left, bourgeois social reformers in the Society for Social Reform drifted toward an alliance with reformist Social Democracy on the basis of a common commitment to parliamentarization and democratization, and of a vision of participation guided and shaped by corporatist institutions; on the right, some conservatives drifted toward radical and increasingly racist biologistic authoritarianism; caught between the two, the monarchical government clung doggedly to its traditionalist conservatism.

The boundaries between these groupings were often rather blurred. In correctional education, as Detlev Peukert has pointed out, the exclusion of "difficult" children from reformatories on the basis of biologistic diagnoses could be presented as the precondition for the introduction of "free" methods and self-government. Progressive enthusiasts of family planning often shared with more authoritarian thinkers an enthusiasm for eugenics; similarly, left-liberal reformers often shared an enthusiasm for imperialism and efficiency with radical-right groups such as the Pan-German League; and while the Pan-Germans increasingly fell out with the conservative government, in correctional education, as we have seen, Christian pedagogues were sometimes deeply skeptical of the materialism of psychiatric theory.

For these reasons, Peukert has seen the development of pedagogical reform as part of the prehistory of fascism and of the murder of "defective" children in the 1940s.

And yet, just as the conservative government called on the services of the radical right in national politics—for example, in the "Hottentot Election" of 1907—so it was conservative Christian, and above all Protestant, practitioners rather than progressive theorists who appealed most often to the notion of "ineducability," and who were most eager to exclude the "defective" from the institutions they controlled. It was surprisingly easy for conservative pedagogues to shift rapidly back and forth between Christian and psychiatric ideas, with organic brain defects standing in for the natural sinfulness of man's will. And Friedrich Wilhelm Förster, in contrast, explicitly held that his pedagogical program was particularly appropriate for "abnormal" youths precisely because "the disorganized personality has a pathological drive for freedom . . ., the reflection of a pathological drive for freedom in the subordinate nerve centers, against cerebral control."[113] It was thus these children who most needed to learn self-discipline, and who were least accessible to a pedagogy based on authority.

Finally, conservative Protestant practitioners were more often moved to criticize the incipient democratic ethos of "free" pedagogy than the materialism of psychiatrists. For those who regarded the will and natural desires of the individual as sinful, the strategy of tolerating and harnessing them was a recipe not for the release of energy but for anarchy. Seiffert, for example, denounced reform proposals as the pipe dreams of "professors" with no experience of the realities of life in the reformatories, and argued that the pedagogical methods appropriate to a republic such as the United States could not be applied in Germany.[114] Before the First World War the influence of the new pedagogy was not great enough to elicit more than grumbling. The divisive potential of this split was, however, obvious, and it would become a central problem of German child welfare in the 1920s.

By 1914, then, the child welfare community was increasingly divided by a complex, cross-cutting set of conflicts. Divisions along gender lines, religious lines, and philosophical lines, between public and private organizations, between conservatives and progressives, reformers and jurists, threatened to develop into open rifts that might have crippled public policy. The failure of the reform of juvenile justice, the breakdown of reform in vocational education, and indeed the government's announcement in 1912 that fiscal constraints ruled out any further social reforms for the near future suggest the vulnerability of progressive reform in this period.

Just as these tensions appeared to be approaching a critical level, however, the outbreak of the war transformed the political and social situation. World War I struck this divided child welfare community with tremendous force, relentlessly revealing, in the space of a few catastrophic years, the cultural and ideological tensions that had been built up over the course of the previous half century. The war gave immense impetus both to the conservative backlash and to the more democratic alternative—as well as to the tendency toward centralization and technocracy. By 1918 German policymakers were faced with the absolute necessity of resolving the tensions within the social reform community. The result was the emergence of a set of fundamental institutional compromises which have underpinned the German welfare state for most of the twentieth century. This process is the subject of Chapter 5.

CHAPTER FIVE

Child Welfare Policy in the Great War, 1914–1918

The Wartime Crisis of Patriarchal Social Relations and the Coercive Response

The surge of patriotic fervor occasioned by the outbreak of the Great War—the *Burgfrieden,* or the "spirit of 1914"—convinced many Germans that their country was experiencing a political and cultural rebirth that would sweep aside the conflicts and divisions of the prewar years. While the Social Democrats in parliament voted for war credits, the trade unions suspended industrial action for the duration. Confessional divisions seemed forgotten as both churches rushed to support the war effort; conservative Christians persuaded themselves that the sacrifices of war would bring about a revival of Christian faith. And the women's movement mobilized to support the war on the home front through a National Women's Service which included even Social Democratic women.

At the outset of the war optimistic observers believed that wartime conditions would prove beneficial for youth. A new national mood of seriousness, high moral purpose, patriotism, and reconciliation would, they hoped, correct many of the "abuses" of the prewar period. J. F. Landsberg wrote in the fall of 1914 that popular "frivolity" and the "vicious entertainments of the masses" were in retreat. Even socialist radicalism among youth would abate, he predicted, as "the struggle forced them into blood brotherhood." And wartime shortages would eliminate "luxury of dress," which was "one source of the moral ruin of many women and girls."[1]

But by the middle of 1915, as the *Burgfrieden* in domestic politics began to unravel, this early optimism was being hastily abandoned, and by 1916 there was a growing consensus, at least on the political right, that the war was in fact immensely exacerbating the crisis of the patriarchal social order.

Excessive patriotism led some boys to steal in order to send care packages to the front, or to hop freight trains to get closer to the action. Many observers complained that girls were allowing their appreciation for soldiers, or their fear of not seeing boyfriends again, to carry them beyond the bounds of respectable behavior. And there was a widespread perception that children's games were becoming increasingly violent and even dangerous. The city government of Stuttgart listed "imitation of the military" and "shoot-outs" among the causes of rising juvenile delinquency, while another report complained of "boys who play war in the streets and do not shrink from attacking each other with knives or secretly purchased air pistols."[2]

Much more important in bourgeois critics' eyes, however, was the fact that the call-up of millions of adult men simply removed from the scene many of the representatives and agents of patriarchal social authority. Worst of all, of course, the sudden disappearance of men from millions of families was felt to be bringing about an alarming collapse of parental authority (since mothers were not believed to have the capacity to discipline children adequately, particularly adolescent boys). But the military also laid claim to a whole occupying army, so to speak, of other social authorities who in peacetime kept youth in line and ensured their orderly socialization. In most towns instruction in the schools was cut back progressively as ever more teachers were called up. Schools had to be closed in winter because they could not be heated; and rural children did not attend in summer and fall because they had to help with the harvest. A growing number of schools were converted for use as military hospitals. By 1917 and 1918 many children were spending half as many hours as usual in school. With fewer police officers about, young people were less likely to behave respectably in the streets, parks, and other public spaces. And the war also compromised the operations of *Jugendpflege* groups.

These problems were heightened by the economic conditions created by total mobilization for war. Reports of the theft of food, particularly the theft of fruit from orchards, with attendant damage to trees, were very common. The uncertainty created by the conflict may well have discouraged saving. There was some concern, too, that the example of profiteering and widespread evasion of the government's economic decrees was undermining young people's respect for the law generally. But above all there was a considerable increase in the proportion of young people and mothers working in factories, and a rise in the wages of unskilled factory workers, which heightened concern over both the relative independence of working-class youth and their future employment prospects. Wilhelm Bloch of Charlottenburg wrote in early 1915 that "high wages create a very great independence, and the behavior especially of young people in big cities toward their parents is not improved," while the conservative Prussian *Kreuz-*

Zeitung complained of the "disappearance of authority and piety" brought about by the war.[3] And of course the higher wages earned by young people also gave them more opportunity to "abuse" their new freedom by engaging in lowbrow cultural consumption. Reports that young people were attending the cinema and public amusements, pursuing "nocturnal adventures" in cafés, buying novels, frequenting bars, and purchasing clothes, sweets, cigarettes, and alcohol in greater numbers were common.[4] The fact that a growing number of mothers were taking factory jobs seemed to threaten the moral and physical well-being of younger children as well.

The combined result of all these influences was, in the perception of the conservative middle class, a frightening increase in the waywardness of youth. Among girls and young women, many believed they could discern a distinct increase in sexual activity, particularly in outright or thinly veiled prostitution—a product of independence and high wages, which accustomed girls to a luxurious style of living. As for young males, by late 1915 there was a growing sense that they were "running wild." Observers complained that "it almost seems as if the children are the masters of the streets," engaging in "blatant disobedience, outrageous lying, thievery and fencing, vandalism, truancy," throwing rocks at citizens strolling quietly in municipal parks, and openly laughing at those who attempted to bring them to order.[5] Others complained of an increase in "loutish behavior," "roughness," "unruly doings," and the like. And though the rate of juvenile delinquency had leveled off after 1900, during the war years it shot upward with unheard-of rapidity: 14,087 minors were brought to trial in Prussia in the first quarter of 1914; 48,977 in the first quarter of 1918.[6] As the political crisis of the authoritarian state deepened toward the end of the war, the association of waywardness with chaos and revolution became more explicit. Paul Felisch, for example, wrote of "immature boys who dream of freedom and understand by that Bolshevik terror," while one Major Treu complained to the district administration in Oppeln on the day before the proclamation of the Republic that "people have no idea of the disobedience and roughness of youths between the ages of 14 and 17 who have been without their fathers for the past four years of war. . . . That is the material with which the Bolsheviks have operated in Austria, Russia, and soon will among us, too. . . . We are headed for the abyss if we close our eyes to this."[7]

As we have seen, such concerns were common well before the war. The state of national emergency, however, was uniquely favorable to determined action. The imposition of martial law presented a golden opportunity to translate the cultural backlash of the prewar period into a program of direct state intervention. As Duchess von der Gröben pointed out with evident satisfaction in 1915, "We live under a military dictatorship. It is now 'possible' to do many healthy things for the common good that were earlier 'impossible.'" Lamenting the spiritual enslavement of youth to the powers of immorality, she called "in the name of the freedom of our people" for military decrees regulating young people's morality.[8]

Beginning in 1915, and intensifying with the establishment of a virtual military dictatorship by 1917, the various army corps with jurisdiction in the Empire responded to such calls by enacting a flood of measures restricting the freedom of young people. According to the Central Bureau for National Welfare (ZVW), of the twenty-four army corps with jurisdiction in the Empire, fully twenty-two issued decrees against "trashy" popular literature; nineteen attempted to limit the consumption of alcohol by young people; seventeen sought to outlaw smoking by minors; fifteen banned youth from all except approved films; twelve adopted curfews or measures against loitering and vagrancy *(Herumtreiben)* by young people; a few imposed mandatory savings plans for young workers.[9] A number of city governments adopted similar measures as well. And in some cases more radical suggestions enjoyed considerable support. The possibility of limiting the right of free movement for young people was seriously discussed in a variety of meetings after 1916, and was a particular interest of Wilhelm Polligkeit's. In at least one celebrated case correctional education was used against a young man who was found to be "no longer capable of feeling German," as evidenced by his attendance at radical socialist demonstrations.[10]

Reluctance, Resistance, and Failure

Despite this rage for order, there was considerable resistance to these measures among middle-class people. Behavior which seemed to some to indicate a state of waywardness seemed to others to be harmless. One Berlin industrialist, for example, observed that smoking or going to the movies did not constitute "running wild."[11] Of the authorities responding to a survey by the head of the state administration in the district of Düsseldorf at the end of 1915 and in early 1916, most reported some "roughness" or "crudeness" among young people but little real waywardness.[12] Many observers suggested that the rising number of convictions was the product of an increase in the number of punishable offenses as well as intensified enforcement. One Guardianship Court judge wrote in 1918 that there were simply "countless decrees which were unknown, and therefore could not be violated, in peacetime."[13] And at a conference titled "Coercion and Freedom in *Jugendpflege*," held by the Central Bureau for National Welfare in late 1916, Aloys Fischer warned that naked coercion would only produce "masses of obedient, unthinking people"—or worse "either hypocrisy and . . . secret rebellion, or open revolt."[14]

But even many conservatives shied away from measures such as mandatory universal paramilitary or physical fitness training. The aversion of Christian groups to the militarization and secularization implicit in such plans was made clear at a conference of the Central Bureau in 1915, at which spokespeople for the religious *Jugendpflege* organizations stubbornly resisted such schemes. Carl Mosterts, the general chairman of the Catholic youth organizations, warned that young workers, already sufficiently fed up with school, work, and military service, would be embittered by any further claims on their time; that the "religious conception of life could suffer damage" if training were held on Sundays; and that this would constitute an "enormous intrusion on family life" and the rights of parents. While Christians might be enthusiastic supporters of greater "discipline," then, they often rejected measures that would create competition between new imperialist institutions and those of the Christian social order.[15]

Regardless of the policy preferences of middle-class people, the decisive fact was that restrictive measures ran up against the same limitations as had correctional education in the prewar period. A number of local courts struck down various of the decrees promulgated by the military authorities; and though the adjudication of the courts was confused and contradictory, they do seem to have prevented the construction of a consistent, universal system of restrictions. More important, young people resisted restraints on their freedom. The most spectacular rejection of such measures was a strike against the imposition of enforced savings by over one thousand young workers in Hannover and Brunswick in the spring of 1916, which forced the local military authority to rescind the decree. Moreover, owners of bars, smoke shops, movie theaters, newsstands and dance halls did not leap to comply with attempts to limit young people's access to tobacco, alcohol, entertainment, or trashy novels, and young people seem to have widely ignored the proclamations of the military authorities.

A report of the ZVW in December 1917 summed up the lessons of two years' experience: "Overall it is evident from the reports received that the early enthusiastic reception of the decrees, in which the intervention of the 'strong hand' was welcomed, has given way to a critical reserve."[16] While the idea of banning sales of alcohol or tobacco to youth retained some support, and censorship of books and films was still quite popular, by the end of the war most observers agreed that punishments for young people were downright counterproductive: they merely criminalized masses of youth and, because they could be enforced only sporadically and arbitrarily, inculcated disrespect for the law and the authorities.[17] By the end of the war, then, it was becoming increasingly clear that the coercive response to the perceived moral collapse was unworkable. The idea of taking positive and preventive measures—such as creating youth clubs, public lectures for young people, youth film theaters, organized entertainments and outings, reading rooms, and so forth—was clearly gaining support by 1918.

The War and Population Power

While the apparent decay of social authority under the impact of the war brought about a proliferation of coercive measures, the immense social catastrophe created by economic mobilization for total war and by the Allied blockade brought about an extraordinary blossoming of social "welfare" measures more narrowly defined. When men left for the front, the state found itself obliged to step in to support their families; and since the elderly, women, and children were clearly not responsible for the hardship they suffered when their men were called up, the system of "war welfare" *(Kriegsfürsorge)* created to assist them had to be kept institutionally distinct from the discriminatory poor relief system. As the war went on, separate systems also had to be created for the dependents of men killed or incapacitated by injuries at the front, for those who lost their income to mounting inflation, and, by the end of the war, for refugees from areas occupied by Germany's enemies. By the war's end, the state's response to these needs had created an entirely new system of public assistance which, for some people at least, realized many of the demands of reformers before 1914. In many cases relief was a legal right, and provided more than merely the minimum necessary for subsistence; and the new forms of assistance were clearly designed to maintain not just life and order but also efficiency and social "health." In other words, these programs were forms of *soziale Fürsorge,* not of poor relief.

Child welfare programs benefited disproportionately from the atmosphere created by this transformation. Most concretely, the slaughter in the trenches gave equal impetus to concern about infant mortality and the declining birthrate. The champions of traditional morality might still argue that "the deciding factors . . . in war lie in the . . . moral character" of the troops, but the lesson of the war as it dragged on seemed to be that that state would triumph which had the most warm bodies at its disposal.[18] The war therefore transformed population policy into a central topic of public discussion. Increasingly, population policy analysts agreed that the end of the war, whatever its outcome, would not mean the end of the struggle against Germany's enemies. In Aloys Fischer's pithy Clausewitzian formulation, most assumed that "peace will be the continuation of the war by other means."[19] Indeed, some even suggested that the military outcome of the war was relatively unimportant: C. Weinbrenner wrote in 1918 that "the fate of our country will not be decided by the victorious conclusion of this war and a . . . favorable peace; the future of our land depends upon the solution to the population problem, which has become the question of economic and political power."[20] From this perspective the future looked rather grim. The absence of millions of men at the front led to a precipitous decline in births—a "birth deficit" which for the first time brought about negative population growth. Even worse, those being killed at the front were mostly between the ages of twenty and forty—precisely the men who, had they lived, would have fathered the next generation.[21] And while the French, with a feeble birthrate and high losses, seemed to be headed for extinction, Russia's population was growing explosively; some population policy enthusiasts hinted darkly of the Slavic Peril.

As the war of attrition dragged on, therefore, interest in the question of population policy and the birthrate soared. The Prussian Ministry of the Interior had established an inquiry into the birthrate in 1912, and it published its report in 1915. Prussia's Interministerial Commission on the Birthrate conducted extensive hearings on population policy from late 1915 through early 1917; the Reichstag established its own Committee on Population Policy in 1916; the Prussian parliament established a commission in 1918; and General Erich Ludendorff, the army quartermaster, published his own suggestions in September 1917.[22] In January 1917 the Central Committee of the DVAW concluded that child welfare was now the "most burning question" in the field of welfare policy generally, and began planning a major national conference on the subject.[23] Even the Catholic paper *Germania* as early as 1915 urged Germans to "*Protect the youth, the future of the nation!*"[24]

One response to this concern was the further elaboration of the moralist themes dominant in the writings of people such as Jean Bornträger before the war. Indeed, the visceral (and propagandistically orchestrated) "return" to the punitive, repressive discourse and moral categories of Christian and authoritarian traditionalism during the war gave tremendous impetus to the moralistic interpretation of the decline in the birthrate. Heinrich Behm, for example, confessed in the *Journal of Population Policy and Infant Welfare* (the new name of the *Journal of Infant Welfare*) in 1918 that the decline in the birthrate filled him with "shame," for he believed that it was a symptom of moral decay and spiritual decline. Dominated by their lustful natural desires, and titillated by the modern mass media, his fellow Germans were calculatingly adopting rational, technical means of preventing conception, the better to indulge in "sensual pleasures." But Behm hoped that the "education by God in our present history"—that is, the war— would finally bring Germans to their senses and spark a return to family, piety, and patriotism. Every married woman, he suggested, "owes the fatherland, as a contribution to national self-preservation, four children." Germans generally, he urged, must "turn our backs on foreign things" such as the "plague of desire" and rationalism (which he believed "came out of the West . . . as a French disease") in order to preserve the foundation of national power: a large population.[25] The technocratic authoritarianism of doctors engaged in infant health programs, in particular, was given greater impetus by the notion that the production of healthy babies was an urgent national need.

Under the conditions created by the war—the Manichean moralism of propaganda and public discourse as well as the fiscal strain on local and national government—and despite the recommendations of the Prussian and Reichstag commissions, which largely favored measures for reducing infant mortality, this kind of conservative, punitive approach prevailed over the more rational and expensive approach of people such as Arthur Schlossmann, who proposed tax cuts, income supports, and other social policy projects. Moreover, the fundamental assumptions of proponents of a *positive* population policy of social reforms were sometimes extremely objectionable to Christians and cultural conservatives. One Dr. Saalman, for example, proposing the creation of foundling homes for illegitimate children, asked whether "the satisfaction of the most forceful instinct is really immoral," and spoke approvingly of the "state-communist tendency" created by the war.[26] Even short of such radical rhetoric, many Christians no doubt sensed that offering economic incentives for fecundity contradicted the ideal of individual familial, sexual, and economic responsibility which was at the core of bourgeois Christian values.

Under these circumstances the government promoted almost exclusively negative measures. A growing flood of pronatalist propaganda was churned out during the war by a plethora of private and semiprivate organizations; restrictions on the sale and use of contraceptives and on abortions were tightened in 1916 and 1917; and efforts were made to censor popular medical books ("nature therapy" literature) and pamphlets on contraception. In 1918, finally, the government, under pressure from the military, introduced three major population policy bills in parliament. There were no positive measures included in these laws. Rather than seeking to encourage women and men to have children, they would have enacted a number of repressive measures, aimed mostly at women, designed to enforce higher fertility. The production, sale, import, and advertising of any contraceptives whatsoever would be prohibited—although condoms, which were considered prophylactic rather than contraceptive, were exempted. Penalties for abortion would be more severe. And police and medical control over prostitutes and "suspect" women would be tightened, on the grounds that venereal disease was responsible for the sterility of many couples.[27]

Passed by committees of both houses of parliament, these laws would have come before the full houses in November 1918; their passage was prevented only by the Revolution. Interestingly, however, the major child welfare and social reform organizations took almost no notice of them.[28] Their indifference probably sprang from the perception that the laws' impact would be minimal. *Coitus interruptus* was the most common form of contraception, followed by condoms, and abortion was already illegal. In fact, Cornelie Usborne has suggested that these bills may have been a mere public relations exercise, which the government did not expect to have much impact on fertility rates.[29] Certainly progressive reformers, who believed that the reduction of infant mortality was the only truly realistic aim of population policy, regarded the repressive strategy with the utmost skepticism. Friedrich Zahn, for example, stated flatly, "Nothing will be accomplished here with pious wishes and cheap admonition."[30] And Saalmann, blaming the declining birthrate on "social conditions" and the "honest desire to get ahead" among the "better workers," warned that such causes could not be effectively addressed by "police decrees and the courts."[31]

Illegitimacy Law and the Contradictions of Conservative Population Policy

Since the war ended before the government's three population policy bills could be passed, their effectiveness remained a matter of speculation. The contradictions and limitations of a policy that was both moralist and imperialist, however, did become unmistakable during the course of the wartime debate over the reform of illegitimacy law.

Such a reform had been discussed since the passage of the BGB in 1900. Seeing the plight of single mothers as a glaring instance of the double standard of sexual morality, the radical feminist League for the Protection of Motherhood (Bund für Mutterschutz) had been agitating since 1905 in favor of granting them state support, and of giving their children a greater claim on the father's resources, including at least a limited right of inheritance and the right to bear his name. As more and more children came under public legal guardianship, child welfare reformers became increasingly impatient, particularly with the delays caused by the necessity of disproving in court fathers' claims to have been only one of many men who had slept with a woman during the period of conception—the *exceptio plurium concumbentum* (paragraph 1717 of the BGB). Though only a tiny minority of cases ended with the child losing its right to support payments, over half of all unwed fathers attempted to use this clause to escape paying, so the delays which a trial caused affected a far greater number of children. Moreover, the father was liable to pay child support only until his child was sixteen, and only in an amount commensurate with the *mother's* standard of living. These limitations virtually ensured that illegitimate children would grow up in poverty and receive no proper vocational training.

As early as 1910, therefore, some members of the Organization of Professional Legal Guardians (ADB) demanded the abolition of the *exceptio* and the expansion of the father's obligations. The war greatly increased pressure on the government to reform the law in this area. By 1914 an important step had been taken toward the principle of legal equality for legitimate and illegitimate children when the government was persuaded by petitions of the ADB and other reform organizations to extend family support payments *(Kriegsunterstützung)* for the dependents of men in military service to illegitimate children. And in 1915 the national parliament also extended pensions for the dependents of soldiers killed in the service to their illegitimate offspring.

In view of the high mortality rates suffered by illegitimate children, illegitimacy law also became one of the primary concerns of the ministerial and parliamentary committees on population policy. The parliamentary committee in fact recommended the abolition of the *exceptio* as the most important step in a possible reform.[32] The Prussian government committee on the birthrate had already unanimously approved abandoning paragraph 1717 at a meeting on May 9, 1916, on the grounds, as Privy Councillor Paul Krohne of the Ministry of the Interior explained, that wartime losses meant that by 1930–1936 "we must reckon with a considerable reduction in the pool of men fit for military service. Given the seriousness of this situation, all fundamental objections . . . must be withdrawn."[33]

But many conservatives were not willing to discard principle so easily for the sake of population power. The framers of the BGB had believed, after all, that the stigmatization and economic hardship which the law imposed on unwed mothers and their children was the price that must be paid for the maintenance of female sexual morality—and thus the control of illegitimacy itself—and the protection of the legitimate family based on the sacrament of marriage. Catholics in particular were unwilling to abandon these principles. The DCV and the KDF both opposed the ADB petition for the extension of full pension benefits to soldiers' illegitimate children, arguing that any step which tended to undermine the legitimate family would "necessarily have antisocial consequences."[34] As Karl Böckenhoff of Strassburg explained, the legitimate family was the "fundamental cell of civil society and the state" and therefore "must be unconditionally protected" against "shortsighted eagerness" in social policy. Most Catholics held that illegitimate children must be helped in some way, but, as Böckenhoff wrote, their exceptional status must be preserved, for "the moral teaching of the church . . . holds . . . that great, indeed heroic sacrifice can be demanded from an individual or a group within society, if the welfare of all makes this necessary."[35]

Indeed, Christian responses to those who carried the pronatalist position to its logical extreme reveal the fundamental contradiction between imperialism and Christian morality that lay at the heart of this debate. In an article in the respected economic journal *Schmollers Jahrbuch* in 1916, R. E. May suggested that, far from stigmatizing single mothers, the state ought to be grateful to them for bringing children into the world, and should undertake to raise them in public institutions. One Dr. Nassauer suggested a similar scheme before the Munich Doctors' Association in December 1915, as did Deputy Warmuth, a member of the Reichstag's Committee on Population Policy, in early 1918.[36] In a scathing attack on such schemes in the Catholic journal *Hochland* titled "Heightened Military Power or Morality?" Wilhelm Feld castigated May as a "representative of the . . . Napoleonic population policy of militarism. In the name of enlightened *raison d'état*, the unlimited production of children is encouraged as a national service. Women who do not have the moral strength to control their drives become not merely welcome war contractors, no, they even become heroes and are surrounded with the halo of patriotic self-sacrifice." From such plans, Feld warned, "the moral consciousness of the people suffers . . . great damage. And that must be decisive for us. Against that, material advantages must never ever come into consideration."[37]

Similarly, a Pastor Boré remarked at the October 1915 conference of the Central Bureau for National Welfare: "The best part of national power derives from the other world. The lectures here could be given by any livestock breeder with respect to . . . his animals. . . . Would it not be possible at another conference for the directors to pose the theme: 'national power and belief in God' or something similar?"[38] And as late as the summer of 1918, A. Hessenbach asked "whether 'readiness for war' or *morality* is more important for the maintenance of the state."[39]

Objections such as these did in fact succeed in blocking reform of the BGB. The lower house of parliament accepted the parliamentary committees' recommendations in February 1918; but the committee itself had rejected inheritance and name rights for illegitimate children, and only narrowly approved abolishing the *exceptio*.[40] In the interministerial commission the national and Prussian justice ministries opposed even that step, arguing that the *exceptio* was a bulwark against immorality.[41] Finally, at a cabinet session of April 1918 the justice ministers successfully prevented a decision on the matter, and as late as October 24, 1918, the government's commission was still meeting to try to find acceptable alternatives to the *exceptio*.[42]

The superheated righteous moralism, the tough talk, and the emergency atmosphere created by the war, then, gave tremendous impetus to authoritarian and moralist reform proposals. In the field of morality legislation, as in population policy, a number of repressive policies were in fact put in place during the war. But by 1918 these policies seemed to be demonstrably bankrupt, and coercive and moralist reform had apparently demonstrated its incapacity to resolve the urgent issues of social order and national power raised by the war. By the last year of the war, therefore, it was already becoming clear that secular, more "social-liberal" or managerial reform would dominate postwar child welfare policy. And in fact progressive reformers were on the verge of realizing the ambition of creating a comprehensive public child welfare system.

The Youth Bureau as Socializing Agency

The opponents of positive population policy themselves suggested an expansion of welfare services as a less threatening alternative to structural changes such as illegitimacy law reform. Wilhelm Feld, for example, preferred "the so obvious and appropriate demand to energetically expand the existing child welfare services, public guardianship, etc. and to orient the whole poor relief system more toward social policy" to the "sentimental phrases" of legal reform.[43] The representatives of the justice ministries argued similarly in March 1918 that "the betterment of care for illegitimate children must be attempted in another direction, namely, in the establishment of a comprehensive system of public welfare for the illegitimate."[44] Child welfare advocates themselves were not enchanted with their new allies, nor with the population policy craze: Christian Jasper Klumker, for example, pointed out in late 1918 that the idea of the Youth Bureau had "only at the moment a superficial connection with population policy," having grown originally out of "the rise in educational standards" created by social progress; and Kurt Blaum, annoyed by the sudden craze for population policy, reminded the ADB in 1917 that the modern child welfare movement had arisen out of economic and social development rather than the war, and that "the state doesn't, after all, exist for the army; the state exists rather for its citizens."[45] But in fact the nationalist upsurge of the war years tremendously reinforced arguments in favor of a broad strategy of social management and political integration; and child welfare advocates were not slow to try to capitalize on it.

A good example is the rhetoric used by a speaker named von Seefeld at the ADB conference of 1916. Modern warfare, he argued, demanded not blind obedience but individual "flexibility" and "independence." Recruits therefore had to be well-educated, capable people. Moreover, "it is essential to our economic well-being that we be capable of thriving in international competition. That our industry can do only if it has at its disposal a labor force of high and varied capabilities, a work force that is mentally active, technically proficient, and also capable of adjusting to changing demands." Finally, the wartime "discovery" of the values inherent in "our Germanness itself" required an overhaul of the entire educational system: young people, he suggested, should be "educated for conscious Germanness" as a means of encouraging "the unity of all citizens in service to the fatherland."[46] Indeed, one public legal guardian, writing in the *Zentralblatt* in 1916, went so far as to argue that "the love which the child receives from the state it shall return. Thus, child welfare is at the same time education for love of the state, education for participation, for the further expansion and strengthening of the state."[47]

In the context of this sort of rhetoric the preventive, social-managerial ambition of the progressive program was, by the end of the war, being articulated much more explicitly and boldly than before 1914. In particular, the idea that the state should be involved directly in the socialization of children, at least in a "supervisory" role, gained far broader acceptance during the war years. The strain the war put on many families, as well as the imperialist ambitions and fears it fostered, rapidly eroded commitment to maintaining the boundaries between state and society.

Still more revealing was the increased wartime concern with the welfare and socialization of preschool-aged children, a group largely neglected by reformers before the war. A 1915 conference of the DZJ had already revealed the potentials of this expansion of the purview of child welfare programs. The dominant tone at the conference was quite cautious and conservative; most speakers were careful to insist that the aim of any measures must be to help parents and to strengthen the family. Indeed, the conference was in part an effort to develop a theory of how the family could be "healed" rather than replaced by day care, through the "education" of parents, and particularly mothers, for the tasks and joys of child rearing.[48]

Nonetheless, their enthusiasm for *Erziehung*, their confidence in their own expertise, and the sense of national crisis carried some speakers well beyond this program. In particular, they insisted, conditions in some working-class families were so bad that they demanded immediate intervention. Frieda Duensing, for example, expressed her shock at the treatment some working-class children received: their parents were often exhausted, impatient, and indifferent; they lived in cramped, dark, airless apartments, played on the streets, and got too little to eat; they were sometimes struck at the slightest provocation, locked in apartments or tied to furniture when the parents were away at work; neglect made some appear to be deaf and dumb or retarded at the age of five or seven.[49] But, as one speaker pointed out, attending to these ills would require not merely "clearing aside hindrances" to proper childhood socialization "but rather above all applying positive measures."[50] In fact, it implied an active intervention in the child rearing practices of the legitimate family. Marie Baum, for example, spoke at the same conference of the need to "politicize . . . the household child-socialization work of women," to make it a part of social policy, and to "shape it according to the grand perspectives derived from the concern for the national good." Another participant remarked more pointedly that "the child is more important to me, as a social policy expert and patriot, than parental rights."[51]

In fact, the war years did see the development of a number of draconian proposals. Legal guardians argued even more energetically than before the war for the transfer of the right of primary care from single mothers to themselves. Kurt Blaum suggested that the Youth Bureau's social workers should have the right to enter any home at any time in order to "determine . . .: is the child being treated correctly?"[52] Aloys Fischer claimed to see "drawbacks, very great drawbacks," in according parents a firm right to raise their own children, since "sometimes the task of socialization . . . is so difficult that quite special knowledge, experience and tact . . . are necessary."[53] Others argued in favor of making it easier to remove children from their families if they were judged to be "endangered."

More common, however, was a further elaboration of the "preventive" program developed before the war. For one thing, the war brought wider acceptance of centralizing and bureaucratic methods. The immense effort of coordination and organization which total mobilization demanded, and the success it achieved, created a new enthusiasm for organization and for industrial power. As the immense fiscal and economic impact of the war became increasingly important, concern over the "fragmentation" *(Zersplitterung)* of public child welfare efforts grew, and the pressure on state and local governments to consolidate and streamline child welfare programs mounted, making the idea of the Youth Bureau ever more attractive. At the same time, the wartime romance with efficiency, organization, and unity led to an even more determined attack on what Marie Baum called the "hopeless fragmentation and aimlessness" of the private welfare organizations.[54] The issue appeared all the more urgent because the outpouring of patriotic generosity sparked by the war resulted in the creation of large numbers of new charitable undertakings.

The private charities did make efforts to impose some cooperation and centralization on themselves; but in general, such schemes soon broke down in the face of confessional and organizational jealousies. Calls for the imposition of order on the private charities by the state therefore grew more common as the war went on. In 1915 the federal upper house (Bundesrat) established a system of state approval for all charitable collections; and momentum was clearly building, too, toward a system of state licensing for charitable activity. In fact, during the war the private associations themselves became one of the most important constituencies lobbying for public supervision of the charities and legislative centralization of public child welfare programs, since the new foundations were often in competition with established organizations. But the Youth Bureau, as a "neutral" public body, was the obvious agency for rationalizing relations among existing organizations locally.

Just as important as these organizational questions, however, was the development during the war of the idea of the Youth Bureau as a "socialization agency," first proposed by Polligkeit and Petersen around 1910. Wartime stresses on the family naturally made this conception increasingly attractive and plausible, as did ideas such as those of von Seefeld regarding the need to educate children for patriotism. At the 1917 conference of the ADB, Kurt Blaum presented a mature program for the creation of such an agency. The Youth Bureau, he suggested, should not limit itself to care for specific, high-risk groups of children, for that would defeat the goal of "preventive" child welfare: "If child welfare, of which it is rightly said that it works . . . preventively, were to take on merely those children in whom the first signs of infection, of moral or physical destruction were already present, then it would come too late. . . . Such a distinction between normal youth and youth in need of protection would have the consequence that precisely those who are in a transitional stage . . . would suffer, for they would remain unnoticed among the great number of healthy youth."[55]

The implications of this program were momentous, for it clearly involved abandoning the traditional theory of familial socialization. The family alone, it suggested, was no longer sufficient for the education of children; the state had to play a role in socializing not just children whose families had failed them in some way or who were clearly identifiable as in danger of becoming "wayward," but *all* children. As Klumker put it, child welfare was not merely a "replacement" for the family but "an independent social-educational task."[56]

The Prussian Bill of 1917–18

The prewar expansion of municipal child welfare services was accelerated considerably by this consolidation of progressive theory, despite the general upheaval in public finances and administration. Encouraged by the wartime shortage of individual guardians, public legal guardianship spread rapidly, as did the centralization of local child welfare programs: a report by the National Municipal League (Deutscher Städtetag, or DST) in 1918 found that fifty-two cities of under 100,000 inhabitants had some form of child welfare office.[57] Not satisfied with such piecemeal progress, however, child welfare advocates increasingly argued that it was now time for the state to impose the new child welfare methods and institutions uniformly—to establish a mature, unified national child welfare system. By January 1916 the DVAW, acting on a petition by Blaum and Klumker, created a special Committee on Children's Poor Relief, the task of which was to devise a draft of a national law for the centralization of child welfare. In November 1917 the DZJ, the ADB, and the DVAW established the Working Group for a National Child Welfare Law, and in December these organizations presented a formal petition to the imperial minister of the interior.

While progress toward legislation at the national level was blocked by the resistance of the Ministry of Finance, in Prussia the government and private organizations forged ahead, and by July 1917 the Ministry of the Interior had completed a draft Law on Youth Bureaus and Public Legal Guardianship. In December it opened confidential consultation on the bill with local administrations and representatives of a broad spectrum of private welfare organizations. The bill was submitted to the Prussian parliament the following spring, and would almost certainly have passed but for the outbreak of the Revolution.[58]

Despite the sense of urgency within progressive circles, however, the resistance to the statist social-managerial reform program did not disappear during the war years. Indeed, the ever more open advocacy of intervention revived many of the fears prevalent in the 1890s and 1910s. One Catholic cleric conceded in 1918, for example, that there was a clear need for an effective "population policy"; but he warned that "we must avoid harming the most elementary child welfare," that of the family: "If we followed the suggestions and demands that come from the circles of overeager theoreticians and shortsighted specialists, we would steer under full sail into the red sea of state socialism."[59] By 1917, however, the question was no longer *whether* the state should intervene; the social hardship and the sense of demographic crisis created by the war made *some* form of action unavoidable. And as the bankruptcy and ineffectiveness of moralistic, repressive strategies became clearer, bureaucratic, social-managerial intervention was increasingly recognized as the only available option. The central issue by late 1917 was therefore simply what form that intervention would take. The debate over the prospective Prussian legislation narrowed during the last year of the war to essentially one decisive practical point: how to reconcile the Christian conservative agenda with social management—and, specifically, the question of the proper relationship between the new public child welfare agencies and the private charities.

For the foremost concern of those in the private charities was that the creation of centralized public, bureaucratic welfare agencies might crowd them out—that they might be, as the DCV remarked in comments on the Prussian bill of 1917–18, "either wholly excluded or at least . . . hindered in their free and independent efforts"—and that Christian values might thus be excluded from the whole field of child welfare.[60] The private charities could not match the financial power of the state and the municipalities; furthermore, the momentum the war gave to the professionalization of child welfare work threatened the activities of the private charities, since it meant that their untrained volunteers might be excluded by law from certain activities. In March 1917, for example, a government decree introduced state licensing procedures for infant care workers *(Säuglingspflegerinnen)*, a step which threatened the work of the Protestant and Catholic religious orders and innumerable volunteers active in this field. A professional association of female social workers was created in 1916, and Catholic and Protestant associations in 1916 and 1917, respectively. The DCV also vehemently rejected proposals to continue the wartime system of state licensing of private charities and charitable collections after the war, partly on the grounds that "it cannot be objected that political or anti-Catholic intentions are completely foreign to the originators and champions of the idea of state supervision."[61] And the expansion of the role of *municipal* governments through the creation of Youth Bureaus was much more alarming still, for both Catholic and Protestant charities believed city governments to be dominated by purely political concerns, and often by socialists or secular liberals. It was partly such concerns about the growing role of local and national government that moved the 1916 conference of the Catholic episcopate formally to recognize the DCV as the representative of the church in the field of welfare, with the intention of coordinating and centralizing resistance to undesired intervention (although the financial problems of the organization played at least an equally important role).

The public discussion of the bill did little to calm their fears. At the meeting called by the Prussian minister of the interior on December 11, 1917, the division between the municipalities on the one hand and the Inner Mission and the DCV on the other was thrown into high relief. Whereas the government's bill would have required the inclusion of representatives of the local clergy in the Youth Bureau, the cities rejected this stipulation, arguing that the clergy did not necessarily have any special interest in or qualifications for child welfare work. Representatives of the cities also argued that the Youth Bureau should not be absolutely required to place children in institutions, or to assign them social workers and public legal guardians, of their own faith—since such institutions or social workers were not always available, and since many cities had only one public guardian for all wards of both faiths.[62] The DCV reported after these meetings that the views of the big city administrations were "completely dominated by the 'liberal' spirit and hostile to the activity of any positive religious confession."[63]

To make matters worse, it was clear by 1918 that the reform of municipal suffrage laws was politically unavoidable; and since a democratic suffrage would drastically increase the representation of the left, and particularly the SPD, Christian groups looked forward to it with foreboding. "It is enough," the Protestant *Rheinische Fürsorgeerziehungsblatt* lamented as early as February 1918, "merely to imagine what form and makeup our city administrations will take on in the age of democracy."[64] But, even short of consciously political attacks on religious groups, the charities worried that "it is *contra naturam sui generis* that a large administration, with money and officials at its disposal, should not, in the natural rhythm of its operation, expand its activity ever further," raising the danger that it would "finally kill all independence" in the charities.[65]

In part, the emphasis on the independence of the charities reflected the strength of mere organizational jealousies—the fear, in effect, that public agencies would be able to do a better job than the private organizations. But many in the religious charities truly believed, as the director of the DCV's child welfare section argued, that "the great pedagogical tasks which saving endangered youth gives society cannot be accomplished on an interconfessional basis. . . . Undeniable experience shows that religious-moral education, the one successful education, can thrive only on the foundation of a specific confession."[66] More broadly, both Christian and nonreligious private associations believed themselves to be the repositories and defenders of the liberty and creative potential of society against the encroachment of a stifling and imperious bureaucratic state apparatus. State intervention, many felt, might actually do more harm than good in the field of child welfare, since, as one judge put it, "the firm foundation of all our private child welfare work is voluntarism. . . . If compulsion is used, the good workers will turn their backs." There was the danger that state intervention might "stop up the spring from which the original joy in dedication to service to youth bubbles, and which dries up in the face of bureaucratic compulsion."[67] State action, in other words, might lead to the atrophy of the sense of individual social responsibility. Since many Christians believed, as we have seen, that no public institution such as public legal guardianship could "socialize" children, this would mean disaster.

Such misgivings were heightened by the pattern of policy-making which began to emerge during the war, in which the boundaries between ministerial bureaucracies and the secular, "expert" welfare organizations blurred as consultation between them became more common and more intensive. A growing number of people involved directly in child welfare began to feel excluded from the process of policy formation.

For instance, in the course of 1916–17 some of the leadership of the liberal women's movement became increasingly outraged at the manner in which the—male-dominated—expert organizations were able to monopolize policy input. At the outbreak of the war the Federation of German Women's Associations under Gertrud Bäumer had established a National Women's Service (Nationaler Frauendienst), which played a crucial role in mobilizing women as volunteer social workers and administrators in wartime welfare programs, and which took a special interest in family and child welfare. As part of the mobilization for total war launched in 1916, furthermore, a Women's Labor Center (Frauenarbeitszentrale, or FAZ) had been created within the War Office, charged with encouraging women to take up munitions work, for example, by providing day care facilities. By 1917 the FAZ, under its director, Marie-Elisabeth Lüders, had established the Commission on Child Welfare (under Anna von Gierke) and was attempting to take a leading role in the formulation of national child welfare policy, publishing its own "Guidelines for Child Welfare" in May of that year. Against the resistance of the established "expert" organizations, however, these women's groups were unable to exert much independent influence.[68]

A far more public debate, and one that absorbed much of the time and energy of the expert organizations during 1917, was occasioned by the attempts of Paul Felisch, director of the Voluntary Educational Council in Berlin, to seize the initiative by organizing a national network of private Youth Bureaus—to, as he put it in the course of the dispute, "go to the people" over the heads of the experts, securing the "collaboration of all classes" in the process of legislation.[69] Felisch was well connected in court circles, and it cost the "experts" considerable time and effort to defeat his independent initiative.

Much more important, finally, the Catholic charities in particular were also increasingly alienated by the behavior of the secular organizations. In fact, it became increasingly evident to the religious charities that their secular counterparts did not regard Christians as child welfare "experts." In particular, in late 1917 the DCV discovered that a grand total of three out of fifty invitations to join the Working Group for a National Youth Welfare Law had gone out to Catholics.[70] The executive secretary of the DZJ, who ran the daily affairs of the Working Group, soon agreed with Catholic representatives that religious issues must be given greater consideration and consented to invite Lorenz Werthmann of the DCV to join; but one Catholic member reported that in fact there was a "steady quiet struggle" within the organization between confessional and nonreligious interests.[71]

Matters came to a head, however, only in the summer of 1918, over the issue of the National Child Welfare Conference called by the nonreligious organizations. The conference, planned by the DVAW as early as January 1917, was intended as a grand "demonstration" (Kundgebung) of support for a national child welfare law, and was to bring together representatives of all the public and private child welfare agencies. Yet once again planning for the meeting, held in Berlin in late September 1918, was carried out exclusively by the secular experts in the DVAW; when a public invitation was circulated, it was signed by representatives of the DVAW, the ADB, the DZJ, the AFET, the ZVW, and even the tiny Society for the Protection of Children—but by neither the Inner Mission nor the DCV. Speakers were to include a number of figures from the nonreligious organizations but not a single representative of the Catholic or Protestant charities. Outraged, Werthmann decided that the DCV would boycott the meeting, and persuaded a number of other Catholic organizations to do the same. Protestants, less fearful for their religious interests and better represented in the nonreligious groups, were much less upset than the DCV. But at the conference the director of the Rauhes Haus in Hamburg, Pastor Martin Hennig, remarked angrily on the fact that "the Protestant and Catholic organizations have been excluded from the discussions occasioned by the Youth Bureau law by the leading circles of this Child Welfare Conference. Given such a position, one could easily come to the conclusion that similar tendencies could prevail in the individual work [of the Youth Bureaus]."[72]

The Corporatist Welfare Compromise

While the preparations for the 1918 Child Welfare Conference and for a national child welfare law seemed to have finally brought about a real rupture between secular experts and the Christian charities, the meeting itself paved the way for a political resolution of this conflict. For despite the breach forced by Werthmann, there were considerable grounds for compromise between the religious charities and the exponents of state action.

In the first place, Catholics had reason to regard Prussian or national legislation as the lesser of possible evils. As the DCV pointed out, any law passed before the end of the war would probably be more to Christian tastes than one passed after the introduction of the political reforms which would inevitably follow. Moreover, legal codification would at least have the benefit of putting limits on the municipalities' actions—for "the danger to the private charities from the liberalism of the big cities is even greater in the present conditions, in which legal limits are completely absent."[73] Finally, there were important figures within Catholic circles who believed that the enactment of legislation on child welfare was inevitable, and argued that Catholics could not afford not to collaborate in drafting it. Agnes Neuhaus in particular was incensed at Werthmann's actions (and refused to boycott the conference), since she believed that "the participation of Catholics is absolutely necessary" in order that "if the inevitable happens, we can so turn it that it does us the least possible harm."[74]

At the same time, the leadership of the "expert" organizations had reason to do their best to reconcile the private charities to the creation of a system of centralized public child welfare agencies, in order to create a politically irresistible consensus for legislation. Moreover, it was clear that the immense amount of labor required by the multifarious public child welfare programs was, especially in rural areas, simply beyond the resources of the state and of a single public agency. Any effective child welfare system would have to rely on the cooperation of private organizations and their volunteers. Equally important, enthusiasts of the professionalization of welfare services shared the charities' fear that the establishment of public agencies might lead to the triumph of bureaucracy and "politicization." For there was the very real danger that local governments would appoint to the Youth Bureaus not professional child welfare "experts" with training in pedagogy and social work, but mere administrators, clerks, and representatives of the political factions in the town council. Such a regime of incompetent hacks and inflexible, overbearing bureaucrats, addicted to routines and lacking all pedagogical sensibility, would do more harm than good. While many in the secular welfare organizations would rather have seen the Youth Bureau staffed by trained professionals, then, almost all would have preferred experienced, committed volunteers from the private charities to administrative clerks.

Partly for this reason, finally, the religious charities and the secular "experts" shared common criticisms of the Prussian bill. Both criticized it for failing to create a sufficient centralization of child welfare programs: it left supervision of foster care in the hands of the police, petitions for commitment to correctional education in the hands of the *Landrat* or mayor, and material aid for poor children in those of the poor relief agencies. Worse yet, in early drafts of the law even the establishment of public legal guardianship was only allowed, not required.[75] Finally, the individual Youth Bureaus it envisioned remained isolated agencies of each county or municipal government. This meant that all tasks requiring cooperation of the Youth Bureaus and uniform procedures would be considerably complicated. There would be no special agency with the resources to undertake the creation of institutions requiring large capital outlays or organizational effort (reformatories, vacation camps, schools of social work, and so on); complaints— for example, by parents or private charitable institutions—would go to the administrative authorities or the courts rather than to an expert agency *(Fachbehörde)*. But most important, the absence of specialized child welfare agencies above the local level would mean that there would be no way to impose "expert" or professional standards on the individual municipal or county Youth Bureau. In fact, even the Social Democrats supported these objections, which were summarized in a counterdraft produced by Christian Jasper Klumker.

In order to correct these shortcomings, child welfare advocates almost unanimously demanded the creation of State (or provincial) Youth Bureaus *(Landesjugendämter)*. And this demand was particularly favored by the religious charities, which were able to exert greater influence on the provinces through their national associations than they could through the individual local associations on local governments. Indeed, since institutions sustained by Christian groups housed most children in correctional education, the Christian charities had already established good working relations with the provincial administrations.

The foremost task of the National Child Welfare Conference of September 1918 was to develop a program which, on the basis of these converging interests, would reconcile the religious charities to the creation of a system of public Youth Bureaus. One means of doing this was an appeal to the "principle of subsidiarity," developed in other areas of public policy during the war, according to which public agencies were to yield precedence to private organizations. Blaum's co-speaker at the 1917 conference of the ADB suggested, for example, that "in all cases in which appropriate and proven private associations carry out their activities, that field of child welfare should be excluded from the work of the Youth Bureau."[76] And at the National Conference of 1918 Friedrich Siegmund-Schultze, director of Berlin's Youth Bureau, went even further, suggesting that "the task of the Youth Bureau is to encourage private charity and further expand it."[77]

Even more important, however, was another product of the experience of mobilization for total war: a corporatist constitution for public agencies themselves. It had been clear from the beginning of the war that governmental agencies alone could not accomplish the immense task of mobilization and coordination which the war would require: the state simply had neither sufficient administrative personnel and resources nor the political power to impose direct intervention. Particularly as the war effort intensified after 1916, therefore, the state resorted increasingly to delegating governmental authority to private organizations. In industry, for example, industrial councils in each branch, which included representatives of the major corporations and unions, as well as of the government and military, were set up to facilitate the distribution of government contracts and the delivery of goods to the military or to the civilian population. A similar arrangement was made in the field of welfare, where much of the administrative and social work personnel of public wartime relief agencies was drawn from the charities. Thus, Else Wex in 1929 wrote of the wartime transformation of administrative structures as "a completely new fusing of official agencies and organs of private charity."[78]

The advantages of this system were immediately evident. On the one hand, private organizations provided the public agencies with an army of unpaid social workers, allowing public programs to take on unprecedented scope, while public policy initiatives could be transmitted immediately and more or less informally to already existing private administrative structures, giving public agencies new flexibility and a shorter response time. On the other hand, association with public agencies and policy gave private organizations unaccustomed legal resources and authority, and coordination with centralized public services went far toward overcoming the drawbacks of "fragmentation."

The corporatist organizational program for child welfare—like the ideal of the Youth Bureau as a "socialization agency"—was first presented in mature form in Kurt Blaum's address to the ADB conference of 1917. Blaum suggested that the effective cooperation of private organizations and public welfare agencies should involve a mutual exchange of members; the Youth

Bureau should coordinate the efforts of the associations by delegating officials to sit on their boards of directors, while a Central Committee for Child Welfare made up of representatives not only of the medical and school authorities but also of the charities and the churches would be established in each Youth Bureau to "lay down the fundamental principles for the Youth Bureau's activities." Such a corporatist, "mixed-economic" structure, Blaum argued, would effectively counteract the danger that the Youth Bureau might become an inflexible and sterile bureaucratic organism. The personalistic individualizing "spirit" and commitment of Christian bourgeois charity would be preserved *within* the Youth Bureau, "preventing it from becoming a bureaucratic institution."[79]

The National Child Welfare Conference of September 1918 developed these themes still further. Aloys Fischer set the tone for the conference in his opening speech, sketching the theoretical foundations for the reconciliation of Christian personalist and social-managerial commitments—or, as he put it, between the social or collective principle and that of individuality. According to Fischer, the "mass character" of modern society created a dilemma for child welfare policy: modern conditions "endangered" the great mass of children, so that "it sometimes seems as if only the . . . collective idea . . . points to the future"; and yet each individual child had to be treated "with regard for the uniqueness of his person and situation." This dual task could be mastered by building the individualist principle, represented by private charity, into the Youth Bureau itself—the "crowning of that welfare activity which is founded upon the collective idea."[80] In order to secure the influence of the individualist principle, the Youth Bureau would have to mobilize or even hire social workers from the charities. But the charities would also have to be given a voice, by the constitution of the Youth Bureau, in its executive.

For the secular child welfare experts this program seemed to ensure that the Youth Bureau would be guided by real expertise, by scientific and practical understanding of child welfare. As the director of Berlin's Youth Bureau suggested, it would create "set forms" which would guarantee that "expert advice . . . is ensured even under such adverse conditions as might appear in one place or another."[81] Yet the private and especially the religious charities responded more favorably to the argument that they were indispensable as the bearers of a special "spirit," as the guardians of individuality, of love, and ultimately of the Christian project of personal regeneration. This "spirit of charitable help from person to person," Blaum argued, "must absolutely be preserved in child welfare if it is not to degenerate into the rigid forms of public bureaucracy . . . [or make] decisions hostile to the family."[82]

Because the Revolution intervened within weeks of its close, it is difficult to gauge the success of the National Conference on Child Welfare, insofar as its aim was to achieve consensus within child welfare circles. There are good indications, however, that the private charities were moving toward approval of the corporatist strategy. The leading Catholic expert, Agnes Neuhaus, summed up the program of the conference in a familiar metaphor that appealed to the most culturally conservative in the audience, announcing that "we must form a firm union, Father State with the masculine force of his laws, with his effective authority, his big wallet—and Mother Charity, with her warm heart, her self-renewing freshness of feeling, and especially with her wholly personal devotion to work with the individual child."[83] The corporatist solution now gave such rhetoric—which, as we have seen, had been used since before the war—concrete content. The archbishop of Cologne, writing to Prussian Minister of Justice Peter Spahn (himself a conservative Catholic) one month after the conference, suggested that the membership in the Youth Bureau of representatives of the private associations would be the best means of counteracting the dangers he saw in the Prussian bill.[84]

Democracy versus the Experts

But if the National Child Welfare Conference achieved unity among child welfare circles on the basis of a corporatist constitution for the Youth Bureau, that same program deeply alienated many of the representatives of the very agencies that would be called upon to put it into practice: the municipal governments. The cities were by no means opposed to the general project of centralizing child welfare services. But the Prussian bill explicitly stipulated that representatives of the schools, the churches, and the state medical authorities would be members of the Youth Bureau's executive, and it dictated the precise administrative structure of the agency. Many municipal officials saw in all this an attempt to limit the autonomy and self-government *(Selbstverwaltung)* granted to them by the Prussian Municipal Code (Städteordnung). Most immediately, they saw the danger that an office made up largely of persons not accountable to the municipality would be assigned the task of spending municipal moneys. What is more, the proposed powers of the State Youth Bureaus seemed to threaten state intervention in municipal affairs.

Beneath these relatively technical questions lurked a deeper philosophical issue. The private associations adhered to a particularist conception of liberty, arguing for the preservation of the complexity and the irreducible variety of social life, which they saw as the source of the vitality and creativity of society. Secular social reformers championed (at least rhetorically) the "right of the child" to be empowered to participate in the life of the polity—and the responsibility of the state to realize that right. Many representatives of municipal government, however, defended against both these social ideals a fundamentally *political* conception of liberty—a democratic, rationalist, majoritarian, and localist tradition. They argued that the bill effectively represented an abrogation of the sovereignty of democratically elected local governments.[85] In fact, in the context of domestic politics in the fall of 1918, it was easy for municipal politicians—and particularly Social Democratic municipal officials—to suspect that the law was being used to soften the blow of constitutional reform, which seemed imminent. Mayor Cuno of Hagen, for example, believed that "the Prussian parliament, if it has enough time remaining, will pass this law quickly, because the majority will feel that it is advantageous for the conservatives to anticipate a democratically constituted parliament. A regressive revision of the Städteordnung, a limitation of the freedom of the communes, is quickly carried out, and the power of the *Landräte* in the countryside is strengthened, by the law."[86]

As early as December 1917, therefore, a number of city governments consulted by the Prussian government suggested that if a law were deemed necessary, it should merely list the tasks which the cities must take on, leaving the organization of their administration to the free decision of the elected city governments. And as for the State Youth Bureau, Mayor Matting of Breslau suggested that if the government wanted to control child welfare programs in detail, then it should institute them itself. "Self-government," he fumed, "means . . . the administration of one's own affairs. That is, in other words, one does not let others interfere with one's own affairs, and one should not interfere in the affairs of others. . . . If the State Youth Bureau wants to give directives like that and have competencies like that, then the State Youth Bureau must also be the one that foots the bill."[87]

All the major organizations of local governments submitted strongly worded protests to the Ministry of the Interior during the last few days of the Empire. That of the Municipal League (Städtetag) in particular rejected the bill's proposed Youth Bureau as an assault on self-government and a "special institution outside the framework of the municipal constitution for which the city is allowed only to bear the costs. . . . Through the delegation . . . to the Youth Bureau of persons who are given seats and votes in the Bureau not as citizens of the commune but as representatives of the state and as representatives of the church, the Youth Bureau ceases completely to be a part of the organism of the commune."[88] All such stipulations, therefore, must be dropped from the law. This was a virtual declaration of political war against the corporatist compromise and the plans of the government and the experts. Indeed, some cities issued thinly veiled threats of sabotage. "The great danger of such disruptions of . . . self-government," Matting warned, "is, in my opinion, that the responsible authorities become annoyed and that they . . . lose the sense of responsibility. . . . The more responsibility one leaves us, the more intensively we apply ourselves to the matter."[89] And the mayor of Guben warned that the law "could come to nothing" if the cities' "interest" in child welfare were compromised by outside interference.[90]

Given the balance of power prevailing in the Prussian parliament under the reactionary constitution, it is probable that the cities could not have prevented the passage of the law. Whether it could have been implemented in the face of their resistance is less certain—particularly as the Prussian finance minister had already, as early as August 1917, told the minister of the interior that no subsidies for municipal or county child welfare programs would be forthcoming.[91] Within a week after the communal organizations submitted their protests to the Prussian government, the Revolution broke out, rendering the question irrelevant. The government of the new Republic thus inherited the task of creating the corporatist child welfare system envisaged by the National Child Welfare Conference in 1918—and the political struggle that doing so would entail.

CHAPTER SIX

Revolution and the National Child Welfare Act, 1918–1924

The Revolution of 1918–1920

After the defeat of 1918, the Revolution which broke out at the beginning of November threatened to sweep away the old order completely and establish a revolutionary socialist society. In the field of child welfare, there seemed to be a real possibility as late as June 1920 that the corporatist program developed during the last years of the war would be abandoned in favor of the purely public and secular welfare bureaucracy favored by the Social Democratic political parties (the SPD and the Independent Social Democratic party, or USPD). What is more, in many municipalities there was strong pressure from the left for the socialization of charitable enterprises. As the DVAW—renamed National Association for Public and Private Welfare (Deutscher Verein für öffentliche und private Fürsorge, or DVöpF) in 1919—remarked in January 1920, the new popular mood "demands rights instead of good deeds, the replacement of private through exclusively public welfare."[1]

The fact that the endowments of many private groups were rapidly disappearing as a consequence of inflation, leaving the charities increasingly dependent on public subsidies, made such ideas all the more popular. In the spring of 1920 the government of Frankfurt circulated a suggestion among city governments for the partial socialization of all private charities.[2] Correctional education seemed particularly endangered—partly because it was uncertain whether, with the separation of church and state on the agenda of the socialist provisional government, the state would continue to support confessional reformatories, but partly also simply because the institution was so hated. As Wilhelm Rhiel, director of the Association for Catholic charitable Education, remarked in 1919, the triumph of democracy threatened the reformatories not only because of the outright hostility of many

Social Democrats to Christianity, but also simply because "correctional education has never yet had the sympathy of those circles for whose benefit the law was primarily made. But precisely these elements of the nation have a very different voice in the new constitution and in legislation."[3] Workers' and soldiers' councils in a number of towns actually did liberate some of the inmates of private correctional homes in late 1918. In Hamburg an association of former reformatory inmates launched a bitter campaign against the institution which was not silenced until 1922.[4] And the number of commitments to correctional education—despite what many Christians saw as a collapse of morality—dropped sharply: 13,774 were committed in Prussia in 1917, but only 9,528 in 1919.[5] But correctional education was not the only program that seemed to be threatened. A rumor circulated in Protestant circles in May 1919 to the effect that the Prussian Ministry of Culture was leaning strongly toward nationalizing child care and requiring that all children attend kindergarten from the age of three.[6]

In the end, the Revolution turned out to be far less radical than many middle-class conservatives had feared. The reformist, revisionist, and nationalist element within the Social Democratic party was unswervingly committed to democratic legitimacy; relieved of more radical elements by the creation of the Spartakist League (later the Communist party, or KPD) and the USPD, and fearing the kind of chaotic civil conflict that was ripping Russia apart, the party refused to allow the provisional government to take any radical steps before elections for a National Assembly were held and a legitimate government was established. While the trade unions negotiated a settlement with employers' organizations, the SPD entered into a defacto alliance with the army and crushed the radical council movement and the Spartakists by military force. Elections for the National Assembly, held January 19, 1919, did not result in a majority for the socialist parties. The new Republic was governed by a coalition of Social Democrats, the German Democratic party (the DDP, successor to the Progressive People's party), and the Catholic Center party. The Weimar constitution, adopted in August 1919, was fundamentally a liberal-democratic one.

In the field of child welfare, as in the economy, plans for widespread socialization soon faded; the government firmly opposed the councils' attacks on correctional education; and article 138 of the new constitution explicitly guaranteed the property of the charities. Within the government, the prewar ministerial bureaucracy was virtually untouched, so that policy was often in the hands of the same middle-level ministerial officials who had been active before 1914.[7] Finally, the national Labor Ministry, which was in the hands of Catholic Center party figures for most of the 1920s, very effectively used subsidies and pressure for centralization to reconsolidate the position of the private charities (see Chapter 7).

Despite such continuities, however, the Revolution and the consequences of the war did create fundamental changes in the social, political, and cultural context; and these changes profoundly influenced the evolution of child welfare policy after 1919. A number of them, moreover, were very favorable to the realization of the ambitions and plans of secular social reformers for the creation of a national child welfare system and a comprehensive social-managerial policy structure.

For one thing, the shattering impact of the war on German society made the expansion of welfare provision seem a simple practical necessity—and nowhere more so than in child welfare specifically. The war left behind over 1 million fatherless or orphaned children; and there were almost half a million disabled veterans, many with dependents. First the Allied blockade, then the hardship of the inflation period, had a devastating impact on popular nutrition, with lasting effects on the health of millions of children. The director of the National Health Bureau, Franz Bumm, stated in early 1920 that 70 percent of pregnant women were undernourished, while in Barmen at the end of the year almost 60 percent of schoolchildren suffered from nutritional deficiencies. In Saxony 50.8 percent of all schoolchildren were undernourished or had rickets, scrofula, or anemia. Doctors employed in the American Quakers' relief efforts found that 15 percent of the children they saw were abnormally physically underdeveloped, and 30 percent were in need of "nutritional therapy."[8] The development of welfare programs adequate to care for these immense numbers of impoverished and hungry children was a pressing necessity.

Moreover, the inflation years also created an acute sense of moral crisis among the Christian middle classes. The cultural upheaval of the Revolution and the general determination to enjoy life after the war encouraged the emergence of new and disturbing patterns of behavior among youth. As one critic remarked in 1921, there seemed to have been an "inversion of all values: what was earlier seen as bad and indecent is now often seen as permissible and modern, as appropriate to our times and right."[9] Complaints about young people's open display of their sexuality (the "shocking social intercourse between male and female youth," as one observer called it), the popularity of the movies, racy theater pieces, and above all the "dance craze" were common. Middle-class observers decried postwar youths' "complete lack of concern for authority and discipline."[10] Rhiel, for example, held that "the Revolution, with its destruction of all authority," had done great moral damage, while Friedrich Siegmund-Schultze, director of Berlin's Youth Bureau, told a conference in Berlin that the "moral suffering" of young people was greater than before the war, "since all objective authority is lacking."[11] The abolition of censorship and certain repressive regulations such as the Law on Servants (Gesindeordnung) seemed to many conservatives to invite chaos and moral disaster. What was more, after 1923 young people suffered from sustained high rates of unemployment, and it was commonly feared that the shortage of work would have a negative impact on morality and character: as one concerned advocate remarked in 1927, the lack of an "orderly life and . . . regular work" was particularly bad for young people, who were "in a developmental stage in which they particularly need order and discipline."[12]

While Social Democrats and left-liberals urgently demanded that the state step in to secure the health of children and employment for young people, conservatives looked to the public authorities to impose moral order. The first lines of the official commentary to the National Child Welfare Act of 1922 reflect the sense of grim optimism with which both groups set about reconstructing their society: "Our German Fatherland is stricken. A dark future, poor in hope, lies before us. But we must not despair. Germany . . . must awaken new powers, slumbering deep within her. . . . We may hope for such strength in our youth and in the unborn generations."[13]

The particular nature of the postwar economic and international situation, however, encouraged the abandonment of the punitive, coercive, and openly imperialistic variety of "population policy" adopted by German governments just before and during the war, and a shift to a policy more influenced by eugenic thought and aimed not only at quantitative expansion but also at improving the "quality" of the population. The horrific losses at the front and at home, the drastic reduction of the birthrate after the war, and the fact that most of the same officials continued to work within national and state ministerial bureaucracies ensured that sheer numbers would continue to be a preoccupation of policymakers. But the end (at least for the foreseeable future) of Germany's role as an imperial power and the strict limitations on the size of its army imposed by the Versailles settlement made the number of recruits a less pressing issue. At the same time, the prewar economic boom did not persist into the 1920s, and the nascent labor shortage of the 1900s gave way to stubborn high unemployment. Finally, the increasing rationalization of industry and sharper international competition helped fuel a greater interest in productivity and "quality" (highly skilled) labor rather than sheer mass of product and population. As a consequence, eugenic thought—in various guises—achieved unprecedented and steadily growing influence during the Weimar years, gaining support within almost every political party and faction. For the first time, eugenics organizations such as the Society for Racial Hygiene and the Federation for National Improvement and Hereditary Science received government subsidies and encouragement. For example, Otto Krohne, president of the former from 1922, retained his post in the Prussian Medical Department, becoming its director in 1926. And numerous officials in the Prussian and national welfare and health bureaucracies were increasingly favorably disposed toward eugenic ideas. The first academic chairs in human genetics and "racial hygiene" were created in Munich and Berlin in 1923, and an institute for the study of human heredity was established in Berlin in 1927.[14] The influence of eugenic thought was particularly marked where hereditarian ideas had always been strongest—among psychiatrists, doctors, penologists, and academics.

One long-term consequence of this development, of course, was to lend respectability to ideas that would in the end form part of the foundation of the coercive and homicidal policies of the National Socialist regime, and in fact to some extent to make the language and demands of Hitler himself sound relatively normal. Particularly in the context of the economic difficulties of the 1920s, the growing popularity of eugenics could form a bridge, as Detlev Peukert and others have argued, between reformist optimism and potentially murderous schemes of eugenic classification and "special treatment" *(Sonderbehandlung);* but already in 1920 Karl Binding and Alfred Hoche were suggesting the possibility of murdering the "unfit."[15]

More generally, the growing interest in eugenics was part of that "medicalization" of social welfare which I discussed briefly in Chapters 3 and 4. During the 1920s the medical profession continued to gain influence within child welfare policy and across the whole spectrum of child welfare programs. The increasing power of the medical profession was also reflected, however, in the growing number of Public Health Bureaus *(Gesundheit-sämter)* established by local governments—around one hundred by 1929.[16] In some cases this expansion of the medical establishment caused conflicts with social welfare advocates; for example, there was a brief but intense debate in 1920 and 1921 between doctors who argued (successfully) that infant and prenatal health programs should be provided by the Health Bureaus and child welfare advocates who demanded their inclusion in the Youth Bureaus. What is more, there was a very real intellectual or ideological tension between social reform advocates and medical reformers. Doctors regarded themselves as the guardians of the health of the nation as a whole; their extensive training and the closed nature of the profession seem to have encouraged elitist and authoritarian attitudes; and since their mission was the diagnosis and treatment of the pathologies of *individuals,* they tended to be skeptical of *social* analyses of the origins of health and behavior. The medical profession as a whole, therefore, was essentially estranged from many of the central traditions of progressive reform, in particular from the language of individual rights and the social analysis of individual behavior. Finally, many doctors developed a general hostility to social welfare programs as a consequence of the unsuccessful struggle to gain independence from the public insurance system. As we will see, in the Nazi period this latent hostility would pose a growing threat to these programs.

In the short term, however, doctors were in most respects not so much competitors as part of a broad common movement of public health and social welfare. The "racial hygiene" advocated by the radical right wing and conservatives (for example in the German National People's party, or DNVP), which criticized welfare programs for securing the survival of the "unfit" and "inferior." languished in the 1920s, while "eugenics" and "social hygiene," which focused on preventive welfarist measures, flourished. It was the latter conception, which favored positive health measures and education over coercive intervention, that was preferred by Center party figures such as Adam Stegerwald, the Prussian minister for national welfare, and his successor Karl Hirtsiefer; by Carl Severing, the Prussian Social Democratic minister of the interior from 1928 to 1930; Alfred Grotjahn and his successor Julius Moses, the SPD's spokesmen on eugenic issues; the Catholic eugenics expert Hermann Muckermann; and almost all of the left-liberal social welfare experts.[17] As a consequence, the growing power of the medical profession and the eugenics craze contributed to an enormous expansion of welfare and public health programs. Maternity allowances (*Wochenhilfe*, which had a prehistory as part of the social insurance system reaching back to 1883) were introduced by a law of September 1919; maternity benefits were expanded in 1926 and 1927; the number of infant health clinics, which had grown from one thousand to about three thousand between 1914 and 1919, expanded further to nearly ten thousand by 1928.[18] A massive campaign of popular health propaganda was launched by government agencies and eugenics organizations in the 1920s, encouraging personal hygiene, improved nutrition, regular exercise, and general prevention. A network of Marriage Advice Centers (224 of them in Prussia by 1928), often subsidized or administered by public agencies such as the health insurance funds, disseminated contraceptive information and devices, partly as an attempt to reduce the number of abortions.[19] And concern for children's "eugenic" health was a major motivation for the expansion of child welfare programs in general. Particularly important in this respect was the expansion of in-school medical services: Saxony, Württemberg and Thuringia all passed laws requiring schools to hire a school doctor; in Prussia, which did not pass a law, by 1926, 81 percent of school-age children were attending schools that employed a school doctor (as against about 4 percent in 1911 and 63 percent in 1921).[20]

A further factor encouraging the expansion of welfare provision was the transformation of the bourgeois women's movement after 1918. A number of developments—including the opening of professions and academic institutions to women, the creation of new employment opportunities for women in sales and clerical work, the development of the consumer economy, and the corresponding massive expansion of more conservative housewives' organizations—shifted the focus of the German women's movement from women's rights toward the representation of women's narrower professional and economic interests. These developments shifted the movement politically to the right, but the influence of more conservative women and the need to avoid party-political issues also encouraged a growing focus on issues such as censorship, prostitution, birth control, and the welfare of children and families.[21]

The rapid expansion of public welfare programs and of the number of schools of social work was also creating new employment opportunities for women interested in social reform and social justice. Schools of social work had proliferated during the war years, encouraged and in some cases established directly by government: there were fourteen such schools in 1913, twenty-seven in 1918, and thirty-three in 1927.[22] By 1933 there were 19,299 women social workers of all kinds (including, for example, kindergarten teachers) in paid employment in Germany, as against only 1,830 men; in the mid-1920s the three major professional organizations of accredited women social workers had some eight thousand members.[23] The introduction of state licensing for social workers in 1920 gave governments greater control over curricula, and they used it to foster a more narrowly professional conception of the female social worker's role, at the expense of the more feminist elements of the curriculum. There was an effort in 1923–1925 to create a specifically secular, liberal feminist welfare association, in parallel to the already established welfare groups and charity groups such as the DCV, the Inner Mission, and the DVAW; but in the end, partly owing to the hostility of the Catholic-dominated national Labor Ministry, this initiative was absorbed by the new "Fifth Welfare Association" (Fünfter Wohlfahrtsverband, founded formally in December 1924 but with a prehistory dating to 1920, and renamed Paritätische Wohlfahrtsverband in November 1932), which was largely dominated by male doctors and was led by Leo Langstein.[24] After 1925 specifically feminist ambitions in welfare were largely confined to the defense of the professional interests of women social workers. In consequence, the growing institutionalization of the female profession of social work actually appears to have *reduced* and channeled conflicts within the social welfare establishment while creating a new lobby for the expansion of public welfare programs.

It was even more important for the development of social welfare programs, and child welfare programs in particular, that the Revolution gave German women the vote and the right to sit in parliament. Relatively few women actually were elected to the Reichstag—forty-one in 1919, over half of them representatives of the socialist parties. But these women were often extraordinarily competent; and their impact was heightened by the fact that almost all of them focused their parliamentary activity on issues of education, welfare, and health. They played a crucial role in securing child welfare legislation in the early 1920s. In 1919 a unanimous petition of women

Reichstag deputies helped to secure the transfer of competence over welfare policy from state to national government; and in 1920 a second women's petition was decisive in rescuing the National Child Welfare Act after financial questions had virtually consigned it to oblivion. Women were also heavily represented in the parliamentary committee established to consider the law, and played a decisive role in working out a compromise between the positions of their various political parties—often, as in the case of Marie Juchacz of the SPD and Agnes Neuhaus of the Center, in the face of stiff resistance from their (mostly male) party comrades.

Furthermore, while the institutionalization of child welfare and social work in the early 1920s helped to rule out some issues and close some options, it did not mean that women had less influence in child welfare policy; the number of women who played key roles in the child welfare establishment in fact grew in the 1920s. German women never achieved the kind of dominance within public welfare bureaucracies that their counterparts in the United States enjoyed, but they did occupy a large number of strategic posts. In addition to keeping most organizations running from day to day in the capacity of executive secretaries (for example, Hilde Eiserhardt at the DVöpF and Ina Hundinger at the Protestant National Educational Association—Evangelische Reichserziehungsverband, or EREV—which was formed in April 1920 out of the Educational Office of the Inner Mission [1913]), a large number of women in high-profile positions played central roles in child welfare policy. They included Gertrud Bäumer, ministerial councillor in the national Ministry of the Interior from 1920 to 1932; Anna Maier, Dorothea Hirschfeld, and Helene Weber in the Prussian Welfare Ministry; Julia Dünner in the national Labor Ministry; Marie Baum in Baden's Labor Ministry; Agnes Neuhaus and Elisabeth Zillken at the KFV; Marie Juchacz at the head of the Social Democrats' welfare organization; the conservative Reichstag deputy Paula Müller; and Ruth van der Leyen, prominent in the care of "psychopathic" children.

The youth movement also played a role in encouraging the development of child welfare policy. Youth groups achieved a new degree of autonomy in the 1920s, orienting themselves increasingly toward the model of the "youth movement" rather than that of *Jugendpflege*—a development reflected in the formation in early 1919 of the National Council of Youth Organizations, the Ausschuss der deutschen Jugendverbände (after 1926, Reichsausschuss). Youth groups also grew very rapidly: by 1926 there were some 4.353 million young people in youth organizations—54 percent of all boys and 26 percent of all girls aged fourteen to twenty-one.[25] The youth organizations did not pay a great deal of attention to welfare issues narrowly defined but focused instead on the effort to secure increased employment among young people, longer paid vacations, improved working conditions, and controls on working hours. But the National Council did actively support important child welfare legislation, and the mere existence of large and increasingly independent youth groups lent added urgency to issues of youth and child welfare. Moreover, as we shall see, pedagogues who derived their ideas from their years in the youth movement were to play a central role in debates over pedagogy, including reformatory pedagogy, in the 1920s.

The single most decisive factor in moving welfare policy forward after 1918, however, was the fact that the Revolution and the democratization of the state and local franchise gave Social Democracy an incomparably greater degree of influence at all levels of government than it had been able to achieve before 1914. For a very brief period, from the Revolution in November 1918 until the elections of June 1920, the Social Democrats were the dominant party in the national government, and they remained a dominant factor in parliamentary politics throughout the 1920s. The party also retained control of the Prussian state government throughout the 1920s (although the new Prussian Ministry of Popular Welfare was held by Catholic Center party politicians). But most important for our purposes here, the reform of municipal franchises gave the socialists control of the governments of many of Germany's major cities. This gave Social Democrats a considerable degree of influence in social policy, since most welfare programs (even those mandated by national legislation) were implemented by municipal government. In the absence of an actual socialist revolution, and with the revisionist and reformist element dominant within the party, Social Democrats by the 1920s regarded the expansion of social welfare programs, and particularly the realization of the idea of social rights—that the citizen has a right to have his or her basic needs met by society at large, a principle anchored in article 163 of the new constitution—as central to the construction of a just and democratic social order. They therefore pushed the expansion of social welfare programs energetically at all levels of government, and Social Democratic municipal administrations were in the forefront of the development of social programs. As Hedwig Wachenheim remarked in 1926, under Social Democratic administration many of Germany's larger cities began to become experimental "proletarian cooperatives."[26]

Given the convergence between Social Democratic and social-liberal thought on social welfare, it is not surprising that Social Democrats cooperated quite closely at all levels of government with the DDP, with social-liberal progressive welfare experts, and even with the reform-minded left wing of the Catholic Center party, particularly figures from the Catholic ("Christian") trade unions.

In fact, many left-liberal reformers welcomed the political transformation of 1919–20 with enthusiasm; and a number received important appointments within the new governments, especially where they were dominated by Social Democrats. Kurt Blaum, for example, accepted a post in Würt-temberg's socialist-led Ministry of the Interior and authored that state's centralizing child welfare law of 1919. Political democracy, in many social reformers' eyes, was essential to the social-managerial program of mobilization and participation—not only as an analogy to and consequence of social integration, but also as a precondition of securing the collaboration of the broadest spectrum of social groups, which was indispensable for its success. Many progressives also hoped that the Revolution would help to consolidate the foundations of centralizing, technocratic social management by abolishing what Christian Jasper Klumker called the "stupid German multiplicity of little states."[27] Failing that, the experts, like the women's groups, demanded at least the transfer of legislative competence over child welfare from the states to the national government. All of these factors contributed to the rapid expansion of welfare programs after 1918: for instance, whereas in 1909 some 12,515 officials were employed in municipal welfare agencies, by 1928 there were 36,072.[28]

Other aspects of the upheaval of 1918–19 also ensured the intensification of some of the conflicts of the prewar years. In fact, the limited nature of the Revolution resulted in the establishment and institutionalization of a set of conflicts which would in the end contribute decisively to the demise of the Republic, in this area as in so many others.

In the first place, the economic problems created by the war, inflation, and the recession in the international economy made the steady expansion of welfare provision extremely problematic fiscally. Funding problems not only delayed and disrupted legislation, as we will see, but they also provided a convenient excuse for those who opposed social-liberal and Social Democratic policies to raise ideologically "neutral" fiscal objections to legislation. Furthermore, as I have already remarked, in the long run fiscal constraints contributed to the growing popularity of a more brutal and discriminatory current in eugenic thought, since it was tempting to argue that the nation could not afford to care for handicapped, asocial, or otherwise nonproductive people. By the onset of the Great Depression, the transition from "positive" to "negative" eugenics—from health education to compulsory sterilization, for example—was an easy step.

Second, the moral panic among conservative Christians which had played an important part in the conflicts over welfare policy in the decade before the war was immensely exacerbated by the cultural transformation wrought by the war, the Revolution, and the Weimar period. During the 1920s many of the patterns of mass culture which had alarmed conservative observers during the war and the subsequent revolutionary and inflationary periods persisted unabated. The "dance craze" *(Tanzwut)* of the later war "years and the inflation period raged on in the later 1920s; indeed, jazz—"Negro music" to which young people performed wild and sensuous dances—grew ever more popular. The spread of contraceptive knowledge and devices produced a significant shift in sexual behavior among the young, as temporary "relationships" gradually replaced prostitution—a development which conservatives regarded as a step backward, since it meant that now *both* sexes were engaging in premarital sex, and one which also contributed to the spread of venereal disease. Christian observers in particular complained of the "matter-of-fact way in which young people discuss intimate matters" and of the "extensive sexualization of public life."[29] The prominence in the late 1920s of ideological apologists for sexual modernism, such as the sex researcher Magnus Hirschfeld and the communist sex educator Max Hodann, the American Ben Lindsey, and the Bolshevik family law reformers, raised the alarm particularly of Catholics to a fever pitch: the Catholic journal *Jugendrettung* saw a storm of sexual libertinism and corrupt materialist philosophy sweeping into "central Europe" from the "two moral low-pressure zones: the United States and Russia."[30] Campaigns for the reform of illegitimacy law, for the decriminalization of abortion and homosexuality, and for the liberalization of divorce seemed to aim deliberately at destroying the moral foundations of the social order; so too did the opening of hundreds of private and public "sexual advice clinics" *(Sexualberatungsstellen)*, the advocacy of family planning by marriage counseling centers and working-class family planning organizations, and the flourishing of nudism. Meanwhile filmmakers and publishers, their critics charged, continued to "speculate with particular refinement on the instinctual drives of half-grown youth," pursuing "the bottom line at the cost of higher community values."[31] The development of the film industry (there were some 1,500 cinemas in 1912, 3,878 by 1925), with its trivial adventure, crime, and love stories, was particularly disturbing to the cultured middle classes.[32] And all of these concerns were exacerbated by the success of the Communist party in presenting itself as a party of youth, and by the fact that young people in particular seemed to be embracing the new forms of mass cultural consumption—trends which, despite the SPD's own stern moralism and its rejection of trivial popular culture, helped to reinforce the association in conservative minds between materialist socialism and immorality.[33]

Yet attempts to create what Theodor Heuss called "a social policy of the soul"[34] were largely a failure. Emergency decrees prohibiting the sale of tobacco and alcohol to minors in 1920 and 1923 were ineffective. A so-called Law for the Protection of Minors at Public Entertainments, which would have denied young people access to cabarets, dance halls, and so on, was rejected by the upper house of parliament in 1927 on fiscal grounds. And even where legislation *was* passed, it was often disappointing to cultural conservatives and social purity crusaders. After a bitter debate over censorship, for example, a Law for the Protection of Minors against Smutty and

Trashy Literature, or the "*Schmutz* and *Schund* Law," was passed at the end of 1926, over the votes of the left. But because there was intense disagreement as to what constituted "smut," and because it was clear that pulp fiction was (as Robert von Erdberg remarked) "a necessity of life for the peoples of the twentieth century . . ., the form in which the spiritual life of broad masses of the people finds expression," the law provided no clear definitions.[35] In the absence of such definitions, however, the corporatist review boards established by the law tended to proceed with extreme caution. By the end of 1929 only 63 books had been banned for sale to minors, and by the end of 1932 only 183.[36] There were similar problems with the Film Law, passed in 1920: only about 1 percent of all films reviewed were banned, no larger a proportion than under prewar censorship laws.[37] And the Law on the Prevention of Venereal Diseases of 1927, which decriminalized prostitution to permit medical supervision, was regarded by many conservatives as a disaster for public morality. Finally, although the government issued important decrees in support of *Jugendpflege* in December 1918 and November 1919, and despite the increasing participation of young people in youth organizations, the growing independence of these groups, the importance of radical political ideas among working-class youth in particular, and the spread of a subculture of gangs and diffuse radicalism among chronically underemployed urban youth caused disquiet among more conservative observers.

By the late 1920s, then, there was a growing sense of near-panic among cultural conservatives regarding what appeared to be the moral degeneration of youth in particular. This sense of moral crisis was critically important *politically* because Christians regarded the moral crisis of the 1920s as an outgrowth of the decline of religiosity and the spread of "naturalistic," materialist philosophy. They therefore associated it with a problem in child welfare policy, the most important and fundamental one of the 1920s: that of the deepening conflict between Christian conservatism on the one hand and democracy and socialism on the other.

There were, of course, fundamental ideological conflicts between Christian—particularly Protestant—conservatism and democratic ideology which made the relationship between the churches and the Republic a problematic one. This was a conflict played out in child welfare policy in a debate over pedagogy which we will examine in Chapter 7. Even aside from these more metaphysical questions, however, there were particular developments in the Weimar period which were deeply threatening to Christian conservatives. On the one hand, the very expansion of child welfare programs seemed to many to undermine the Christian family, and thus to be a step in the direction of socialism. The Catholic child welfare advocate Ina Neuendörfer, for example, wrote in early 1920, "The more the expansion of welfare measures . . . proceeds, the closer the public educational and school system comes to the socialist ideal."[38] The Social Democratic or left-liberal convictions of many municipal officials only made this phenomenon more worrisome. On the other hand, in the latter half of the decade Social Democrats were increasingly developing their own conceptions of child welfare policy, inserting their own "experts" and volunteers into public agencies, and building their own organizations and institutions of child welfare. This development was largely the work of the Social Democratic party's new welfare association, Workers' Welfare (Arbeiterwohlfahrt), which grew out of the work of the Child Protection Commissions of the prewar period and took definite shape in 1919–20.[39] In part its growth reflected precisely the *success* of the middle-class parties in containing socialism politically; as one Protestant observed in 1921: "The revocation of our independence or of the Christian character of our institutions through state measures which we still feared two years ago hardly threatens us anymore. Social Democracy has set about establishing an independent welfare activity in the service of its ideas with all the more zeal."[40]

Workers' Welfare never remotely rivaled the financial and institutional resources of the middle-class charities; and it was confined virtually exclusively to the larger cities, since in rural areas the culture of deference still defeated socialists. Nevertheless, in urban Germany Workers' Welfare developed considerable influence through its success in enlisting volunteers. It claimed to have 1,200 local chapters and 24,000 volunteers in 1924, and was represented in 24 percent of all the Youth Bureaus established by the National Child Welfare Act of 1922; by the end of the decade it claimed to have 2,300 local chapters and 114,000 members, and was represented in about a third of the Youth Bureaus. Particularly in some large cities it was an impressive organization indeed. By 1926, for example, Cologne's chapter claimed to have a budget of half a million marks.[41] More important, Workers' Welfare training programs for social workers and volunteers were particularly successful. In 1929 the KFV's secretary, Elisabeth Zillken, admitted in private that Workers' Welfare volunteers were often the most capable available to the Youth Bureau; and in some larger cities (such as Hamburg) those trained by Workers' Welfare came to dominate the ranks of volunteers working for public welfare agencies.[42]

The growing influence of Workers' Welfare was particularly frightening for the Christian charities and the Christian churches because the organization argued that, since the citizen had a right to social services, all social welfare programs should be publicly administered by municipal government—and the private charities, accordingly, abolished. The control of many municipal governments by Social Democrats, and the success of Workers' Welfare in breaking into social work, also raised for many Christians the frightening possibility that public child welfare programs might be used to indoctrinate their children with atheistic, revolutionary, and democratic values, even against the wishes of their own families.

The efforts of Workers' Welfare were supplemented, moreover, by those of the Friends of the Children (Kinderfreunde) movement, a socialist group for young children and parents begun in Austria in 1908. The Kinderfreunde spread rapidly throughout Germany after 1922: a national association was created in November 1923 (with the support of the socialist unions, Workers' Welfare, the SPD teachers' association, and socialist youth groups, and under the leadership of Kurt Löwenstein). There were 183 local chapters by 1925, and 441 by 1929; in 1928 these groups cared for over 200,000 children daily; a weekly newsletter was received by 251,000 subscribers; and the annual children's camp, in which children became "accustomed to democratic and social life-styles" through self-government, involved 10,000 children.[43] Even more frightening for conservative Christians was the development of a number of atheist and communist child welfare groups. By 1931 the national association of atheist welfare organizations claimed to have 112 local member associations.[44] Communist organizations such as the International Workers' Assistance (Internationale Arbeiterhilfe) and the Red Aid (Rote Hilfe), while largely engaged only in supporting the families of political prisoners and victims of state terrorism, were increasingly active in Germany in the late 1920s. The Rote Hilfe, for example, claimed 1,590 local chapters with 437,535 members by 1926.[45] From 1928 a coalition of these groups (the Arbeitsgemeinschaft sozialpolitischer Organisationen, or ARSO) published its own journal, *Proletarische Sozialpolitik,* which offered communist criticism of the existing welfare system. ARSO attacked the child welfare system in general as a weapon of class oppression, and denounced especially the "confessionalization" and "priestification" *(Verpfaffung)* of public welfare programs; it also played an important role in bringing to light abuses in correctional education.[46] Again, all these organizations seemed to conservative Christians to be part of a broad attempt at the systematic de-Christianization of German youth.

Finally, this battle within child welfare policy was all the more threatening because it appeared to be merely one part of a much larger struggle. With the (at least partial) separation of church and state, the issue of the state's involvement in the nation's cultural life sparked intense conflicts in a whole range of fields. The most heated of these battles was the bitter dispute in the latter half of the decade, particularly in Prussia and Saxony, over religious instruction in the schools—to which one historian has referred as "the school civil war," and which was one of the central political issues of the period.[47] Particularly within this context, the development of socialist child welfare organizations gave many in the Christian charities the sense, as one member of the Inner Mission put it in 1926, that they were engaged "in a cultural war."[48]

As we will see in Chapter 7, this political and ideological conflict had fateful consequences for child welfare policy later in the 1920s. After the revolutionary upheaval of 1918–19, German child welfare policy passed through a period of extraordinary legislative and institutional activity, lasting into the middle of the decade. The establishment of a centralized structure of child welfare programs, however, inevitably led to the realization and institutionalization of the potential for conflict inherent in the political and ideological divisions and compromises that grew out of the revolutionary period. By the end of the 1920s—even before the onset of the Great Depression—the German child welfare system was increasingly wracked by conflict. The rest of this chapter treats the first period of legislation and institution building; in Chapter 7 I will examine the logic of escalating conflict later in the 1920s.

The RJWG within the Government and in the Reichsrat, 1919–1921

The urgency of the problems created by the war and inflation, and the sense of possibility which the creation of the new Republic instilled, resulted in an outpouring of legislative measures in the field of child welfare policy in the early 1920s. The extension of maternity benefits, the new *Jugendpflege* decrees, and the passage of the film and "*Schmutz* and *Schund*" laws, were part of this surge of legislation. So was the Law on the Religious Education of Children of July 1921, which formally established the rights of parents to determine their children's confession or "worldview" (*Weltanschauung*, a particularly troublesome term politically and for the courts). Services for survivors of the war (including orphans and widowed mothers) were consolidated in May 1920. In the field of child welfare more narrowly defined, the reform of juvenile justice (which had been frustrated in 1913) was finally achieved in 1923. The National Juvenile Justice Act (Reichsjugendgerichtsgesetz, or RJGG), also of 1923, was something of a disappointment to many reformers, but as the minister of justice put it, it did at least achieve "what has been for over a decade and a half a self-evident demand" by mandating the establishing of a juvenile court in every judicial district, raising the age of criminal responsibility from twelve to fourteen and of conditional responsibility to eighteen, excluding the public and the press, and permitting the courts greater flexibility in sentencing minors (for example, by introducing judicial warnings and suspended sentences with probation) or in forgoing all punishment if "educational measures" seemed more appropriate, and even allowing public prosecutors to drop charges.[49] In 1925 the government at last submitted a bill to parliament for the reform of illegitimacy law. A Prussian law of 1927 expanded prenatal care and maternity benefits. And a number of other laws had important implications for child welfare—notably the Law for the Combating of Venereal Diseases of 1927, a Prussian law of 1920 on services for crippled children (an initiative of Arthur Schlossmann), and a large number of social insurance laws passed in the early 1920s.

This surge of legislation and of social policy enthusiasm, however, bogged down in the second half of the decade in a complicated and angry conflict among progressives, "Manchester" liberals, conservatives, socialists, and the targets of policy themselves. Jurists, for one thing, continued to suspect and resist those who favored extensive state intervention in the private sphere. One judge wrote in 1924 that "welfare fanatics," including "nearly all the responsible administrative organs," were intervening "ever more deeply in private life" and were "ever more inclined" to extend correctional education to "all elements who are in any way burdened by the milieu of their parental home."[50] And while Heinrich Webler was, by 1929, demanding the complete abandonment of criminal prosecution of all those aged fourteen to eighteen, the pedagogue Carl Mennicke saw in efforts to raise the age of legal responsibility to sixteen (a measure on which most juvenile justice reformers were in agreement by the end of the 1920s, and which was narrowly defeated in the *Reichstag* in 1931) an "uncontrolled educational fanaticism" which threatened the legal rights of young people.[51] A number of crucial high court decisions, perhaps partly inspired by such fears, strictly limited the number of "preventive" commitments after 1929. In the case of illegitimacy law, the government's bill became the subject of a drawn-out struggle among welfare advocates, who sought to retain the powers of the public legal guardian; socialists, moralists, and feminists, who demanded full legal equality for illegitimate children and parental authority for their mothers; and conservative Christians, who opposed any changes that might suggest an accepted alternative to marriage. The debate in parliament and in the public dragged on until the project died with the end of parliamentary government in 1930.[52] Plans for a comprehensive system of vocational education also broke down over the issue of financing. And, as we have seen, the morality legislation of the 1920s was disappointing at least to a large number of conservative observers.

The most important piece of child welfare legislation in the 1920s, however, was the National Child Welfare Act—Reichsgesetz für Jugendwohlfahrt, or RJWG—of 1922, which grew directly out of the progressive reform program developed between 1910 and 1918. It established the institutional framework for all child welfare programs in the 1920s; and its history perhaps best illustrates the potentials and problems of child welfare policy in this decade.

The Ministry of the Interior, it will be recalled, had begun work toward a national law on child welfare as early as March 1918. Seeing in the creation of a national child welfare system an important opportunity to push the Social Democratic program of social justice and democratization, the new SPD minister of the interior, Eduard David, had made it a high priority immediately after the Revolution. A special commission made up of representatives of the SPD, the DDP, and the Center party began drafting a new bill in the winter of 1919, and commissarial discussions of early drafts began in early May.[53] The bill drafted by the ministry comprised five separate laws, treating respectively the structure and responsibilities of the Youth Bureaus, State Youth Bureaus, and National Youth Bureau, including an almost limitlessly expandable list of preventive welfare measures in paragraphs 4 and 5 (section 2); supervision of foster care (section 3); public legal guardianship (section 4); and material relief for poor children, which was to include the costs of education and was to be paid by the community in which the child lived rather than its "hometown" (section 5). At the insistence of the Social Democrats a fifth section was later added, which amounted to a national correctional education law (section 6). The law as a whole was prefaced by a general statement of its purposes (section 1).

While the Social Democratic Child Protection Commissions had, by the last years before the war, been laying the foundations for a coherent Social Democratic child welfare policy, those organizations were drastically disrupted by the war years and largely absorbed by the National Women's Service; so in 1918 and 1919 Social Democratic thought and policy on child welfare were still quite underdeveloped. The socialist-dominated Ministry of the Interior therefore relied heavily on the proposals of middle-class welfare experts in drawing up the new law.[54] This first draft, presented to the commissarial committee of ministers by Privy Councilor Otto Köbner of the Ministry of the Interior, therefore derived quite unmistakably from the progressive tradition. Its first paragraph established the "right of the child to education," to be secured by the public child welfare agencies wherever the family could not do so. And Köbner quite explicitly hoped to create a "socializing agency" of the kind envisioned by Johannes Petersen and Kurt Blaum. The "people and particularly the youth itself," he told his colleagues in the first meeting of May 5, must not be allowed to believe that "we are dealing in the Youth Bureau merely with an institution for the mentally or physically deficient, fallen, or endangered youth. We cannot put enough services for healthy children in the Youth Bureaus, in order to give these the character of real welfare agencies and thereby to secure them the popularity without which they would be condemned to bureaucratic barrenness."[55]

Moreover, Köbner clearly saw the system created by the bill as an important part of the structure of the new, unitary democratic state. The ministry repeatedly insisted that the bill was important "not only for the sake of the thing itself but from the perspective of the consolidation of the national idea," which it would strengthen by bringing government into the daily lives of the citizenry and by creating a powerful, flexible, unitary national bureaucracy.[56] The National Youth Bureau had the power to promulgate guidelines for the activity of the local and State Youth Bureaus; State Youth Bureaus would hear appeals against decisions of the local Youth Bureaus and have authority to issue guidelines for the local bureaus; and the Youth Bureaus, organs of the self-governing cities and counties, would centralize virtually every program and agency bearing on the welfare of children. The bill explicitly reserved to the national, state, and local governments the right to expand the functions of the Youth Bureaus at will, through legislation or administrative directive.

Nevertheless, the draft also clearly reflected certain fundamental items on the agenda of Social Democracy. In particular, the open-ended assignment of responsibility for the well-being of all German children to public agencies reflected the Social Democrats' desire to create a purely *public* system of child welfare—and angered many progressives, such as Klumker, who argued that the bill was simply too ambitious. What is more, in line with Social Democratic hostility to private charities, the charities were not mentioned in the bill at all; there was no provision for their inclusion in an executive board of the Youth Bureau. The draft represented, in other words, an abrogation of the corporatist compromise worked out in the last year of the war.

Despite the technical complexity of the material and efforts of the Prussian Finance Ministry to defend the interests of the charities and the treasury, the Ministry of the Interior made a determined effort to ram the bill through the initial process of consultation among the ministries and through the upper house of parliament as quickly as possible. It clearly wanted a national law passed before the individual states had time to complicate matters by enacting their own (as Württemberg in fact did in 1919). The SPD government also hoped to be able to bring the law before the National Assembly before elections to the new national parliament could be held—partly in order to enhance the prestige of the new Republic, but probably also because it was apparent that the elections of 1920 would yield an even more conservative result than those of 1919. Some of the ministries also hoped to avoid the inclusion of financially insupportable measures by precluding a detailed discussion and amendments.[57]

The deliberations within the government were therefore completed at a breakneck pace in seven meetings between June 16 and July 3, 1919. No formal consultation with private experts ever occurred before the bill was submitted to the upper house on February 25, 1920, though informal meetings were held with the DZJ.[58] The cities were virtually ignored. And the individual states received the same treatment: the government's bill was sent to them for comment only a month before submission—a procedure hotly protested by the governments of the south German states.[59]

The bill therefore arrived in the upper house of parliament much as it had been drafted by the Ministry of the Interior. In particular, despite the objections of several ministries and private organizations, no mechanisms for securing the rights or influence of the charities were written into the bill, and neither were what conservatives regarded as adequate protections of the rights of parents. The right of national, state, and local governments to expand the duties of the Youth Bureau was not curtailed. And while the Ministry was persuaded to require that the Youth Bureau be made up of an executive and a "council" *(Beirat)*, the list of prospective members included representatives of a number of public agencies and "especially the trade unions"; the requirement that clergy and others sit on it in an official capacity, added in the course of the deliberations, was dropped after it became clear that the cities and socialists would reject the idea. The corporatist solution proposed in 1918, then, was still conspicuously absent from the government's bill when it was submitted to the upper house.

At that point, however, the ministry's efforts were completely derailed. The monarchist Kapp putsch of March 1920, and the radical socialist risings in the Ruhr that grew out of the general strike that defeated it, further polarized the political situation and discredited the republican parties. In the elections held on June 6, 1920, they suffered a crushing defeat, and the Social Democrats left the government to make way for a coalition of the center-right. Eduard David was replaced as minister of the interior by Erich Koch of the DDP. The new government did not pursue the passage of the RJWG as energetically as the socialists had. In addition, as the financial situation deteriorated, the states—including the Social Democratic Prussian Ministry of Finance—were increasingly able to force the government to take their objections to the costs of the bill seriously. The Erzberger tax reform of 1920, by transferring important sources of revenue from local and state governments to the national government, increased their leverage. The result was that the bill was stalled in the upper house for just over one entire year by complicated financial negotiations, which twice nearly torpedoed it completely. It was rescued only by a petition of women deputies in the Reichstag.

That delay gave the states an opportunity to undertake a serious revision of the law. Led by the strongly Catholic south German states, and notably by Bavaria, the upper house decided on a whole series of important changes designed to hem in the public child welfare system with negative controls. On the petition of Baden and Württemberg, the upper house abolished the National Youth Bureau—which the southern states regarded as a threat to their autonomy from "Red" Berlin and an expensive luxury. Fearing that public child welfare agencies might undermine the family, Baden secured the addition in section 1 of the stipulation that the Youth Bureau could intervene against the will of the parents only if a law expressly allowed it to do so. A motion supported by both Bavaria and Hamburg resulted in the striking of the list of possible members of the Youth Bureau: the law now required only the membership of "men and women experienced and proven in child welfare from all groups of the populace."

But, most important, the Bavarians feared that allowing local governments to expand the duties of their Youth Bureaus would permit them to take over activities hitherto in the hands of private organizations, and that "in light of the great differences of opinion over religious and moral education of youth," the Youth Bureau might consciously set out to destroy the private charities. Bavaria therefore secured the expurgation of the expansion clause and the inclusion of a clause in section 1 making it clear that the intervention of private organizations, as well as socialization by the family, must take precedence over the activity of public agencies—which could act only "without detriment to the collaboration" of the charities.[60]

By the spring of 1921, moreover, the private charities were rapidly reconsolidating their position. In the face of the danger of socialization, nonreligious groups and organizations of both confessions began in 1919 to discover their common interests, while the DVöpF and the DZJ increasingly saw themselves as lobbying organizations for the private associations. The refusal of the government to consult the experts in the writing of the RJWG in particular helped to draw the private organizations together. By May 1920 the DZJ was seeking the cooperation of the DCV in defending private charities' "appropriate place in the structure of German child welfare," and even conservatives within the Catholic charities were counseling collaboration.[61] In May of the following year these connections were formalized by the creation of the National Union of Associations of Private Welfare (Reichsgemeinschaft von Hauptverbänden der freien Wohlfahrtspflege), renamed Deutsche Liga der freien Wohlfahrtspflege (National League of Private Welfare) after reorganizing in December 1924. In 1923 the DZJ was transformed into an organization exclusively of private child welfare associations (and renamed National Center for Private Child Welfare, or Deutsche Zentrale für freie Jugendwohlfahrt).

By the time the draft of the RJWG reached the lower house, then, the private charities were well prepared to lobby the various bourgeois parties to secure their interests. Within the Reichstag committee set up to review the bill, the bourgeois parties had a solid majority of sixteen votes to twelve; it was chaired by Wilhelm Marx, a Center party deputy and later chancellor with ties to Catholic reform circles in the Rhineland, and dominated by women deputies with close ties to private welfare organizations (including Marie Juchacz of Workers' Welfare).

But the private organizations did not risk relying only on their representatives in the parliament. In order to increase their leverage, in April 1921 they created an independent "Expert Commission" of forty-nine representatives from virtually every major welfare organization in the country, as well as of youth groups, teachers' associations, local government associations, and so on. Six of its members also served on the parliamentary committee. This commission achieved semiofficial status and extensive influence: it advised the members of the parliamentary committee on the complex technical aspects of the law, published a position paper in which its suggestions and demands were summarized, and peppered the committee with countless petitions.[62]

The Expert Commission and the Catholic Response

The proposals put forward by the Expert Commission, which was dominated by the DVöpF and the DZJ, were virtually identical with those which had guided those organizations' views on the Prussian bill of 1917–18. By 1921, however, the experts' concern over the possibility that the Youth Bureaus might be dominated by mere bureaucrats had been considerably sharpened. As they had during the war, some experts and social workers feared that in the new parliamentary-democratic state, party-political considerations would play too great a role in hiring. As the Association of Public Legal Guardians of Greater Berlin warned in April 1921, the directors of Youth Bureaus "will not always be chosen on objective grounds, since they will be chosen by the local governments. These . . . are almost always chosen in elections, which are almost everywhere guided by party-political considerations."[63] Moreover, reductions in the size of the armed forces and local administrations made it tempting to use the new child welfare bureaus as a repository for unemployed officers and public officials. Accumulating evidence seemed to support these concerns; a survey of 1921, for example, found that of 114 public legal guardians questioned, two were trained as social workers, while twenty-three were officer candidates and fifty-four were administrative officials.[64]

As a result, the Expert Commission laid even greater emphasis than the secular experts had in 1917–18 on the pedagogical mission of the Youth Bureau and on the need to professionalize child welfare work to ensure the influence within the Youth Bureaus of the humanitarian and pedagogical spirit of the private welfare organizations.

The suggestions presented to the parliamentary committee by the Expert Commission therefore carried the ideas expressed at the National Child Welfare Conference to their logical conclusion. Most important of all, the commission recommended that two fifths of the seats on the governing boards of the Youth Bureaus be reserved for representatives of the private charities. In addition, the commission was adamantly in favor of giving the state Youth Bureaus substantive powers. It supported the guarantees of "subsidiarity" demanded by the southern states in the upper house of parliament. And, finally, it recommended that only people with experience in child welfare be accepted as members of the Youth Bureau, and that all full-time employees have adequate training.[65]

Given the central role played in the committee and in the Reichstag as a whole by the Catholic deputies, and the fact that the Center party controlled both the Prussian Welfare Ministry and the national Labor Ministry after 1920, the position of the DCV and the Catholic Center party was decisive for the fate of the law. That position was hammered out in late 1921 and 1922 by a special DCV commission on the RJWG, established in November 1921.

The initial response to the bill in conservative Catholic circles was very negative. The Catholic newspaper *Germania* declared in July 1921 that the law's fundamental outlines "undeniably rest on Marxist principles," that it was an attempt to "socialize the child" and would tend toward the "de-Christianization of child rearing."[66] Some within both the Protestant and the Catholic charities had already announced in 1919 that they favored basing the Youth Bureaus on the politically "neutral" and culturally conservative courts.[67] The semiofficial Bavarian and Badenese State Committees for Child Welfare denied the need for a national law.[68] And these views were seconded particularly by some Catholics from the eastern diaspora, who feared that, as a sometimes tiny minority, they would be unable to force the Youth Bureaus to respect their rights. These fears, reinforced by alarmist reports regarding Württemberg's new Youth Bureaus, very nearly turned the commission against the law.[69]

But the DCV's commission was dominated not by the conservatives, but by the more worldly members from the Rhineland, people accustomed to dealing both with the central authorities and with municipal governments. They argued, in the first place, that taking a stand against the bill would be politically unacceptable, given the self-evident need for a public child welfare system.[70] And Neuhaus warned again—as she had in 1918—that since the law would be passed either with or against Catholic votes, it would be better to collaborate in making it than to oppose it in vain; the "locomotive is going forward," she wrote, "whether we take our seats in the train or not."[71] More important, the moderate members of the commission pointed out that national legislation which enforced the corporatist forms advocated by secular experts might be the best protection for Catholic rights, particularly in states with strong Protestant and nonreligious majorities. Without the law, Neuhaus told her colleagues, "the socialists and the liberals have it in their power in every community and in every state to shape the Youth Bureaus as they see fit. . . . I must stress that the situation is better for us with the law than without it."[72]

The initial response of the commission was essentially defensive: an attempt to have written into the law guarantees of the religious education of Catholic children and of the independence of the charities. The DCV's first position paper on the bill, worked out in the commission's meeting in Dortmund in May 1920, demanded the explicit imposition of the principle of subsidiarity of public to private programs, and that the law require children's confession to be taken into account whenever they came under the authority of the Youth Bureau—for example, in placement in foster care or the choice of legal guardians. It also demanded that section 1 guarantee the child's right to religious education, and that the field of the Youth Bureau's duties be more narrowly circumscribed.[73]

In discussions within the commission in Dortmund in December 1921 and March 1922, however, a decisive transition was accomplished. At the December meeting Albert Lenné, a leading figure in Catholic child welfare in the Rhineland, objected to the stipulation that the Youth Bureau could intervene only "without detriment to the collaboration of private philanthropy," which had been written into section 1 to protect the private charities. In order to preserve the independence of the charities, he suggested, the term "work" should replace "collaboration" (*Arbeit* rather than *Mitarbeit*). Otherwise, Lenné argued, the charities would appear to be a mere "appendage" of the Youth Bureau. But here a City Councillor Kaiser and Curate Riekes of Dortmund pointed out that article 124 of the constitution guaranteed the independent existence of the charities, and that what must be secured in the law was their right to be involved directly in the work of the Youth Bureaus. The majority of the commission—including Lenné—was won over by these arguments, and supported both the use of the term "collaboration" and the proposal of the Expert Commission that the charities have a legal right to two fifths of the seats in the Youth Bureau's governing board.[74]

By the time the commission convened again in Koblenz in March 1922, the full implications of this step had become clear. Pastor Karl Neuendörfer of Mainz, in response to critiques of the bill from less optimistic southerners, stated the implications of the two fifths clause clearly. "We must," he insisted, "get into the communal government, we must have a voice there, and we accomplish that through this law." Lenné seconded this view: "The law speaks explicitly of the activity of local government. . . . We wanted to get into this activity; it was not to be allowed to happen without us. In contrast, we have preserved complete freedom in our field. If we consider that, we have more than parity. In this law private activity is even given a privileged position."[75] The two fifths clause and the guarantees of the subsidiarity of public child welfare, in other words, allowed the private organizations to make an end run around majoritarian democratic government. They would sit on the Youth Bureau even in communities where their own political power would not otherwise have allowed them to secure representation.

This shift was not accomplished without creating dissension within Catholic ranks. Several members of the commission rejected it vehemently; one, Christian Bartels of Paderborn (spiritual counsel to the KFV and director of the KMFV), even resigned in protest.[76] In the course of 1921 resistance to the law from conservative Catholics mounted steadily. On May 20, 1922, Adolf Cardinal Bertram, Prince-Bishop of Breslau and spokesman for the German Catholic episcopate, went so far as to reject both the bill and the resolution of the DCV's commission. "The law may bring improvements in infant welfare, child support, and the like," he wrote, "but religious education will be endangered."[77]

By that time, however, the matter was entirely out of the hands of the church and the more conservative members of the Catholic charity community. The Center party was more impressed by the credentials of its representatives in the parliamentary committee than by Bertram's, and it supported Neuhaus's and Marx's efforts. Perhaps to their surprise, they found that their demands virtually represented a consensus position among private welfare organizations. Already in July 1920 Klumker and the DZJ had published a "counterbill" which anticipated the general form of the Expert Commission's suggestions.[78] A position paper put out by the DVöpF made virtually identical demands.[79] Although it was less well organized and less active than either the nonreligious organizations or the DCV, the Inner Mission made similar demands. And in the Expert Commission it was above all Wilhelm Polligkeit, now director of the DVöpF, who pushed the other members toward demanding the two fifths clause, while Klumker demanded half the seats for the charities.[80]

The Emergency Decree of February 14, 1924:
The Experts, the Charities, and the Cities

By the time negotiations within the parliament reached their decisive phase in late 1921 and early 1922, then, experts of both confessions and the secular organizations could present a united front. The result was a resounding triumph for the charities, and for Catholics in particular. The bill produced by the Reichstag's committee gave every German child the right to "physical, spiritual, and social" competency (rather than merely "physical, mental, and moral"). At the insistence of Neuhaus, the phrase "without detriment to the collaboration of private activity" was added to paragraph 1. The Youth Bureau was required to take the child's faith into consideration when placing it in a reformatory or foster family. Paragraph 5, which allowed the expansion of the tasks of the Youth Bureau through legislation, was struck entirely. Paragraph 11 even allowed the transfer of entire programs to private organizations. And, most important, the two fifths clause was written into paragraph 9 of the law.[81]

In the plenum Neuhaus explicitly recognized the significance of this measure, admitting that "never before in any law has private charity been so elevated, been set on such solid ground." Kurt Löwenstein, the spokesman for the Independent Socialist party, came to the same conclusion. "In the place of a Youth Bureau," he complained, "has been put nothing other than a cartel of the private organizations under the protectorate of the administrative authorities and the national government." Nevertheless, the law was passed on June 14, 1922, with a strong majority. The SPD voted for it because they believed that establishing the "right of the child to education" would allow for the passage of more comprehensive laws in the future.[82] And even the Independent Social Democrats acquiesced. The only defeat for the backers of the law was that the Bavarians won an amendment allowing the states to delay putting it into force until April 1924.

If the RJWG itself must be seen as a victory for the private charities, however, many of the laws for its implementation *(Ausführungsgesetze)* passed by the individual states gave middle-class activists even more cause to celebrate. The national law left it in the power of the individual states to pass more specific stipulations regarding the constitution and makeup of the individual Youth Bureaus. In one large state, Saxony, the parties of the left and the representatives of local government won this battle. Here the state law required only that two fifths of the Youth Bureaus' members be nominated by the charities, as the national law required. But legislation in most of the large German states reserved seats on the Youth Bureau board for various state and church officials, creating the clear possibility of the outright domination of the Youth Bureaus by the charities and by religious interests.[83]

Prussia was a particularly blatant example. There the draft bill presented by the Ministry of Welfare revived the Prussian bill of 1917–18 in its entirety, stipulating that the county school and medical administrations and the churches were to be represented in the Youth Bureau, in addition to the private charities. It went even further than its predecessor, however, by expressly declaring that the Youth Bureau was not to be bound by directives from the local government, which could do no more than establish the agency's budget.[84] In the Prussian parliament the medical and school officials were struck from the list of Youth Bureau members, and the stipulation regarding municipal government directives was defeated; but two teachers were then *added* as members of the Youth Bureau. One adviser to the DCV, after doing the arithmetic, concluded that the "danger of a substantial preponderance of the official members or of the influence of the local government is therefore in my opinion not to be feared in *any* case."[85] As far as the cities were concerned, then, the law passed by the democrati-

cally elected parliament of Prussia was actually worse than that which the
monarchical state had nearly forced upon them in its dying moments in late
1918.[86] Similar laws were passed in Baden, Württemberg, and Hessen; and
Bavaria even placed child welfare programs within the competence of the
state government; formally, they were merely "delegated" to the municipalities and counties.

The charities did not believe that the battle had been won with the
passage of these laws, however; rather, they regarded the abstract paragraphs of the RJWG as no more than a brilliant opportunity to secure
their influence in practice. Agnes Neuhaus believed that united and rapid
Catholic action to exploit the new law would "succeed . . . in avoiding its
dangers and making lively and effective the forces for the good of our
young people and our church that are latent in it." And Pastor Gottfried
Schlegtendahl, a leading figure in Protestant child welfare in the Rhineland,
concluded that if the charities would centralize and expand, the law could
be "greeted in its present form without serious reservations. It can be a
good thing for the youth. But it can also become a strong weapon or a successful tool for the church, if she will prepare herself in good time to use it
effectively."[87]

By 1922–23, then, the private charities were laying plans for a comprehensive organizing drive to meet the challenge of the law. In the Catholic
camp a set of guidelines for the proper response to the law was developed
by the DCV's child welfare section in November 1922. It called for the formation of child welfare organizations locally, the centralization and com-
pletion of the national Catholic organizations, the establishment of training
courses, and so forth. A similar set of instructions for the diocesan and
local church authorities was promulgated in a pastoral letter of the German
bishops the following year.[88] The KFV expanded with particular rapidity: it
had 219 local chapters at the beginning of 1924, and 383 by the end of
1926.[89] On the Protestant side, plans were made for an elaborate hierarchical organization which would activate Protestant energies for child welfare at every level from the province or state down to each individual
synod. In some provinces, notably Westphalia and the Rhineland, these efforts bore fruit as early as 1921 in the formation in each community of a
"Protestant Youth Bureau" parallel to the public Youth Bureau.[90] By centralizing their organizations at the top and by extending their local activities to every city and county, then, the charities hoped not only to make it
impossible for the new public child welfare agencies to overlook or tyran-
nize them and their constituencies but also to use the law to transform their
own social role, making themselves an indispensable part of the new welfare state.

Once again, however, the private organizations had completely failed to
take the interests and power of local government into account. Secular wel-

fare experts argued that the special needs of children justified breaching the principle of municipal self-government by imposing a corporatist structure and particular members on the Youth Bureau. The keynote speaker at the ADB's August 1924 conference argued that since the work of the Youth Bureau as a "socializing agency" demanded "engagement of the force of personality," child welfare "unquestionably falls outside the framework of the rest of the communal administration," and insisted that the "Youth Bureau must have an independent position within the administration."[91]

In contrast, the private charities once again insisted that *they* were the representatives of the "people." They defended, of course, their particular constituencies' interests; the Catholic charities, for example, saw themselves as the champions of minority rights. But they also viewed the charities as the embodiment of the authentic ethical energies of the people at large, which were threatened by bureaucrats and by the politicians at City Hall. As Joseph Beeking suggested in an essay of 1925: "Public welfare in a democratic state is not something which can be done independent of the people's will or without direct participation of the people by a group of bureaucrats. . . . But that part of the people which can here in the best sense represent the people, which most effectively anchors welfare work in the people, is private charity."[92] Similarly, Neuhaus wrote to Beeking in early 1924 of the need to avoid the "tyranny of the self-governing local governments."[93] And Constantin Noppel, a leading figure in Bavarian Catholic youth welfare, blithely explained to the 1924 conference of the DVöpF that the charities were "honestly struggling toward new forms . . . for self-government. It is clear to us all: something is wrong today with self-government. . . . In a certain sense contact has been lost between the community and local government, which self-governs more than others govern themselves through it. Forms must be found which restore the balance, which really bring about self-government by the whole community."[94] The creation of a truly democratic system, in other words, required new forms in which "the people" would participate directly rather than through the mediation of political parties, parliaments, and bureaucracies.

From the perspective of municipal politicians committed to majoritarianism—and often Social Democracy—the arguments both of the charities and of the secular experts seemed outrageous and dangerous; and the two fifths clause and related provisions of the RJWG represented an assault on democracy. The socialist city councillor Gottlob Binder of Bielefeld told the 1924 conference of the DVöpF that "things cannot go so far that we reject the idea of the sovereignty of the state [*den Staatsgedanken*]." It must not be forgotten, he reminded his listeners, that the democratic local government "is the sum of all the citizens, and therefore of the private charities as well."[95] That being the case, he could not understand why the latter should be granted a privileged role in the Youth Bureau, bypassing the authority of the elected representatives of the community and circumventing the democratic process of elections and parliamentary local government.

Not surprisingly, local governments rejected the inclusion in the law of detailed provisions regarding the makeup of the Youth Bureau. Some socialist governments argued that it was inappropriate to include the charities in the work of welfare agencies.[96] Others argued that the Youth Bureau "council" proposed by the government's bill would "politicize" the Youth Bureaus by bringing into them the representatives of the warring ideological camps—the very reverse of the charities' and the experts' fears. Moreover, throughout 1920 and 1921 the cities repeatedly and almost universally rejected the supervision of State Youth Bureaus over their own agencies and their power to issue binding general directives and hear appeals against local Youth Bureau decisions. The functions of the State and National Youth Bureaus, they suggested, could be performed more efficiently by organizations of local governments, such as the National Municipal League (Deutscher Städtetag, or DST) or the DVöpF. Finally, they insisted vehemently that they could not pay for the Youth Bureaus—and particularly for poor relief for children.[97] Material aid for children should be reformed only in the context of the reform of the entire poor relief system.

To their growing frustration, however, the cities found that they were unable to exercise significant influence in parliament. After submitting an initial set of petitions in April 1921, the DST and the National Association of Rural Counties both vented their frustration over the lack of response from the parliamentary committee on the law in another set in February 1922; these new petitions requested as an absolute minimum the striking of section 5 of the law and a solution to the problem of costs.[98] Instead of responding to their demands, the committee passed the two fifths clause. The cities had equally meager success in shaping the state laws.

In late 1923, therefore, the National Municipal League decided to use the occasion of the complete collapse of German finances under the impact of hyperinflation to defeat the law by nonparliamentary means.[99] On November 10 representatives of the Municipal Association met with the national Ministry of the Interior to argue against the whole corporatist apparatus established by the law, reiterating the view that it was "inappropriate to force upon the free forms of self-government a special section with rigid forms," and that "child welfare should be in principle attended to by the general organs of self-government, without any special provisions being necessary." Only in very large cities, they continued, was it really necessary to establish an autonomous child welfare agency: in other places "the creation of special institutions means only that the restricted means which will in future be allocated will be spent for administrative apparatus rather than for the youth itself"—perhaps a veiled threat to cripple the Youth Bureaus by giving them insufficient funding. The State and National Youth Bureaus they characterized as instances of "unnecessary overorganization." Except for section 4 (public guardianship), therefore, the law should be set aside.[100]

These arguments did not persuade the Ministry of the Interior of the necessity of suspending the law. In December and early January the Prussian Ministry of the Interior, the Prussian finance minister, and the national finance minister (himself a former director of the DST) all announced that they considered doing so a "financial" necessity.[101] They suggested that the government should use the emergency powers granted to it in October 1923 to suspend the law indefinitely.

In the end, a compromise was struck. Under an emergency decree of February 14, 1924, based on a DVöpF proposal, the states were given the power to allow local government to forgo the establishment of a Youth Bureau and transfer its tasks to another agency, such as the general Welfare Office. After a complicated set of political machinations, the two fifths clause was retained for whatever agency those programs were transferred to. At the same time, however, paragraph 4 (preventive programs) was made nonbinding, and section 5 (material relief) was set aside. A simultaneous Emergency Decree on Welfare Services (Fürsorgepflichtverordnung, or FpVO) reformed the entire poor-relief system. Finally, a third decree restored considerable powers of taxation to local government and the states.

These decrees relieved some of the financial concerns of municipal governments. During the discussion surrounding them, however, it had become clear that in fact the cities' financial objections were largely a cover for the more political aim of overturning the two-fifths clause. This aim was defeated. In fact, the FpVO itself included a clause requiring representation of the charities in the new poor relief agencies *(Bezirksfürsorgeverbände)* as well.[102] But the victory achieved by the Christian charities was, in retrospect, clearly a pyrrhic one. The mutual mistrust that the struggle had created was apparent at the 1924 conference of the DVöpF, where one municipal politician complained: "It is deeply regrettable that a battle for the soul of our youth is now being opened by . . . private charity. . . . Just as party politics is not statesmanship, so the child welfare of the different orientations of private charity is not child welfare in the sense intended by the law."[103] The restoration of taxation power to the cities made such remarks particularly ominous for the charities; for, as Agnes Neuhaus had remarked as early as 1920, "our greatest security is the financial emergency" faced by the cities.[104] By the mid-1920s the charities would find themselves locked, at least from their own perspective, in an existential struggle with expanding municipal child welfare bureaucracies.

By that time, however, this organizational struggle had become inextricably entangled in and freighted with the much broader cultural confrontation between Christianity and (majoritarian) democratic socialism. That conflict was in many ways merely an escalation of the struggles between social-liberals and Christians in the years before the war. But by driving Christians rapidly to the cultural and political right, it contributed to the destabilization of the fragile compromise embodied in the National Child Welfare Act. By the time the Great Depression struck the child welfare system in 1929, it was already reeling, torn by increasingly politicized and bitter conflicts among democrats, socialists, communists, social managers, Christians, and welfare administrators. In Chapter 7 we will look at these conflicts.

CHAPTER SEVEN

Child Welfare, Bureaucracy, and "Cultural War," 1924–1929

"Social Pedagogy"

After the beginning of 1924, when the RJWG came into force in all of Germany, child welfare advocates increasingly turned from organizational issues to the question of the Youth Bureau's role in the socialization of youth. Curiously, in this respect child welfare thought in the Weimar years was marked by a distinctly more conservative tone, and specifically a more explicit concern with the preservation of the family, than had characterized the rhetoric of Petersen, Klumker, Blaum, and others in the prewar period. In the practice of social agencies, this conservatism was reflected in the growing influence of the idea of "family social work" *(Familienfürsorge)* developed by Marie Baum, in which social workers attempted to "treat" the entire family rather than individual members (children, for example, or alcoholics)—and in particular to practice "preventive" social work, stabilizing the family by educating women in hygiene, home economics, child rearing skills, and so on.[1]

A number of factors contributed to this change. The social conservatism of the mainstream and conservative women's movements, for one thing, was now institutionally anchored in the new profession of social work. The perception that the war had placed unbearable strains on millions of families also played a role, and wartime fears for the stability of the family were confirmed and exacerbated by the catastrophic impact of inflation and hyperinflation, the rising rate of divorce in the 1920s, and changing patterns of behavior among women—in particular the emergence of the "New Woman" and the continued growth of women's paid employment. The new tone also reflected the influence in the 1920s of the often antirationalistic and antimodernist ideas of the youth movement, and of "reform pedagogy" *(Reformpädagogik)* and "social pedagogy" *(Sozialpädagogik)*, which were rapidly establishing themselves as a kind of theoretical and philosophical foundation for public child welfare work. The new awareness of constraints on social engineering and state action which the fiscal crisis imposed was also important, as was the desire to avoid costly duplication of visits to any given family by the social workers of specialized agencies. Finally, increased emphasis on the preservation of the family as the healthiest environment for children's development also reflected the continuation of long-term trends among child welfare advocates—toward greater concern with the prevention of "waywardness," toward environmentalist theory, and accordingly toward an increasing focus on early childhood.

Typical of this more cautious approach was a 1927 essay by Aloys Fischer. Reiterating the themes of Christian social theory and of Paul Natorp's earlier "social pedagogy," he asserted that the family is "the pattern and ideal for all other forms of community building and socialization, the practice and planting ground of social life as such. . . . All community spirit . . . is nourished at bottom . . . by the world of familial experience and feeling. . . . The family is the foundation of society and culture." All sociological theories of the decline of the patriarchal private family and all the theories of the "pedagogical professionals" notwithstanding, Fischer declared that nonfamilial institutions and experiences could not create the basis for a healthy society. Social policy must therefore aim neither to replace nor to complement the family, but rather to "overcome those elements in our spiritual-cultural and economic-social situation which are harmful to the family."[2] In the same year (and volume) Gottlieb Storck, director of Lübeck's Youth Bureau, put the same point in more negative language: "State, municipality, and private associations have competed in supporting the family . . . through the creation of day care centers, kindergartens, crèches . . ., supervisory agencies . . . etc. And what was the result. . .? That the family . . . was not complemented but further weakened."[3] There was a danger, in other words, that public child welfare might undermine parents' sense of responsibility and thus make the situation of children even worse. Similarly, Hermann Nohl, the leading intellectual within the social pedagogy movement of the 1920s, warned against the tendency to blame circumstances rather than people for social need. Such an approach, he suggested, ignored the fact that "the greatest need is always in the soul"; it fostered passivity and might weaken the sense of responsibility, the "will to self-help."[4]

Yet beneath such rhetoric there often lurked an ambition no less grand than that which had motivated the early progressive child welfare movement, and the same ideal of the Youth Bureau as an independent agent of socialization, an *Erziehungsamt*. This ambition was now often expressed in more antimodernist terms. For example, Wilhelm Hertz, director of Hamburg's Youth Bureau, wrote in late 1927 that the Youth Bureau's "cultural mission" was "to collaborate in the overcoming of the amorphous metropolis, its anomie and irresponsibility—toward a new national community. . . . Mass must be given form, a new proletarian life-ideal must be found."[5] Similarly, Hermann Nohl held in 1926 that the aim of welfare must be to combat the "'massification' and 'superficialization'" of modern (proletarian) life. But in a second article, published in 1928, Nohl criticized child welfare programs for not being "preventive": it was, he suggested, "a serious constitutional error in the construction of the whole work [that] an accident always has to happen" before public agencies would intervene. Instead, the task of the moment was to give "the work of child welfare a positive direction which would make the Youth Bureaus independent organs of popular socialization." Public child welfare, he complained, was currently "concentrated on the sickness, but it should be concentrated on maintaining health."[6] Its goal, he said, must be not to take care of people who were in need but to enable them to avoid needing such help. Improved social integration must be achieved not through reactive and punitive intervention (nor through socialist revolution, which would bring the atrophy of "self-help") but through heightened individual productivity, made possible by public programs.

Nohl summed up his argument with a vivid analogy that went to the heart of the social-managerial tradition: "Child welfare today is concerned principally to put cars back on the rails once they have jumped the tracks. But the rail system itself is completely destroyed today." The *proper* task of public child welfare, therefore, must be "to create for the child such a rail system. . . . Herein . . . lies the autonomous *raison d'être* of the Youth Bureau, in this organization of healthy possibilities for growth for our . . . youth."[7] Gertrud Bäumer put this argument with exceptional clarity before the DVöpF in 1930, holding that child welfare services were not merely "help in need":

> Rather we are dealing here . . . also with . . . a healthy change. . . . It would be wrong to regard the social change which has made child welfare programs necessary merely as one which makes more emergency services for youth necessary. . . . *Pedagogical* services have also grown up around the *family*, for the need of the child for nonfamilial socialization has grown with the growing collectivism of modern life. . . . Child welfare must be seen as . . . a work of culture, and not merely welfare.[8]

The Youth Bureau, in other words, would not merely compensate for the failings of individual units of the familial social order; rather, it would be an autonomous and integral part of a *new* social order for which the family alone could no longer adequately socialize children. Again, this was obviously a restatement of Petersen's or Blaum's program of the 1910s for creating a "socialization agency."

An article published by the academic Gerhard Steuk in 1928 suggests how far some thinkers were willing to take this line of reasoning by the late 1920s. Steuk admitted that the debate among welfare experts over the role of the family in socialization had been decided in the family's favor. But, given the decay of the family as an economic unit, a binding legal institution, a religious community, and a determinant of social status, he suggested, the concentration of all efforts on the preservation of the family amounted to a "tragic pose: one pretends to be forced . . . to struggle for a cause which is lost from the beginning." It was time, he suggested, to acknowledge that the family was merely one social expression of the "human desire for essential community" and to recognize the validity of other, newer social forms which met the same need.[9]

The Experts, the Charities, and the Youth Bureaus

The growing importance of social pedagogy in the conception of the Youth Bureau's social function created an urgent belief—as we have seen already in the context of the debate over the RJWG—that the bureau must be staffed by people with some understanding of pedagogy and of the processes of childhood socialization, and that they must have the independence to follow the dictates of their pedagogical expertise. The hiring and administrative practices of the cities after 1922–1924, however, realized all the fears of the child welfare experts regarding the insensitivity of municipal governments and bureaucrats to the special nature of child welfare work. The cities often refused to hire personnel with special training or experience in child welfare, preferring to rely on proven administrators and the normal rules of seniority and preferment. Fiscal constraints, in any case, prohibited them from hiring new officials. And many male administrators refused to place women (who were more likely to have social work training) in positions of responsibility, regarding them as by nature irrational and overly emotional, or as inexperienced upstarts.

As a result, only a small proportion of the directors of the Youth Bureaus had any social welfare or pedagogical training. Of 10,712 officials and employees of the Youth Bureaus in 1928, only 2,667 were accredited social workers, and 2,013 had other forms of training (such as seminars or workshops of several weeks' duration). Moreover, although of those 2,667 licensed social workers only 129 were men, the Youth Bureaus were dominated entirely by male administrators, and the women employed as social workers usually had little say in the running of their agencies.[10] They were, in any case, often overwhelmed by mushrooming caseloads. As one observer put it, the work of the Youth Bureaus was dominated by "middle-level bureaucrats" who were "one-sidedly oriented toward administrative and fiscal concerns." The "welfare-pedagogical" perspective, warned

Immanuel Fischer in 1928, was in danger of being overwhelmed by the "administrative" perspective.[11]

To make matters worse, the emergency decree of 1924 had permitted local government to create the Youth Bureau as a dependent division within another agency, such as the Welfare Office (*Wohlfahrtsamt*). In fact, of the 1,251 Youth Bureaus in 1928, only 383 were independent agencies.[12] This fact, many child welfare experts believed, also tended to militate against the creation of a real "socialization agency," for subordination to the officials and procedures of the Welfare Office led to an overemphasis on mere material relief. The setting aside of paragraph 4 of the law, which listed preventive programs such as *Jugendpflege,* further reduced the "pedagogical" orientation of the Youth Bureau and led to an overemphasis on *reactive* and repressive measures. As the Social Democratic city councillor Gottlob Binder of Bielefeld remarked in 1925, without *Jugendpflege* the Youth Bureau might become merely "a well-functioning new police . . . agency."[13]

For all of these reasons, then, many private social welfare experts concluded soon after 1924 that the public system of child welfare was not functioning as they had hoped, and that it was in fact headed for disaster. By 1925 experts close to the ADB were already concluding that the Youth Bureaus suffered, as Immanuel Fischer put it, from the "creeping disease" of bureaucracy. And Wilhelm Hertz told a meeting of policymakers in the Ministry of the Interior in June 1928 that the experts believed the dearth of appropriately trained officials and employees in the Youth Bureaus, and their domination by the Welfare Offices, together constituted a state of "crisis" for public child welfare.[14]

By that date, in fact, many child welfare experts were expressing growing doubts about the whole concept of child welfare as bureaucratic social management which had guided the creators of the RJWG. Otto Wehn, for example, warned that in the Youth Bureaus real welfare work "threatens to suffocate . . . in a desert of paper and files. . . . If a fundamental change is not accomplished here . . . we are headed with our whole promising welfare legislation and our carefully constructed organization of child welfare irresistibly toward ruin."[15] Heinrich Webler, Klumker's deputy and director of the ADB, spoke more pointedly in 1927 of the "overvaluing of generalization, organization, and routine"; using distinctions drawn from fashionable sociology between mechanical "civilization" and spiritual "culture" and between modern, contractual-individualist "society" and organic "community," he warned that the child welfare system "threatens to fall victim to civilization, technics, and bureaucracy. . . . We must . . . find ways to lead this movement back to its *spiritual* sources. . . . We must find forms of work which allow us to undertake *child welfare as socialization work.*"[16] And Klumker himself—who had held from the beginning that the RJWG was too ambitious and the Youth Bureaus too burdened with multifarious duties—had concluded by 1930 that the whole development of public welfare had been a mistake. By the end of that year his rhetoric had taken on an intensity that bespeaks a virtual conversion experience. "Welfare work," he wrote, "has become rigid and superficial through state help and organizational busyness." Elsewhere he raged,

> We have prayed long enough to this idol [organization]. . . . The Babylonian structure of organization which law and administration have created . . . must be torn down, perhaps it will collapse of its own weight. It obscures our view of the real situation. . . . Such ignorance was the main result of this fury of organizing . . . We must find a new inner orientation. . . . We want to hear no more of all the sonorous nonsense that so often filled our deliberations in the last few years.[17]

This tirade—which moved one socialist critic to suggest that Klumker was "brown" (Nazi) at heart—was extreme, and informed by the awareness that the public child welfare system had proved utterly unequal to the challenge of the Great Depression.[18] But it suggests the extent to which, even before 1929, the child welfare experts were demoralized and doubtful.

This mood was reinforced, furthermore, by the specific concerns of women social workers. While the feminist traditions from which the social work profession sprang stressed the need for judgment, insight, and independence in social workers and the nonrational, individualizing, "motherly" quality of social work, in fact female social workers found themselves in the late 1920s subject to the authority of male bureaucrats and their rational routines, forms, and procedures, and overwhelmed by inflated caseloads. Rather than performing "individual work with human beings, for human beings," one critic remarked, social workers found themselves reduced to cogs in an administrative machine which pursued mere "schematic expedition [*schematische Abfertigung*]" of cases.[19] In what Marie Baum called the "fight against the 'machinery [*Apparat*],'" women social workers appeared to be losing.[20]

If the secular child welfare experts were disappointed by the development of the Youth Bureaus, the leadership of the Christian charities was frightened and antagonized. In 1922 the charities had put their faith in the corporatist compromise embodied in the RJWG. By the end of the decade—indeed as early as 1927—they were increasingly convinced that that compromise had been a failure, that they had been unfairly locked out of the public child welfare agencies, and that they were fighting for their survival and for the survival of their religion against a hostile and aggressive welfare bureaucracy.

This outcome was not immediately foreseeable in 1924. In the early 1920s both the national charity associations streamlined their organization considerably. Bolstered by official government recognition as *Spitzenver-*

bände (umbrella or "peak" organizations of the charities) and by the special status granted them in the RJWG and the FpVO, the DCV and the Inner Mission took on an increasingly active coordinating role among the religious charities. The Red Cross (formed in 1921) and the Fifth Welfare Association did the same for the nonreligious groups. All seven recognized national associations—Inner Mission, DCV, Red Cross, Fifth Welfare Association, the Central Welfare Association of German Jews, Workers' Welfare, and the tiny Central Welfare Committee of Christian Workers— benefited as well from considerable subsidies from the Catholic-controlled National Ministry of Labor (almost 14 million marks each went to the DCV and the Inner Mission and 39 million marks total to the central associations between 1924 and 1932, with a further 30 million going to lower-level organizations),[21] where Catholic officials saw in them a counterweight to the attempts of liberal and Social Democratic municipal governments to control welfare policy. Partly because of their role in carrying out public policies, partly because of their importance in distributing subsidies, and also because of their ties to important figures in the political parties, these organizations were able to establish a far closer working relationship with national and state ministries than they had enjoyed before the war. Both Catholic and Protestant charities also expanded their publishing activities, and the two religious child welfare journals (*Jugendwohl* and *Evangelische Jugendhilfe*) became increasingly vital to the child welfare establishment as a whole. Both the DCV and the Inner Mission developed a more differentiated and specialized administrative structure, forming, for example, special sections for child welfare in 1920 and 1925, respectively (in parallel to the existing EREV and Association for Catholic Charitable Educational Activity, Vereinigung für katholische caritative Erziehungstätigkeit). Despite persistent religious tensions, moreover, the Inner Mission and the DCV increasingly worked together to influence government policy and in organizations such as the AFET, on the basis of opposition to socialism and secular humanism. Finally, as I noted in Chapter 6, the National League of Private Welfare (Deutsche Liga der freien Wohlfahrtspflege, formed in 1921) and the DZJ became increasingly active in representing the interests of private welfare as a whole.

Yet, despite this impressive development, the charities found after 1924 that they were unable either to persuade or to force local governments to conform to their hopes for the cooperation of public agencies and private organizations. Formally, local governments did not attempt to circumvent the terms of the RJWG: compliance with the two fifths clause of the law was virtually complete. Moreover, the Youth Bureaus showed considerable readiness to cooperate with private organizations. Most local private groups reported a satisfactory working relationship with the Youth Bureaus. The private associations were extensively involved in carrying out or providing volunteers for essential programs such as protective supervision, nomination and supervision of legal guardians, recruitment of foster families and supervision of foster care, investigation and assessment in correctional education cases, juvenile court assistance, and so forth. But the private charities had aimed at much more than mere peaceful coexistence and cooperation. The terms of the law and the discussion surrounding it had seemed to promise the creation of a genuinely hybrid public-private agency, in which the charities would be able to help form and direct local policy and programs rather than merely assisting in their implementation. This expectation was proven false from the very outset. Generalized "passive resistance" on the part of the cities, as one critic called it, very often thwarted the private organizations' hopes for an active role in the direction of the Youth Bureaus.[22]

For one thing, the governing boards of the Youth Bureaus were usually consulted only regarding general policy decisions, major expenditures, or other such decisions; they had little or no input into the daily operations of child welfare programs. Many in the private organizations believed, moreover, that their fears of a "politicization" of child welfare (usually a code word for the growth of Social Democratic influence) by the communal governments were being realized after 1924. Pastor Niemöller of Münster, for example, wrote in early 1926 that administrative appointments in the Youth Bureaus were guided by "political considerations."[23] And in discussions within the DVöpF in early 1925, one official complained that in some towns appointments were made according to the relative strength of the political parties in the communal parliament.[24] The most effective and widely used means of reducing the influence of the corporatist board of directors, however, was simply not to hold meetings. A government study in 1928 found that fully 26 percent of Prussian Youth Bureaus' boards had never met. An additional 33 percent had met only once, 36 percent had met two to four times, and only 5 percent had met five or more times.[25] When meetings were held, local records indicate that the administrators often attempted to limit their role narrowly—for example, to passing official acts transferring public guardianship from one official to another.

Much of the leadership of the private charities saw in these problems evidence of the predominance of an arrogant and jealous bureaucratic spirit among Youth Bureau administrators, who they believed were simply impatient with interference by meddling charity workers. Maria Kiene of the DCV had concluded by 1927 that "the executive directors of the Youth Bureaus see themselves more and more as officials of the municipal agencies, without consideration for the nature of the Youth Bureau as a center for the cooperation of public and private child welfare."[26]

In fact, however, while private organizations resented the "politicization" of youth welfare work by the communal governments, those same governments sometimes accused the charities of "confessionalizing" the Youth Bureaus.[27] Gottlieb Storck complained in 1928 that "the mandated participation of the private welfare organizations is leading today in part to an inward and outward fragmentation of the work of the Youth Bureau, because members from these organizations see themselves not as members of the Youth Bureau, but rather see their task as being to represent the particular interests of private welfare organizations."[28] As a result, conflicts among the charities represented in the Youth Bureau sometimes disrupted its smooth functioning. As the political and organizational struggle between the socialist welfare organization Workers' Welfare and the religious charities heated up in the later 1920s (a topic discussed later in this chapter), this problem became increasingly acute. Indeed, by 1926 the formally interconfessional Red Cross saw its own work and that of the Youth Bureaus threatened with disruption and even paralysis by the escalating battle between Workers' Welfare and the religious charities.[29]

Whatever factors may explain it, the failure of the RJWG to create an organic synthesis of public and private child welfare organizations gave rise to bitter disappointment and growing fear among the charities. Pastor Adolf Stahl, a leading figure in the Inner Mission, wrote in August 1926 that the two fifths clause in paragraph 9 of the RJWG "has led to politicization; the Youth Bureaus as public agencies are of no use to us. Everywhere, in spite of paragraph 9, bureaucratization."[30] And Friedrich Grüneisen of the Red Cross reported that while the intention of the law had been to create a "committee in which the representatives determine . . . how the Youth Bureau is to work," in fact "this kind of collaboration—in which the representatives of the private associations feel themselves responsible for the work [of the Youth Bureau] as members of the public agency—appears, probably through the fault of both parties, to be almost nowhere in force."[31] Although there was no generalized assault on the charities, the Youth Bureaus did not seem eager to "support," "encourage," and "enlist" them, as paragraph 6 of the RJWG required; nor did they make much use of paragraph 11, which allowed them to transfer whole programs to private organizations.

By 1926, then, it seemed to many in the charities that the municipalities regarded the private charities as at best mere "drudges" for public child welfare (a charge with which even Workers' Welfare was not entirely unsympathetic), while at worst the insensitivity, bureaucratic arrogance, and expansionism of the Youth Bureaus threatened to crush them.[32] "The fact is," wrote Joseph Gillmann, "that, measured by really decisive influence, the private forces have, in the shortest time, been thrown completely in the shadow of the public." Joseph Beeking used an even more vivid metaphor: the charities, he concluded, had their "backs to the wall."[33]

Throughout the late 1920s the private associations attempted to use the central government and the State Youth Bureaus, in which they were far better represented than in the local Youth Bureaus, to influence the practices of the latter. The government did issue a decree in December 1925 urging closer cooperation between the Youth Bureaus and the private associations.[34] At bottom, however, there was very little that the charities could do to change the way Youth Bureau policy was made. As representatives of both the Prussian and the national government pointed out at a meeting of the DVöpF's child welfare committee in April 1925, any steps that reduced local government's control over the Youth Bureau would also reduce the "interest" of the local governments in child welfare programs—and thus their willingness to fund them.[35] Litigation would merely further alienate the public agencies. And any attempt to pass state laws actually removing the Youth Bureau from the direct competence of local governments would, in the North, have sparked a bitter battle with the cities and probably crippled the Youth Bureaus completely.

In the second half of the 1920s, therefore, the Christian charities pursued a program of expansion and centralization which was designed not only, as in the more optimistic period of the early 1920s, to take advantage of the opportunities offered by the RJWG but also to counter what they saw as growing threats from public programs. By 1929 all observers agreed that an extraordinary renaissance of the private charities was taking place. By that year no fewer than 527 individual associations involved in child welfare work were affiliated with the Inner Mission, and they supported 789 residential institutions for children and 3,227 day care institutions; the DCV included 420 member groups with 749 residential institutions and 3,498 day care institutions.[36] The KFV grew with particular rapidity: it had 344 local chapters and a combined work force (paid and unpaid) of 13,041 in 1925, 472 and 26,503, respectively, in 1932; it handled 77,894 cases in the former year and 122,151 in the latter.[37] Indeed, the expansion of private organizations, the training of their staff, and the growing number of private schools of social work were just as important in the development of the profession of social work as was the development of public agencies. The Catholic charities in particular moved rapidly to establish their own schools of social work and to professionalize both their staff and their administrative personnel, a process that had already begun during the war years.[38] Most of the day-to-day work of private organizations, however, continued to be done by Catholic nuns, Protestant deaconesses, and female volunteers; and the women's organizations which supplied those volunteers expanded rapidly: the Protestant Women's Auxiliary had 200,000 members in 1910, 500,000 in 1925, and 1 million by 1933, while the Catholic women's sodality, which transformed itself from a strictly religious into a social service organization in the late 1920s, had 250,000 members in 1925 and 900,000 in 1933.[39]

The Expansion of the Youth Bureaus as "Socializing Agencies"

In this context the expansion of the Youth Bureaus into programs involving direct socialization of children was particularly fateful. For despite the complaints of secular experts, the Youth Bureaus were in fact making efforts to become real "socialization agencies" and to construct the kind of "rail system" for youth imagined by Nohl. And what seemed far too little to the experts seemed far too much to the Christian charities.

The expansion of the Youth Bureaus was clearest in the case of paragraph 4 of the RJWG, which assigned to the Youth Bureau the task of creating or supporting "preventive" child welfare programs: counseling programs for mothers and young people, prenatal care programs, organized leisure activities for children and teenagers, and so on. The decree of February 1924 made the implementation of this paragraph a matter of administrative discretion; but with the recovery of municipal finances after the currency stabilization and tax reforms of early 1924, a growing number of cities did move into this area of policy.[40]

Most common were "preventive" health programs such as school lunch programs, pediatric clinics, and so forth. Also very common were recreation and convalescence programs *(Erholungsfürsorge)* such as organized daytime sports in city parks or vacation and health camps. Slightly less widespread were municipal day care programs such as kindergartens and day schools *(Tagesheime)*. A number of large cities in particular became involved in various ways in "youth cultivation" *(Jugendpflege)*—by building swimming pools, sports centers, playgrounds, youth hostels, and particularly youth centers or *Jugendheime* (of which there were at least 1,136 by 1927); or by establishing special cultural institutions such as municipal movie theaters for young audiences, youth libraries, lecture series, and regular slide shows.[41] Finally, by the mid-1920s the Youth Bureaus had also begun to expand into institutional care for orphans and wayward children, building their own reformatories, homes, and public orphanages. Their number was relatively small; but that the cities built them at all was an important precedent. In addition, the Youth Bureaus became involved more directly in correctional education through what came to be called "voluntary educational assistance" *(freiwillige Erziehungshilfe,* or FEH), in which parents voluntarily placed their children in the care of the Youth Bureau.

The Christian charities reacted to these activities with intense alarm. They feared that municipal Youth Bureaus might undertake a limitless expansion of such programs at the expense of familial socialization. More immediately, the construction of public convalescent homes, vacation camps, orphanages, day care institutions, and so forth struck a blow at the financial and organizational interests of the Christian charities. This prospect was all the more threatening because private institutions were suffering from underoccupancy in the late 1920s, owing to improving general health and the political crisis of correctional education. Most important, public agencies were usually not guided in their pedagogy by explicitly Christian principles. The Catholic charities, in particular, complained that the public authorities in the Catholic diaspora (outside the Rhineland and the South) often disregarded the legal requirement that children be placed "insofar as possible" (paragraph 69 of the RJWG) in institutions or families of their own confession. Maria Kiene cited one case in which a provincial administrator held that he had the legal right to place a Catholic child in a Protestant home if it cost less to do so.[42] Protestants voiced fewer specific complaints regarding the placement of children; but they shared Catholics' concern with what they saw as the growing indifference of public child welfare officials to Christianity. A Pastor Eggebrecht reported that in the Prussian province of Saxony the dominant attitude of Youth Bureau officials was "that it is modern to replace confessional with general religious education" and that "belief in progress and culture, in the ideal of freedom of conscience . . ., combined with a deep consciousness of duty, is the best foundation for education for proper citizenship."[43] There were fears, too, that children in public institutions (for example, health camps) were not encouraged to attend religious services. Again, as we saw in Chapter 6, this development was all the more alarming because it seemed to parallel the drive to eliminate religious instruction from the public schools.

Partly in response to these developments and to the challenge of secular humanism and Social Democracy, many in the Christian charities moved rapidly in the mid-1920s toward a more consciously religious perspective on their own work. The official religious neutrality of the new Republic, the cultural confrontation with radical socialism, and the development of mass culture since the beginning of the century had already fostered a kind of siege mentality among conservative Christians. The passage of the RJWG and the expansion of state welfare programs had then confronted the charities with the immense task of securing their interests in the Youth Bureau of every city and county in the country. They were thrown back of necessity on the financial, organizational, and ideological resources of the churches.

As the DCV and its subsidiaries closed ranks for the defense of the faith against secular communal administrations, Catholics turned to the church to provide the money, personnel, organization, political clout, and access to the broader Catholic public required to build up a comprehensive Catholic child welfare system. The Diocesan Caritas Associations, closely associated with the diocesan administrations, became increasingly important in the organization and coordination of local Catholic charitable activity, while after 1924 the clergy became increasingly involved in child welfare organizations. At the same time the Catholic charities turned inward, and to the church, to recover or reinforce the ideological sources of their autonomy, their independent pedagogical mission, and the commitment of their volunteers.

For Protestants the turn to the church was a more difficult transition, since the relationship between the Inner Mission and the Protestant churches had historically been less close. Like their Catholic counterparts, however, Protestant organizers necessarily relied on the church for the organizational and financial resources to construct a Protestant child welfare system parallel to the public Youth Bureaus. The Protestant Youth and Welfare Offices established after 1922 relied heavily on the support of local church authorities and the involvement of the clergy, as did the new Protestant State Welfare Services, which served the same functions as the DCV's diocesan offices. And in contrast to older associations, the myriad new Protestant child welfare organizations formed after 1922 had much closer ties to the church than to the state bureaucracy. Moreover, by 1922 voices within the Inner Mission were urging greater attention to religious fundamentals as the best guarantee of the continued independence of Protestant charities from the expanding public bureaucracy. Wilhelm Backhausen, for example, wrote in that year, "In the face of the united, powerful front of public welfare agencies . . . the Inner Mission must pull itself together . . . and above all recall to mind its own unique character" rooted in the gospel.[44] The revival of conservative (or, better, fundamentalist or fundamentalizing) Protestant theology under Karl Barth, Friedrich Gogarten, and others encouraged this trend in the course of the 1920s—in part by injecting a "neo-pietistic" note into the Protestant churches which brought them closer to the traditions of the Inner Mission.[45] In 1931 the *Evangelische Jugendhilfe* argued that "the Protestant organizations must once again recall to mind their real 'employer,' Christ."[46] The Christian charities' response to the growth of public welfare, then, involved not only the organizational expansion mentioned earlier but also a deepening of commitment to religious principles and to the missionary role of charity work.

Religion, Pedagogy, and the Youth Bureau

The revival of self-consciously confessional pedagogy was an important part of this "reconfessionalization" of the charities. The expansion of public child welfare programs brought home to Protestants the need to "call up," as Pastor Hermann Beutel told the Inner Mission in 1924, "a whole army of pedagogues . . . to grapple with and rebuild Protestant pedagogy."[47] In 1928 Joachim Beckmann voiced the perspective of the emerging Protestant pedagogy in the *Evangelische Jugendhilfe*:

> We have neither a personal nor a social ideal, not even that of a Christian person or society. . . . The Protestant pedagogical goal can only be oriented to the Word of God, the Gospel, from which the Protestant faith springs. . . . There is, then, no Protestant pedagogical ideal in the sense of an ideal of man, state, society, people, church. Protestant faith sees through the fundamental sinfulness of every ideal. . . . We become members of the community of Jesus Christ through faithful and obedient hearing of the Word of God. . . . We have in fact nothing more to do than to preach the gospel. Precondition, means, and goal of our pedagogy are one and the same: the Word of God.[48]

Catholics, as representatives of a much more culturally, intellectually, and socially coherent community and a more liturgical faith, tended to take the specificity of their pedagogy for granted and to concentrate on securing Catholic education for Catholic children. Here, too, however, there was a growing sense of the centrality of religion to socialization. Joseph Beeking, for example, argued in 1926 that the bureaucratic spirit and religious neutrality of the new Youth Bureaus demanded not only the expansion of Catholic organizations but also a "further deepening of the . . . consciously Christian ethos" guiding their work.[49] This emphasis was reflected and reinforced by papal condemnation of Italian fascist education and the papal encyclical on the Christian education of children published on December 31, 1929.

This confessional orientation necessarily led Christian thinkers to reiterate traditional conceptions of pedagogy which emphasized the imposition of values on the pupil by a teacher whose own religious beliefs are well thought out and deeply held. In the words of Adolf Stahl, a leading figure in the Inner Mission, the "Protestant personality" was both the goal and the means of "Protestant education."[50] Otto Wehn stated this traditional approach in eloquent terms in the *Zentralblatt* in 1927: what was decisive in the pedagogical relationship, he argued, was that the teacher possess "superiority of person in all things" and the will to express his inward "force of character" through the "creative shaping of the young . . . person."[51] Christians of both faiths agreed, too, that without the common ground of a shared ideology or faith, the necessary relationship of trust and mutual understanding could not develop between teacher and child: the "necessary collaboration" of the pupil, Pastor Otto Ohl, director of the Inner Mission in the Rhineland, argued in 1926, "is possible only if the psychic orientation, the orientation of the will of the person in need, is in conformity with that of his helper."[52]

The implication of these ideas was clearly that *all* education must be religious, or at least ideological. If the task of socialization was to impart values, then it must be clear *which* values were to be imparted. And if (as the Catholic Karl Vossen wrote in 1927) "socialization is possible only on the basis of a firmly founded specific worldview," then it was clear that only people with firm ideological or religious commitments could socialize children.[53] Furthermore, most Christians did not believe that humanism could form such a positive foundation for individual morality. As Karl Neuendörfer remarked in 1925, education "must proceed from the inner connection between order and religion. . . . For the final foundation of the imperatives of a moral order can only lie in God."[54] In any case, Christians did not believe that, as public administrators often assumed, humanistic principles were "neutral." As one Protestant critic put it, the Youth Bureau "has no right to socialize Protestant children on the basis of ethical humanism."[55] Nor, finally, could religious faith be simply tacked on to an otherwise neutral humanistic education—by means, for example, of separate daily religious instruction. Rather, it must suffuse the entire life and rearing of the child.

These conclusions were fateful for the relationship between the charities and the Youth Bureau. For the republican state was avowedly ideologically neutral: indeed, in order to be a democratic "state of the whole people" *(Volksstaat)* in an ideologically and culturally divided nation, it must necessarily be so. The obvious conclusion was that the Youth Bureau could not socialize. The political and religious neutrality of the state, Joachim Beckmann pointed out, "necessarily implies the renunciation of any pedagogical goal. . . . A concrete pedagogical goal is possible only on the concrete, individual basis of a specific worldview or religion. Here the state must fail."[56] Otto Ohl concluded similarly that "because the state, public welfare, is neutral, it must surrender its pedagogical tasks to the specific ideological private welfare organizations."[57] And in a series of seminal publications in 1926 and 1927, Karl Vossen held that the private associations had legally enforceable "jurisdiction" over children belonging to their ideological or religious communities, and that the Youth Bureau must hand over each individual case to the proper private organization—a suggestion supported in 1925 by the annual conference of the KFV.[58]

The Peace Conferences of 1925

To the secular child welfare "experts" these demands appeared to threaten the very existence of the entire public child welfare system. As Immanuel Fischer commented, simply handing children over to the religious charities would mean a disastrous "hollowing out" of public welfare.[59] The socialist journal *Arbeiterwohlfahrt*, which supported the absorption of all child welfare work by public agencies, accused the Christian charities of attempting to reduce the Youth Bureaus to mere "official distribution points" for their own work.[60] Worse still, many feared that such a system would give rise to divisive struggles over individual cases which could cripple the Youth Bureaus entirely.

There were some attempts in the late 1920s to evade this cultural conflict through an appeal to science. The pedagogical reform movement claimed to be developing methods which could be adopted by educators of any confession or ideology. Erich Weniger hoped that the "autonomous laws" of correctional pedagogy, expressed in "purely methodological rules," would impose themselves on all ideological camps.[61] As Aloys Fischer observed, pedagogy in this form sought to "remove itself from the battle of the ideological parties and stabilize itself through the form of a scientific falsifiability which is binding for all."[62] Psychoanalytical and psychotherapeutic child psychology similarly laid claim to the mantle of science, promising to provide the foundations for a neutral method at least in correctional education, as did the emerging discipline of therapeutic pedagogy *(Heilpädagogik)*, which applied modern psychological theory to correctional education.

But "scientific" pedagogy was still in its infancy in the 1920s, and the radical democratic rhetoric and left-liberal identification of much of the youth movement and "reform pedagogy" were objectionable to conservative Christians. So was its rejection of the idea of sin. Psychoanalytic thought, moreover, was at this stage flatly rejected by most nonsocialists. Nonreligious pedagogical traditionalists such as Otto Wehn considered psychotherapeutic theories "not even useful as food for thought."[63] And though Catholics were relatively open to Adlerian ideas by the end of the decade, for the time being they just as often rejected psychoanalytic theory as dangerously naturalistic and even perverse.

The failure of these scientific disciplines to provide the basis for cooperation between religious and ideological camps was fateful, for it meant that a growing number of child welfare advocates turned to a set of quasimystical, quasi-racialist ideas that quite possibly predisposed them toward acceptance of National Socialist rhetoric. These ideas were articulated with striking clarity in 1925, at a series of confidential conferences between selected representatives of the Red Cross, the DCV, the Inner Mission, and Workers' Welfare called by the DVöpF in the hope of establishing an intellectual or programmatic foundation for cooperation. At the initial meeting (held in Eisenach in late April 1925) the first speaker, Mayor Carl Neinhaus of Heidelberg, attempted to develop a theoretical foundation for public welfare programs. Neinhaus, operating from the Protestant nationalist political tradition, interpreted the flourishing of corporatism in the Weimar state—of which the RJWG was but one example—as an existential crisis of state sovereignty. The recent literature, he said, constituted "a great obituary for the state"—an obituary justified by "a glance at the events of the past few years, in which newly formed economic interest organizations of employers and employees and other groups of people, rapidly growing in importance, have more and more sought to set themselves in the place of the state." The Weimar state was "corroded by parties and conflicts"; Germany suffered from an "atrophy of the idea of the state and the will to the state"; and "ideologically based communities" were attempting to "depose the state intellectually." He discovered an antidote in the Romantic concept of the *Volkstum,* the people and its unique qualities, which was currently being rediscovered in neo-Romanticism and organological theories of the state. The *Volkstum* was a *"corpus mysticum,* from whose invisible bonds we cannot loose ourselves, without which intellectual and moral individual life is not imaginable. . . . It is the one really natural community which, despite all the disintegrative tendencies of our times, encompasses the people of today, just like the family." And just as Christians were involved in child welfare for Christ's sake, so the state created welfare programs "for the sake of our common *Volkstum.*" The cultural and political tensions which were rending the corporatist system, in other words, would be transcended through a common allegiance to a quasi-racial, nonrational, ideal "national community." "German" Catholics, socialists, Protestants, and Jews could all cooperate in service to the *Volkstum.*[64]

Otto Ohl elaborated further on these themes at a second meeting, held in Heidelberg in August 1925. He too posited the existence of a racial, nonrational "community" which transcended all ideological divisions and could therefore serve as the basis of a universal welfare system. This shared community was "the biological," "what is in the blood," "unconscious will and life." And both public welfare programs and private philanthropy served this community, the *Volkstum.* Thus, Ohl concluded, it was not so "that diametrically divergent movements and aspirations are in fact leading us completely apart." Instead, "an ultimate will, outside of ourselves and yet working through us, transcendent and immanent at the same time, is guiding us"—whether it be called God, the *Volkstum,* or history. The charities, he said, must recognize that "*Volkstum* without the state, without law and power," would dissolve into anarchy; and yet governments must recognize that the *Volkstum* expresses itself "not only in the legally regulated, bureaucratic state, but . . . in the greatest degree also in freely growing life expressions . . . [and] above all also in the great . . . ideological groups."[65]

These ideas were attractive to some participants in the conference. At the April meeting in Eisenach, Grüneisen of the Red Cross, for example, saw in it the potential salvation of private interconfessional welfare work; he announced that Neinhaus's ideas summed up the "inner program of the Red Cross." Polligkeit, too, while he remained neutral with respect to Neinhaus's metaphysics, spoke of the common "longing for unity," of the "oppressive feeling of being isolated, of not being completely united in a community with the other orientations," and of the need to "spiritually deepen" welfare work to overcome these divisions.[66]

But most remained unconvinced by Neinhaus's and Ohl's arguments. In particular, the Catholics and more conservative Protestants rejected the speakers' concept of the "national community" *(Volksgemeinschaft)* outright. Rejecting the "organic" ideal of the state, they championed instead the principle of natural law and that more voluntarist conception of the relationship between state and society which we have seen expressed in the conflicts of the 1910s. At the August meeting, the Catholic Karl Neuendörfer in particular completely rejected Neinhaus's analysis and conclusions. The state, he held, was not a spiritual unity but a creature of law and power; only the charities represented the "vital source" of society's ethical life-energy. For this reason the distinction between public and private welfare must remain clear. Moreover, the church could not surrender to the state on the basis of any high-flying theories about the nature of the German *Volkstum* or its claims on its members. Above all, the state must not enter into competition with Christianity on the basis of a quasi-mystical ideology of the *Volkstum:* "That would be a new paganism, if the state wanted to make . . . a god of itself."[67]

Stahl concurred with his Catholic colleague. He pointed out that it was not so easy to transcend in fact the conflicts that Neinhaus wished away in theory: the "empirical state is not the same as the ideal state," he said, and while the latter might be an "organism," the former was a mere "organization." That being the case, there was no getting around the fact that the different parts of the *Volkstum* were at war with one another. With some prescience he pointed out that in order to impose "organic" unity "one would have to extinguish the contrasts, and that we don't want. The life force springs from the wealth of variety and tension." The strength of each ideological camp's welfare work lay precisely in the conviction of absolute correctness: therefore, attempts at reconciliation in theory—the "method of coming together inwardly"—necessarily has limits, "and will not alone lead us to the goal."[68]

As Stahl's and Neuendörfer's comments reveal, the authoritarian potentials of Ohl's and Neinhaus's ideas were not hidden from contemporaries. Although the latter two men both attempted to use the idea of the *Volkstum* to stabilize the corporatist Weimar system, it was already clear by the mid-1920s that such ideas *could* form the foundation of a fascist alternative to pluralist, corporatist democracy and its conflicts. In any event, after 1933 Otto Ohl became perhaps the most perceptive and persistent critic within the Inner Mission of National Socialism, while Neinhaus joined the NSDAP in May of 1933 and was active in Nazi welfare work until 1945.

But for the time being, in 1925–26, the threat of this racialist, organicist populism receded in the minds of Christians before another threat: that of democratic socialism.

Socialism, Christianity, and Public Child Welfare

As we saw in Chapter 6, it was not only the expansion of public programs that seemed to threaten Christian culture and the Christian social order with creeping socialism. In the 1920s the socialist welfare organization, Workers' Welfare, was also growing rapidly, establishing itself as an effective competitor of the Christian charities.

Workers' Welfare rejected virtually every central assumption on which the Christian charities were founded. It argued that the bourgeois, capitalist social order itself *necessarily* led to the moral and physical "endangerment" of children, which would be abolished only by the socialist revolution. In an article in the organization's journal in 1928, Paula Kurgass argued that "in our social situation we are all more or less endangered. . . . One cannot make people believe that one should be 'good' in a society built on injustice and lies."[69] Accordingly, bourgeois child welfare served the interests not of children but of the capitalist social order, imposing false consciousness on children (for example, in Christian reformatories), obscuring and depoliticizing the destructive essence of capitalism, and reinforcing class power by creating relations of dependence and deference between middle-class "benefactors" and working-class clients. In some cases, in fact, Workers' Welfare seems to have acted locally partly as a kind of self-defense organization against correctional education: the president of the Regional Court in Dortmund, for example, complained in 1925 that Workers' Welfare was "directly hostile to all official socialization measures"—that is, correctional education.[70]

More important, Workers' Welfare argued that the private charities should be abolished in favor of a purely public welfare system. It denounced subsidies for the private organizations (although it also received considerable sums) as a means of creating an alternative private administration alongside and in opposition to "the real and legal bearers of welfare work, the self-governing communes."[71] It refused to join the *Liga* of private welfare organizations. It rejected the principle of "subsidiarity" as an assault on freedom of conscience (forcing those in need to seek aid from Christian charities). And it saw the corporatism of the RJWG as a simple power grab by the middle class. In Hedwig Wachenheim's words, the "insertion of private charities" into the Youth Bureau had "succeeded in preserving old privileges for the bourgeoisie."[72] Its own aim was to bring about the democratization of the public welfare system by recruiting working people as volunteers and social workers. At the same time, in its training of those social workers and volunteers for the Youth Bureaus, Workers' Welfare was guided by the sense that children must be educated, as Rudolf Schlosser put it, to be "the makers and the bearers of a new society"; it was therefore "not the main point that the child get along well in the world, but that the will to community is strengthened in it, and that the existing social order therefore become intolerable to it."[73] Its aim, in other words, was to prepare children for the revolution and for life in the society of the future. And as we have seen, Christianity did not seem to have a place in that society.

By the end of the 1920s, Workers' Welfare was still a small organization compared to the Christian charities; it claimed to handle only some 10,000 child welfare cases in 1929, for example.[74] Nevertheless, it appeared to be growing rapidly both in size and in confidence and competence, and it seemed to many Christians to pose a terrible threat. A Catholic observer summed up Christian responses to the growth and program of Workers' Welfare in 1929: "We are dealing," he wrote, "with a threat to the roots and foundations of our Christian culture."[75]

Not surprisingly, the conflict between the Christian charities and Workers' Welfare came to a head in Cologne, a city at once dominated by the Catholic establishment and home to one of the most successful chapters of Workers' Welfare. In 1926 a bitter fight erupted within the Youth Bureau there, sparking a national debate on the problem. By spring the struggle threatened, as Otto Ohl remarked, to "be the death of our German welfare system."[76]

The conflict in Cologne centered on a simple question: Under what conditions should the Youth Bureau assign a volunteer social worker or legal guardian connected with Workers' Welfare, or place a child in a foster family found by that organization, and in which cases should it choose a volunteer or family suggested by a Christian organization? Protestants and particularly Catholics held that children should be raised in the faith in which they had been baptized. The rise of Workers' Welfare, however, created a gnarly problem, for millions of socialists were practicing or at least nominal Christians; and very few had bothered to leave the church officially. As Workers' Welfare pointed out, for example, in the Rhineland 95 percent of the population were baptized Christians, yet in elections in 1925 the socialist parties had received about 30 percent of the vote. Workers' Welfare argued that the children of these socialist voters should be cared for by socialist organizations, since for them Christian thought and ritual—including baptism—had become essentially meaningless.[77] As Rudolf Schlosser remarked, the "inherited religious world has collapsed for the class-conscious proletarian."[78] In any case, because so very small a proportion of the population had officially renounced membership in the

Christian churches, the demand that church membership be the basis for the assignment of cases amounted to an attempt to exclude Workers' Welfare (as well as other nonreligious groups such as the Red Cross or the Fifth Welfare Association) from child welfare work almost completely—if not also to "reclaim" the children of socialist parents wherever possible. The struggle, Hedwig Wachenheim protested, appeared to be a "cultural war [*Kulturkampf*] against socialism."[79]

Socialist representatives therefore rejected all formal rules and routine procedures, and argued that the Youth Bureau must decide in each individual case which private organization to rely on. In this socialists were supported by nonreligious "experts" such as Neinhaus and Storck, on the grounds that the Youth Bureau as a neutral agency should be the "protector of the freedom of the child's personality" against the competing ideological groupings.[80]

But for committed Christians such a solution was completely unacceptable, for it meant that whoever controlled the Youth Bureau controlled the distribution of cases to the private organizations. In fact, at the conference of 1925 Workers' Welfare spokesman Erich Heimerich had deplored the fact that the corporatist system created by the RJWG had created "a kind of parallel government by the associations . . . a kind of class state" in which the exploitation of the workers was perpetuated; but whereas Neinhaus insisted on the ideological *neutrality* of the "community" of the *Volkstum/* state, Heimerich insisted that the idea "of 'freeing welfare from politics'" was simply "a chimera," since "there is no such thing as a neutral state."[81] The implication of this statement was clear: not theoretical discussions but a struggle for power within the Youth Bureaus would determine the outcome of the ideological conflicts plaguing child welfare. The Christian charities demanded, therefore, that distribution of cases be made on the basis of objective facts—in other words, baptism. Protestants were less adamant than Catholics, since the Protestant population was less bound to the church and religious practice; moreover, some hoped to achieve a "permeation of Workers' Welfare with the ideas of the gospel" (in Ohl's words), and argued against taking the all-or-nothing position of the Catholics. Yet in the end Protestants too had to conclude that baptism must, in principle, be the decisive factor: as Niemöller put it, Protestants could not afford to "take the standpoint that baptism is a farce."[82] In any case, Protestants too soon became convinced that Workers' Welfare was seeking a "political solution" rather than reconciliation.[83]

By 1929, then, the Christian charities were bracing for a political battle with Workers' Welfare and socialist municipalities. One important aspect of this preparation was the creation of a more centralized and cooperative organizational structure: in November 1928, for example, Protestant organizations involved in day care and reformatory work formed a new National

Conference of Protestant Child Care (Reichskonferenz für evangelische Kinderpflege), while Catholic youth groups, the DCV, the *Volksverein,* the Catholic trade unions, the Catholic parents' groups, mothers' associations, and the KDF all came together to form the Catholic Task Force Child Welfare (Katholische Reichsarbeitsgemeinschaft Kinderwohl) in March 1929.

Democratic Pedagogy

For Christian groups this sense of impending conflict was reinforced by the simultaneous threat from the communal Youth Bureaus. The chairman of the DCV's Committee on Child Welfare told its members in April 1929 that the "assault from the socialist side on confessional institutions and confessional welfare work on the one hand, and the attempts at expansion by the state and other organizations on the other hand, demand from us united action in all questions which arise." And the EREV concluded in April 1928 that both the "bureaucratization of the Youth Bureaus and their permeation by Workers' Welfare" might lead to the complete exclusion of the Protestant charities from public child welfare.[84] Secular social reform and public child welfare programs were becoming associated in some Christians' minds with socialism, as parts of a whole complex of developments threatening the values, social institutions, and political arrangements of Christian society.

The identification of socialism and public child welfare programs was lent credibility, moreover, by the fact that in the late 1920s both socialists and some pedagogues from the youth movement were creating a new pedagogy which was self-consciously democratic. They regarded this process as a logical part of the consolidation of democratic culture in the new Republic. The central ideas of left-wing reform pedagogy were developed primarily, however, by people involved in correctional education; and they were a response to precisely the crisis of correctional pedagogy—an extension, in fact, of what I have called the "new" pedagogy of the immediate prewar years.

Drawing the obvious conclusions from the observations of middle-class reformers in the prewar period, socialists in the 1920s explicitly argued that classic bourgeois pedagogy was inappropriate for working-class children, since the latter were simply not accessible to appeals to religious sensibilities or the Christian conception of authority. In Walter Friedländer's words, the proletarian child gained from its milieu and from its experiences no understanding of "authoritarian discipline . . .; in line with his experience, the proletarian in no way sees in the adult and in his teacher a godlike creature."[85] Moreover, socialists in particular held that the whole idea of transmitting values through instruction made no sense in the case of proletarian children. While Otto Wehn spoke of the need for the teacher to be

possessed of spiritual "superiority in all things," Karl Mennicke, director of
the Workers' Welfare school of social work in Berlin, argued that most proletarian children lived not from intellect but "from instinct, because the
preconditions for the formation of a personal intellectual world of values
are lacking."[86] For this reason the most impressive and coherent "pedagogical personality" would fail to have much impact on proletarian children.
What was most important was that the child take part in a healthy *community,* learning sociality and morality in the course of daily life.

As Mennicke himself noted, his views on the subject placed him at odds
with Hermann Nohl, Eduard Spranger, and the whole intellectual world of
bourgeois pedagogy, "reformed" or not. Nevertheless, there were many
middle-class pedagogues who agreed that it was necessary to develop a pedagogy appropriate to a class society. At the 1927 conference of the AFET,
Walter Hoffmann asserted: "The social stratification of our people is connected with a differentiation of understandings of life and life goals. . . . It
is therefore not in our discretion to choose which ideals we wish to implant;
rather we must [determine] . . . what social and ethical forces slumber in
the child."[87]

Whatever their position with regard to the question of class, however, the
pedagogical left—socialist or middle-class democratic—was united by precisely this conviction that pedagogy must proceed "from the child" *(vom
Kinde aus)* rather than from the educator's ideological commitments. It thus
abrogated the authority-centered and value-centered models of accultura-
tion on which traditional and above all religious pedagogy rested. Invoking
Rousseau, Fröbel, Pestalozzi, and the traditions of Idealism, the left argued
that the child must be allowed and encouraged to discover and construct
the world, its own character, and its relationship to society on its own terms.
As Mennicke put it, the teacher must be able to "'give the youth a chance,'
as the Americans say, that is, to create opportunities for experience, experimentation, and to prove themselves."[88]

The argument was made most forcefully—and in its most extreme
form—by Wilhelm Paulsen. The child, he held, "understands its surroundings with the resources within it. . . . Every arbitrary intervention in the development of the child is therefore ruled out automatically; its psychic imperatives must be unconditionally respected. . . . Compulsion and authority
are—in psychic terms—destructive forces . . .; the *goal* imposed arbitrarily
from without ruins the clear . . . vital line which the child's individuality
follows." With this realization, he continued, traditional pedagogy becomes
untenable; for with it "the *ideological* basis of socialization falls; every attempt to impose a religious, political, ethical, or aesthetic belief through
compulsion or suggestion falls. Schools of ideology . . . prevent spiritual
progress because they . . . destroy the creative powers of imagination." The
child, he concluded, "should be a creator, and not one who is created."[89]

Few people, whether socialists or reform pedagogues, would have carried these ideas to the logical conclusions that Paulsen did: but many shared his assumptions. Storck, for example, remarked that the child had "equal rights as the bearer of new values for the future," while Nohl called the child "not wax, but a seed."[90]

For committed Christians these ideas were incompatible not merely with the teachings of their faith but with social order and indeed with human freedom. Less conservative people were more sanguine: both Alfred Fritz of the Inner Mission and Joseph Beeking of the DCV hoped that it would in fact be possible to reach agreement on common pedagogical methods. The influence of Montessorian pedagogy made Catholics in particular fairly receptive to the idea of socialization "from the child," as did the work of Don Bosco, whose Salesian order renounced the use of corporal punishment. The Catholic child welfare journal for the Rhineland, *Jugendrettung,* remarked in 1929 that "the well-developed sense of autonomy is the natural foundation for the sense of moral dignity: coercion at every turn . . . leads to the build-up and perversion of drives. . . . If freedom must then be granted after all, then there is often a relapse into indiscipline and dissolution."[91] There was even Catholic interest in Adlerian psychoanalytic theory. And Protestants could base a more democratic approach to pedagogy on the concept of the brotherhood of student and teacher imposed by the shared burden of sin. But Christians could hardly have agreed with Walter Hoffmann that to view the wayward child as a "sinner" was a sign that one was beholden to "the ideas of past times," with the psychiatrist Isemann that "religion is not the goal of life but a means, which can be replaced by ethical and general social ideas," or with socialists that religion was irrelevant to the entire working class.[92]

More fundamentally, conservative Christians viewed socialization as a process by which the child was prepared to become a member of a preexisting social and cultural order through the internalization of the principle of authority and the authoritative inculcation of a set of positive values and beliefs. They therefore genuinely feared that the coddled products of the new democratic pedagogy would be unable to restrain their animal passions, and that the result would be crime, abandonment, corruption, and chaos. Subject to the internal tyranny of their appetites, they would also be slaves to the outward tyranny of the mass; they would become mere "herd people," unable to oppose the arbitrary will of the majority from the solid ground of allegiance to any principle.[93] It was all very well to speak of class-specific pedagogy, argued Alfred Fritz, but one had to ask whether educators "should create characterless people whose standard is 'people say and do such-and-such,' or people of character, who can if necessary stand in painful contradiction to their surroundings. . . . The pressing question arises here of a . . . community which is formed not by blood and class but by obedience to conscience."[94] In light of later events, of course, this position appears extraordinarily sympathetic. At the time, however, it was a criticism of the *left* rather than of fascism. The remarks of the Protestant Pastor Wilhelm Backhausen in 1921 neatly sum up the spirit that moved pedagogical conservatives: "Freedom through freedom is utopia, [for] moral freedom can come only through obedience, that is, by way of authority."[95]

What made the new pedagogy particularly frightening to Christians, however, was the fact that its proponents saw themselves as the creators of a pedagogy which was appropriate not only to the psychology of modern youth but also to the structure of the modern state. They believed that a just and harmonious modern society must be based on the active participation of its citizens, and that only a free pedagogy could prepare children for that kind of participation as adults. Otto Flug announced in 1928 that "the new democratic state . . . finds in that ideal of life which has come out of the youth movement the proper form of socialization for responsible citizens."[96] And Erich Weniger summed up the situation cogently—and ominously: "There are today people working in correctional education who have derived from the fact of the present state and its present form—if you will, from the ideology of this state—certain motives and goals for their pedagogical work and who felt in their conscience responsible to this state, as its agents, for the accomplishment of these goals."[97] Such pronouncements seemed to raise the possibility that the Youth Bureaus would abandon the idea of neutrality and seek to impose a democratic and anti-Christian ideology on children. The fact that in Westphalia in 1927 and 1928 both the KPD *and* the SPD called in the provincial parliament for the deconfessionalization of correctional education only confirmed these anxieties.[98]

This fear that a relentlessly expanding public welfare system would become committed to de-Christianization, or at least to secular humanism, was by the late 1920s part of a much larger complex of anxieties sparked by developments in many different areas of welfare and public health policy. The decriminalization of prostitution in 1927 was intended to make way for a more effective medical response to venereal disease, but it horrified conservative Christians. A law of May 1926 which made abortion a misdemeanor rather than a felony (and accordingly reduced penalties) and a growing campaign for further reforms, discussions of a further reform of divorce law, and official toleration and even encouragement of family planning propaganda and services also seemed to threaten the family. And again, the struggle over religious education provided a threatening backdrop for this struggle within welfare policy. By 1930 some conservative Christians—among them Elisabeth Zillken of the KFV—were concluding that the entire Weimar welfare system was contributing to the hollowing out of Christian culture and thus to a collapse of morality and individual and social responsibility, establishing a downward spiral which could end only in complete anarchy. When the depression struck, a number of voices within the charities welcomed it as the only effective antidote to this looming disaster.[99]

The Crisis of Correctional Education

The disillusionment of the charities was heightened by a deepening crisis of the system of correctional education—a program whose troubles provide a kind of summary of the problems of child welfare policy in the late 1920s.

In the first place, the new pedagogy was developed particularly in correctional education, and there were some efforts throughout the 1920s to put democratic or at least less authoritarian pedagogy into practice in the reformatories. Between 1917 and 1921 Karl Wilker, a youth movement member, introduced a panoply of radical reforms at the Lindenhof public reformatory in Berlin. He stopped shaving inmates' heads upon arrival; allowed them to paint their rooms colors other than institutional green; removed the iron bars on the bedroom doors and windows; abolished the most boring and grinding work; read aloud not only from the Bible but from Lao-tzu, Nietzsche, and Rabindranath Tagore; permitted inmates to organize their own recreational activities; allowed parents to visit on Sundays and winked at the presence of "secret brides" posing as sisters; established representative "self-government" (in consultation with himself) and a "Boys' Court"; allowed nude gymnastics; took his charges to museums; and so forth.[100]

Yet such experiments were quite rare. The vast majority of those who actually staffed and operated the reformatories were conservative Christian pedagogues or penal reformers. The Revolution failed to do more than frighten and anger these people; from the beginning of the Republic to its demise, they remained indifferent and often hostile to newfangled "democratic" ideas. And they were able to retain control of almost all reformatories; despite the support of the director of the Berlin State Youth Bureau, for example, Wilker was eventually forced to resign from the Lindenhof by a rebellion of older staff members.

By the late 1920s, in fact, the efforts of the pedagogical left to penetrate the reformatories had sparked a self-conscious reaction among more conservative practitioners, particularly in the Inner Mission. At the AFET's annual conference in 1926, Pastor Hermann Büchsel issued a virtual declaration of war against the new pedagogy, demanding that educators have the "courage" to impose "a strict and joyous discipline," denouncing "democracy in the reformatory," and proclaiming his allegiance to "patriarchalism." "Evil," he reminded his listeners, "rules the world, and even children . . . in reformatories are subject to the mysterious and terrible power of evil and of sin"—from which they must be rescued through unconditional obedience to the director's will.[101] Büchsel's Catholic co-speaker rejected this tirade, suggesting that authority was effective only if it were recognized and affirmed; and the director of Hamburg's Youth Bureau remarked, "The previous century speaks."[102] But many practitioners seem to have agreed with Büchsel: Otto Flug noted of the AFET conference in the following year, at which the keynote speaker elucidated many of the arguments of reform pedagogy, that there was a "broad undercurrent in the assembly . . . which hardly corresponded to the new pedagogical spirit and . . . the intentions of the leading personalities."[103] An attempt within the AFET's steering committee to reach agreement on a few basic principles—including the idea that socialization was possible only on the basis of a distinct worldview, and yet that children should be educated for "freedom and self-determination"—broke down, in 1927, just as had the DVöpF's special conferences in 1925.[104]

The result of the perpetuation of traditional methods was the continued escalation of the struggle within and over correctional education. The attacks on correctional education which had characterized the last years before the war resumed with redoubled force after the stabilization of early 1924. Socialists and communists in state and provincial parliaments were most active in condemning the system and demanding its reform. But some critics within the reform pedagogy camp were also unsparing in their criticism. In 1928 the Gilde Soziale Arbeit, a group of left-liberal, socialist, and youth movement social workers founded in 1925, formed a "Task Force for the Reform of Correctional Education." The mass press, too, was relentless in its sensationalist coverage of scandals and revolts in correctional education. The culmination of this publicistic campaign was the production of a play by Peter Martin Lampel in December 1928 titled *Revolt in the Reformatory*. Enthusiastically received by the public, the piece unleashed a storm of discussion and criticism which included public meetings (at which former inmates told all) and inflammatory pieces in popular papers. By 1930 Gustav von Mann of the DCV would speak of a "frontal assault" on correctional education by the mass media.[105]

The escalation of resistance within the reformatories themselves was equally significant. This resistance may have been reinforced by the growing influence of communism among young workers. Berlin's State Youth Bureau reported that "the great majority of minors committed after graduation from school are influenced by and oriented toward radical politics. In this orientation they often come into the reformatories with a fanatical hatred and deep-seated defensiveness toward their future teachers and plot revolts and disorders."[106] Probably more important was the fact that the RJWG had raised the latest age at which young people could be committed from eighteen to twenty, making for an older and less tractable institutional population. Most important still, however, was surely the poor standard of pay and training among reformatory staff, and the survival in many institutions of methods and attitudes appropriate to the late nineteenth century at best. But whatever the reasons, by the end of the decade the growing opposition of reformatory inmates climaxed in a veritable wave of mass revolts. There were at least four in 1927 and 1928, two in March 1929 (including one at the Lindenhof), and one each in September and November 1929 and January, February, March, September, and October 1930.[107] In the aftermath of the revolt at Scheuen, near Celle, in February 1930, one inmate was beaten to death and others were seriously injured. The ensuing scandal was made all the worse by the attempts of Knaut and the State Youth Bureau of Berlin (which placed children in Scheuen) to discredit the revolt as the product of psychopathy, communism, and press sensationalism. A revolt and subsequent trial in Waldhof-Templin brought to light sexual abuse and brutal beatings by a staff including six Nazis. A third, in Rickling, ended the career of a director whose success in extracting labor from his charges had earned him the title "the Stinnes of the Inner Mission." These revolts and the attempt to cover them up or dismiss them wrecked the credibility of correctional education. One pedagogical reformer, Kurt Bondy, summed up the general mood on the left in 1930: "Better no reformatories," he concluded, "than bad ones."[108]

It was decisive for child welfare policy that the growing opposition of the populace to correctional education threatened to compromise the work of the Youth Bureaus in other programs that were less confrontational in character and often affected many more people, such as infant welfare programs and general *Familienfürsorge*. One administrator in the Rhineland reported in 1927 that a social worker in his district had been greeted in a rural community with curses and rock throwing after a child there had been removed from its family; the parents told her, "We thought you were here for the poor people. But you spy and turn us in to the courts. So, you're one of *those*." Teachers and clergy who cooperated with the Youth Bureau in finding cases for correctional education, the administrator reported, were in the same situation. As he remarked, this problem "is of a kind which could destroy at one blow everything that has been achieved in welfare work" in rural areas.[109]

The persistence of the repressive strategy in correctional education, in other words, threatened the success of other programs based on a more participatory, integrative model. As a result, many people who worked in the Youth Bureaus were increasingly alienated from correctional education—which was in most states administered by provincial rather than local agencies and carried out for the most part by private Christian organizations. In 1930 Leo Pelle, the director of a county Youth Bureau and an important figure in child welfare after World War II, asked whether the Youth Bureaus could still petition the courts to commit children at all, given the abuses which were coming to light and the fact that they had no influence on the reformatories themselves.[110]

One response to this deepening crisis, as prior to World War I, was a growing emphasis on the organic, inherited mental "abnormality" of children in correctional education. While psychiatry seems to have made little progress in creating an empirical foundation for itself, the growing influence and prestige of the medical profession generally consolidated the influence of biologistic models of "deviancy" in the 1920s. In fact, estimates of the proportion of children in reformatories who were "hereditarily tainted" *(erblich belastet),* "inferior" *(minderwertig),* or "abnormal" sometimes reached new heights. In a classic study of 1918 Adalbert Gregor and Else Voigtländer concluded that between 85 and 95 percent of reformatory inmates were *"erblich belastet,"* and even the Prussian government conceded that 31 percent of those in correctional education were not "normal" (up from 9 percent in 1906).[111]

By the middle of the 1920s a growing number of psychiatrists were increasingly cautious in their assessment of the nature of "hereditary abnormality." Whereas in the 1900s it had been common to speak of a "hereditary tendency to theft," a "hereditary lack of discipline," "hereditary vagabondism," "born whores," and so on, by the 1920s many were arguing instead that particular "abnormal" character traits—for example, "oversensitivity" or exaggerated "liveliness"—created tensions and conflicts within families, which then gave rise to poor socialization and problematic behaviors. As Werner Villinger, head of the medical section of Hamburg's Youth Bureau, remarked in 1927, "With respect to heredity there are only potential criminals, potential ineducables."[112] In some cases psychiatrists were even able to discern the social origins of "abnormal" behavior: Ruth van der Leyen, for example, discovered that many children who wet the bed, ate food found on the streets, tortured animals, or ate their own excrement—behaviors previously regarded as hereditary—were the victims of frequent moves from one foster family to another, of "poor socialization, a lack of love, a bad environment."[113] And yet, even skeptics such as Villinger and van der Leyen persisted in calling these children "abnormal" and "psychopathic." Above all, they increasingly demanded that such children be separated from "normal" reformatory inmates and placed in special institutions.

Of particular concern were those children who were allegedly so "abnormal" as to be "psychopathic"—another vague term, but one that was becoming increasingly popular. "Psychopath welfare" *(Psychopathenfürsorge)* became a prominent fashion among child welfare experts, a reflection of the growing influence of eugenic thought and medical models in social welfare. A National Association for the Care of Young Psychopaths, led by Ruth van der Leyen, had been founded in October 1918, and played a prominent role in debates about correctional education in the late 1920s. Between 1920 and 1927, in fact, fifty-eight special homes, clinics, and sections within existing reformatories were opened for "psychopathic" youth.[114] The concept of psychopathy was particularly popular among reformatory administrators, who used it to lend legitimacy to frustration and simple prejudices. The work-shy, the vagrant, the politically radical, the sexually active, girls who dressed fashionably, those who read too many detective stories—all were liable to be branded "psychopathic" or "ineducable." Above all, psychopathy was used to label those who made trouble for reformatory staff. Some, in fact, even went so far as to suggest that reformatory revolts were caused by "degenerates" who were drawn to radical political ideas precisely because they were by nature morally inferior. But from the mid-1920s even many of those who had been active in developing the "new" pedagogy began to voice a new pessimism, and a new conviction that it was necessary to recognize what Theodor Litt, in 1926, had called the "limits of pedagogy"—limits that were frequently believed to be defined by "organic" disorders.[115] Whatever form it took, in any case, the demand that "psychopathic" and "ineducable" children be ejected from the reformatories became increasingly common.

Paragraph 73 of the RJWG stipulated that "ineducable" children could be released from correctional education only if provision were made for their placement in some other institution; but for children who were not "insane" or mentally handicapped, there were few such institutions. As the crisis of correctional education deepened, many practitioners became obsessed with obtaining legislation providing for the indefinite institutionalization, or *Bewahrung,* of "abnormal" or "ineducable" children—despite the skepticism of people such as Klumker, who insisted that if ordinary methods failed with a particular group of children, then extraordinary ones must be developed.[116] The first draft of a law on *Bewahrung* (intended for use particularly against young prostitutes) was presented to the national parliament in 1921 by Agnes Neuhaus and the Catholic Center party. When it died in committee, the DVöpF established a commission to work on the problem of *Bewahrung* not only for psychopathic children but also for alcoholics, the mentally ill, and the homeless; its proposals were finally presented to parliament (by the Center and the German National People's party) in 1925. At the same time, the Social Democratic party introduced its own bill, worked out by Workers' Welfare. Only the Communists denounced the whole idea.

As Detlev Peukert has shown, the appeal of *Bewahrung* was in part a logical consequence of the development of the pedagogical reform movement. For as the Hannoverian administrator Rudolf Hartmann pointed out at the

1927 conference of the AFET, the new methods relied on the fundamental rationality, even the goodwill, of young people: if "the formation of character can be achieved only through self-education," he said, then clearly "we must renounce this goal in . . . cases of abnormality."[117] The exclusion of "abnormal," "psychopathic" children was therefore often seen as a precondition for a progressive reform of correctional education.

Again, however, the more common motivation among practitioners of correctional education was sheer frustration and the desire to be rid of children who disrupted and discredited their institutions. As the keynote speaker at the same conference noted, emphasis on hereditary abnormality could easily lead to "pedagogical nihilism"; and he remarked "how often already today the slogan 'hereditary defect' serves as a disguise for the neglect of pedagogical duties."[118] The psychiatrist Otto Mönkemöller's list of youth who should be excluded from correctional education included those with "insufficient ethics and morals," the "eternal runaways," the "born whores," and the "eternally discontented elements who always feel discriminated against and insulted, who secretly and openly resist their education."[119]

Although *Bewahrung* appealed to a broad spectrum of those engaged in correctional education, its champions were unable to secure passage of legislation. The enormous assault on personal freedom which the law would represent, the potential for abuse, the difficulty of defining the group or groups of people to whom the law might be applied, and above all the problem of financing dragged out the debate through several sessions of parliament. By 1928 the government was clearly signaling that no bill would be introduced in the near future.

Efforts to respond to the crisis of correctional education by reducing rates of institutionalization, or at least by reducing the level of confrontation between parents and child welfare programs, were much more successful. Among the most widespread was the now fully legal institution of protective supervision *(Schutzaufsicht)*, which expanded at a tremendous rate after the implementation of the RJWG. By 1930 there were fully 73,000 children under protective supervision.[120] Most of the German states also adopted some form of "voluntary educational assistance" *(freiwillige Erziehungshilfe,* or FEH), in which parents voluntarily committed their own children to the care of the Youth Bureau. In many cases, this system responded to the needs of parents themselves, and merely duplicated the practice of the Houses of Salvation prior to 1878. In other cases, however, parents were pressured into committing their own children by threats of formal action before the Guardianship Court. For its most enthusiastic supporters, in any case, FEH promised to rescue the reputation of correctional education, not only because it was ostensibly less coercive and confrontational but also because the children committed were often younger and less "wayward." The numbers involved in FEH were relatively small in most areas: it was introduced only late in the 1920s and was resisted with some success in many areas. Nevertheless, such programs were clearly growing rapidly; in the Koblenz district of the Rheinprovinz, where FEH was introduced in 1927, the number of children committed voluntarily exceeded the number committed by the courts by 1930.[121]

A third alternative to direct intervention was voluntary or court-ordered "educational counseling" (Erziehungsberatung). In such programs families with troubled or delinquent children were referred to pedagogical and psychological experts employed by the Youth Bureau, or in a few cases by private organizations, for advice, support in dealing with children, or psychotherapy. Although such an approach had been proposed as early as 1905 by Polligkeit, and again in 1916 by Aloys Fischer before the ADB, only a few big city Youth Bureaus, mostly those dominated by Social Democrats, had set up counseling stations by the end of the 1920s; there were about eighty in the country at the end of the decade.[122] But Erziehungsberatung was extremely important because it offered a radically different approach to child welfare services as a whole. In an article of 1928 Lene Mann of the Frankfurt Youth Bureau outlined the role that educational counseling might play in bringing about a fundamental shift in child welfare policy. With Nohl she insisted that the work of the Youth Bureaus must become more preventive if the public child welfare system were to be effective at all, and if it were to escape from the immediate crisis which threatened it. The problems the reformatories had with older children, she pointed out, indicated that the Youth Bureaus were not identifying early enough cases in which socialization by the family was failing. At the same time, late intervention meant that the Youth Bureau had to use the most draconian measure at its disposal, correctional education. As a result, "the activities of the Youth Bureaus are easily judged, in the eyes of the parents, as an attack on their rights, as an often arbitrary coercive measure which is directed only at a certain class of the population." The obvious answer to this double crisis, she argued, was simply to transform the Youth Bureau into an "educational counseling station." [123] Since, as Franz Becker put it, "in our times, what with the general disquiet and the lack of clarity in our cultural relations, well-meaning parents are often at a complete loss in the face of the for them unbelievable opinions, tensions, disasters, and struggles—unknown to them from their own youth—of their sons and daughters," there was some hope that such a system would be warmly welcomed by parents.[124]

As we will see in Chapter 9, Mann's short article was prescient: "educational counseling" would in fact become the keystone in the structure of child welfare programs after World War II. For the time being, however, the growth of alternatives to correctional education deepened the crisis in the reformatories. By the mid-1920s a rapid decline in the number of children committed each year had set in. In Prussia, for example, 10,885 children were committed in 1925, but only 6,626 in 1929; and whereas there had been 56,455 children in Prussian reformatories in 1913 and 64,384 in 1925, by 1930 there were only 50,197.[125] In Germany as a whole, there were 97,561 children in correctional education in 1928, 89,593 in 1930, and 78,632 in 1931.[126] In the Rhineland, fully 22.1 percent of all available spaces in reformatories were unfilled in 1929.[127] Equally important, the courts were committing ever fewer young children. In the country as a whole, 43.5 percent of those committed in 1926–27 were under age fourteen, but only 22.8 percent of those committed in 1931–32. This aging of reformatory populations, of course, probably only contributed further to the frequency of revolts.[128]

State governments also attempted to deal with the crisis in correctional education by reducing the level of coercion in the reformatories. During the late 1920s they encouraged reformatories to abandon many more degrading practices of the reformatories, such as shaving the heads of new arrivals or the rule of silence. In Prussia corporal punishment in the reformatories was restricted in the early 1920s, and was finally ruled out for all girls and for boys over age fourteen in 1929; Berlin and Baden abolished it completely, as Hamburg had done in 1923 and Saxony in 1928.[129] At the same time, steps were taken toward a greater refinement of the methods of the reformatories. Toward the end of the decade individualized "education plans" for each child, including specific intermediate goals and measures, became increasingly popular.[130] Particularly after the disasters at Scheuen, Rickling, and Templin, many critics demanded the institution of state licensing for reformatory staff. In 1929 Workers' Welfare published a proposal for the complete overhaul of correctional education, calling for the introduction of self-government by inmates, adequate vocational training, differentiation of reformatories, better training for staff, closer inspection of private institutions, and expanded rights for inmates, as well as arguing that the administration of correctional education should be transferred from the provincial and state authorities to the Youth Bureaus—a measure proposed by Klumker and others as early as the 1910s.[131]

Christians themselves were increasingly disillusioned with correctional education in the later 1920s. Some, in fact, suggested that it be abandoned altogether. A Pastor Petto recommended to the DCV's commission on "difficult" children that Catholic reformatories should simply refuse to accept any who "refuse to let themselves be educated as Catholics."[132] Similarly, the Protestant Pastor Wendelin argued in 1930 that "our institutions have been badly harmed by correctional education *laws*" which had destroyed the freedom that Wichern had recognized as indispensable: it would be better, he suggested, "to abandon all coercion."[133] And at least some in the charities supported each of the reform proposals mentioned—from FEH and educational counseling to the abandonment of corporal punishment.

Yet every single reform proposal made in the 1920s alienated some members of the Christian charity leadership. Catholics, for example, initially regarded FEH as part of a general cultural offensive by secular humanist and socialist Youth Bureaus, since children in FEH remained under the control of the latter rather than the (presumably less politically left-leaning) provincial correctional education authorities. They rejected placing correctional education in the competence of the Youth Bureaus for the same reason. Practitioners of correctional education had argued since the inception of the RJWG that "protective supervision" simply allowed children to escape correctional education until they were too old to be effectively resocialized. Those large cities with the resources to establish "educational counseling stations" were often socialist dominated, and the methods of the stations were guided by purely humanistic (often Adlerian) psychotherapeutic theory. Christian reformatory staff balked at the idea that they might be required to attend courses (no doubt taught by secular humanists) and obtain licenses in order to continue doing what they had been doing for decades. They complained bitterly about the prohibition of corporal punishment, arguing that it was inconsistent with their values and with the reality of life in the reformatories, and that the whole crisis had been produced in the first place by a relaxation of discipline which had positively invited revolts.

In fact, there was a certain temptation for conservative practitioners to regard the whole crisis of correctional education as a public relations problem, and perhaps even a communist plot. For all his willingness to give up the existing system of correctional education, the Protestant Helmuth Schreiner criticized Lampel's *Revolt in the Reformatory* as a piece of shameless agitation. It was an attack, he wrote, "not only on the system in its methodological implementation . . . but on order as such, on the state. This is evident even in the portrayal of sexual problems, but above all in the unbridled hatred for every outward restriction. Seen from this standpoint the real background of the . . . multiplying attacks on our institutions comes to light."[134]

Correctional education therefore stumbled into the depression in a state of complete disarray—hated among the general public; discredited among pedagogical reformers and secular experts; riven by conflict over methods; facing a rapidly declining and steadily more obstreperous institutional population; racked by revolts and scandals; and the subject of bitter ideological disagreements among Christians, socialists, humanistic psychologists, and municipal governments. The budgetary collapse, when it struck in 1930–31, was the final straw. By the end of 1931 the system was in a crisis from which it seemed that only the most drastic measures could rescue it.

In all of this, however, correctional education presented only the most extreme case of a malady that afflicted the child welfare system as a whole—and indeed the entire social and political constitution of the Weimar state. As historians of the Weimar economy have discovered, there was a "crisis before the crisis": the Great Depression merely revealed and exacerbated problems built into the structure of the Weimar system.

Perhaps what is most striking about the crisis of the late 1920s is that in many respects it appears to have been the product precisely of the *success* of progressive reform since about 1905 or 1910. It was the rapid expansion of the Youth Bureaus and their growing tendency to move beyond merely fulfilling the letter of the law (for example, by becoming involved in *Jugendpflege* or preventive programs or correctional education) that antagonized the Christian charities. And yet, the intense ideological and organizational conflicts of the 1920s were in large part the product of a tremendous mobilization of private energies for social work—of the massive expansion and centralization of the charities and the growing participation of the working-class movement, developments which were entirely in keeping with progressive principles. And the municipalities, of course, were alienated precisely by the success of the child welfare "experts" in securing a considerable degree of control over the Youth Bureaus, and by the aggressive attempts of the Christian charities to impose their own agendas on the child welfare system. Even in correctional education it could have been argued in the late 1920s that progress toward the modernization of the reformatories was being made, as the failure of older pedagogical methods became increasingly apparent. The irony of the entire situation by 1930 was of course that this broad success in creating a more effectively managed and a more participatory society had generated conflicts that threatened to spin out of control. German society, in child welfare as in so many other fields, seemed to be increasingly mobilized against itself.

Whether the Weimar system of child welfare—much less the Weimar state as a whole—would have become completely paralyzed, as many people feared, is not clear; for at the precise moment at which ideological tensions seemed to be coming to a head, the catastrophe of the Great Depression struck. The fiscal crisis called the whole structure of the Weimar welfare system into question and seemed to make it imperative—and possible—to create an entirely new structure, one that would achieve mobilization without creating wasteful and divisive conflict. In Chapter 8 I discuss briefly the dimensions of the crisis which the depression created, and then turn to the development of child welfare policy under National Socialism.

CHAPTER EIGHT

The Great Depression and National Socialism, 1930–1945

The Great Depression

The Great Depression struck a staggering blow to child welfare programs. Despite demands from experts for an increase in spending on preventive child welfare as a means of blunting the long-term effects and costs of the economic disaster, the Youth Bureaus were gutted by fiscal cuts. In 1928–29 public expenditures for child welfare were 45.2 million marks; by 1930–31 they had sunk to 22 million, and by 1932–33 to 14.4 million. In the midst of the fight against sheer hunger, programs specifically for children took second priority. Whereas in 1928–29 fully 5.2 percent of the expenditures of the public relief system went to child welfare programs, by 1932–33 less than 1 percent did.[1] Moreover, the specific nature of the cuts was particularly disturbing. Staffing cuts affected the younger, less senior staff members, who were more likely to have social work training (and of course to be women). The first programs to be cut were the "preventive" programs listed under paragraph 4 of the RJWG, which were not mandatory; day care centers, youth centers, and counseling centers were being closed throughout Germany by 1932. Subsidies to private organizations were similarly vulnerable. These developments vastly exacerbated the problems of routinization and bureaucratization I examined in Chapter 7. By 1932 any possibility that the Youth Bureaus might become true "socialization agencies" seemed to have been destroyed. Some in the charities in fact saw the depression as potentially a golden opportunity to regain ground lost in the 1920s; one representative of the Red Cross announced in September 1930 that "the private charities' day has come once again."[2]

Correctional education suffered as badly as the Youth Bureaus. By 1930 it had become clear that correctional education would be reformed; and government decrees limiting corporal punishment and the election of Hedwig Wachenheim and Rudolf Schlosser (both of Workers' Welfare) to the central committee of the AFET in 1930 and of Walter Friedländer as chairman of the DZJ in 1931 had seemed to bode well for a relatively progressive approach. The financial crisis decisively shifted the terms of the discussion. Funding for correctional education plummeted—falling in Prussia, for example, from 41 million marks in 1928–29 to 15 million in 1932–33 (with annual expenditure per pupil dropping from 683 marks in 1929–30 to 570 marks in 1932–33).[3] By 1932 it had become plainly imperative that the number of children in correctional education be reduced, and those who argued that the institution's problems could be resolved simply by expelling "difficult" children—what they called the "cleaning out" of the reformatories—gained ground rapidly. At the same time, the political crisis of the reformatories only deepened, partly owing to the creation, in June 1931, of a "Committee for Struggle against Correctional Education" by communist and radical socialist organizations, which demanded the abolition of private reformatories, a system of financial support for poor families, self-government in new public institutions for wayward youth, better training for staff, vocational training and the payment of wages to inmates, and improved labor legislation as an alternative to the existing system.[4]

On November 4, 1932, responding to pressure from state governments and private organizations, the government published an emergency decree which prohibited the commitment of children in whose case there was "clearly no prospect of success" for correctional education, decreed the termination of correctional education at age nineteen for all children, and allowed the release of children who showed "considerable intellectual or mental abnormalities."[5] At the end of fiscal 1931 there were still 44,666 children in correctional education in Prussia; by the end of fiscal 1932 there were only 30,084.[6]

And yet in response to a number of adverse court decisions in 1929 and 1930, the decree also stipulated that children should be committed to correctional education if their removal from their own families was required but "placement elsewhere cannot be accomplished without expenditure of public funds"—precisely the wording of Adolf Schmedding's petition of 1913, which the RJWG had abandoned. While the decree temporarily reduced the number of children in correctional education, then, it also clearly aimed to bring younger children into the reformatories—and laid the foundation for an *expansion,* at some future date, of correctional education. It was thus a clear defeat for those who advocated a transition from correctional education to other forms of intervention such as FEH or educational counseling.

All these developments were particularly demoralizing in the context of the impact of the depression on young workers. Already in October 1930 about 13 percent of all young people of working age (fourteen to twenty-five) were officially unemployed, a total of 450,000 youths; by July 1932 there were 1.457 million young people unemployed.[7] Given the fact that meaningful work—a *Beruf,* or calling—was regarded as critical for the moral development of a young person, this situation was perceived as disastrous for the socialization of the young. In fact, there was a close relationship between unemployment and juvenile delinquency and gang activity. Moreover, the unemployment insurance system was overwhelmed by the sheer numbers of people involved. By an emergency decree of June 5, 1931, the legal age at which a worker could qualify for unemployment benefits was raised from nineteen to twenty-one for those living at home—potentially disqualifying about 50 percent of working youth. The local relief agencies, on which the remainder had to rely, proved to be financially incapable of taking up the slack. Local agencies, subsidized by the national government, attempted to keep young people off the streets and out of trouble by offering vocational training courses, in which 330,000 young people took part in 1931–32 and 527,000 in 1932–33. Such courses lasted only six to twelve weeks, however, and only ten to twelve hours weekly. A "voluntary work service" (*Freiwillige Arbeitsdienst,* or FAD) scheme for young workers, largely organized by private agencies but consolidated by an emergency decree in July 1932, occupied young people in make-work projects, mostly in camps, for twenty weeks at a time: in August 1932 there were some 96,000 young people involved; by December 285,000.[8] A few cities opened day centers, and many private organizations attempted to occupy unemployed youths' time with games, outings, dances, and the like. In the face of mass unemployment, all these programs amounted essentially to well-meaning gestures.

In the face of this failure, a sense of helplessness spread among child welfare advocates. In June 1932 a member of the DCV's Committee on Child Welfare concluded simply, "Our pedagogical arts are not equal to this immense emergency."[9] Social conditions among the young seemed to confirm this judgment: there was a massive increase in vagrancy as young people migrated in search of work; prostitution and juvenile delinquency rose precipitously; there was a revival of youth gangs; and young people were increasingly involved in political violence and radical organizations of both the left and the right.

In fact, by mid-1932 the disaster of the depression and the collapse of most of the institutions of the Weimar state from parliament down to the Youth Bureaus was inducing a kind of general paralysis on the noncommunist left, even as it galvanized the right and drove cultural conservatives to call for a return to the simple fundamentals of traditional authoritarian culture—or for the adoption of radical, racist solutions.

One important instance of this development was the growing appeal of eugenics within social welfare circles, and particularly of the idea that resources should not be "wasted" on cases in which there was little hope of full reintegration into society—a pattern which was of course also apparent in the correctional education decree of 1932.[10] In the context of the fiscal emergency and of seemingly unmanageable social problems, the promise of eugenics not merely to manage but actually to *eliminate* social problems— or rather to eliminate biologically those groups of people whom it was economically inefficient and irrational to support—was increasingly attractive.

This trend was also influential within the Christian charities. In the Inner Mission Hans Harmsen, a doctor, economist, student of the Social Democratic eugenicist Alfred Grotjahn, and head of the Task Force for National Regeneration (Arbeitsgemeinschaft für Volksgesundung, a central organization of moral purity associations established in 1924), rapidly gained influence as a kind of missionary for eugenics. In fact, this medicalization of thinking within the Inner Mission proceeded in parallel with the reconfessionalization process described in Chapter 7, from the mid-1920s on. Harmsen became head of the newly formed Protestant Hospital Association (Deutsche Evangelische Krankenhausverband) and at the same time director of the Inner Mission's new Health Care Section in 1926, and used his growing intellectual and organizational influence to lead the effort to "modernize" the Inner Mission's conception of welfare policy on the basis of a "eugenic reorientation."[11] With the onset of the depression, Harmsen's ideas began to make rapid headway and became more radical. His Special Conference for Eugenics, established by the Inner Mission in January 1931 and made up almost exclusively of medical men, adopted a resolution at its first meeting that May in favor of voluntary eugenic sterilization and "differentiated welfare": those who could not be restored to "full productive capacity [*Leistungsfähigkeit*]" and reintegrated into society, it suggested, should be given the minimum of institutional care and maintenance "consistent with human dignity" and prevented from reproducing while efforts and resources were focused on those who could be rehabilitated.[12] By 1932 Harmsen was denouncing "exaggerated welfare" and "a Christianity which consciously turns its back on the healthy, strong, and natural, destroys the national spirit and will to self-preservation (pacifism, conscientious objection), and essentially has as its content only care for those who are sick, miserable, and unworthy of life."[13] In Catholic circles Joseph Mayer, editor of the DCV's journal *Caritas,* had organized a conference on Eugenics and Welfare in 1929, and Hermann Muckermann worked closely with Harmsen in the Arbeitsgemeinschaft für Volksgesundung. After the promulgation of the papal encyclical *Casti conubii* (December 31, 1930), which explicitly condemned the idea of eugenic sterilization, Muckermann and Mayer were forced to adopt a lower profile; but they continued, more circumspectly, to support eugenic ideas.[14]

State and national governments, too, took a rapidly growing interest in eugenic solutions to social and fiscal problems. A National Commission for Population Questions, in which leading eugenicists were influential, was established by the Ministry of the Interior in 1930. Within the Prussian Ministry of the Interior, work on a sterilization law went ahead within a special commission of the health administration: a draft law was in fact prepared by July 1932 which would have allowed for voluntary sterilization (including, for example, at the request of the director of a mental asylum on behalf of mentally incompetent inmates) on eugenic grounds.

In a not unrelated development, discussions of the possibility of *Bewahrung* for "ineducable" youths became more urgent as well. In November 1931 the Prussian provincial administrations proposed placing such youths in workhouses, a provision included in the first draft of the emergency decree of November 1932. Outraged child welfare advocates were able to secure the deletion of this clause from the final draft; but even among reformers, conceptions of what an eventual *Bewahrung* law would look like were increasingly draconian. One Catholic administrator suggested that for those placed permanently in institutions, conditions would have to be "very simple; in particular, food and clothing must not exceed the necessary minimum."[15]

While nothing came of these legislative projects, under the von Papen and von Schleicher governments in late 1932 there was an intensification of an already extant trend toward a more repressive administration of welfare programs. The juvenile courts began to adopt a harsher approach: they imposed no punishment in 20.7 percent of all cases in 1931, but in only 18.2 percent in 1932 and 16.5 percent in 1933; and the percentage of convictions which resulted in imprisonment fell from 56.8 in 1925 to 48.6 in 1929, then rose to 57.4 in 1932 and 62 in 1933. At the same time, progressive administrators and institutions became targets of an incipient purge: the progressive Berlin juvenile court judge Herbert Francke was transferred in November; Curt Bondy was relieved of his position as director of a youth prison in December; the Prussian Ministry of Welfare had already been abolished in July 1932, after the deposition of the Prussian government.[16] In response to political radicalization, by October 1932 the von Papen government proposed raising the voting age to twenty-five, and Schleicher and Wilhelm Groener developed schemes for creating a state-controlled paramilitary organizations for young men as a means of disciplining them and preparing them for "service" to the state. There were proposals, too, for the use of FAD work camps as sites for the rehabilitation of "ineducable" youths.[17] And the further rapid decline of the birthrate brought about a revival of conservative pronatalism in government circles.

The growing crisis within the pedagogical left was equally revealing. As we have seen, even before the onset of the depression some Christian pedagogues, particularly within the Protestant Inner Mission, had been deepening their commitment to the fundamentals of conservative Christian thought. But by the early 1930s conservative Protestants were being joined by a growing secular conservative critique of pedagogical modernism, one that sprang from the same "conservative revolution" among intellectuals which (often unintentionally) helped to pave the way for the National Socialists. An article by Martin Havenstein, published in the journal *Die Erziehung* in 1930, was typical of both the content and the tone of this critique. Havenstein argued that aversion to the death penalty and the demand that young offenders should be resocialized rather than punished was a sign that German society was "in a state of dissolution," since it lacked the moral commitment and social integrity "which are required for judgment and punishment." Modern parents, he complained, let their children "grow up almost as does the bitch her litter, and of this renunciation of all socialization they make the ideal of a 'natural' and truly 'humane' socialization." Reform pedagogy merely spoiled children, failing to develop firm moral commitments in them; the final result was that they were prey to every form of immorality and could never apply themselves seriously. Modern democratic values, in short, were not really values at all but only spinelessness; they could be the basis neither for socialization nor for social order. As a corrective Havenstein suggested that "we" should "be honest, and admit that one cannot get by without punishments, including corporal, in the socialization of children. . . . Children have this in common with our favorite house pets, that they only really love those by whom they have been punished and whom they therefore fear a little bit."[18] Nor was Havenstein alone. Already in 1928 Werner Villinger warned a conference on therapeutic pedagogy that the prevailing "sentimental education" based on "pity," the lack of a "unified goal for socialization," an "exaggerated ideal of freedom," and the "erotic emancipation of youth" were generating a widespread "loss of willingness to be socialized" among young people.[19]

Social Democrats, for whom class provided (at least in theory) a binding set of values and an ideal of community, were generally unimpressed by such rhetoric. But it is a measure of the demoralizing impact of the depression—reinforcing doubts already present, as we have seen, in the second half of the 1920s—that arguments like these gained an ever greater audience among bourgeois pedagogues, and particularly among pedagogues from the left wing of the youth movement, who by 1932 were beginning to seek an accommodation with their conservative peers.[20] In the context of what appeared to be the final crisis of economic and political liberalism, the optimistic and democratizing thrust of the pedagogical reform movement was broken; what supplanted it was disorientation and drift to the right.

A meeting of the Task Force for the Reform of Correctional Education in October 1932 illustrates this process. Here Hermann Nohl announced that modern pedagogy had unfolded in three stages: that of "liberal individual pedagogy"; that of the "democratic-social turn" and of "community" (that is, Social Democratic and youth movement pedagogy); and the third, just beginning, that of "the idea of service" and of the "commitment [*Bindung*, or binding] of the liberated energies." It was time to balance love with authority, play with performance, and individuality with the great "objective forces." Similarly, Curt Bondy denounced authoritarian methods, but conceded that the sentimental spirit and extravagant individualism of the youth movement—its tendency toward "pampering"—was not suited to a new, harder era. Confronted by heckling from an audience that included many Social Democrats, Bondy became embarrassed and "so confused that he broke into a helpless, stumbling speech."[21]

While men such as Bondy and Nohl stumbled about in search of a new formulation of their idealistic theories, others were much more realistic about what was ultimately at issue. In 1931 Hermann Herrigel, commenting in *Die Erziehung* on Friedrich Gogarten's conservative theological tirade "Against Disrespect for Authority," had contrasted realistic liberalism with the metaphysical, "mechanistic, atomizing collectivism" of communism and fascism. Rejecting Gogarten's demand for obedience to God's authority as the only root of good, Herrigel spoke for the good which is produced by man's acting in history, by man's own *constructive* will. It was true, he conceded, that "anarchy reigns." The question was, however, "whether anarchy can *only* be overcome by a dictatorship."[22]

Such pleas for a policy of reasonable reform had little appeal in the midst of social and political chaos, however. Disgusted by political paralysis and internecine strife, overwhelmed by the economic and political collapse, most middle-class Germans were convinced by the winter of 1932 that a drastic revision of existing arrangements was inevitable, but they remained fundamentally at a loss to construct a solution that could command a minimal consensus. In this situation people of many different persuasions could see in the energy, self-assurance, and apparent competence of the National Socialist movement at least the best available chance of bringing about necessary changes. This hope—or better, despair—shaped initial responses to the Nazi seizure of power at the beginning of 1933.

The Response to National Socialism

The enthusiasm and lack of critical distance with which many people in the child welfare establishment greeted the Nazi seizure of power cannot be explained merely in terms of the demoralization wrought by the depression. In fact, the Nazis played very skillfully on the political, ideological, cultural, and organizational tensions and frustrations that had been so evident since the mid-1920s, *before* the onset of the economic crisis, which I described in Chapter 7. An astonishing number of people within the Christian charities and the secular progressive welfare establishment were able to convince themselves that the creation of a Nazi regime would give them the opportunity to solve long-standing problems.

In the field of child welfare—as in many other areas—this self-delusion was encouraged by the relative vagueness of the Nazi program. The Nazi welfare organization, the National Socialist People's Welfare (National-sozialistische Volkswohlfahrt, or NSV) under the leadership of Erich Hilgenfeldt, had been established in 1931–32 as a self-help organization for SA men and their families; at the end of 1932, despite the patronage of Josef Goebbels, it was still very much in its infancy, and it was not even officially recognized by the party until May 3, 1933. Programmatic statements by Hitler and the party, which stressed the biological evils and economic irrationality of supporting the "sickly," weak elements in the "national community" *(Volksgemeinschaft)*, made it clear that welfare policy would be strongly influenced by eugenic considerations. But by 1932 this stance did not clearly distinguish the Nazis from many other conservative or progressive reformers, or, for that matter, from social reformers in other countries. Similarly, Nazi denunciations of the Weimar system for raising up armies of welfare slackers, and stressing the need to inculcate discipline and an ethos of self-help, did not sound eccentric in the context of the depression, of the nineteenth-century traditions of poor relief, or of traditions and debates and legislation in other European nations. The Nazis made it clear that they regarded the German population as a measure and tool of national power; but again, while Christians might have regarded their rhetoric as somewhat too "hard-headed," such ideas were very much a part of the vocabulary of modern child welfare, and specifically echoed the pronatalism of the imperial state. These ideas, then, did not appear to amount to a coherent or distinctive program at all; and a large number of people seem to have believed that the Nazis were in agreement with them, or even that they could guide Nazi policy themselves.

In general, the Catholic leadership regarded the Nazi movement with considerable skepticism before 1933. In the early 1930s the Catholic hierarchy had explicitly rejected the National Socialists' racial ideology, as had leaders of the Catholic women's organizations; some bishops had even threatened to excommunicate anyone who joined the National Socialist German Workers' party (NSDAP). The troubled relationship between the Catholic Church and the Fascist regime in Italy made Catholics deeply suspicious of German fascism as well. The Catholic political movement, moreover, had helped to establish the Republic, and had thrived and achieved an unprecedented degree of integration and influence in it, while both the church itself and popular Catholicism had experienced something of a renaissance in the 1920s. In 1933, however, many Catholics were attracted to the social and cultural conservatism of the National Socialist movement, and particularly to its antisocialism. Equally important, after the signing of the Concordat between Hitler and the church on July 20, 1933, the Catholic hierarchy ceased criticizing Nazism and even encouraged Catholics to support the efforts of the new regime. In late 1933 and 1934, therefore, Catholic organizations—including the charities—sought to negotiate and cooperate with Nazi organizations in the hope that a reasonable division of labor could be achieved. Throughout the 1930s the Catholic leadership would seek above all to avoid open confrontation with the NSDAP and the regime.[23]

Protestants were from the beginning much more susceptible to the charms of National Socialism, and far less equipped by their intellectual traditions—their long-standing connection to the state, the strength of conservative nationalism among Protestants, the theological tradition of obedience to the secular authorities and of political passivity, the prevalence of anti-Semitism within the churches, and more recently their greater acceptance of eugenic proposals—to oppose it. The receptivity of the Inner Mission to Nazism was also reinforced by a serious financial scandal within the organization in 1931–32, which forced the resignation or firing of a large number of employees and officials of the organization, some of whom then transferred to the Nazi welfare organization.[24] Most of the leadership and members of the Protestant churches and the Protestant charities (and indeed most Protestant officials) detested the Republic and the socialist and Catholic political movements that had helped to create it, and believed that National Socialism was a conservative Christian and specifically Protestant movement. They welcomed Hitler's accession to power, often with immense enthusiasm, as the beginning of the spiritual, cultural, and political rebirth of the nation. Just under 10 percent of German Protestant pastors became members of the Nazi party, and in 1933 up to a third were members of or sympathized with the Nazi "German Christian" movement, which aimed to nazify both the church and its doctrine.

Not surprisingly, therefore, the Red Cross, whose leadership was drawn largely from medical circles and from the old conservative Patriotic Women's Leagues, was thoroughly nazified, and was virtually absorbed by the NSV in December 1937. But within the Inner Mission, too, the majority had been hostile to the Republic and oriented politically toward the conservative, nationalist German National People's party, the coalition partner of the NSDAP; and a large minority became active and committed Nazis. Hermann Althaus, for example, became a sort of chief ideologist for the NSV (and Hilgenfeldt's proxy [Stellvertreter]) after transferring from the Inner Mission.[25] Several members of the Inner Mission's governing central committee were NSDAP members, and most members of the organization as a whole—including the Protestant religious orders (the deaconesses) and women's organizations which did the bulk of the Inner Mission's work—were at least sympathetic toward the party and movement, and often glowingly enthusiastic.[26]

The Christian charities had several specific reasons to believe that they might profit from the National Socialist dictatorship. While some Nazi intellectuals professed anti-Christian *völkisch* ideas, Hitler himself carefully concealed his own radical and racist anti-Christian convictions, repeatedly emphasizing that the Third Reich would be a Christian state. In his speech to the Reichstag on February 1, 1933, Hitler declared that the new regime would "take Christianity, the basis of our morality, and the family, the fundamental cell of the state, under its firm protection."[27]

The most important concrete evidence of this Christian character of the new regime was its hostility to socialism. The party and the SA demonstratively stressed that they saw themselves as fighting in alliance with the churches against "Bolshevism," and this was perhaps the most important element of the Nazi appeal to Christians. Even the Catholic bishops enthusiastically welcomed the dismantling of the Social Democratic and Communist parties—and their welfare organizations. In a pastoral letter of June 3, 1933, the episcopate, while clearly rejecting (albeit in cautious language) racist persecution, welcomed the fact that "no longer will unbelief and the immorality that it unleashes poison the . . . German people, no longer shall murderous Bolshevism threaten . . . the German national soul with its satanic hatred of God."[28]

For the Christian charities, not only did the destruction of Workers' Welfare and communist welfare groups remove a threatening competitor, but also it seemed to resolve at a blow the political crisis of correctional education by silencing the critics of the system. The new director of the Inner Mission, Horst Schirmacher, recalled with glee "how the whole of Marxist Germany raised a hue and cry when some brat got his ears boxed," while at the EREV conference of 1934 the director of the Rauhes Haus greeted the "overthrow of Bolshevism" by the "fists of the SA" as a great contribution to the work of the reformatories.[29] The silencing of German communism also removed what many reformatory administrators saw as one of the main causes of the rebelliousness of their charges. And the emphasis in Nazi rhetoric and ideology on authority, obedience, duty, conformity, and discipline seemed not only to vindicate the methods and ideas of conservative practitioners but also to bode well for the future of the institution itself. In any event, the authoritarian state did indeed undertake a rapid expansion of the number of children committed to correctional education. In fiscal 1933 only 6,000 children were committed; by 1937 that number had surged to 10,000; and by 1941 there were some 100,000 children in reformatories and foster care, including those committed "voluntarily" under FEH (in 1928 the total number in correctional education had been 97,000).[30] What is more, children were being committed at a younger age in the 1930s than in the 1920s: in fiscal 1939 just under half the children committed in Prussia were aged fourteen and over (as opposed to nearly three quarters in 1930).[31]

More generally, many Christians of both confessions welcomed the Nazis' rhetorical allegiance to traditional values such as discipline, morality, and responsibility; and they were delighted by the flurry of early Nazi decrees aimed at the suppression of public indecency, pornography, contraceptives, and the sex reform movement—decrees which extended measures already taken under the von Papen and Schleicher governments. For Christians these steps seemed to promise salvation from the moral corruption of the mass culture of the 1920s. In 1933 one Catholic reformatory celebrated the fact that "the dark forces which plagued our youth with the poison of godlessness, of moral corruption . . . have, thank God, been defeated, to the good of the whole people."[32] And Elisabeth Zillken of the KFV proclaimed in May 1933 that if "the state combats godlessness . . ., if it wants to use its power to end the impudent immorality of the past few years, then we have reason to be thankful to it."[33] At the EREV, Alfred Fritz (director since 1932) welcomed the "earnest and determined will of the new regime to stop up the wellsprings of waywardness," while for Ina Hundinger the seizure of power was "liberating."[34] Equally important was the Nazis' antifeminism and their promise to revitalize the family. Their vehemence in proclaiming the virtues of family life and their commitment to the twin domestic virtues of maternal love and paternal authority seemed to cultural conservatives eager for allies to place them among the opponents of moral decline and of the collapse of the patriarchal family—and of the further "social-pedagogical" expansion of public child welfare. The Nazis' enthusiasm for discipline and order also appealed to the authoritarian, punitive, and moralistic prejudices of many conservative Christians, as did their rejection of individualism. Pastor Johannes Wolff, head of the AFET, observed approvingly in early 1934 that in the new state "the community is not there for the individual . . ., rather . . . the individual is there for the community."[35]

Furthermore, the Nazis' denunciation of the Weimar welfare state for breeding irresponsibility, and their rhetorical allegiance to the ideal of self-reliance and self-help, not only represented a rolling back of the concept of social rights in favor of older notions about the "moralization" of the poor by social workers, but also seemed to promise a systematic paring back of public welfare programs—which, as we have seen, by the end of the 1920s some in the charities were beginning to view as their only salvation. In 1933 the Nazis seemed to be in the process of making good on this implicit promise. A decree of the national minister of the interior in June 1933 indicated that the new regime might respond to many of the concerns of the charities—indeed, that it might even reduce public welfare agencies to the role of supporting, encouraging, and coordinating private organizations and distributing cases to them. "The striving of the past to fulfill the tasks of national welfare principally through public agencies and institutions," it stated, "has proved itself to be a fateful error," since it had encouraged public agencies to build new institutions "even where sufficient institutions of private welfare were present," thereby making "the entire welfare system considerably and needlessly more expensive. At the same time, welfare has been politicized and bureaucratized and so estranged from the hearts of the people; and private and especially confessional welfare has been pushed back." In contrast, the new regime, "inspired by patriotic and Christian spirit," would "correct the mistakes of past years through extensive involvement of private charities."[36] Needless to say, the private charities welcomed such pronouncements warmly.

Early discussions of a reform of the RJWG were equally promising. A revision of its liberal-individualist definition of the goal of state child welfare measures (the securing of the child's "right to education") was clearly unavoidable. Moreover, the "leadership principle" *(Führerprinzip)* seemed to demand the abandonment of the "parliamentary," corporatist form of the Youth Bureau; indeed, in many cases it was already being ignored. By the summer of 1933, therefore, plans for a reform of the law were being discussed within the national association of private welfare organizations—now rebuilt as the Reichsgemeinschaft der freien Wohlfahrtspflege (formed in July 1933) and administered by the NSV. Since the NSV was itself formally a "private" organization, throughout 1933 it seemed possible that the charities might achieve a radical "privatization" of child welfare programs. The DCV, while conceding that the Youth Bureaus must perform all acts requiring the exercise of state authority *(Hoheitsakten)*, suggested that in future the Youth Bureaus should delegate all "tasks of socialization" to the private charities. And though concluding that the adoption of the *Führerprinzip* in the Youth Bureaus was inevitable, it argued that there must still be an advisory Leaders' Council, which would meet four times yearly by law, and which would have the right to appeal the Youth Bureau director's decisions to the State Youth Bureau.[37] The Inner Mission's spokesman, Pastor Adolf Stahl, even maintained that the Youth Bureau should in future simply delegate all cases to the private charities.[38] Even the National Municipal League (Gemeindetag), now "coordinated" and under the influence of the decree of June, made very similar recommendations in August 1933.[39] The Youth Bureaus, in other words, were to be more or less reduced to distribution stations for cases, according to the program developing among the charities in the late 1920s. At the same time, the DCV and the Inner Mission hoped to be able to include Christianity explicitly in the new definition of the goal of socialization (the RJWG spoke only of education for "spiritual competence") and to secure further guarantees of the rights of parents.[40]

In a number of instances, more generally, the Nazi regime seemed in the mid-1930s to be acting concretely and successfully on the promises implicit in its rhetoric about the family. After 1936 working-class families were paid a small amount monthly for each child. New legislation punished abortion more harshly, and public family planning clinics were closed. A censorship law of 1935 continued the assault on "indecent" literature. A marriage loan scheme helped to raise the marriage rate by almost 50 percent by 1939, helping to cut the illegitimacy rate in half (12.2 percent in 1926–1930, 7.7 percent in 1936–1939); and the fertility rate had by then recovered its level of 1924. The National Socialist Women's Organization (National Sozialistische Frauenfront, or NSF) and the NSV also established a training program for mothers in 1934; by 1939, 1.7 million women had taken part.[41]

Finally, although Harmsen's Conference on Eugenics had rejected forcible sterilization in 1931, and some participants were clearly shocked that the Law for the Prevention of Hereditarily Diseased Progeny (Gesetz zur Verhütung erbkranken Nachwuchses) of July 1933 mandated compulsory sterilization, Harmsen himself and many others in the Protestant charities actually welcomed the law with "gratitude and joy."[42]

The secular experts of the DVöpF and the ADB, however, were just as hopeful that National Socialism would realize *their* vision of a rational, ubiquitous system of public social management. Many committed social-liberals soon recognized the evil of the new regime: Christian Jasper Klumker, for example, was forced into retirement after calling a boycott in protest of the firing of Jewish faculty members at his university (Frankfurt). But there was much in Nazi rhetoric that seemed to justify the hopes of less perceptive and less principled people. Above all, Hitler and other major Nazi figures again and again made it clear that the "national community" *(Volksgemeinschaft)* was responsible for and dependent on the well-being of each of its members, and that children were the greatest "resource" of the nation. These postulates seemed to bode well for the extension of the structure and powers of the public child welfare system.

Some secular experts rushed to build on this apparent theoretical common ground in the first years of the regime. The DVöpF—whose director, Wilhelm Polligkeit, welcomed Nazism with some enthusiasm[43]—published a position paper in June 1933 which attempted to establish general guidelines for the expansion of public programs on the basis of "national and social principles." The Nazi state, it argued, "demands a unitary youth policy in the sense of National Socialist education" and would therefore impose a "unitary goal" on child welfare policy. This ideological re-foundation of child welfare programs would end the crippling conflicts that had resulted from the regrettable fact that "the different socializing agencies and communities oriented their work with youth according to completely differing values." Under National Socialism there would be no struggles over individual children and programs because all would recognize that their role in child welfare derived not from their own particular agendas and "rights" to particular children but from their capacity in each case "to serve the socialization goal of the state." The "parliamentary" form of the Youth Bureau would be abandoned, and the "board" would become an advisory body. Finally, National Socialist principles demanded that the Youth Bureaus' work be concentrated on the task of preserving the moral and physical health of all children—on the "preventive" programs listed in paragraph 4 of the RJWG. With a clear goal for the socialization of youth and a unitary structure, and working in cooperation with the Hitler Youth, the Youth Bureau would at last "become a real socialization agency, assisting, encouraging, and supervising the family in fulfilling its socialization duties."[44]

An article published in early 1935 by Heinrich Webler—who ousted Klumker to take control of the ADB in late 1933—reveals even more clearly the appeal of Nazism to enthusiasts of social management. The "dissolution of the closed domestic economy by the liberal-private-capitalist economy," Webler argued, had destroyed the patriarchal family and with it the justification for the absolute right of parents over their children. Unfortunately, however, the "liberal-individualist selfishness of the holder of parental authority . . . has known how to protect itself even until the present day." But National Socialism would do away with the outdated legal system which protected this selfishness, for "National Socialist legal policy derives . . . the new law of socialization solely from the needs of the *Volk*" rather than of the parent or the child. In the new state there would be no contradiction between public law and private law:

> Child, parents, and state no longer stand more or less singly . . . as bearers of rights. . . . There will be in future only *one* unitary legal order, from which all rights flow. . . . The right of the parents to educate their children thus becomes . . . a duty in the service of the *Volk* and under the supervision of the state. The *völkisch* state does not recognize an independent, original, and fundamentally inalienable right of the parents. . . . Rather it entrusts the national posterity to the family out of insight into the capacity of the blood-related community of the family as the essential cell of the national community.[45]

This argumentation was transparently intended to undermine parents' capacity to resist the intervention of public child welfare agencies. Gustav von Mann, director of the DCV's child welfare section, even suggested that it derived from "the same point of view that underlies also the Bolshevik system."[46] At the same time, however, its derivation from the progressive tradition is obvious; in particular, Webler's article followed rather closely the original programmatic statement of the progressive position, Polligkeit's 1908 essay "The Right of the Child to Education," in its conception of the "organic" state and of the proper relationship between the state and the family.

In fact, there were some striking similarities between the agenda of secular progressive child welfare advocates in the 1920s and the program of the NSV as it emerged in the first years of the National Socialist regime. The organization's agenda emphasized preventive programs and focused on the task of helping to stabilize families—for example, through assistance in finding work or adequate housing, advice on child rearing, vacations or household help for exhausted mothers and vacation camps for children, and day care facilities. This was in large part simply a continuation of the trend toward *Familienfürsorge* which had begun in the mid-1920s. Nazi child welfare advocates also insisted that child welfare programs, or at least youth policy more broadly defined, should target not just troubled or abused children but *all* children, and particularly "healthy" children—much as, for example, Nohl and Bäumer had suggested in the 1920s. In the Nazi period the distinction between *Jugendfürsorge,* or child welfare, and *Jugendpflege,* or youth cultivation, which had started to erode in the late 1920s as Youth Bureaus became more involved in creating recreational programs, was reinforced by the organizational imperialism of the Hitler Youth. Nevertheless, the drive to get all young people involved in some sort of organization was very similar, and was clearly rooted in the tradition of youth cultivation and citizenship education, in the desire to create citizens positively committed to the state and to the values that underpinned the regime.

Given these commitments, it is not surprising that the NSV was extremely active in providing vacation camps and health camps for urban children, gradually pushing the religious charities out of this field.[47] The NSV's activities in the field of day care in particular were also extraordinarily impressive. It maintained 1,061 day care centers *(Kindertagesstätten)* in 1935 and 14,328 in 1941, as well as 600 seasonal "harvest day care centers" for rural children in 1934 and 8,700 in 1941.[48] And much of the NSV's work was done through local "advice stations." While these appear to have been largely merely the local offices of the NSV, in theory at least they were intended to provide services and advice to all comers, and to perform many of the functions of the old infant welfare stations, maternal advice clinics, and educational counseling centers (although, unlike the educational counseling centers of the Weimar period, the NSV determinedly rejected psychoanalysis). There were 25,552 such stations in 1935 and 33,325 in 1940, most of them staffed by women of the NSF.[49] After 1940, moreover, as the war created growing problems among young people, the NSV appears to have attempted to establish genuine educational counseling centers, rather like those established in some major cities in the late 1920s.[50] In light of all these "preventive" programs, Andreas Mehringer, active in the NSV in Berlin, was even moved in 1938 to boast that "our child welfare work is no longer care for defectives [*Minderwertigenfürsorge*]."[51]

The NSV's program with respect to correctional education also continued to some extent trends established in the second half of the 1920s. It favored, for example, limiting disruption of families in cases of "waywardness," recommending membership in the Hitler Youth or voluntary (not court-ordered) protective supervision for "mild" cases. Where institutionalization was necessary, it favored brief stays in reformatories or, better yet, voluntary correctional education (FEH) in semi-open institutions. Increasingly in the 1930s, correctional education was used "preventively" for neglected or poor children; and as we have seen, the average age of children in correctional education fell. The NSV also established a few smaller and more open "youth homes" *(Jugendheimstätten)* for "normal" children, and FEH was given a formal legal foundation by a law of 1943.[52] And Nazi spokesmen advocated (in theory at least) a pedagogical style for the reformatories that was in some respects quite "modern," arguing that socialization was best and most naturally accomplished through common life in peer groups, through appeals to the individual and collective sense of honor and responsibility, and through reliance on "natural leaders" among inmates, on pride in work well done, and on the development of the sense of self-worth and belonging. In some cases Nazi experts even recommended a more relaxed attitude toward runaways. All of this was to be made possible, of course, by the exclusion of "inferior" or "defective" children; but that, too, was an idea that had been gaining support in the late 1920s.

The National Socialist ambition of achieving the mobilization of the populace in and for the regime—for example, through mass organizations such as the NSV, which by 1939 claimed to have 12.5 million members and a million volunteers—also echoed, in a new and authoritarian key, the progressive ideal of participation.[53] The organization's use of propaganda campaigns and collection drives, too, echoed the hygiene propaganda of the 1920s.

This relationship between progressive and Nazi programs, moreover, was by no means characteristic only of child welfare policy narrowly defined. Nazi legislation on divorce, for example, "liberalized" existing law appreciably, and Nazi population policy realized some of the demands set forth in the previous two decades regarding, among other things, public child support payments and tax policy.

Finally, the Nazis' fixation with the rational use of national resources—including the NSV's insistence that it would help only those "normal" people who could be rehabilitated and made useful and productive members of society, a point to which we shall return—clearly reflected not merely the radicalizing impact of the disastrous consequences of the Great War and the depression but also the economistic arguments of, for example, Seiffert in 1906 or even Pagel in the 1890s. And, more fundamentally, it derived in part from the progressive ideal not only of efficiency but also of economic and social participation and integration, of a society of skilled, productive workers and active contributors to the general good. Indeed, ironically enough, in some respects—for instance in the belief in the central importance of productive work, or of public supervision over the family—Nazi rhetoric was reminiscent of nothing so much as the language of some Social Democrats in the early 1920s.[54]

The organismic social and political theory and the ideal of a mobilized, powerful, efficient, harmonious society which progressives shared with the Nazis, then, made it easy for men such as Webler to believe that they could reach an accommodation with the new regime, that they could continue to pursue their own agendas within it. The Nazi ideal of the *Volksgemeinschaft* broke with the dominant traditions of progressive thought, of course, in that it was authoritarian and antiliberal; it projected the establishment of harmony not on the basis of individual rights, self-interest, and creative endeavor, but of self-sacrifice, obedience, and conformity. But as we have seen, the social-managerial program of progressive reform also fostered a technocratic authoritarianism of the welfare "experts" and administrators; and by 1933 many appear to have been more interested in seizing the opportunities created by the new dictatorship for clearing away legal, organizational, and individual resistance than in assessing the possible meanings of this shift. As we saw in Chapter 3, moreover, the relationship between the rights of the individual and the needs of "society" in progressive thought meant that the shift, as Gottlieb Storck put it, from "the individualistic right of every child" to the "right of the state to educate the youth" was not a particularly difficult one for many progressives to make. Indeed, at times Nazi rhetoric quite precisely replicated that of more conservative early secular child welfare advocates. For example, Erich Hilgenfeldt, head of the NSV, wrote in early 1933 that "the right of the individual is less than that of the community, and . . . must yield if the needs of the community require it," an eerie echo of Appelius's formulation forty years earlier (see Chapter 2).[55]

As the demoralization of people such as Nohl and Bondy suggests, the apparent failure of liberal and democratic models of a participatory, mobilized, powerful national society in the 1920s made at least some progressives more accepting of authoritarian ones. In 1933 it was not yet clear that this shift would create an entirely new political dynamic completely beyond the control of established "experts"; and a remarkable number of them blithely attempted, in 1933–34 and even later, to present long-standing agendas as logical outgrowths of Nazi ideology—including, for example, Nohl and Bondy, who both urged their students to join the Nazi movement in order, as one of them put it later, "that the movement amount to something [good]."[56]

The Character of the Regime Revealed, 1933–34

Despite the high hopes harbored by some child welfare advocates, it rapidly became clear that the Nazi program and regime were in fact compatible neither with a Christian conservative agenda nor with that of secular social managers. There were several related reasons for this.

In the first place, it became apparent that the totalitarian character of the movement—its ambition to direct every aspect of national life and to infuse every sphere with National Socialist ideology—made it impossible for NSDAP party organs to cooperate with any other agencies, public or private. At the same time, even sympathizers soon could not overlook the fact that while certain elements of Nazi rhetoric echoed the concerns and ambitions of either the Christian charities or secular experts, in fact they were integrated into a comprehensive racist ideology that was independent of either tradition, and ultimately compatible with neither.

Certain structural characteristics of the new regime, moreover, had fateful consequences for welfare policy. Although Nazi rhetoric stressed unity and efficiency, in practice the different Nazi agencies and governmental departments—each under its own "leader"—operated largely independently of one another, and in competition for resources and for control of policy areas. This system frequently created paralyzing conflicts between different ministries and agencies. The reform of the RJWG, for example, bogged down in jurisdictional disputes in 1934, and limited changes were in fact introduced—by decree—only in 1939. Similar debates defeated the reform of illegitimacy law. And bureaucratic infighting and the objections of the Ministry of Justice delayed even the attempt to introduce permanent institutionalization *(Bewahrung)* until the spring of 1944 (although local authorities created their own *Bewahrung* programs—the Rhineprovinz as early as 1934).[57] What is more, the struggle between rival leaders and organizations precluded rational formulation of policy by the cabinet. It was often unclear what organization or ministry was in control of a particular area of policy, and this made it even more difficult to gain any kind of influence over policy formulation. Most often, in fact, policy was made on a more or less ad hoc basis, through administrative decrees, interagency agreements, or even informal administrative initiatives, and largely without consultation with or input from nonparty and nongovernmental agencies. More important, the struggle between these bureaucratic empires encouraged them to become steadily more aggressive and ideologically radicalized as each strove to gain political advantage by appearing more orthodox, and more essential to the struggle against enemies and weaklings, than its rivals. The dictatorial powers of the regime, the isolation of the party leadership and the government from public opinion (and from unwelcome "expert" advice), and the bureaucratic chaos it created finally permitted the Nazi leadership to pursue its own particular obsessions to their "logical" extremes, and to translate them secretly into policy through the creation of new bureaucracies and agencies. Within just seven years the Nazis were pursuing a program of secret mass murder which would have seemed almost unimaginable to both secular progressives and conservative Christians in 1933.

The relationship of both the Christian charities and secular reformers to the new regime first began to sour as a consequence of organizational offensives launched by Nazi party organizations. A whole phalanx of Nazi agencies in fact set out to conquer all or part of the field of welfare policy, and child welfare policy in particular, especially the Hitler Youth under Baldur von Schirach, the National Socialist Women's Organization (Nationalsozialistische Frauenschaft, or NSF) under Gertrud von Scholtz-Klink, and the Labor Front under Robert Ley. The most important Nazi organization in the field of welfare, however, was the NSV, under Erich Hilgenfeldt. The NSV grew rapidly following its official recognition by Hitler in May 1933, supported by the vast annual "voluntary" collection drives—the *Winterhilfswerk* collections, which netted some 900 million marks in 1940–41, two thirds of which went to the NSV. Despite continued competition from other Nazi groups, by the mid-1930s it clearly dominated Nazi welfare work; and by 1943 it was one of the largest and perhaps the most visible of Nazi organizations, with 17 million members.[58] In July 1933 the NSV became one of four recognized national "peak organizations," and the association of these groups (the old *Liga,* renamed Reichsgemeinschaft der freien Wohlfahrtspflege in March 1934) was placed under the "leadership" and administration of the NSV, which also absorbed the resources and institutions of Workers' Welfare, the Paritätische Wohlfahrtsverband (the old Fifth Welfare Association), and the Christian trade unions' welfare organization.[59] In November the NSDAP erected a Central Office for National Welfare (Hauptamt für Volkswohlfahrt, or HAV) within the party headquarters; its director was Erich Hilgenfeldt. The practical welfare work of the NSV was done in large part by members of the National Socialist Women's Organization; there were some 6 million women working in the NSF and the associated *Frauenwerk* by 1939.[60]

The imperialist and racialist concerns central to Nazi thought made it inevitable that the NSV would regard the efficient management of the quality and quantity of the population as its particular goal in welfare policy; in fact, it regarded itself as an instrument for the creation of a numerous, healthy, and pure "Aryan race." In the words of its own "Guidelines," the NSV's aim was to devote itself to the care only of the "healthy," of those who could be or were willing to become productive members of society, "to help wherever healing is possible. The improper relationship between expenditures for the healthy and the sick members of the *Volk* which existed up to now must be ended."[61] It was fundamentally unwilling to support "unhealthy" or "inferior" *(minderwertige)* institutional populations such as the mentally ill, the handicapped, or the asocial (who were all, presumably, to be dealt with by the medical authorities). The organization's charter, therefore, heavily emphasized preventive programs. In practice this meant that child welfare—the Hilfswerk Mutter und Kind directed by Hermann Althaus of the HAV's Office of Welfare and Child Welfare—was the central focus of its activities. Already by 1937 the organization claimed to be handling over 200,000 individual child welfare cases annually, making it the largest "private" child welfare organization in the country.[62]

The fundamental incompatibility of the Nazi agenda in child welfare with that of the Christian charities was revealed in discussions over the reform of the RJWG in 1933 and early 1934. Initially these consultations, held within a special commission of the Reichsgemeinschaft der freien Wohlfahrtspflege, proceeded amicably enough. The NSV endorsed the right of parents to raise their own children so long as they did not neglect their duty to do so properly; it recognized the participation of the churches and other social organizations in child welfare work; it conceived of the Youth Bureau as a coordinating body which would for the most part delegate actual implementation of policy to the private welfare organizations; and it recognized the need for a council of experts to advise the director of the Youth Bureau.[63] Above all, it gave assurances that the imposition of a single, unifying National Socialist goal for the socialization of children—to be enshrined in the first paragraph of the RJWG in place of the original liberal formulation—would preserve Christian values even in the context of a noncorporatist institutional structure.

It soon became clear, however, that the NSV's conception of guarantees of religious education was very different from that of the religious charities. The latter saw themselves as being the only forces capable of guaranteeing a sound religious education. In September 1933, however, the NSV claimed "that the National Socialist ideology stands on the foundation of Christianity and includes and bears within itself both the Christian confessions. Religious education is therefore not an addition to but rather an ingredient of National Socialist education."[64] This position, of course, implicitly denied the justification for the autonomous existence of the Christian charities; as the DCV's commission on reform of the RJWG remarked as early as August, "The claim to totality of the church and the claim to totality of the state contradict each other here."[65] A draft of the new legislation, produced in mid-October of 1933, failed to mention the churches at all in its first paragraph, stating merely that the goal of education must be to create healthy, moral, competent people "rooted in blood and soil, sustained by the vital energies of Christianity, committed and bound to the *Volk* and the state."[66] The draft's fifth paragraph specifically acknowledged the role of the "Christian churches," but in mid-December the Nazi representatives demanded that even this clause be removed.

In the end a compromise was struck in a draft National Youth Law of January 1934, which gave the Christian churches "the right and the duty to contribute in a deciding capacity to the achievement of the goal of education."[67] More important, the Nazi drive to change the law simply broke down. By early 1934 not only the Reichsgemeinschaft der freien Wohlfahrtspflege but also the Ministry of the Interior and the Reichsjugendführer, Baldur von Schirach, were working on drafts of a new law; and by the summer they were all challenged by the Ministry of Science and Education, which had just been formed in May. It would be another five years before the regime would introduce a revision of the law. Nevertheless, the course of the discussions made it unmistakably clear that the Nazis posed a profound threat to the charities.

If these disagreements over the RJWG were disillusioning, the opening moves in the organizational offensive of the NSV and other Nazi organizations were even more alarming. As the NSV's and NSF's resources expanded in the second half of 1933, the local and regional leadership of these organizations began to harass and compete with the Christian charities. Given the early enthusiasm of the Protestant welfare establishment for National Socialism, the Catholic charities were a favored target; but committed Nazis were in fact determined to achieve the complete "deconfessionalization" of child welfare, and did not spare Protestant organizations. Locally Nazi administrators attempted to disrupt charitable collections or to insinuate Nazi staff into private orphanages and reformatories; insisted that those appointed as legal guardians be members of a National Socialist organization; ignored children's confession in favor of placement in NSV institutions and Nazi foster families; pressured kindergartens to accept cosponsorship by the NSV; refused to pay daily rates for children placed in private institutions or canceled local government subsidies to private organizations; raised bogus hygienic objections; and even seized institutions, such as kindergartens or maternal advice clinics, outright.[68] Moreover, while the Hitler Youth successfully "coordinated" and absorbed the Protestant youth groups, it did so by a rather underhanded process which angered many Protestants.[69] The NSF, too, angered Protestant women's groups by attempting to absorb the Protestant deaconesses, and, when that failed, by creating its own "NS-*Schwesternstationen*" staffed with "Brown Sisters."

The aggressive efforts of "German Christians" to gain control of the church sparked a bitter struggle which helped to alienate much of the Protestant church leadership—and was defeated at the end of 1933. Similar struggles within the Inner Mission and even the Protestant Women's Auxiliary, which had chosen a German Christian pastor as its director in 1932, had similar outcomes.[70] The Hitler Youth, while it was more or less welcomed in Protestant reformatories, angered Catholic institutions by claiming access to their charges.[71] More generally, it soon appeared to some that the Hitler Youth and related recreational and work service programs posed a threat to the family by laying claim to an ever-increasing proportion of children's time and loyalties—and thus realizing precisely the threat which the Christian *Jugendpflege* groups had seen in compulsory premilitary training during the First World War.[72]

Within the Catholic charitable establishment, difficulties like these soon ended the brief honeymoon that had followed in the wake of the Concordat. By January 1934 Gustav von Mann, now director of the DCV, reported that "a shooting war has already begun on all fronts," and that the Nazis "are trying with all their power to drive the church . . . out of the field of . . . child welfare."[73] In fact, church officials and representatives of the Catholic educational and charitable establishment were beginning to speak out against the principles of National Socialism as early as the autumn of 1933. Otto Hipp, for example, writing in *Jugendwohl*, welcomed the Nazis' stress on the family, and particularly on paternal authority; but he denounced as a "complete reversal of natural law" what he provocatively called "the notion, first formulated by Danton, that children belong first to the state and then to their parents."[74] Anna Zillken similarly welcomed the Nazis' assault on the "exaggerated individualism of past times" but warned that "there is now a clear danger that the state is attempting to absorb the personal sphere."[75] Elizabeth Zillken, drawing on the papal encyclical on Christian education of 1929, attempted to establish strict theoretical limitations on the state's intervention in family life.[76] And Hans Wollasch, director of the DCV's school of social work in Freiburg, published a blistering review of the ideas of the Nazi pedagogue Ernst Krieck in *Jugendwohl* in the fall of 1933 in which he denounced virtually every major postulate of Nazi ideology—its worship of the nation as the highest ethical value ("Even the state . . . must recognize an objective order of values"), the idea of the historical and racial contingency of truth, territorial conquest, imperialism, chauvinism, the concept of racial purity, the Law for the Prevention of Hereditarily Diseased Progeny, and the one-sided emphasis on martial virtues.[77]

Responding to pressure from the new regime much as they had to the challenge of the Weimar state in the late 1920s, the Catholic charities embarked on a massive recruitment campaign after 1934. The St. Elisabeth

Associations (*Elisabethenvereine*), in which much of this recruitment drive was focused, had 120,000 members in 1934 and 535,000 in 1939; the Catholic women's sodalities grew from 900,000 in 1933 to 1.3 million in 1939; the KFV's personnel grew from 26,163 in 1932 to 35,033 in 1935 (though the number of full-time and paid staff and the number of local chapters fell slightly, and the number of cases—with the collapse of referrals from public agencies—fell from 122,151 to 81,547); and the DCV itself grew from 500,000 in 1941 to 1 million by the end of the war.[78]

Protestants, again, generally embraced the nationalism, authoritarianism, and cultural conservatism of the Nazis, and responded more positively also to their eugenic program. But by 1935 it was already becoming clear to a growing number that the Nazi movement was not in fact a conservative Christian one, and even more were simply determined to defend the autonomy and traditions of their own organizations against the apparently mindless and pointless expansionism of the Nazi ones. By March 1934 Ina Hundinger warned that despite early hopes for a blossoming of Protestant charity work in the new state, "unbridgeable spiritual clefts and fronts" seemed to be forming; three months later Fritz Trost complained that "sometimes it appears that the struggle of liberalism and materialism [against Christianity] has merely taken on a new and much more dangerous form."[79] By late 1934 and early 1935 the Inner Mission was centralizing the operation of the Protestant charities and steering a cautious course of defensive acquiescence while itself coming under growing pressure, particularly in child and maternal welfare programs. Most Protestants continued to believe in and support the political, economic, and broader cultural policies of the regime; but they stubbornly and fairly successfully resisted its interference in their religious and organizational affairs. By 1936 the NSV had alienated even many of its most enthusiastic allies within confessional Protestant circles by its unrelenting drive to gain control of all welfare organizations and personnel.[80]

As the Catholic critiques cited earlier suggest, however, the conflict between the Christian charities and Nazi groups was not just a product of the intention of the latter to establish a monopoly. Increasingly it became clear to Christians that Nazi organizations were guided fundamentally by racist principles incompatible with Christian faith. Most strikingly, in November 1933 certain members of the leadership of the Nazi German Christian movement publicly advocated abandoning the ("Jewish") Old Testament; and within six months the Protestant churches were bitterly divided between German Christians and the "Confessing Church," led by Pastors Niemöller and Barth, which issued its own statement of principles in May 1934. While the Catholic hierarchy rejected eugenic sterilization and equivocated, maneuvered, and in some cases even attempted to protect their "hereditarily diseased" charges by promising to prevent them from breeding through permanent institutionalization in locked-down institutions, much of the Protestant leadership, as already noted, appears to have welcomed the Law for the Prevention of Hereditarily Diseased Progeny (which was passed in July 1933 and came into force on January 1, 1934); and Protestant institutions generally cooperated, sometimes enthusiastically, in carrying out the sterilization of their charges.[81] In the course of 1934, however, the law was extended by the courts to include eugenic abortion, a step that horrified Protestants as well as Catholics, and drew clear protests, though not actual calls to resistance, even from enthusiasts of sterilization such as Hans Harmsen.[82] While both churches were extraordinarily tardy in condemning the persecution of Jews, particularly after the passage of the Nuremberg Laws in 1935 the issue of the validity of marriages between Christians and converted Jews, the application of legal disabilities to converts, and the status of converted Jews who had become pastors and priests confronted Christians with the religious implications of Nazi anti-Semitism. What is more, it eventually became clear that the regime's commitment to the patriarchal family and its return to the kind of moralistic and punitive pronatalism that had characterized government policy before 1918, which was gratifying to conservative Christians, did not rule out discussions, for example, of the possibility of polygamy as a means of boosting the birthrate, or of the possibility of simply eliminating the legal distinction between legitimate and illegitimate children—recognizing "biological marriage," and thus undermining the sacrament of marriage—as a means of reducing infant mortality and recognizing the bonds and responsibilities of "blood."[83]

More generally, the hostility of the Nazi regime to the charities grew in part out of the racist principles at the heart of National Socialism. For as Nazi "experts" consistently stressed, Christian charity, insofar as it supported the weak and "unhealthy," was a "waste" of valuable national resources and actually compromised the health of the "race" as a whole. As one critic put it in 1934, the charities sustained "worthless elements" of society by "flooding" them with "exaggerated Christian mercy."[84]

In fact, after 1935 the racist and organizational offensives of the Nazis clearly began to converge, as financial constraints were eliminated and as the regime began to pursue its racist program and the organizational assault on the charities more openly. As early as the end of 1935, the HAV suggested that the Youth Bureaus should simply delegate all cases to its own local branches, which could then distribute them to other organizations as necessary. This measure—which would clearly mean, as one Catholic commentator put it, "the death of all private charity"—was defeated at the national level by the united opposition of the DCV and the Inner Mission.[85] Nevertheless, in June 1936 the NSV, DCV, Red Cross, and Inner Mission did reach an agreement to form local branches of the DZJ under the leadership of the NSV (Althaus was now director of the DZJ's national offices) which would distribute those cases that were delegated by the Youth Bureau to private organizations.[86] At the same time, the NSV also demanded that it retain responsibility for all "genetically healthy" children, while the Christian charities would care for the hereditarily inferior and asocial. Again, this principle was already being adopted by a number of local and regional NSV branches; and after 1936 Nazi officials in some localities even began removing "genetically healthy" children from private institutions.[87] In the face of such measures, even Protestants began to insist, by early 1935, on their right to care for all children who were baptized Protestants; Ina Hundinger spoke of a "decisive struggle for the Christian basis of German national life."[88]

In 1936 and 1937 the rhetorical assault on the Christian and particularly Catholic charities in the NSV's journal *Nationalsozialistischer Volksdienst* and in the *Zentralblatt* (edited after mid-1935 by Althaus, succeeding Heinrich Webler) heated up. By June of the latter year H. Edwards assured the former journal's readers that it was clear "that the Catholic-oriented welfare and child welfare organizations of the DCV have decided not to conform to the fundamental reorientation of German welfare," while Heinz Vagt accused the Christian reformatories of exploiting their charges, and of having thereby sparked the revolts of the early 1930s.[89] From 1937–38 on, the NSV's national leadership, which had publicly disavowed the aggressive actions of zealous local chapters even as it secretly encouraged them, progressively abandoned its cooperative stance in favor of the confrontational approach long adopted by local leadership. After 1937 charitable collections for organizations other than the NSV were not permitted; and national subsidies to the private charities were steadily reduced. Increasingly the police were called in to assist with wholesale seizures of private institutions, so that by 1939, for example, some 1,200 Catholic kindergartens (out of 4,000 total) had been seized, while the Protestant charities lost 500 by 1940.[90] By 1938 the DCV reported that only the NSV's severe shortage of competent personnel prevented the complete "socialization" of correctional education.[91] Already by January 1937 Alfred Fritz, while still believing that "committed Protestantism not only does not rule out loyalty to the National Socialist state, it demands it," nevertheless wrote of a "battle of ideologies" and indeed a "struggle between good and demonic forces."[92]

After the annexation of Austria in 1938, the NSV simply absorbed all private and religious day care institutions there. Moreover, after 1937 deteriorating relations between the churches—especially the Catholic church—and the regime led to more open persecution. In that year the pope was at last moved to issue an explicit condemnation of the political totalitarianism and racist ideology of National Socialism, and thereafter Catholic denunciations of Nazi racial policy became more frequent. From 1937 on, mem-

bers of both the Inner Mission and the DCV were subjected to growing political persecution, including the arrest of large numbers of members of the
"Confessing Church" and trumped-up morals charges against the Catholic
religious orders. In 1939 the Catholic women's sodality, which recruited
large numbers of volunteers for the Catholic charities, was banned. The
NSV's shortage of personnel—and the lack of training and the incompe-
tence of many of its volunteers—allowed the Christian charities, for the
time being, to maintain more or less the level of activity they had reached
by 1933, by expanding their membership and increasing reliance on the institutions of the Christian churches; but it was clear that time was on the
Nazis' side.[93]

While opening a piecemeal assault on the charities, the Nazi authorities,
through a decree revising the RJWG in February 1939, finally excluded
them formally from the public child welfare administration. The decree
clearly amounted to a complete break with the Christian rhetoric still present in the drafts of 1933–34 in favor of racial principles, establishing the
creation of the "physically and spiritually healthy, morally firm, mentally
developed, professionally competent German person, conscious of his race,
rooted in blood and soil, and committed and bound to the *Volk* and the
Reich" as the goal of socialization. It also expelled the charities and the
clergy from the executive boards of the Youth Bureaus; consistent with
the establishment of the "leadership principle" in local government in 1935,
these now became merely advisory bodies, and included only two teachers,
a judge, and representatives of the Hitler Youth and the NSV.[94] By 1939, of
course, these organizational changes had already been introduced informally in most localities.

Finally, by 1939 it was becoming increasingly obvious that the logic of all
these developments was ultimately homicidal. On the one hand, Nazi theorists argued that the cost of supporting those who could never become
"fully valuable [*vollwertige*]" and productive members of the *Volksgemeinschaft* was a burden the nation could not afford, and the NSV declined
to care for the "hereditarily inferior." On the other hand, the "long-term
goal" of the NSV and the Nazi regime—already in the early stages of implementation by 1938—was the elimination of the private charities, to which
care of the "inferior" was assigned.[95] In the end, the logical consequence
was that there would be no place at all within welfare policy for the "inferior."

In fact, the mass murder of "defective" and Jewish children (and adults)
in public and private institutions for the mentally ill or handicapped began
as early as August 1939, under the T4 "euthanasia" program, which was
carried out by a special medical bureaucracy created specifically for that
purpose.[96] Needless to say, "eugenic" mass murder was an abomination in
the eyes of the vast majority of Christians, and was rejected even by those

who had been most convinced of the necessity of eugenic sterilization. While horrified and shocked by the mounting evidence of a secret murder program, both church hierarchies and both the Christian charitable establishments moved with agonizing deliberation to try to stop it. Their caution reflected partly fear that their protests would be used by foreign propagandists and thus compromise the war effort; partly fear that too energetic and public a protest would compromise their other responsibilities; but perhaps also partly of the widespread stigmatization of the handicapped even within Christian charitable circles—just as their even more shameful failure to defend the Jews reflected the widespread anti-Semitism within both churches, which derived in large part from the common association between the Jews and communism, commercial entertainment, and modern "immorality" generally. Even when it became widely known that handicapped people were being killed, most—not all—institutions could not bring themselves openly to resist the classification (the relevant forms had to be filled out by the institutions themselves) and transfer of their charges. Nevertheless, the Christian churches did exert gradual pressure on the regime, and in the summer of 1941 some of the Catholic hierarchy at last launched a blistering public attack on the program itself and on the racist principles underlying it. In response, Hitler ordered the partial suspension of the program in August 1941—though by that time the program had in any case achieved its initial goal of murdering 70,000 people, and tens of thousands more would be killed in smaller groups and less obviously (for example, by starvation or injection rather than mass gassings) until the fall of the regime. In the meantime, a very few institutions had discovered ways to resist the murder of their charges: on the Catholic side, for example, twenty-one institutions managed to save 1,500 inmates, while something over 11,000 were murdered; and the director of the Protestant institutions at Bethel was able to protect most of his wards.[97]

As we have seen, there were striking continuities between the progressive agenda of the 1910s and 1920s and that of the Nazi welfare leadership. And yet in the end Nazi policy proved as inimical to the aims of secular child welfare experts as to those of the Christian charities.

In part, again, this was due to the expansionism of the NSV and other Nazi organizations, which did not spare public agencies dear to the hearts of progressives. Most generally, the Nazis' demand for complete ideological conformity and the consequent wave of purges of both paid staff and volunteers created serious personnel problems for child welfare agencies, particularly in cities where Workers' Welfare had been very active. In Hamburg, for example, the Nazi official responsible for welfare policy had to admit by the summer of 1935 that "the quality of personnel in the field of social welfare, it is universally agreed, has deteriorated alarmingly."[98] And in some cases the Youth Bureaus found that the volunteers provided by the

NSF and the NSV were not sufficiently competent to replace those of the Christian charities, or that local branches of those organizations could not implement programs delegated to them.[99]

The Youth Bureaus in particular found themselves assaulted by Nazi organizations eager to expand their jurisdiction. The Hitler Youth made a concerted effort in the late 1930s to gain control over the personnel policy of the Youth Bureaus, and argued in 1937 that the Youth Bureaus should in future have "the character of Hitler Youth centers."[100] Needless to say, this would have had a devastating impact on their efficiency as child welfare (as opposed to indoctrination) agencies. But the NSV posed an even greater threat. Already in 1935–36 some in the NSV were arguing that the development of their organization made the Youth Bureaus superfluous, while others were suggesting that the officials of public agencies might not be entirely politically reliable, or might pursue policies not compatible with the goal of raising good Nazis.[101] In January 1936 the NSV and the association of local governments—the Gemeindetag—were brought together in a National Union of Private and Public Welfare, within which the NSV usually had the upper hand. By 1937 many local and regional NSV leaders, particularly Althaus in the NSV/HAV, were claiming jurisdiction not only over all private welfare work but also over all public welfare programs. By 1938 the national NSV leadership was going over to an aggressive and confrontational approach against public welfare as well as the private charities (though here again the NSV wanted to leave the care of "inferior" people and "defectives" to the public authorities); and rumors circulated throughout 1939 that public programs would soon be transferred to the NSV in order to eliminate what Martin Bormann called the "more than irrational" concurrent operation of public and private welfare programs.[102]

In fact, the local chapters of the NSV had for the previous two years engaged in mounting efforts to absorb, through agreements with Youth Bureaus, certain public child welfare institutions, such as kindergartens or vacation camps, as well as to monopolize foster care supervision, the selection of individual legal guardians and of volunteers for supervision, juvenile court assistance, and so on.[103] Despite a shortage of trained personnel and resistance from municipal administrations and the Hitler Youth (which was increasingly successful in placing members in the Youth Bureaus), in some areas the NSV had considerable success in absorbing public functions. In 1939 an NSV official from Munich pointed out that his organization "has difficulties insofar as locally people sometimes do not know whether it is a public or a private agency of child welfare."[104] A similar assault was made on the provincial and state correctional education authorities, and the NSV virtually gained control of correctional education by late 1941.[105]

Beneath these organizational struggles, however, lay a deeper ideological discongruity between Nazism and progressive thought. For one thing, despite all autocratic and technocratic tendencies among welfare experts (and particularly medical men), the Nazis' vehement condemnation of the principles of liberalism marked a very real departure from mainstream progressive thought. The "progressive" elements of Nazi child welfare policy were coupled with a deeply reactionary emphasis on authority, conformity, and order that drew in part on themes first sounded in the pedagogical reaction of the late 1920s or even in the cultural backlash of the 1910s, and was radicalized by the Nazis' commitment to complete ideological unanimity. Participation in the life of the *Volksgemeinschaft* was for the Nazis an obligation rather than an opportunity; and individuals' energies were to be directed exclusively toward accomplishing the ends of the party.

The case of reformatory education is particularly revealing. Despite the theoretical commitment of the NSV to "preventive" use of correctional education, the reformatories were increasingly being used for blatantly political purposes—as a tool not for social reintegration but for the brute enforcement of ideological conformity. Children of socialists and communists had of course been targets from the early 1930s. By 1937 a number of courts were ruling that parents who were members of the International Society for Bible Study (*Bibelforscher*) or the Jehovah's Witnesses "endangered" their children morally and socially by inculcating values incompatible with those of the National Socialist *Volksgemeinschaft,* and that their children could therefore be committed to reformatories or Nazi foster families. In addition, in some cases their commitment to an ideal of enforced active participation in the life of the *Volksgemeinschaft* clearly led Nazi administrators and courts to expand the definition of "waywardness" in an extraordinary manner. In one celebrated case a boy was removed from the care of his mother because she had allegedly turned him into a lazy, "pimply" loner without discipline, strength of will, or "sense of comradeship."[106]

What is more, despite the "progressive" elements of Nazi theory, the Nazis in fact instituted a return to the ideal of complete obedience and—all theory aside—to the practice of corporal punishment and coercion. The "Guidelines for [Our] Work" put out by the NSV in July 1933 held that "the position of the reform pedagogues in the last few years led to negation, to disintegration and dissolution. National Socialist child welfare must be built up against waywardness and rebelliousness, on the basis of the will of youth to discipline, to community, to honor."[107] And Lothar Koeppchen, director of the Provincial Youth Bureau of Hannover, argued that "no new pedagogical truths can or should be discovered," and that Nazi principles demanded a return to "education for inner discipline, that is, obedience, conformity, reliability, love of work."[108] Needless to say, bans on corporal punishment were ignored from 1933 on; the Prussian ban was officially lifted by decree in July 1935. Thus, while Nazi thinking, like reform pedagogy, emphasized the need for education through and for "community" and self-government, Nazi pedagogues dropped the other central demand of reform pedagogy—that socialization proceed "from the child," allowing it to develop in freedom. Again, like the Nazi *Volksgemeinschaft* itself, the "community" of inmates established in the reformatory was to be authoritarian and strictly regimented, based on duty, discipline, and conformity and on ideological indoctrination and uniformity rather than on rights and on the autonomous, creative social and cultural capacities of children. There would be no experimentation with democratic self-government or the encouragement of creativity and spiritual exploration.

Even more important, however, was the fact that the Nazi regime was motivated by a consistent obsession with biology and race that went far beyond the concerns of mainstream progressive thought and was fundamentally incompatible with the progressives' appreciation of the *social* origins of "waywardness," delinquency, and other forms of "deviance" among young people. While the final consequences of this obsession with biology only became clear in the course of the steady radicalization of the regime in the late 1930s, the potential for that radicalization was clearly present at the outset. It is typical of Nazi thinking that in 1933 Erich Hilgenfeldt drew conclusions from the argument that the individual's rights must give way before community needs which Hugo Appelius could not yet have imagined when he made the same suggestion in 1892: that "the unfit must be ruthlessly exterminated."[109] Again, there was a clear continuity between the Nazis' biologistic approach to social problems and the growing influence of doctors within the social reform community since the 1890s—and particularly the widespread acceptance before 1933 of the idea that "deviance" was the product of inherited biological defects (*Anlage* or *erbliche Belastung*). But the Nazis, and particularly Nazi medical experts, carried this medicalization of social problems to extremes that would not have appeared legitimate in mainstream child welfare discussions before 1933. In fact, it is precisely the obsession with health that explains in good part the Nazis' condemnation of liberalism and the growing emphasis on coercion: whereas progressives before 1933 had seen the release of individual energies through guaranteeing individual social rights and assistance—in short, *inclusion*—as the source of social harmony and efficiency, for the Nazis harmony and efficiency were to be achieved through the manipulation of the physical substance of the nation by experts, and specifically the *exclusion* of the "inferior."[110]

In the case of correctional education, this division led to considerable debate between Nazi doctors, who were happy to brand virtually all children in reformatories "inferior" and "defective" (despite explicitly admitting their incapacity to make a scientifically viable case for this belief), and the established child welfare organizations, which were unwilling to see their charges dismissed as irredeemable enemies of the *Volksgemeinschaft*.[111] At the same time, while the language of doctors involved in welfare programs had long been characterized by a particularly autocratic and moralistic tone, the explicitly punitive quality of Nazi language and policy was also new. Its potential significance was by no means lost on contemporaries: as early as 1934, for example, the DCV's journal *Caritas* was warning against conflating *Bewahrung* (permanent institutionalization) with the "preventive" permanent institutionalization *(Verwahrung)* of criminals.[112] And even in the final years of the regime, while the Nazis proceeded with the internment of "asocial" youths in labor camps and the murder of "defectives," the DVöpF leadership continued to speak of the possibility of rehabilitation in the context of *Bewahrung* right up until 1945.[113]

The destructive potential of the Nazis' obsession with biology was in any case not entirely hidden from contemporaries even in the first years of the regime. In 1935 Gertrud Bäumer, while defending pre-Nazi welfare policy against the Nazi charge that it had been dominated by liberal individualism and ignored biology, also warned that a nation that refused to care for those who were "not a part [of] but rather a burden on" its creative energies would "lose one of its noblest qualities," and that the application of an "ethic of biological usefulness [*biologische Nützlichkeitsmoral*]" would give rise to a "brutalization [*Verrohung*]" that would have consequences far beyond the field of welfare policy."[114]

In its single-minded focus on biological determinism, Nazi policy owed less to the traditions of "welfare" than to those of population policy, psychiatry, and eugenics—and specifically not the more liberal "social hygiene" wing of the eugenics movement, which had been dominant in the Weimar years, but rather its more conservative, authoritarian, and antiwelfarist "race hygiene" wing. Although the NSV was highly visible and vocal, as the regime became increasingly radicalized, medical and racial concerns and organizations came increasingly to dominate Nazi "social" policy. Indeed, the Nazi medical establishment under "National Health Leader" (*Reichsgesundheitsführer*) Leonardo Conti was one of the few organizations that was able to defend itself effectively against the expansionism of the NSV. This development was not without organizational consequences for child welfare policy: during the Nazi years the Youth Bureaus were starved of resources and personnel, even as the state-controlled Health Bureaus—created by the Law on the Unification of the Health System of 1934—expanded rapidly. At the same time, the Health Bureaus also absorbed jurisdiction over many "preventive" child welfare programs: after 1935 infant welfare, counseling for mothers, school health programs, and other programs focused on children's hygiene and health were all placed under their authority. Since the Health Bureaus' mission was precisely to act as the focus for the eugenic and racial policies of the regime, these changes entailed an important shift in emphasis within social policy as a whole.[115] Finally, the role of the Youth Bureaus themselves was reconceived by Nazi "welfare" experts largely in terms of their racial policy: they were to assist in the elimination of human "rubbish" (Hermann Hübner) so that Nazi organizations could concentrate on caring for the "healthy." Again, this was precisely the opposite of the ambitions of progressive reformers in the 1920s, who had hoped to make the Youth Bureaus real "socialization agencies" for *all* children. In 1939, not surprisingly, authority over welfare programs was transferred within the Ministry of the Interior from the Local Government Section to the Public Health Section (under *Reichsgesundheitsführer* Leonardo Conti).[116]

The progressive program was transformed in a similar manner in other areas of policy. In NSV kindergartens racial and military preoccupations ensured that the emphasis was as much on "physical fitness, the formation of character, and steeling the will" as on Frobelian learning theory.[117] In educational counseling, the network of centers established by the NSV was increasingly seen as merely a useful system for sorting children according to their ostensible "racial" or "biological" qualities.[118] In population policy, the liberalization of divorce law and the introduction of "eugenic" abortion were accompanied by a return to moralistic and punitive pronatalism, including prohibitions on contraception and more severe punishment of (noneugenic) abortion which was fundamentally alien to the concepts of family planning that had become prevalent in the 1920s. Abandoning the more progressive, "social hygiene" strand of eugenic thought dominant in the 1920s, the Nazis favored instead the "race hygiene" tradition and the theorists of "Aryan" superiority, who had been regarded by most eugenics experts in the 1920s as unscientific cranks.[119] And while the NSV pursued the goal of a "preventive" child welfare system through day care and counseling facilities, the establishing of innumerable "educational" camps for young people—Hitler Youth camps, summer camps, work service camps (the FAD had been "nationalized" with the creation of a compulsory National Labor Service for boys in 1935, and in 1939 for girls), health camps, "preparation camps" for beginning university students, work camps for unemployed youth—was more important to the Nazi ambition of creating a system of extrafamilial socialization for all young people.[120] Again, this system in fact represented a massive politicization of "welfare" policy, since the camps' central aim was the political indoctrination of those who passed through them.

Finally, the Nazis very early took up the question of a reform of illegitimacy law, which had bogged down in the Reichstag between 1925 and 1930; but their commitment to paternal power, to the idea of individual responsibility, and above all to biologistic thinking led a number of jurists in the NSDAP's legal department to issue proposals for the granting of full parental authority to the fathers of illegitimate children, and of all the legal rights of legitimate children to their children.[121] The churches, of course, feared that this step would undermine the sacrament of marriage and with it the Christian family (the journal of the SA even spoke of "biological marriage").[122] But since few fathers took any interest in their illegitimate offspring, and granting them parental authority would have meant the end of public legal guardianship, secular reformers were horrified, too. In the end, nothing came of these proposals; but they indicate how unhinged from rational considerations Nazi policy could become under the impact of ideological imperatives.

War and Radicalization

In some important respects the outbreak of the war checked the expansion of Nazi agencies and created a breathing space particularly for the charities. In January 1939 Hilgenfeldt, writing in the *Nationalsozialistischer Volksdienst,* had baldly stated that "the Nation . . . recognizes no welfare work by classes or confessions"; but plans within the NSV for a new welfare law which would bring about the final destruction of the charities were defeated by Hitler's own concern over the political costs of continued confrontation with the churches—a concern which may have played a role in the halting of the eugenic murder campaign—and by the need for cooperation in caring for victims of the war.[123] By 1943–44, in fact, the NSV was forced to abandon tacitly entire fields of its activity, as members were called up for the war effort and as it had to concentrate on responding to the bombing campaign.

But the state of emergency and the growing role of the police, the intensification of ideological radicalism, and the need to economize and reduce inefficiencies on the home front also gave Nazi agencies new opportunities for expansion. The NSV in particular was able to pursue its ends increasingly through simple administrative coups and reliance on the police and on threats and coercion. In February 1940, for example, in the wake of steps taken by the Inner Mission and the Protestant church to close ranks against the NSV, the Inner Mission's headquarters were searched and its employees questioned by the secret police. During 1940 the NSV began to take over numbers of reformatories and other institutions, especially in northern Germany, again with police assistance. Between the spring of 1940 and the summer of 1942, eight hundred Protestant kindergartens came under NSV control.[124] And by the summer of 1941 the NSV was able to bring about outright mass seizures of private day care institutions. By 1942 there was even talk within the NSV of requiring all children to attend Nazi kindergartens.[125] In 1940, moreover, a decree forbade healthy persons to enter cloisters—a measure aimed at solving, in the long term, the central problem of the NSV: its inferior numbers.

At the same time, in the summer of 1941 a series of administrative "agreements" brought about greater "cooperation" between the NSV and other agencies. In particular, in September the NSV reached an agreement with the municipalities according to which the Youth Bureaus could delegate cases or programs only to the NSV, which endeavored in particular to secure the delegation of preventive programs, a step which many social pedagogues must have deplored as the equivalent of reducing the Youth Bureau to a police agency. The NSV also established its exclusive right to found new day care institutions.[126] Despite a decree of the national Ministry of the Interior in October 1941 which attempted to establish a clear division of labor between the NSV and local Youth Bureaus, in mid-1942 Althaus explicitly stated that the NSV wished to gain control over legal guardianship, protective supervision *(Schutzaufsicht)*, and the supervision of foster care.[127] In fact, it was above all the NSV's inability to recruit sufficient personnel, as well as the increasing demands of care for wounded soldiers and civilian victims of bombing, that prevented the organization from absorbing all private and municipal welfare programs.

But while the NSDAP's influence in child welfare was growing rapidly, the Second World War, like the first, unmistakably demonstrated the self-contradictory character of a radical right-wing agenda which sought to combine authoritarian moralism with imperialist expansionism. Even before the war many observers had reported that the Nazi regime was having a negative impact on youth: delinquency was rising, gang crime was more common, "life is completely dominated by the profane," and in "the area of sexuality a destructive precociousness is apparent."[128] The war immensely exacerbated this development. By 1941 child welfare authorities were complaining of a rise in juvenile delinquency, adolescent sexuality and illegitimacy, gang-related crime, escapes from reformatories, public disorderliness, and other symptoms of a decline of moral order. Toward the end of the war, as public order and the economy in urban areas completed disintegrated, youth gangs increasingly engaged in acts of brigandage and even outright opposition—attacking Hitler Youth patrols; spreading critical graffiti; carrying out armed thefts of money, food, and weapons; and even, in the fall of 1944, killing the head of the Gestapo in Cologne.[129]

As during the First World War, the perceived moral crisis of youth was believed to be the product above all of a crisis of patriarchy: the excessive freedom created by the absence of fathers, teachers, policemen, Hitler Youth leaders, clergy, and social workers, as well as the employment of large numbers of young people at relatively high wages in munitions factories, permitted the resurfacing of the anarchic and asocial urges of the young. There is no need to recount the discussion of this problem here; the arguments presented were quite the same as those we have seen deployed in World War I.

Under certain circumstances, however, the fundamentally amoral character of Nazi imperialism was unmistakably exposed. For example, since 1937 SA and SS organs campaigning against existing illegitimacy laws on population policy grounds had praised "biological marriage" and the "courage to have children," and denounced the "Jesuitical moral theology" of "fat and hypocritical burghers."[130] This agitation culminated in Himmler's decree of November 28, 1939, encouraging German women to become the mothers of children sired by men departing for the front.[131] Similar contradictions between the Nazis' "traditionalist" social values and their imperialist policy developed in other fields at the same time: in employment policy, for example, the Nazis eventually found themselves forced to *encourage* women to take up factory work, while complaints about brawling among young people contradicted the systematic celebration of violence and physical prowess in Nazi pedagogy.

In any case, the steady deterioration of discipline and order on the home front brought about an accelerating shift in Nazi policy as a whole from ideological and social integration toward repression and punishment, a shift that complemented the growing importance of "negative" measures in race policy. By the end of the First World War, the growing resistance of young people to coercive measures and the evident failure to bring about noticeable changes in public and private behavior had led most child welfare advocates to accept the idea of abandoning such programs in favor of more positive and preventive ones. The Nazis, in contrast, were willing to accept any cost and any measures necessary to make such a coercive approach work—up to and including mass murder.

Predictably enough, then, the National Socialist regime responded to growing "waywardness" among youth primarily with a proliferation of police measures and with an increasingly punitive, harsh, and racist approach to social problems. A National Center for Combating Juvenile Delinquency was established in May 1939, while a law of October 1940 introduced special procedures and more severe penalties for young offenders who committed serious crimes. Administrative "youth arrest" *(Jugendarrest)* of up to three months in solitary confinement was introduced (as an "educational" measure) in 1940. A police decree for the "protection" of young people in March 1940 attempted to prevent young people from attending dances, cabarets, and amusement parks after 9:00 P.M., and to forbid "loitering" after dark, smoking, and drinking; and an even more restrictive new law for the "protection" of youth was put in place in June 1943. Indeterminate sentences for young offenders were introduced in 1941, and a new National Law on Juvenile Courts came into force in 1944 which allowed

judges greater latitude in sentencing, lowered the age of criminal responsibility from fourteen to twelve, and introduced the death penalty for juve-
niles. After 1943 the police could place young people who showed unwillingness to work in "work education camps." In 1944 a series of decrees
finally introduced permanent institutionalization for "asocial" people. It
had in any case already been introduced by the police, under a law for "preventive" detention, and by local authorities.[132] After 1940 the police were
empowered to place young offenders in "youth protection camps" *(Jugend-
schutzlager).*[133] While only two concentration camps exclusively for young
people were established, the expanding role of Himmler's police and the SS
in child "welfare" reveals the gradual drift of National Socialist policy toward wholesale incarceration and extermination. The murder of "ineducable" reformatory inmates had in any case begun as early as 1941.[134]

The response of the child welfare establishment to the Nazi regime, at
least through about 1934, makes it clear that the appeal of fascism
within the child welfare establishment derived from the political crisis of
the late 1920s and the economic crisis of the depression, and not primarily from the micro-political logic of ever-intensifying state intervention in social life, or from monolithic consensus at the top in favor of authoritarian social manipulation. It is best explained as a response to a
crisis induced by the incapacity to achieve consensus within the organs of
the formal and informal government of society, from conflicts over the
purposes, forms, and content of state intervention in society. The National Socialist regime, in its pronouncements regarding welfare policy,
played very deliberately on the antagonisms and frustrations that those
conflicts created. In this sense, Nazism seemed to many of those active in
the field of child welfare merely to offer new solutions to already existing
political problems.

As we have seen, the ambitions of NSV theorists corresponded quite
closely in many ways with those of secular progressives, and of some conservative Christians, in the 1910s and 1920s. Both the ideal of integration
through productive participation and the habit of calculating the costs of
failing to ensure such integration in individual cases were central to the progressive tradition. In its emphasis on prevention and on the family, Nazi
policy merely intensified trends already long present in child welfare policy
and theory. And eugenic theories, the medicalization of social problems,
and the idea of expelling disruptive "psychopaths" from the reformatories
had all been gaining influence well before 1933, and a kind of technocratic
authoritarianism was common, especially among doctors, even at the turn
of the century. Nor was the politicization of child welfare policy entirely
without precedent: as we have seen, the possibility of pursuing the systematic political indoctrination of young people had been discussed as early as

the imperial period. And the punitive and moralistic tone of Nazi thinking in this field appears to owe something, too, to the style of the conservative cultural backlash in the 1910s and 1920s.

In fact, the dual nature of Nazi policy—prevention and services for the "healthy," repression for the "unhealthy"—reflected a tendency inherent in progressive child welfare policy from its inception (see Chapter 3). In some cases, moreover, there was a clear personal continuity, particularly among doctors and psychiatrists, between child welfare activism and the most radical policies of the Nazi regime. Werner Villinger, for example, was director of the medical section of Hamburg's Youth Bureau in the 1920s and a member of Harmsen's conference on eugenics within the Inner Mission in 1931 and 1932; he went on to become chief doctor of the Protestant institutions at Bethel, where he recommended that 1,700 of his 3,000 wards be sterilized; and by 1939 he was one of those who selected "defectives" for murder under the T4 program—although he appears to have recommended against killing the victims in almost all cases.[135] Finally, as the ideas put forward by Otto Ohl and Karl Neinhaus in 1925 (see Chapter 7) suggest, even the utopian racialism of National Socialism may have been in part an outgrowth of the cultural and political crisis of the 1920s, a form of compensation for insurmountable social and ideological divisions. The only element of Nazi thinking and practice that had *not* been clearly present in mainstream discussions of child welfare before 1933, apart from the idea of actually murdering "defective" children, was its radical and genocidal anti-Semitism. And even there it is clear that the line between psychiatric or eugenic theories of "inferiority" and ethnic racism was always quite thin, a good example from the field of child welfare being the treatment of Gypsy children, mentioned in Chapter 3.[136]

And yet, despite these continuities, in many respects the Nazi regime brought about a clear *dis*continuity in child welfare policy. That discontinuity is perhaps clearest in institutional terms. On the one hand, the corporatist relationship between public and private agencies that had been fifty years in the making, the symbiotic relationship between public policy and the private charities, was decisively abandoned. On the other hand, the development of public child welfare agencies was substantially disrupted, both by the expansion of the Nazi party's own welfare organization and by the shift in emphasis within welfare policy from social to biological and political concerns, or in organizational terms from the Youth Bureaus to the Health Bureaus, the police, and the SS.

This organizational discontinuity reflected important ideological and intellectual shifts as well. Again, there is no very clear break here: the Nazi obsession with biology was built on trends that appear to have been gathering momentum in the second half of the 1920s, if not since the turn of the century. Nevertheless, the intensification of these trends, and particularly the way in which Nazi theorists pursued them to their logical (and insane) consequences, clearly brought about a crucial qualitative change, just as it created important institutional changes. While eugenics and the hereditarian theories of psychiatrists, penologists, academics, and doctors had been important in the 1920s, they had not yet led to the complete "biologization" of conceptions of the ideal society or of the function of social policy. That transition took place only during the depression and under National Socialism. Similarly, the radical authoritarianism of the Nazis, which attempted to impose obligatory activism, clearly differed profoundly in its implications and dynamic both from the liberal tradition on which Weimar child welfare programs were founded and from the authoritarianism of Christian pedagogy and Christian social conservatism.

In the field of child welfare, then, National Socialism presents us with the paradox of a set of unmistakable continuities which nevertheless amount to a discontinuity, a "mere" reorientation so profound that it amounts to a revolution. In fact, what made Nazi policy different—again, with the crucial exception of ethnic racism—was above all the extraordinary and uncompromising radicalism of the Nazi regime, the open-ended, unhinged, hyperlogical dynamic that it created. That dynamic allowed for a new and fatal development which was nevertheless rooted in extant traditions.

In the broadest terms, Nazi policy seems to have been based on a new and immensely radicalized combination of particular elements of the very same traditions which had been built into the Weimar compromise. Specifically, certain aspects of the Nazis' racist and totalitarian program echoed both progressivism's biological imperialist conception of the nation and its ideal of mobilization and participation, while others echoed (in a new, "naturalized" language) the conservative Christian concept of the relationship between authority and morality (and between morality and national strength). Indeed, National Socialism may have seemed to hold out the promise of a reconciliation—and not merely an elaborate and fragile institutional balancing, as was achieved by the Weimar state—of the ideal of mobilization with that of authority, of dynamism with stability, modernity with order, science with Christian values, and perhaps even of a new racial variant of the liberal conception of popular sovereignty with the conservative tradition of hierarchy and transcendental metaphysical imperatives.

This capacity to combine elements of opposing agendas helps to explain the appeal Nazism had for representatives of very different and divergent ideological traditions, and thus to explain the conditions under which the Nazi dictatorship could emerge. But it may also help to explain why Nazi policy veered so tragically toward mass murder. For it seems possible that, at least in the field of child welfare, it was precisely the combination of the "scientific" ambition of secular social reform with the punitive strain of Christian moralism and cultural criticism—a combination readily apparent

in the writings of some psychiatrists interested in reformatory inmates—
that explains the uniquely destructive character of Nazism.

In the field of child welfare as in every sphere, this attempt to resolve the
tensions which had crippled the Weimar system by abandoning corporatism and democracy in favor of an authoritarian "organic" state failed,
by any rational standard, in the most spectacular manner. It created a
policy-making system that was even more paralyzed by internal conflicts
than democracy had been. It paved the way for an intense politicization of
administrative bodies and practice, and succeeded in bringing political
hacks to the fore to a degree unknown in the Weimar Republic. It brought
about an immense expansion of the welfare bureaucracy, a proliferation of
paperwork, and a renewed "fragmentation" of welfare work and competition and conflict between agencies. It gave birth to a regime that was inevitably driven by the logic both of its political economy and of its racist,
biological-nationalist ideology into an imperialist war that undermined the
social order and the very system of social and personal morality which
Nazism had promised to preserve. Rather than achieving a new synthesis of
state and society—and thus fulfilling the hopes of reformers since the turn
of the century—it gave birth to a system in which the party-state increasingly absorbed all independent social organizations. It thereby realized precisely the danger that the advocates of corporatism and participation had
sought to avoid: the stifling of autonomous social energies by bureaucracy,
the limitless assault of the state upon society. Rather than reconciling Christian conservative and social-managerial reform programs, increasingly it
combined the worst elements of both, each in a hysterical and compulsive
form. National Socialist policies were shaped by authoritarian moralism
without commitment to an objective and autonomous ethical system, by
scientific brutality without therapeutic ambition, and by social-managerial
ambition without commitment to voluntary participation. With all institutional and intellectual restraints removed by the creation of a totalitarian
regime, Nazi policy carried each of these principles toward its "logical" extreme, developing relentlessly and by rapid stages toward mass murder.
Rather than creating a system of efficient social management and moral
order, in the end the new regime resorted to ever-expanding criminalization
of both children and adults, and the creation of an ever more irrational machinery of punishment and death.

Ultimately this monstrous regime brought about the destruction of
the German state and discredited the German political tradition. The National Socialist regime pursued the strategies of coercive social and political integration and mobilization, punitive denial of cultural divisions,
and aggressive, murderous "final solutions" to social problems to their self-
destructive end.

From this perspective, while it is clear that fascism offered one possible way of constructing and organizing child welfare policy, in this field as in most others it was ultimately a nonviable one, doomed by its very nature to consume itself. Historically, moreover, its self-annihilation brought about a fundamental transformation of the German political and social landscape, a transformation that paved the way for the (re)establishment of a stable corporatist-democratic child welfare policy. The failure of the authoritarian "organic" state made possible the rebirth and success of the democratic system it had destroyed. We will examine the foundation and consolidation of this system in the years 1945–1961 in Chapter 9.

CHAPTER NINE

Child Welfare Policy in the Federal Republic, 1945–1961

The Post-War Context

The destruction of the National Socialist state in 1945 brought about very few changes in the structure and personnel of the major private and semi-public organizations. The NSV, of course, was dismantled, and the Red Cross and Workers' Welfare recovered only slowly. But the AFET, ADB, DVöpF, DCV, KFV, Inner Mission, and EREV all survived the war largely intact. The most important new foundation was the Working Group for Child Welfare and Youth Cultivation (Arbeitsgemeinschaft für Jugendwohlfahrt und Jugendpflege, or AGJJ, formed in May 1949); composed of representatives of the private organizations, the ministries of the states, and local governments, it essentially replaced the DZJ. Encouraged and relied on heavily by the government, it gave the private charities and the municipalities unprecedented influence over child welfare policy in the new Republic. The leadership of both private and public organizations remained much the same as it had been before, and often after, 1933. Johannes Wolff, for example, was chairman of the AFET from 1924 to 1969, despite having, in his capacity as head of the Stephansstift in Hannover, urged his deacons to join the SA. Elisabeth Zillken was general secretary of the KFV from 1916 to 1958. Heinrich Webler headed the ADB, in its various incarnations, from 1923 until 1966, despite joining the NSDAP in March 1933 and being essentially a consultant in the Ministry of the Interior until 1945. Wilhelm Polligkeit was active in the DVAW leadership from 1911; became the organization's chairman in 1922; "coordinated" it in 1933 and then became its executive director *(Geschäftsführer)* after being replaced as chairman by Hermann Althaus in 1934; resigned and remained in Frankfurt (where he held an academic post) when it was moved to Berlin in 1936;

and was once again its chairman from 1947 to 1950. Hans Muthesius was active in Berlin's welfare bureaucracy from 1915 until 1933, moved to the DVöpF after his dismissal, returned to public service in 1935, joined the NSDAP in 1939, rose high in the child welfare bureaucracy of the Ministry of the Interior, and in 1950 succeeded Polligkeit as chairman of the DVöpF, a post he held until 1964. After the war Werner Villinger, whose activities in the Nazi period were mentioned in Chapter 8, became director of the Institute for Medical-Pedagogical Child Welfare in Marburg. The list of examples could be continued indefinitely.[1]

Moreover, though the structure of the German state was radically altered after 1945, the impact of this change on child welfare programs was not very great. The states were given considerably broader powers than before 1933, and the occupation regimes did overturn some Nazi laws (particularly regarding censorship). But child welfare policy remained in the competence of the national government, and the RJWG and the RJGG remained in force in the forms given them in 1939 and 1943.

What the war *did* decisively change was the context in which child welfare policy was made and implemented. In the first place, Hitler and Stalin accomplished the complete destruction of the revolutionary socialist left in West Germany; the West German Communist party was easily harassed and contained, and finally outlawed in 1956. Those radical socialists who did not die in the concentration camps or in the great purges in the Soviet Union either moved to East Germany or found themselves almost completely isolated in the West. Within Social Democracy the postwar years saw the final triumph of reformism, culminating in the formal abandonment of Marxism in the Bad Godesberg program of 1959 in favor of "libertarian-democratic socialism" *(freiheitlich-demokratischer Sozialismus).* By the late 1950s the SPD was moving toward a new profile as a *Volkspartei* (party of the whole people) and gaining the votes of many who might have voted Democratic in the 1920s.

A similar fate overtook the authoritarian right. The partition of Germany removed the conservative Prussian landowning class from West German political life; and it also relieved the Federal Republic of Saxony and Thuringia, which had been among the most politically volatile (and "brownest") regions of the old state. Both traditional authoritarianism and the radical "conservative revolution" of the 1920s were discredited by the disaster of the Nazi regime, and the political institutions of German conservatism were demolished. Among Christians, moreover, the appeal of authoritarian social, political, and pedagogical theory was immensely reduced both by its obviously catastrophic instrumentalization by National Socialism and by the totalitarian state's assault on the churches. The new vitality and depth of the Christian commitment to democracy was reflected in the replacement of the actively antidemocratic German National People's party and the lukewarm republican Center by the interconfessional Christian Democratic Union (CDU). And of course the dominance of democratic thought was vitally reinforced by the fact that the absence of a domestic revolutionary socialist threat removed the occasion for a reactionary politicization of the Christian critique of modern culture. In the 1920s Christian critics had directly associated the materialism and "naturalism" of consumer culture and modern sexual mores with the materialism of revolutionary socialism; but while in the 1950s politically and socially active Christians (and particularly Catholics) remained *culturally* deeply conservative, this *political* element of cultural criticism became considerably more moderate with the collapse of the radical left. The rock 'n' roll craze, for example, did not spark the same panicky reaction as had the raunchy popular songs of the 1900s or, particularly, the jazz craze of the 1920s; one important reason was that whereas the Communist party had attracted a considerable following among young people in the 1920s, it virtually disappeared in the 1950s. The youth riots of the mid-1950s, Walter Becker wrote in 1961, had expressed a tendency toward "rebellions but not revolutions."[2]

The majority within the Protestant churches had in any case broken with the tradition of uncritical commitment to the conservative state and social order at the Barmen synod of 1934 (a process that had begun earlier, in the 1920s, among pacifist theologians such as Günther Dehn and Friedrich Siegmund-Schultze). That break was reinforced by the admission of collective guilt at the Protestant church conference in Stuttgart in October 1945, and by the second half of the 1950s the Protestant churches were emerging as an increasingly progressive force in German society. This development was reflected in the growing vitality of political debate within Protestant circles in the 1950s, in powerful Protestant resistance to rearmament, in the reconciliation between the Protestant churches and the (now "nonpolitical") trade unions after the synod of 1955, and even—to use an example from the purview of this volume—in the growing prominence of practicing Protestants within Workers' Welfare.[3] Heinrich Albertz, director of Workers' Welfare from 1949 to 1965, was a Protestant pastor.

The Catholic hierarchy, in contrast to the Protestant, was unready to acknowledge any responsibility for the disaster of fascism; and in the 1940s and 1950s the Catholic church labored hard and successfully to reconstruct the comprehensive and closed social milieu and the monolithic political unity of German Catholicism. The Catholic leadership was, in the 1950s, intolerant of both internal dissent and secularizing liberalism, and it devoted much of its energy to leading the ideological crusade against communism. But within the Catholic community, too, the experience of fascism had greatly encouraged the maturation of a commitment to democracy which had already been developing in the 1920s. In fact, the experience of National Socialism, the perceived threat of atheistic totalitarian communism, and the centrality of a self-consciously conservative, Christian liberal-democratic ideology to the Allied regimes created an unprecedented flowering of democratic thought within the Catholic community in the 1940s and 1950s, a process reflected in the endorsement of democratic pluralism by the second Vatican Council (1962–1965). If anything, the continued commitment of the Catholic leadership of the new Christian Democratic Union to a conservative cultural and social agenda helped to stabilize the democratic constitution; for it meant that the CDU and its more conservative Bavarian branch, the Christian Social Union (CSU), were able in the course of the 1950s to sweep up most of the remnants of German conservatism, including many former Nazis. These people, too, while hardly enthusiastic about democracy, accepted the Republic partly because of the strong and sometimes even strident anticommunist, antirevolutionary stance of the CDU government.

Within child welfare policy, these developments were reflected, first, in the virtual disappearance of the radical socialist pedagogical program and much of the organizational élan of the 1920s. Workers' Welfare, rebuilt from the ground up after 1945, still sometimes vehemently rejected both corporatism and the principle of "subsidiarity," demanded the creation of a purely public welfare system, and strenuously objected to public subsidies to the private charities. Under the conditions of postwar political and economic stabilization, however, the radical agenda and rhetoric of the 1920s steadily faded. Since the American occupation authorities did not permit political organizations to be active in the field of welfare, Workers' Welfare abandoned its connection to the SPD in 1947. Profiting from the distribution of NSV property, the organization greatly expanded the number of institutions it maintained (41 in 1930, 152 in 1949), thereby tacitly abandoning its hostility to private charitable activity. It increasingly resembled the nonsocialist charities, too, in its dependence on public subsidies, which by 1958–59 accounted for almost 70 percent of its income.[4] In fact, sobered by the statism of the Nazis, Workers' Welfare also increasingly abandoned its hostility to the existence of private welfare organizations, and whereas it had not been a member of the *Liga* of private welfare organizations in the Weimar period, it did join the AGJJ in the new Republic. At the same time, in the early 1950s its definition of its own goals in child welfare reflected the de facto abandonment of the ideal of creating a distinct, revolutionary socialist pedagogy in favor of a general and fairly vague humanism. Lotte Lemke wrote in 1950 that Workers' Welfare could "perhaps more easily see the person in the person" because it was not committed to a particular class or faith; its goal was "the development of the individual to harmonious humanity."[5] And as I have already remarked, explicitly Christian values became increasingly accepted within the organization: by the mid-1950s the Bavarian Workers' Welfare organization regarded socialism as simply "the

Sermon on the Mount applied practically."[6] Finally, the distinct proletarian subculture within which Workers' Welfare had thrived had disintegrated under the impact of the depression, Nazism, the hardship of the immediate postwar years, and then the economic "miracle"; one consequence was a steady decline in the number of members and volunteers that Workers' Welfare (like the SPD itself) could muster in the early 1950s.

Looking back in 1985, Richard Haar argued that the "stagnation" of child welfare within Workers' Welfare in the 1950s and 1960s resulted from the fact that the "goals and content of pedagogy were excluded from discussion" by the adoption of the language and goals of middle-class pedagogy.[7] In fact, this assessment was too pessimistic; as we shall see, Workers' Welfare regained its vitality in this field by the late 1950s, becoming the most active and influential element within a broad spectrum of left-leaning welfare reform built on a convergence of reformist Social Democratic and (now explicitly democratic) progressive traditions, and, as one spokesman put it in 1953, on the goal of "education for social responsibility, for the great ideals of freedom and respect for the dignity of others."[8] But the abandonment of the goal and rhetoric of social revolution did bring about a difficult process of reorientation and rethinking in the first decade after the war, when the fundamental institutions of the West German state were being created.

In the early 1950s many Protestants seem to have remained committed to a somewhat defensive piety, perhaps inherited from the "Confessing Church": the *Evangelische Jugendhilfe,* for example, was almost entirely devoted in the early 1950s to the work of the *Rettungshäuser* and to meditations on the Protestant faith. By the middle of the decade, however, the growing vitality and openness of political and social discussion within the Protestant churches paved the way for a much more positive engagement with child welfare more broadly defined. Particularly important was a growing reconciliation of Protestantism with "social pedagogy" and even with Social Democratic pedagogy and child welfare policy—a reconciliation which was quite deliberately pursued, for example, in the pages of the journal *Die Sammlung,* the more self-consciously Protestant successor to *Die Erziehung.* By 1959 the name of the Protestant *Evangelische Jugendhilfe* was even exchanged in favor of *Sozialpädagogik* (Social Pedagogy).

Catholic child welfare policy in the 1940s and 1950s did not go through as profound an evolution as did its Protestant counterpart. The influence of Montessorian thought and of psychotherapeutic models—which were, as we shall see, also crucial in shifting Protestant circles away from a narrowly confessional perspective—did encourage a new degree of acceptance of "social pedagogy" and "reform" pedagogy. But the vitality of Catholic activity in this field was less the product of any intellectual transformation than of an aggressive cultural conservatism, a determination to defend the Christian family and Christian values against the interventionist state and the commercialization of culture. As we shall also see, Catholic policy in child welfare in the 1950s amounted less to an embracing of modernity than to an effort to contain and control it.

Given this fact, it was of critical importance to the history of social policy—as of the Federal Republic in general—that the division of Germany after 1949 decisively changed the confessional demography of the country. Whereas Catholics had made up about one third of the population of the Empire and the Weimar Republic, the new Federal Republic was over half Catholic. Perhaps equally important, the Christian churches were the strongest surviving German institutions in 1945, and they played a decisive role in laying the foundations of the new state. Given the new confessional balance and the greater unity of the Catholic community, the practical result was that Christian Democracy was dominated by the Catholic leadership. Since the Christian Democrats governed in coalition with the Free Democratic party (itself a relatively conservative force into the early 1960s), and even held an outright parliamentary majority between 1957 and 1961, this ensured that Catholic social thought achieved a degree of dominance over social and cultural policy greater than at any time previously—and this despite the increasingly secular tone of public and private life in the land of the "economic miracle."

In addition to these political and ideological changes, of course, the war also brought about an immense social disaster. Malnutrition was common until the currency reform of 1948, particularly in urban areas; and many observed that children suffered from low blood pressure, fainting spells with exertion, weakness, and inability to concentrate. In Berlin at the end of 1947, 125,000 children had no proper shoes; in Fürth in Bavaria, 60 percent had none. The flight of millions of ethnic Germans from the East, the division of Germany, the collapse of the economy, and the destruction of housing stock set literally millions of people in motion across central Europe. Conditions in the East created a long-term influx of young people from the Soviet zone into the West. At the end of 1949, there were 1.55 million refugees aged fourteen to twenty-four in West Germany, almost half of them living in camps and emergency shelters.[9] Between 15 and 18 percent of all children in West Germany in 1952 were refugees.[10] Many feared that the straining or shattering of these children's emotional and social ties and the experience of the anomic, often monotonous, hopeless, and squalid life in the camps and overcrowded dwellings (in 1946 there were 14 million households but only 8 million habitable dwellings in the western zones)[11] would make it difficult for them to integrate themselves into a stable social order. The shortage of housing forced countless families to live in overcrowded apartments and children to sleep two or more to a bed. By the end of 1949 there were over half a million homeless people under the age of twenty-one.[12] Of particularly grave concern was the widespread unemployment and underemployment of young people: as late as 1951 over half a million young people were without work or training, a situation that seemed to threaten the political and social stability of the new state.[13] Some states passed draconian labor and vagrancy laws, but in the prevailing chaotic conditions they could have little effect, and most were soon struck down by the occupying authorities. A Youth Reconstruction Project similar to the FAD had little more success.

Other problems seemed even more difficult to resolve. The fathers of some 16 percent of all German children were either dead or in captivity, and nearly one third of households were headed by single women—a situation which, in the eyes not just of conservatives, threatened both the material well-being and the psychological and moral development of millions of children. Moreover, many men were more or less incapacitated, particularly emotionally, by their experiences in the war and as POWs. Marriages were severely strained or broken, and the divorce rate rose sharply; also women were being drawn into the work force in unprecedented numbers in the process of reconstruction. These developments were not reversed with the economic recovery of the 1950s; climbing rates of divorce and of women's participation in the labor force became matters of increasing concern to policymakers in the 1960s.

To many people this social dislocation and hardship seemed to be creating a real moral collapse, the symptoms of which included the rising illegitimacy rate (7.1 percent in 1941, 10.6 percent in 1948), rising divorce rates, a precipitous increase in the number of cases of venereal disease, expanded informal prostitution, the large number of illegitimate children fathered by occupation troops (94,000 by 1952), and a sharp rise in juvenile delinquency.[14] Most observers blamed these trends on the difficult conditions of the immediate postwar period, particularly on the food shortage. But they feared that such temporary causes could lead to lasting moral corruption. Gustav von Mann, for example, remarked that 70 percent of crimes committed by young people in Berlin were "poverty crimes," but worried that crime might "become a habit" if conditions did not improve soon.[15] Some Christians believed that children who grew up without fathers would not have an instinctive understanding of God's authority and of that of teachers, magistrates, and the law. Many feared, too, that the experience of Nazism might have lasting effects on youth; the DCV's Committees on Child and Youth Welfare, for example, deplored the effects of "the reversal of all moral and spiritual values through National Socialism and its emphasis on this world."[16] Finally, many observers in the early postwar years discerned a disturbing "new waywardness." Walter Cimbal found in 1948 that postwar youth suffered from an alarming "infantilism": they shunned responsibility, were interested only in gaining the "most narrow professional training," and displayed a lack of "capacity for creative thought," a certain flatness and superficiality of feeling, a lack of interest in ideological questions, a lack of "civil courage." Children no longer revolted in reformatories, he complained; indeed, they were often thankful to be relieved of responsibility for their own lives. "Waywardness," in short, "has become passive." One Social Democratic commentator reached a similar conclusion in 1953, claiming that waywardness was now the product not of "an overabundance of unused or misdirected energies" but of "depression and inner disorientation."[17]

In addition to these specific problems of youth, the postwar situation—the divorce rate, women working outside the home, increasing illegitimacy, the "surplus" of women in the age cohorts affected by the war, the vast number of "rootless" refugees from the east—further heightened fears, already prevalent in the 1920s, for the long-term stability of the family as an institution. And the continued decline of the birthrate seemed to many observers to threaten economic and social recovery. Also, the efforts of both National Socialism and communism to penetrate and instrumentalize the private sphere made it seem all the more imperative after 1949 to reconstruct and restabilize the family—by which was meant, particularly but not exclusively among Christian Democrats, the nuclear family with male breadwinner—as the foundation of a liberal, democratic social order.[18] The fact that social policy in East Germany abandoned the ideal of the single-breadwinner family in favor of universal public day care can only have reinforced this tendency. Indeed, there was a great deal of concern during the occupation period, particularly but not exclusively among Catholic leaders, that hardship and disorientation would drive the populace into the arms of communism. The reestablishment of orderly domestic and family life was regarded as an important means of preventing such a development. More broadly, of course, heightened concern over the fate of the family in the 1950s merely continued a trend already apparent in the 1920s and under the Nazi regime. In any case, the new Ministry of Family Affairs, headed by Franz-Josef Wuermeling, embarked on a profoundly conservative "family policy" (Familienpolitik) in the 1950s, attempting, for example, to make divorce more difficult to obtain, to limit access to contraceptives, and to encourage women not to work in paid employment. Its efforts were not entirely unsuccessful: divorce was made more difficult in 1961 (though the number of divorces actually increased by 75 percent in the 1960s), and the proportion of married women working outside the home in 1955 (33.6 percent) was lower than that in 1939 (36.2 percent).[19]

The Triumph of Management: The Federal Youth Plans

And yet, just as the emphasis on the family in "social pedagogy" in the 1920s was coupled with grandiose interventionist ambitions, so the influence of Christian cultural conservatism in the early years of the Federal Republic did not lead to a simple "restoration" of an imagined family order. In the circumstances created by the general collapse of both state and society in 1945–1948, that would have been an impossibility. Social policy under a CDU government, it was clear, would be guided by fundamentally conservative values; but it was also clear that a massive expansion of public welfare programs and of social engineering was inescapable.

In the field of child welfare specifically, the new government of the Federal Republic in fact responded to the problems of the postwar years with remarkable energy. In the course of 1949 work was begun within the national Ministry of the Interior and the AGJJ on reforming the RJWG and RJGG, illegitimacy law, adoption law, morality legislation, and so forth. A parallel set of initiatives emerged in the sphere of family policy, where work began on a law (passed in 1954) providing supplementary payments to those with more than three children, and on a reform (finally passed in 1957) of the BGB that, in accordance with the requirement of the Fundamental Law, granted men and women the same rights. Between 1949 and 1953, then, there was an extraordinary outpouring of legislative activity that matched that of the first years of the Weimar Republic.

In this effort a clear pattern is discernible: in virtually every field the repressive, coercive approach which had become more and more characteristic of Nazi policy was abandoned in favor of a return to a social-managerial strategy of prevention, and to corporatist and consensual forms for child welfare institutions and programs. Perhaps the most impressive example of this approach was the development of the annual National Youth Plan (Bundesjugendplan, or BJP) after 1950, which directed tens of millions of marks in federal subsidies to child welfare organizations, the states, and youth groups.[20] The aim of these annual plans was twofold. In the first place, they were intended to support programs designed to overcome the problem of youth unemployment and training, since policymakers feared that unemployed or untrained youth would form an unstable and restless proletariat and that German industry would face a serious shortage of skilled labor in the late 1960s. In 1951 the AGJJ warned that some half million young people faced the "lack of an opportunity to take up a lasting, socially integrative professional training and employment that corresponds to their natural right to development and secures their existence," and that the consequences might include "demoralization, indifference, moral dissipation and confusion, deficient social integration and uprootedness, waywardness and criminality," emigration, and "increasing radicalization"— and that after 1955 the shortage of skilled labor would be a major economic problem as well.[21] At the same time, the development of a skilled work force seemed essential to economic recovery. One advocate of the reform of the RJWG asked in 1952, "How shall we one day survive in the ever more heated . . . economic competition between nations, if in those other nations every last maturing young person is comprehensively educated, while among us . . . so many young people are ruined inwardly and outwardly owing to lack of . . . timely development?"[22] The Youth Plans therefore provided subsidies for vocational training, and particularly for the construction of hostels and dormitories for apprentices and students in areas where work was plentiful but housing was in short supply.

This effort under the Youth Plans, moreover, was merely part of a much larger and less focused effort of social engineering which aimed, again, to stabilize modern society and counteract the anonymity and fluidity of "massification" *(Vermassung)* by establishing a rational career pattern and life pattern for young people. That larger program gave rise to a proliferation of state, local, and private vocational training and apprenticeship programs, and eventually to unified national legislation in 1969. And it was complemented—just as in Franz Pagel's conception in 1896—by efforts to reconstruct the family and gender order through legislation such as the establishment of legal equality between men and women (1957 and successive reforms to 1977) or the Law for the Protection of Mothers (Mutterschutzgesetz) of 1952.[23]

But the Youth Plans also aimed at political as well as economic and social integration. The massive political indoctrination undertaken by the National Socialist regime seemed to demand the reeducation of youth for democracy and international cooperation. At the same time, it still seemed necessary in the early 1950s, as a meeting of the states' Youth Plan officials remarked in June 1951, to "protect youth against radicalization in political life."[24] Most important, it was essential that the new state overcome the widespread political indifference and passivity fostered by fascism, by popular culture, and by the disastrous outcome of the war, and create a citizenry actively committed to the democratic political order. The Youth Plans aimed to foster a minimal democratic consensus and, even more important, the strength of character, civic courage, and active personal political engagement on which a democratic polity might confidently be founded—a program obviously derived in part from the progressive and social-liberal conception of "civic education" and political participation developed in the 1890s and 1900s.

To accomplish this aim, the government poured millions of marks yearly into the religious, sports, and political youth groups, now gathered in a national association, the Bundesjugendring, or BJR. Sizable subsidies were directed, too, to various domestic youth conferences and meetings, international youth exchanges, "political education" courses, youth libraries, and so forth. A small percentage of the annual plan budget was allocated to child welfare organizations.

The results of the Youth Plans were impressive. By 1956, 641,000 young people had passed through the 800 dormitories funded under the plans, and some 152,000 had studied at 4,600 institutions established for vocational training; another 300,000 had taken part in international conferences and youth exchanges, and 400,000 in political education courses.[25] Most important, by 1954 perhaps 40 percent of all German youth between the ages of ten and twenty-one were members of youth groups—more than in the late 1920s, before the destruction of all non-Nazi youth organizations. And, in part because they were regularly consulted regarding the distribution of Youth Plan funds, these organizations had developed a close and friendly relationship with the national and state governments. In that year the minister of the interior declared that the Youth Plans and the youth groups were succeeding in their greatest aim: "Youth," he announced, "is abandoning its indifference toward the state."[26]

Correctional Education in a Democratic State

In the context of such a grand preventive and democratic-participatory agenda, the form and methods of correctional education seemed increasingly anachronistic in the early 1950s. Despite the effects of the emergency decree of 1932 and the Nazis' expansion of FEH, correctional education was still generally detested by the populace after 1945. Moreover, the standards of child welfare experts were, if anything, increasingly out of step with the real experiences and values of the working-class population. As councillor Elisabeth Bamberger of the Bavarian Ministry of the Interior observed at an AFET meeting in 1950: "In an age of mass waywardness, 'waywardness' has become a problematic concept. . . . People have often become accustomed to conditions which would earlier . . . have been considered irregular. . . . In this situation there is the danger that intervention . . . might meet with no understanding and appear merely ridiculous."[27] At the same time, the concept of waywardness itself was expanding, so that as the expectations of policymakers and educators for conformity and "adjustment" rose, children who might once have been considered merely nervous or rough came to be regarded as wayward.[28]

In these circumstances drastic intervention seemed more and more problematic to many involved in child welfare. The early years of the Federal Republic therefore saw the return to the trend, begun in the Weimar period and reversed by the Nazis, away from traditional correctional education. The AFET itself, at its meeting of 1950, demanded that wherever possible children be committed voluntarily, by their parents, rather than by court order.[29] By fiscal 1954–55 more children were being committed through FEH than by the courts, and by 1961 just over half of all children in correctional education had been committed through FEH.[30] At the same time, the number of children who were "placed" by the courts in their own families (which gave social workers access to the home and the child and allowed them to threaten to "transfer" the child to another family or a reformatory, but did not otherwise disrupt the family) rose from 19.2 percent in 1951 to 27 percent in 1959.[31] A similar development affected protective supervision: by 1950 there were more cases of "voluntary" than of court-ordered protective supervision.

Within the reformatories, moreover, the new appeal of democratic pedagogy led to the complete triumph, at least in theory, of more "free" *(freiheitliche)* methods. The methods and aims of correctional education remained conservative and conformity-oriented; and older, authoritarian ideas and practices, and the biologistic theories of the psychiatrists, proved extraordinarily tenacious. But the trend was clearly toward liberalization. Increasingly practitioners, especially on the left, argued that life in large institutions was too monotonous, impersonal, and oppressive. Children in such institutions were bound to be unhappy and resentful; but equally important, since large institutions required order and conformity above all, they tended to crush individuality and initiative, creating passive, weak, undisciplined "herd people" who could not shape their own lives rationally after their release.[32] These ideas, of course, had been put forward in the 1910s and even earlier, in the debate over the Prussian Law on Correctional Education in the 1890s; but it was only in the early and mid-1950s that German correctional educators were converted en masse to the ideal of the "familylike" *(familienhafte)* reformatory, which would be not an "institution" *(Anstalt)* but a real "home" *(Heim)*. Children were to be divided into groups of ten to fifteen, of various ages and both sexes; to be placed under the care of an individual female social worker (a nurturing substitute "mother" rather than an authoritarian "house father"); and to be kept in one institution rather than transferred upon reaching a particular age or stage of development. There was a gradual trend toward smaller, better-staffed reformatories; and by the end of the 1960s, there were few of the old-style "closed" (locked-down, barred, fenced-in) reformatories remaining. By the late 1950s the opinions and practices that had dominated correctional education in the early twentieth century—the insistence on order and authority; the use of harsh and degrading punishments, uniforms, and drill; the use of terms and concepts such as "ineducability" and "psychopathy"—were increasingly seen as quaint at best, and often as primitive and horrifying.

Much more important than the effort to reform correctional education, however, was the almost universal conviction that it should be avoided wherever possible in favor of "preventive" methods. Since it was increasingly clear that "waywardness" was a product of social dislocation and hardship, the obvious solution seemed to be to attack the problem at its social roots. The institutionalization of wayward children was, so to speak, not only too much but also too late. And, in fact, after 1959 the gradual decline of court-ordered commitments to correctional education was only partly compensated for by FEH. There were 73,000 children in correctional education in Germany in 1939, 75,000 in 1949, 53,000 in 1959, but only 48,000 in 1969.[33]

The Reform of the RJWG

Discussion of a reform of the RJWG in the late 1940s and early 1950s was dominated by this preventive agenda, and by the need to redemocratize and rebuild the Youth Bureaus, which were still operating under the "leadership principle," and which had been gutted by the organizational empire building of the Health Bureaus, the NSV, and the Hitler Youth. Work on reforming the law began immediately after the war. The DVöpF published drafts of a new law in 1946, 1947, and 1949, and in June 1950 a full draft was published by a joint committee of the DVöpF and the AGJJ.[34] That draft aimed above all at reimposing the two fifths clause in order to ensure that bureaucratic routine and "political influences" did not dominate the work of the Youth Bureaus.[35] Meanwhile, the power of the cities and of democratic ideology in the new state and the influence of municipal administrations and Workers' Welfare in the AGJJ ensured that certain concessions would be made to municipal power. The Youth Bureaus were to be freed from oversight by the State Youth Bureaus but subjected to the direct authority of the municipal government; and medical and school officials, teachers, and clergy were all evicted from the executive boards, now renamed Child Welfare Committees (*Jugendwohlfahrtsausschüsse*, or JWAs) of the Youth Bureaus. In return the charities were given two fifths of *all* seats (not just two fifths of the seats not held by officials of the Youth Bureau), and the JWAs were given the right to be consulted by the city council before decisions were made regarding the Youth Bureau.[36]

In addition to these structural changes, however, the AGJJ argued for the restoration as compulsory programs of the "preventive" programs listed in paragraph 4 of the RJWG, set aside by the emergency decree of February 14, 1924. Prevention, it suggested, was cheaper, and less objectionable to parents, than later intervention. What is more, postwar social dislocation, poverty, and commercial popular culture "endangered" *all* children. "Experience shows," argued the Inner Mission, that it was "impossible to make a real distinction between healthy and endangered youth. The situation of our youth is such that this distinction, which was meaningful at one time, has largely been erased. To a great extent the youth has arrived at a situation of generalized endangerment . . . under the influence of the repercussions of the war."[37] The creation of the kind of "rail system" envisaged by Hermann Nohl in the late 1920s was thus imperative. In effect, the AGJJ had adopted the agenda of the "social pedagogues" of the 1920s.

These proposals were accepted almost without exception by the government, and passed into law by the national parliament in 1953, after extended financial negotiations. The new law therefore preserved the corporatist structure of the Youth Bureaus; but it clearly aimed to establish a public child welfare system that was both more (majoritarian-) democratic and more managerial-interventionist.

The Triumph of Prevention and Psychotherapy

The restoration of paragraph 4 of the RJWG did in fact lead to a considerable expansion of public programs for "nonendangered" children, particularly in urban areas. By 1957–58 over 40 percent of Youth Bureaus were spending over 40 percent of their budget to support youth organizations and their activities *(Jugendpflege)*, which continued to be particularly well developed in the larger cities.[38] In 1950 the district Youth Bureau of Kreuzberg in Berlin, for example, helped to support 162 youth and children's groups, seven youth centers (and their libraries), a children's library, and an annual summer camp; it showed forty-nine films and organized fifteen entertainment events and forty-three lectures, handiwork courses and public works projects, and the like.[39]

Jugendpflege, however, was not the only key to the preventive strategy in child welfare. Instead, an even more important role fell to psychotherapeutic family and child counseling, which in Germany is called "educational counseling" *(Erziehungsberatung*, or EB). Just gaining recognition in the 1920s, particularly in Social Democratic circles and in Workers' Welfare, "deep psychology" *(Tiefenpsychologie*, as it was called in German) had been crippled in Germany by the National Socialists, but it was reintroduced and strongly supported by the Americans and the British after 1945.[40]

Psychotherapeutic thought and EB appealed in the 1950s for a whole range of reasons. Most simply, as we saw in Chapter 8, the idea of placing counseling (at least for "normal" children) at the center of public child welfare policy was already well established, since it had been a central part of the NSV's program. There were, in fact, a large number of people active in EB in the 1950s who had begun their careers in the Nazi period and simply continued them in the postwar years. At the same time, however, by the early 1950s the discipline of psychotherapy had become mature and established enough to make powerful and plausible claims. As Berlin's State Youth Bureau remarked in 1950, psychotherapy had "achieved a degree of precision which allows its . . . findings to be practically, directly applied in the field of social work." Psychological counseling was embraced also because it was a comparatively cheap option: the Berlin Youth Bureau, for example, pointed out that "through tactful investigation by school and parents into the special problems of these children and through psychotherapeutic treatment decisive assistance is possible. In this way many children could stay in their families, and considerable costs for institutionalization . . . would thereby be saved."[41]

Furthermore, the experience of the war, the almost universal social dislocation of the early postwar years, and the new social problems of the postwar period—divorce, post-traumatic stress, anomie—seem to have created severe psychological stress among young people. In this context policymakers began to be more receptive to the policy implications of the fact that delinquent and wayward children came disproportionately from stressed families; they were the products of traumatic experiences, bad marriages, broken homes and single, indigent, or overworked parents. Again, by the late 1950s, despite continued enthusiasm in some cases, the biologistic theories of early psychiatry (and the punitive moralism of conservative Christian theory) seemed at best silly to a growing number of people; and they were in any case discredited by the Nazi abuse of biologistic thought and of psychiatry in particular, and often ridiculed by American social workers.[42]

Equally important, educational counseling appealed to policymakers because it was less confrontational than, for example, correctional education, and therefore less likely to generate a political backlash against child welfare policy. In fact, the promise of psychotherapeutic counseling fit precisely the progressive project of preventive social management. The educational counseling centers were designed to "take on those cases in which psychic conflicts and complexes—originating in an unhealthy environment—are the cause of faulty development and in which therefore the usual measures do not promise sufficient guarantee of success. The educational counseling stations have the mission of recognizing such faulty development in time, and preventing it from becoming chronic. They are intended to lead the young person to social integration and at the same time to assist him to an inner life free from *Angst*."[43] In other words, by assisting individuals to overcome the weaknesses created by the social order, counseling would contribute to their personal and social integration and so to the harmony and stability of the social order as a whole—a striking parallel to the social reform vision of progressives and of social-liberals in particular. At the same time, psychological counseling was obviously less disruptive of the family than other forms of intervention, and it thus fit well the conservative "familialism" of the 1950s.

Most fundamentally, however, psychotherapeutic theory may have appealed to child welfare agencies and advocates because it provided precisely that neutral foundation for child welfare programs which had been lacking in the 1920s, and thereby promised to defuse the conflict between conserv-

ative Christians and secular progressives. In this sense the scientific, culturally "neutral" language of psychotherapy replaced the scientific, "neutral"
language of racism as the means of escape from the cultural conflicts that
had paralyzed the Weimar child welfare system—an issue to which we will
return later in this chapter. It was of critical importance, however, that psychotherapeutic theory brought about a revival of that therapeutic optimism
that had characterized child welfare reform through the 1920s, and which
the Nazis' racist, biologistic ideas had so decisively and disastrously repudi-
ated. It is symptomatic of this shift, for example, that when a new draft of a
Bewahrung law was introduced in 1951, the major criticism—put forward
by Workers' Welfare—was simply that permanent institutionalization was
no longer needed because psychotherapy permitted the successful treatment
of problems which had up to then been regarded as incurable.[44]

In short, the adoption of "preventive" psychotherapeutic counseling as
one of the linchpins of child welfare policy promised to stabilize that policy
by helping to defuse the confrontation with parents and children, and between secular and Christian reformers, which had wracked the child welfare establishment in the 1920s, and at the same time to lower costs and to
make progress toward eliminating—this time in a positive rather than a
negative sense—the problem of those who simply could not be integrated
into an efficient, harmonious social order. It thus provided a critically important bridge or mechanism by which technocratic and social-managerial
progressive theory and practice could accomplish the shift back from the
totalitarian key to the democratic key, from a language of duties and authority to one of rights, needs, and incentives.

The restoration of paragraph 4 of the RJWG in 1953 thus brought about
a massive expansion of psychotherapeutic child welfare services, centered
on a network of *Erziehungsberatungsstellen* modeled on the British and
American child guidance clinics. Berlin led the way in 1950 by planning a
comprehensive psychotherapeutic child welfare system to include twelve
district educational counseling stations, day schools and day care centers,
recreational facilities both in Berlin and throughout the Federal Republic,
small homes *(Pflegenester,* perhaps modeled in part on the NSV's *Jugendheimstätten)* for wayward children staffed by psychologists, special schools,
personnel training at the Institute for Psychotherapy, and sanatoriums for
overstressed mothers.[45] The state government of Hessen similarly erected
numerous counseling stations aimed at foster children, illegitimate children,
children of broken homes, war orphans, and so on.[46] Other Youth Bureaus
and states soon followed suit, and in 1954 the AGJJ published a set of "National Uniform Guidelines for Educational Counseling."[47] By 1957 there
were 320 educational counseling stations in Germany, 45 percent of them
supported exclusively by public agencies such as the Youth Bureaus and
State Youth Bureaus; and in 1959 the Youth Bureaus rendered "informal

assistance" *(formlose Betreuung)*, much of it in the form of therapeutic counseling and interventions, in 291,000 cases.[48]

Again, the parallels between the program embodied in these changes and that of the NSV in the 1930s—prevention, counseling, informal assistance, preservation of the family, relief for mothers, smaller institutions—should be obvious. In the 1950s, however, this program was a self-conscious part of the creation of a democratic welfare system, one founded on rights and incentives, and one in which the extermination of the "unfit" played no part.

This is not to say that psychotherapy did not blame parents for their children's problems. On the contrary, if anything, by locating the cause of "maladjustment" in early childhood, it helped to shift responsibility from general social conditions to the parents. And the theorists of psychotherapeutic child welfare policy were particularly eager to blame mothers—explicitly—for their children's problems: mothers who loved too much or too little, clinging mothers or cold mothers, domineering or indifferent mothers, but above all mothers who left their children in day care and went out to work. Echoing a rhetorical tradition already at least half a century old, many observers held that women worked for essentially trivial reasons—for example, in order to pay for remodeling the kitchen or a "fetching permanent wave."[49]

Moreover, social work guided by psychotherapeutic theory was often very little different from social work guided by Christian theory, by hereditarian theory, or by any other theory: it remained a complex process in which social workers attempted to guide and control the behavior of "clients." In the negotiation between clients and social workers, assistance in securing various forms of material aid (family supports, time out for mothers, public housing, even the institutionalization of children) could be used as incentives to get clients to conform, to accept advice; and the threat of sanctions (the institutionalization of children in particular) often was used as a form of implicit or explicit blackmail. And though the new "educational counseling" was less coercive than earlier forms, it was also more ubiquitous. Social agencies in the 1950s claimed the capacity, the desire, even the right to establish a relationship with families in which they could help, advise, inspect, persuade, negotiate with, bully, and hound their clients; and increasingly they had the resources (the personnel and the theory) to do so.

Nevertheless, in the context of *voluntary* counseling this arrogance and imperiousness was in a sense "invisible," since it was so difficult to identify or resist; and it was certainly less objectionable than coercive legal intervention. Even in the early 1950s parents seem to have resorted on their own initiative to the educational counseling centers in considerable numbers. One educational counseling station in Kassel reported in 1952 that 37 percent of its cases were referred by parents; around 25 percent seems to have been typical.[50] Youth Bureaus soon faced the problem of coping not with resistance but with waiting lists of parents seeking material or psychological assistance. In any case, even where parents were referred by the Youth Bureau or the courts and resented the intrusion of these agencies into their private affairs, counseling sessions presumably did not alienate them as much as the seizure of their children would have. The political implications of an expertise that seeks to *prescribe* certain behaviors and relationships are very different from one that seeks to forbid and *punish*.

The Reform of the RJWG: The Ambitions of Social Pedagogy

The 1953 revision of the RJWG accomplished a number of important changes. The restoration of paragraph 4 of the law helped to fuel the expansion of psychological counseling services. And whereas 70 percent of Youth Bureaus in the Weimar Republic had been mere departments within the general Welfare Offices, by fiscal 1957–58, 80 percent of Youth Bureaus were independent agencies (in 1928 only 30 percent had been).[51] Significant advances had also been made in the number of staff who had social work training.

Nevertheless, the development of the Youth Bureaus in the mid-1950s was disappointing to many social welfare advocates. The expansion in the 1950s severely strained the financial resources of the Youth Bureaus, and as a result the growth in the number of trained staff was slow: in 1958 half the Youth Bureaus had no social workers of their own, relying on those employed by the general Welfare Offices; and 22 percent had no personnel with any training specifically in child welfare. Moreover, the Youth Bureaus continued to be dominated by male bureaucrats without social work training, while the subaltern social workers—78 percent of them women—had little influence on administrative decisions.[52] Also, many Youth Bureaus remained rather sleepy institutions: in 1957–58 half of the JWAs had met three times or fewer, and only 6.9 percent had met more than six times, since 1953; 6.1 percent of Youth Bureaus did not even have a JWA yet.[53] Many Youth Bureaus were badly understaffed, too, and hard-pressed to carry out even the basic functions required of them, such as public guardianship or foster care oversight. One reported in 1953 that its three staff members, sharing one typewriter, had to attend eight to ten court hearings, see 220 clients, and write eighty-six letters each week.[54] Finally, the very expansion of EB—flexible, noncoercive, and cheap—called the inherited forms of Youth Bureau programs into question.

At the end of the 1950s, therefore, child welfare advocates seized on the opportunity for discussions of a comprehensive reform of general social services—which gave rise to the Federal Social Services Law (Bundessozialhilfegesetz, or BSHG) of 1961—to agitate for a second reform of the RJWG as well. By 1958 proposals had been presented by the AGJJ, Workers' Welfare, the AFET, the Gilde Soziale Arbeit (a group of left-leaning social workers first founded in 1925), and a special commission established by the Federal Council for Youth Affairs.

For a broad spectrum of German public opinion on the Social Democratic and liberal left, including the SPD, the FDP, the Gilde Soziale Arbeit, Workers' Welfare, and even many on the Christian Democratic left, the codification of welfare law and the unification of social services represented an important step toward the consolidation of a more just and democratic political and social order. The BSHG was intended from its inception to create a comprehensive system of social services divorced from the discriminatory and repressive heritage of poor law and the paternalist heritage of social policy. The appropriate corresponding step in youth policy seemed to be the creation of a system of public child welfare that could effectively realize the "right of the child to education" while abandoning more repressive child welfare programs in favor of child welfare "services" and prevention.[55] A revised RJWG would finally abandon the narrow focus on "deviant" or otherwise abnormal youth, instead creating a unified policy structure securing the social integration of *all* youth.

Advocates of such a reform argued, first, simply for a new and less threatening terminology—for example, "public educational assistance" rather than correctional education, "educational support" rather than protective supervision, and "educational emergency" rather than waywardness. More concretely, they suggested the replacement, insofar as possible, of court-ordered correctional education by FEH, and of both forms by educational counseling. Still more important, they argued that the inherited forms of child welfare programs, which were directed at specific "categories" or groups of young people (the criminal, bastards, the wayward, foster children, the impoverished), were inherently discriminatory and ineffective. They forced agencies to respond only to particular problems, and only in particular ways, often precluding intervention or imposing inappropriate treatment of individuals and their problems. The Youth Bureau, forced to focus only on specific groups and to intervene in "emergencies," was thought of by the general populace as a police agency, a "youth persecution office" *(Jugendverfolgungsamt)*, and both parents and young people were therefore reluctant to call on it for assistance.[56] And rather than securing the right of *all* children to an education, the Youth Bureau merely offered certain forms of protection to (or intervention against) certain groups of children. Dividing the Youth Bureau's work according to these categories encouraged a narrow, often authoritarian and punitive bureaucratic spirit. "Precisely if the young person is to be raised to be not a well-functioning subject but a responsible, thinking, socially committed citizen," wrote

Christa Hasenclever in 1953, "then the tasks of child welfare policy must be defined much more broadly."[57]

But proponents of such a thorough reconstruction of child welfare programs not only argued that the existing system was not compatible with the new, democratic political order; they also held, as we have seen, that the social dislocation caused by the war and the changing nature of capitalism—growing commercialization, the impact of technology, the rising level of employment among married women, and so on—demanded the extension of welfare services to groups not traditionally regarded as "endangered." As Hanns Eyferth (active in the NSV in Berlin before 1945 and in the cities' expansion of EB thereafter) told the AGJJ conference of 1958, it was no longer "special groups on the lower margin of society" that were threatening to fail to socialize their children adequately: rather, "our average family is in danger of no longer mastering its child rearing task. . . . Preventive . . . educational assistance can become necessary in all families and in all classes, and must stand ready for every young person."[58] And Ernst Bornemann argued in 1957 that the changing structure of the family—including the absence of grandparents, mothers working outside the home, the loss of social contacts and the resulting growing expectation of and need for intimacy and emotional intensity in the nuclear family—made it increasingly necessary to provide counseling to resolve familial problems.[59] Others pointed out that there was a steadily increasing need for day care. And still others held simply that the nuclear family was incapable of preparing children for life in a complex, modern industrial society.

For all these reasons, many child welfare advocates on the left argued more vehemently than in the 1910s and 1920s that public programs were needed not only to *support* familial socialization but also to *complement* it. Indeed, some believed that in certain respects public programs should actually *counteract* the influence of the family. Eyferth's co-speaker Gerhard Wurzbacher was nearly so bold as to welcome the collapse of the "patriarchal" family. The traditional family, he observed, seemed "almost oppressive" by the standards of a modern, democratic society, since it left "little room for the development of individual independence." Although the traditional patriarchal family was disappearing as an economic and legal reality, the hierarchical, authoritarian values and behaviors rooted in historical family forms survived in many modern families. Such families often failed to prepare children for life in a democracy, for the "civic participation, responsibility, and initiative" crucial to the survival of the democratic state, a position which echoed Social Democratic thinking on the private family from the 1920s and even earlier.[60] As Eyferth put it, there were "tensions between the personal and familial attitudes, virtues, and forms of relationships and the conditions of public life, which seems to be built ever more upon formal equality and on anonymity. This tension makes it difficult for the family to serve as a model and example also for those tasks which . . . [confront the child in] the so differently structured world of profession, mass leisure, and political organization."⁶¹ In other words, the state must secure the democratic socialization of citizens by creating a less class centered educational system, reducing economic constraints on working-class lives, and encouraging democratically structured organizations for young people.

The entire system, therefore, had to be overhauled. The Youth Bureau had to cease being a special police agency for problem groups and become instead a truly "social-pedagogical" agency, offering services to *all* children and to society at large. It should be required to respond appropriately in each individual case; and in order to broaden the Youth Bureaus' work to include all children, and to reduce the identification of the Youth Bureau with programs for "wayward" and "abnormal" children, a catalogue of tasks of the Youth Bureau should be written into the RJWG that explicitly included not only child welfare programs narrowly defined but also support for youth policy generally—including in particular vocational training, family counseling, and *Jugendpflege*.

These arguments clearly echoed the assertion of Wilhelm Polligkeit in 1908 that the family was incapable of educating youth for participation in modern society. More particularly, they clearly built on the arguments of Gerhard Steuk, Hermann Nohl, and Gertrud Bäumer in the 1920s, all of whom had seen the Youth Bureau as a socialization agency with an autonomous role to play in the socialization of children *beyond* merely supporting the family. And of course the explicitly political thrust of Eyferth's comments echoed, in a new and democratic key, the program implicit in the Nazis' politicization of youth; for he was suggesting that the (now democratic) state must ensure the proper political socialization of children—if necessary in opposition to the parents' own influence and to the traditions that guided their child rearing practices.

Cultural Pessimism and (Christian) Democracy

These demands brought left-liberal and Social Democratic reformers into bitter conflict with Christian Democrats between 1957 and 1961, a conflict in which the arguments of the 1920s regarding the role of ideology in education and the role of private associations and communal governments in a democratic state were recapitulated almost word for word. In contrast to the stalemate and crisis of the late 1920s, however, in the late 1950s Christian cultural conservatives and the charities achieved an extraordinarily successful response to the new social and political environment and to the reform program of the left.

The destruction of the radical socialist left, the crucial role played by the Christian churches in the years immediately after the defeat, the long-term hold of Christian Democracy over the federal government, and the economic boom of the 1950s created an extremely congenial environment for the Christian charities. Their recovery was very rapid; already by the early 1950s their activities were more extensive than in the 1920s and early 1930s. By 1957, for example, there were 666,000 beds available in the various institutions supported by private charity, as against only 534,000 in 1930.[62]

Nevertheless, Christian social observers were no more approving of the development of German culture and society in the 1950s than in the 1920s. As we have seen, the social disaster left behind by the war created a sense of moral crisis in more conservative middle-class circles, fueled by high rates of delinquency, illegitimacy, divorce, venereal disease, and so on. The defeat of the Nazis and their conservative allies and the social upheaval of the 1940s undermined many traditional cultural and social authorities and patterns of behavior, allowing the development of a more open, less "respectable" society. Particularly alarming was the widespread skepticism of youth regarding the older generation and their values and agendas. And while the symptoms of social pathology and mistrust that were so disturbing in the late 1940s soon eased in the 1950s, the economic boom of that decade brought its own problems. In fact, conservative Christians saw the social and cultural developments of the 1950s as part of—even as the culmination of—a process of decline and decay which they traced back to the 1890s or even to the mythical Christian-patriarchal golden age which they located at the beginning of the nineteenth century, before the onset of the age of iron. The central problem of the 1950s was, of course, precisely the problem which had concerned Christians since the 1840s—what the Catholic ministerial official Friedrich Rothe called the "dissolution of the organic human life-communities [*Lebensgefüge*] of marriage and family" under the impact of divorce, modern patterns of work, the decline of the extended family, and modern conceptions of the "nature and purposes of marriage."[63] While left-leaning "social pedagogues" concentrated on the economic origins of this sociological crisis of the family, Christians—in accordance with a century of analysis—tended to regard it and the decline of the family's capacity to socialize children as more fundamentally the product of a parallel "dissolution of ethical principles," the declining importance of ethical norms and religious ideals in everyday life, and their replacement by goal-rationality, the cult of material success, and cultural massification.

This process had been enormously accelerated, of course, by the teachings of the Nazis; but it was also driven by the postwar boom and consumerism. The destruction of organic human communities and meaningful

individual and collective experience by the ongoing processes of urbanization, industrialization, and mechanization (and the attendant alienation of
labor) were the deepest root of this development. The growth in the 1950s
of consumer capitalism, and particularly of commercialized and techno-
logically sophisticated entertainments (radio, the movies, television, the
phonograph, pinball games, and so on) only made matters worse by over-
whelming authentic human relationships and drowning out deeper spiritual
values and insights, particularly among the young. In the words of an internal KFV document, "The public sphere is today different in aspect" than
before the war, "more aggressive, more intensive in its offerings, etc. The
public sphere reaches out for the child earlier and influences it in a more
unfiltered manner."[64] While the intensification of labor processes, the triumph of technology, and the uniformity of urban society were crushing
individuality and authentic social relationships from without, then, the entertainment industry was achieving a parallel cultural massification, trivial-
ization, even dehumanization from within.

This critique of the triviality and soullessness of modern mass society
soon matured in the 1950s into a sophisticated analysis of the spiritual
poverty of consumer society. Although Christians and particularly Catholics were most concerned, this critique was by no means limited to Christian Democratic circles; conservative and liberal sociologists such as Arnold
Gehlen, Hans Freyer, and even sociologists of the left such as Alexander
Mitscherlich, Theodor Adorno, and Max Horkheimer, played a particularly important role in its development and popularization; Helmut
Schelsky, whose 1957 book *The Skeptical Generation* popularized the conservative critique of postwar youth culture, was perhaps most influential in
child welfare circles.[65] At the DVöpF conference of 1953, Schelsky argued
that the war had created a widespread desire to rediscover personal security, a "retreat into the intimate sphere"; but the economic imperatives of
the postwar period, the striving for social advancement, and the penetration of technology into the home had led to a "superficialization" and "objectification" of the family. Work had undergone a similar objectification,
as the "calling" of the individual came to be seen as nothing more than a
way to earn money. The result was a generalized "cultural and social loss of
substance."[66] The ethical, emotional, and religious life of the masses was
being hollowed out, becoming empty and impoverished.

The Catholic Dr. Fleckenstein was equally pessimistic in a *Jugendwohl*
article of the same year. There could be, he wrote, no "moral maturation"
without the experience of "domestic security" *(Geborgenheit)*, "in which
alone the child can overcome the most dangerous enemy of maturation:
fear." In addition, however, the child must also experience "limits," must
learn that some of its instincts could be followed and others not; there must
be a "rational system of wish fulfillment and wish denial," an "authorita-

tive moral code." Either lack of love or too much love, by creating an imbalance in the relationship between security and limits, could prevent the development of moral character and strength. Both, of course, were the expressions of egoism—whether that of people who had so weak a sense of their own worth that they exaggerated their own authority, or of people who devoted insufficient time and care to their parental duties.[67] But as the Jesuit Franz Prinz argued in the same issue of *Jugendwohl,* the conditions of life in a consumer-capitalist society fostered precisely this kind of egoism. The fact that often both parents worked meant that children grew up without love or a consistently applied set of limits. Familial instability induced by the war threatened the sense of security and reduced domestic happiness. The "mechanization of life," of both leisure and labor, robbed people of the sense of meaning in their lives and actions, and so of their sense of responsibility.[68] The result for modern children, Fleckenstein held, was a spiritual "loss of heart" (*Entmutigung,* literally "dis-courage-ment"), a demoralization expressed in childhood in the form of stubbornness and asociality, lack of discipline, selfishness, impulsiveness, hunger for sensation, precocious sexual activity, and masturbation. In adolescence and adulthood "loss of heart" appeared in an incapacity for self-discipline and rational self-direction and in a lack of internal defenses against the dangers of independent life; the "destruction of spiritual values" led to "cruelty, dishonesty, dissipated living out of the animal instincts, the triumph of the lowly over the higher goals." Such adults developed an "inauthentic and sick" way of life, dominated by a neurotic and amoral striving for passive pleasure. The commercialization of mass culture—through film, rock 'n' roll, jazz, pinball, "shopping," compulsive social drinking, trashy literature, comic strips—bespoke merely the relentless need of selfish, frightened, lonely people to escape from one another, from their own emptiness, from their incapacity to face up to reality and the moral challenges it presented.[69]

One product of this sense of crisis was a renewed spate of morality legislation at the beginning of the 1950s. The Nazi censorship law of 1935 and the decree of 1943 for the "protection" of youth had been struck down by the occupation authorities, leaving German youth at the mercy (in conservative eyes) of the entertainment industry after the war. The replacement of these laws and the development of an effective system of "youth protection" *(Jugendschutz)* was therefore a high priority among child welfare advocates after the creation of the Federal Republic in 1949. A system of voluntary self-censorship was established by the film industry in 1949 to forestall the passage of a new film law.[70] A Law for the Protection of Youth in Public (at dances, in bars, at the movies, on the street at night) was passed in late 1951. And in September 1952 a new law on smutty and trashy literature was passed.

These laws were based on a deeply conservative conception of the politics of cultural life, one best summed up, perhaps, by the remark published in *Jugendwohl* in 1953 to the effect that too eager a defense of freedom of the press was "treason against authentic freedom. . . . No one has the right to be immoral."[71] And many, such as Elisabeth Zillken, also continued to couple the ideal of freedom for the normal with its revocation for the deviant, calling for laws allowing the institutionalization of those "so morally weakened that they cannot take their own lives in hand."[72] In fact, the perennial discussion of the possibility of *Bewahrung* (permanent institutionalization) was also revived in 1951. And by the mid-1950s conservatives, alarmed by the development of the entertainment industry and the negative potentials of the "leisure society," were bitterly criticizing the new morality laws, arguing that even the more draconian measures of the Nazi period were preferable.

Yet such criticisms reflected precisely the fact that these laws did *not* attempt to revive the coercive approach of the Nazi period. Instead, they represented a return to the strategy of the 1920s. The film industry escaped direct regulation by establishing its own standards.[73] And the laws on "smut" and "trash" and for the "protection" of youth punished not young people but those who gave them access to "corrupting" materials or entertainments. Their intent was not to punish immoral youth, not to crush commercial culture and purify the entire public sphere; they aimed, rather, to protect the private sphere, especially childhood, from unlimited penetration by commercial capitalism, to create a protected cultural space around the child. And, increasingly, advocates of *Jugendschutz* also attempted to offer positive measures: "good" books and films, parents' organizations and family counseling, "humane enlightenment about sexuality," and especially youth groups and "open-door" youth centers that offered opportunities for the "cultivation of new social relations in order to drive back anonymous, anomic 'sociability' (for example, public dances)."[74] This was true particularly on the left, for example, within Workers' Welfare; but it was also one central function of the Youth Plans and of the reform of the RJWG in 1953. In other words, the "protectors" of youth were adopting a managerial strategy of offering incentives and benefits rather than imposing prohibitions. As Walter Becker wrote, "*Jugendschutz* does not consist only of the negative defense against the dangers of hypercivilization, but rather [includes] the encouragement of youth in a *positive* sense, and the waking of the forces for the good slumbering in the youth itself."[75] Finally, in the 1950s *Jugendschutz* enthusiasts concentrated less on police measures than on the mobilization of public opinion and the creation of what Rothe called a "minimum of public *ethos*," a consensus on standards of behavior and on moral principles, particularly with respect to the young.[76] Local "Youth Protection Weeks" involving book exchanges, lectures, and displays were particularly important in this effort; 250 of them were held between 1948 and 1956.[77]

In fact, by the early 1950s—despite the obvious continuities between the Christian antimodernism of the 1850s and the cultural criticism of the 1950s—there was a distinctly new tone to the complaints of cultural conservatives. In line with the discovery of the "new waywardness," they increasingly perceived immorality as a problem not of nascent social rebellion but of consumerist passivity. Of more concern to them than the occasional riot at an Elvis Presley movie was the fact that the rapid spread of new technologies such as television, the phonograph, and the movies seemed to pose a new threat to young people's morality, taste, and health, and especially to their capacity for self-directed activity. The great evil of these technologies was that they cultivated a thirst for passive entertainment and for fictional spectacle. The expansion of the film industry, for example, was dangerous merely because of the content of many films; but *Jugendwohl* was equally concerned by the fact that, as it found in 1951, 50 percent of boys and 62 percent of girls went to the movies merely to "kill time," only 29 percent of boys and 26 percent of girls out of active interest in the film in question.[78] By 1956 a Professor A. Tesarek, for one, was so alarmed by the general passivity of youth that he suggested at a meeting of *Jugendpfleger* in Berlin that "we need revolutionaries," and that young people should be encouraged to reject the uniformity imposed by consumerism.[79]

The authors of this cultural criticism in a new key gave their analysis a political dimension very similar to that expounded by their predecessors in the 1910s, but one appropriate to a democratic rather than an authoritarian political order. It was no longer merely the collapse of all moral restraints on individual appetites and the egoistic, anarchic revolt of the masses that they feared; instead, they worried that mass consumerism might be creating a passive, indifferent citizenry incapable of supporting democratic institutions. Having accepted the mobilization of the masses as a political and ethical imperative, they feared not mass action but mass apathy; they were afraid that a democratic state structure could not survive in a society of selfish, amoral adventurers and freebooters. On the one hand, they feared the anarchy of individual amorality. Fleckenstein, for example, believed that "if greedy love does not become the authentic love of well-wishing, which brings to others respect, consideration, and willingness to sacrifice for their own sake, then all human community atrophies, and at the same time individual moral personality. Then there remains only one possibility for ordering human community relations: the coercive collective."[80] On the other hand, they also feared that individual apathy would lead people to delegate all meaningful social action to the state, a tendency which Helmut Schelsky saw as particularly characteristic of modern, skeptical youth.

The terms of this new cultural criticism precluded any return to a repressive cultural strategy. Since it was passivity and weakness rather than the anarchic rebellion of the sinful self that made people asocial, repression would only exacerbate the problem. The ideal of moral freedom—the freedom to do as one should—central to Christian social thought had been transformed from a discourse about the crisis of authority into a discourse about the crisis of democracy, of self-government. In a society held together by participation rather than obedience, the lack of the capacity for self-government, rather than the refusal to obey, was the central concern. Christian cultural conservatives in the 1950s therefore increasingly advocated a strategy of actively and constructively inculcating healthy (and democratic) habits and values; their answer to the problem of massification was not merely to crush unhealthy impulses but to foster healthy ones.

Certainly Christians and secular cultural critics did not abandon their conception of the role of authority in pedagogy and in society. The experience of National Socialism and the decline of authoritarian family structures made even conservative intellectuals very skeptical of authority after the war; but the cultural critics of the 1950s continued to argue that *legitimate* authority, authority which came from God and served his ends, and which played a necessary and just role in social organization and social life, was indispensable. Indeed, by the late 1950s there were signs of a new groundswell of concern about the decay of respect for authority. And Christian theorists often explicitly rejected "liberal" or "free" *(freiheitliche)* educational theory as it had been espoused in the 1920s. It was not true, they held, that the goal of education was to realize whatever was in the pupil or to allow the pupil to become merely well adjusted and comfortable with himself or herself. Man was called to be good, "to natural and supernatural perfection!"[81]

One current within Christian pedagogy, of course, had always seen in authority merely a means toward the end of moral freedom. This commitment had been characteristic particularly of Catholic pedagogical thought, and to some extent the shift in the terms of cultural criticism in the 1950s reflected simply the new predominance of Catholicism and the self-destruction of conservative Protestantism in the Third Reich; but it had been evident, as we have seen, also in the thinking of conservative Protestants such as Wilhelm Backhausen. The goal of Christian pedagogy had been not to forbid the bad but to teach children actively to will the good.

There was, however, a subtly but decisively important new element in the reformulation of this heritage which was increasingly adopted in the 1950s. For whereas traditional Christian theory had emphasized the importance of learning self-control, of internalizing *obedience* as the path to the creation of morally free persons, the emphasis now shifted toward the learning of *self-direction*. Ernst Ell held that Catholic education was not "authoritarian" but "authoritative." Obedience must prepare the child not for further obedience but for self-governance.[82] As the Protestant Wolfgang Fischer argued, education must teach children to "harmonize their own desires with what is allowed"; but "that is possible neither where one . . . breaks the will of the young people . . ., nor where one merely lets them have their way. . . . Education . . . is the building of motivation for proper desire."[83] And the Catholic Franz-Josef Wehnes—precisely echoing Friedrich-Wilhelm Förster's arguments of 1914—was more explicit. In any effective response to the demoralizing impact of consumer society on children, he wrote in 1957, "what is decisive is not yet accomplished . . . through mere education for self-discipline, [since] only the restraining energies are developed; only the constructive energies can work in a really positive manner. Everything therefore depends . . . on the energies of self-direction being added, on activity and spontaneity being awakened in the child, so that later the person can stand on his own and shape his own life himself."[84]

This shift, then, clearly brought about a striking convergence between the "new" pedagogy of the left and Christian pedagogical thought, a project on which Protestants and surviving leaders of the pedagogical reform movement had in fact been working quite self-consciously in *Die Sammlung* (successor to *Die Erziehung*) since 1945. In fact, even in the late 1950s, when cultural pessimism led to a growing sense of crisis and denunciation of the pathologies of prosperity, those making such denunciations rarely abandoned this "democratic" stance. Andreas Mehringer (whose celebration of the preventive character of the NSV's work was cited in Chapter 8) spoke in 1955 of the "danger of an emancipated youth," and held that there was "too little child rearing" being done in modern society. But the "exaggeration of material concerns" was not the "fundamental evil of our time": the essential problem was "lack of inner contact" between children and their parents, and "despite all negative phenomena . . . we should be less worried about lack of discipline today than about a return to the overemphasis on the value of outward discipline." He demanded a more self-consciously *democratic* pedagogy to meet this challenge.[85]

Obviously this change in perspective was not a revolutionary one; it was, again, a shift in emphasis rather than a great innovation. But it was not easily accomplished, for it implied an assumption that was fundamentally foreign to more conservative Christians, and particularly Protestants: that sinful man could will the good. As in the case of secular, social-managerial progressivism, psychotherapeutic thought played a critically important role in the accomplishment of this shift from authoritarianism to democracy. By locating the origins of the specific direction of man's will in early childhood experience rather than in his unalterably and universally sinful nature, and by positing a complex relationship between outward behavior and inward state, psychotherapy shattered the equation between authority and morality that was central to Christian theory. If the active will of the child could be directed toward the good, then it was no longer something merely to be controlled and broken; and if "bad" behavior could be merely a sign of the "neurotic processing of experience,"[86] then one might more effectively help a bad child become good by giving it love than by giving it justice. Psychotherapy, in other words, banished the idea of evil from pedagogy.

Many conservative Christians objected to the complete abandonment of the idea of moral waywardness in favor of mental illness; and Catholics in particular feared that psychotherapy might become a surrogate for religion. In the end, however, most of the Christian reform leadership—including the pope himself—concluded that psychotherapy was compatible with Christian teachings.[87] Indeed, by the end of the 1950s psychotherapy was so influential that Christian counseling centers were being opened all over Germany in order to compete with the public, secular centers, while the journals of the Christian charities overflowed with articles by licensed psychotherapists and with the commonsense humanism of modern psychological "science." As Waltraud Krützfeldt-Eckhard observed in an article of 1952, social work was increasingly dominated by "democracy and psychoanalysis," a combination which amounted to an "ideology" alien to the Christian understanding of sin and redemption. But the method and the insights of such social work could, she believed, be adopted by Christians, since they "are given meaning and significance by the values of the person who uses them." "Slowly," she concluded, "a solution to our problems is beginning to crystallize: many 'ifs' and 'buts'—but in the end a 'yes.'"[88] Within the context of a Christian culture, in other words, democracy was acceptable.

This transition was made easier by the fact that "scientific" psychotherapy was open to a self-consciously Christian interpretation. Christian pedagogical and social theory, after all, had always argued that the child learns to be moral and social in the family and through the peculiar psychological dynamic of family life. Moreover, the goals of psychotherapy could be defined in terms very much compatible with Christian theory. The aim of psychotherapy is to allow the individual to take control of his or her own actions and feelings, to overcome inward weakness and become free. This project, again, clearly paralleled the progressive reform strategy: by liberating energies and resolving internal conflicts, integration and effectiveness would be increased. But it was also compatible with the Christian conception of inward freedom, of the freedom to do what is right. As the Protestant Karl Janssen wrote: "There is . . . a threat from within. Man can fall under the tyranny of his instincts, his lusts and desires and become . . . a slave to his own false and dangerous inner dynamics and addictions. At present this state of affairs is often described as endangerment through neurosis. . . . As soon as the person is made capable of controlling himself, he is free, he is capable of freedom . . . because he has mastery of himself. With that falls also the need to subject him to any restraints."[89] What is more, in a sense psychotherapy and "social pedagogy" took the place, in the Christian rhetoric of the 1950s, of the religious revival at which their predecessors in the 1840s or even the 1890s had aimed. The AGJJ's "Guidelines" for EB, for example, remarked that the cause of the "decline of the pedagogical capacity [Erziehungskraft] of the family" resulted from a "disappearance of binding, generally recognized values," but went on to argue that this problem had to be mastered by "expert educational counseling and constructive educational assistance" which would reawaken the pedagogical "strengths and insights" of parents.[90]

In fact, psychotherapeutic social work ("educational counseling") established a critically important bridge between Christian and progressive reform, for it opened up the possibility of adopting a preventive, managerial, "modern" reform strategy without having to accept the collapse of traditional social structures and the potential collectivism of "social pedagogy." It permitted the creation of a system of child welfare institutions—educational counseling centers—which did not themselves socialize children, or in any way relieve their parents from doing so, but rather assisted the family in carrying out its traditional functions. The Catholic Kurt Nachbauer warned in 1956 of the "fateful tendency toward collectivism" apparent in the fact that "we are today often too quick to capitulate before the failure of family function, before the pedagogical failure of many families, and to seek salvation in institutions outside the family." But he went on to suggest that "educational and marriage counseling stations" provided an antidote to this tendency because they offered to *reconstruct* (rather than replace or even complement) the family.[91] In terms of the spectrum of social pedagogy in the 1920s, the development of educational counseling allowed Christians to develop a model of child welfare policymakers very much like that of Aloys Fischer, who held that state policy must reinforce the family, without accepting the more radical social pedagogy of Gerhard Steuk, who held that policy must accept the obsolescence of the family in the modern world (Chapter 7). If psychotherapy helped to defuse the conflict between child welfare reform and its targets, then, it also helped to reconcile Christians to the social-liberal, social-managerial reform strategy.

The Struggle over the Reform of the RJWG in 1961

The adoption of this conservative managerial strategy did not reconcile Catholics to the kind of preventive social management envisaged by the Social Democratic and social-pedagogical left. On the contrary, conservative Christians, and particularly Catholics, viewed these ambitions with the deepest mistrust. In Catholic circles even the reform of 1953 had appeared threatening. The increased power of local government over the Youth Bureau seemed to open the door to precisely the kind of bureaucratic and plebiscitary tyranny from which they had just been delivered. Karl Peters warned of the "growing danger of state omnipotence . . . communal omnipotence . . . [and] majority omnipotence"; the chairman of the DCV's committee on child welfare feared the creation of an expensive "totalitarian state welfare system"; and the new president of the DCV spoke of a "strong tendency toward dictatorship, autocracy, democracy in the socializing sense."[92] Within the AGJJ, Catholic representatives had argued in the early 1950s—just as they had in the 1920s—in favor of a very different, corporatist conception of democracy. Elisabeth Zillken of the KFV demanded that an alternative structure "must be found that leads to a real democratization. That can happen only through the direct involvement of the people in administrative affairs. Appropriate decisions can be made only by people involved in the actual work."[93] And Gustav von Mann argued that "public" child welfare programs were the responsibility both of public agencies and of the private charities, for in a truly democratic state the implementation of policy must be entrusted not "one-sidedly to parliaments and public agencies" but also to the people themselves: anything less would mean the "end of a healthy democracy."[94]

The restoration of paragraph 4 of the RJWG seemed to make these dangers all the more acute, since it appeared to invite financially healthy cities to shoulder the private charities aside, as well as to encourage their "tendency to ignore the principle of the subsidiarity" of public welfare measures to the family. While not questioning the need for services such as kindergartens and day care, the DCV argued—in contrast to Social Democrats—that mothers' participation in the work force and the need for EB and day care could not be accepted as permanent features of modern life. There was the danger, the DCV warned, "that the family will be socialized and its children, even where it is not necessary, entrusted . . . on principle to kindergartens, day schools, day care, and so on. This is a life-threatening danger for our nation." Such institutions should therefore be controlled by the private charities since, "if the cities create these institutions themselves, dismantling them [in the future] will be difficult, and there is the danger that tasks which normally would fall to the family will be lastingly socialized. It will always be easier to dismantle or transform private welfare institutions."[95]

These views were opposed in the early 1950s, however, by the state governments, the secular reform organizations, the Inner Mission and Workers' Welfare, and even by the Bundesjugendring and the national organization of Catholic youth groups.[96] More cautious Catholics were able to secure only a declaration in the official commentary *(Begründung)* to the law to the effect that it was important to "delegate joint responsibility to those citizens who have shown their civic-mindedness through voluntary activity" in order to prevent "the development of a merely representative democracy," and a resolution passed by the upper house stating that the Youth Bureaus must "preserve the principle of the subsidiarity of public child welfare with respect both to the pedagogical tasks of the family and to the voluntary activity of the private child welfare associations."[97]

By the late 1950s it seemed evident to the Catholic charities that this declaration had not been sufficient to stem the advance of public child welfare programs at the expense of private initiative. While secular social pedagogues and Social Democrats expected from the new reform initiative a deepening of the majoritarian democratic spirit of the law and an extension of state welfare services, the Catholic charities were determined to use the new initiative to accomplish exactly the opposite—the legal anchoring of corporatist democracy and the containment of public child welfare programs.

The Catholic attempt to redirect the reform of the law did not take the form of an outright repudiation of social pedagogy. Both Catholics and Protestants agreed that the state must support private *Jugendpflege;* more important, as we have seen, they also supported the creation of programs that would help and support families. The draft bill of the AGJJ, which was written by von Mann of the DCV and Elisabeth Bamberger of the Bavarian Ministry of the Interior, suggested a catalogue of Youth Bureau tasks as extensive as any. Indeed, Bamberger even made the slogan of Klumker and Petersen her own, demanding that the new Youth Bureau "must become a socializing agency."[98]

But there were fundamental differences between the Catholic view of "social pedagogy" and that of the left. Whereas social pedagogues of the left spoke of the need to relieve overburdened families through the introduction of day care or EB, Catholics were much more cautious, emphasizing assistance to the family in the mastering of its own problems rather than attempts to provide extrafamilial measures and institutions. Even Bamberger, who represented the most liberal perspective on these issues within the Catholic child welfare community, insisted that assistance from public agencies must be introduced "not in order to relieve lazy parents but rather to strengthen the educative powers of overburdened parents."[99]

Furthermore, whereas the secular experts and Social Democrats deplored the failure of the Youth Bureaus to become more "lively" after 1953, once again, as in the 1920s, Catholics were more concerned by their very liveliness. The Catholic charities had hoped that the financial strain of expansion after the 1953 reform would force the Youth Bureaus into closer cooperation with private organizations; but they had been bitterly disappointed. The massive expansion of EB, day care, public *Jugendpflege,* and so forth was, in this sense, very disturbing. Moreover, as they had in the 1920s, many Youth Bureaus simply failed to call meetings of the JWA, discharging the business of the Youth Bureau without input from the charities. And by the late 1950s the Catholic charities increasingly remarked on the *diminishing* readiness of municipal administrations to work with private associations, perhaps in part a product of the growing financial strength of the municipalities. This situation seemed to raise once again, precisely as it had in the 1920s, the threat that public agencies would impose an irreligious education upon youth. The DCV's Gustav von Mann reported that some local administrators argued that it was financially impossible for small communities to support separate kindergartens or public legal guardians for Catholic, Protestant, and nonreligious children, and that in any case the ideologically neutral democratic state should not be in the business of encouraging religious divisions.[100]

Even short of this religious threat, Catholics argued that the family alone, and not public day care institutions and "social pedagogy" generally, was capable of counteracting the pathologies that currently endangered youth—massification, egoism, the loss of respect for authority, monotony and mechanization, loneliness, workaholism, the loss of a sense of spiritual meaning.[101] Failing the revival of the family, of course, intervention by a *private* organization was, from a spiritual point of view and in the long run, the next best solution. In public programs, Toni Thurnreit believed, "the young person is given money, it is true, but no absolute norms and values. . . . What the young person needs in his mental-spiritual situation is a unified worldview and an absolutely binding order, upon which he can build his life. But our state . . . a secular, metaphysically colorless state, no longer has any connection to values standing above itself. Who else but the private charities could give the young person what he needs?"[102] In fact— again echoing Christian arguments of the 1920s—Friedrich Rothe of the Ministry for Family and Youth Affairs argued that state intervention in positive *Erziehung* was unconstitutional, since the ideological neutrality of the state was a condition for the existence of pluralistic democracy, while all *Erziehung* aimed at the inculcation of values and was thus by definition religious or at least ideological *(weltanschaulich).*[103] Furthermore, the spread of public child welfare institutions, with their bland, neutral humanistic and psychologistic philosophical foundations and methods, seemed to be contributing to the hollowing-out and massification of culture. Such methods and values, von Mann warned, could not "do justice to the vividness of life, the variety of humanity"; they could only create "mass-produced human beings," contributing to the development of a depersonalized, superficial mass culture of indifference and passivity.[104]

Finally, again, for conservative cultural critics the development of welfare "services" seemed to encourage the tendency of modern people to shift their personal and public responsibilities onto the state, often in favor of an amoral pursuit of wealth. This in turn could undermine the self-help organizations of society, such as the charities, the churches, and the family. Elisabeth Zillken warned against allowing parents to develop the habit of calling on the educational counseling center in every little family crisis, since doing so would undermine the self-reliance, initiative, and pedagogical capacities of parents. And Friedrich Rothe insisted, "We cannot make it too easy to run to anonymous social agencies," for "through this kind of policy . . . the solidarity of neighborly help will be strangled, and human community life will dry out and die."[105]

This fear had been lively in child welfare circles since the beginning of the twentieth century. It was evident, for example, in the remarks of Frieda Duensing at the inception of the Youth Bureau in 1910, and in the discussion of its structure and functions at the National Child Welfare Conference of 1918. It was all the more pressing, however, in the context of the cold war, for totalitarian communism seemed to provide a frightening example of the consequences of disregarding it. In fact, many Christians believed that the massification of society and the atrophy of its "autonomous energies" (in Rothe's words) was undermining the foundations of Western democracy and opening the way for its ultimate defeat by totalitarian collectivism. As Rothe told the Federal Council of Youth Affairs in December 1957, the "dissolution of ethical principles" was "unconsciously preparing our delivery into the hands of totalitarian forces" by undermining the capacity for real social solidarity and commitment to ethical and political values, while the development of a massive public welfare bureaucracy threatened to destroy the habit of active self-government and political engagement. A state that did not "educate people for freedom and responsibility" would "pave the way for the totalitarian state."[106] And in 1960 Franz-Josef Wuermeling, the CDU minister for family and youth affairs, remarked that the values "given us by the family and the sentiments it instills are in the final analysis also the foundation of our powers of resistance in the worldwide confrontation with communism."[107]

Nor was it only Catholics who entertained such fears. Hugo Möller, writing in *Die Sammlung* in 1954, saw in the impersonal rules and procedures of the welfare state a glaring example of a process of dehumanization and alienation—the loss of concrete, "face-to-face" contact between people and the resulting evaporation of any socially meaningful sense of "self" and "other"—which began with Kant's commitment to abstract moral imperatives and the replacement of the ideal of charity by that of justice and ethical "duty," and culminated in a program of mass murder that sacrificed individual persons in the name of abstract "humanity." The "modern mass-welfare state," he suggested, was rooted in the ideal of humanity, but in it "a new, until now unimagined inhumanity has its origin." In early 1956 the same journal carried an article in which the Hayekian neoliberal Alexander Rüstow denounced the "total[itarian] welfare state" and warned of the decline of "responsibility for self, independent self-help, readiness and eagerness to take risks, daring, and pride in independence—all qualities on which the achievements of Western civilization still largely rest." The coercion that the state would have to employ to extract sufficient revenues to replace such qualities with public welfare programs, he believed, would lead to the creation of "a totalitarian dictatorship." West Germany was thus on "a path which, even if only in a wide and elegant curve, leads in the end to Moscow."[108]

One response to this looming danger, in the 1950s as in the 1900s and the 1920s, was the expansion of the private associations. And in fact, at least with respect to numbers of institutions, talk of a public monopoly over child welfare was rather paranoid, since Germany's "economic miracle" and public subsidies permitted the charities to expand at a dizzying rate. In 1955, 60 percent of child welfare institutions were operated by private organizations, a figure that in 1959 had risen to 73 percent.[109] The private charities were in fact establishing themselves as immense bureaucratic empires. For example, the KFV had 461 local chapters in 1953, employing 385 full-time professional social workers and 60,227 volunteers; it had 45,095 wards (as against 31,045 in 1949).[110] By 1957 Workers' Welfare—which itself claimed in 1951 to have 5,000 local chapters and 70,000 volunteers—even feared a "preponderance" *(Übergewicht)* of the private charities in social welfare.[111]

The prospect of simple competition with the state, however, was unappealing to the charities. Instead, building on arguments developed in the debates over the RJWG in 1922 and 1953, the Catholic charities proposed to protect civil society by establishing in law and in practice the "principle of subsidiarity." Public agencies should be required to allow and encourage the family and private organizations to meet the needs of the populace rather than stepping in themselves. Only in this way could the citizenry be educated for self-help and self-reliance. For this reason, Catholic spokespeople and the AGJJ itself referred to subsidiarity as a "litmus test of democracy."[112]

In contrast to the outcome of 1953, the power of the Catholic establishment within the ministries, parliament, and the AGJJ, and also the unity created by the sense of threat from public welfare programs, enabled the

Catholic charities to impose their will on the legislative process between 1958 and 1961. The draft bill published by the AGJJ in April 1958 was a triumph for the Catholic organizations: it stipulated that "public child welfare consists of the child welfare of public agencies and of private child welfare"; established their "common responsibility" for youth; allowed the Youth Bureau to implement most programs only "insofar as they are not taken on by private child welfare organizations"; and explicitly stated that the Youth Bureau did not fall under the terms of the constitution of communal government *(Gemeindeordnung)*, and that the local government of which the Youth Bureau was an organ could nullify decisions of the JWA only where they were illegal. The charities were to be given half of the seats in the JWA, which was required to meet at least six times yearly.[113] The recommendations of the Federal Council on Youth Affairs virtually reproduced these demands.[114] Finally, the minister for family and youth affairs, Franz-Joseph Wuermeling, was so militant a Catholic that he occasionally caused severe embarrassment to his own party and government,[115] while Friedrich Rothe was the official responsible for drafting the government's bill. Not surprisingly, therefore, the first drafts of the new law closely resembled that published by the AGJJ. They granted the private associations only two fifths of the seats in the JWA; but they did explicitly guarantee the "precedence" *(Vorrang)* of both the family and the private charities over public child welfare measures, and introduced various guarantees of parents' rights to determine the ideological or religious orientation of their children (even those in public care). Most important, the government's draft law required the Youth Bureau to encourage and support the efforts of the family, the private charities, and even of the churches "in the necessary degree" for the accomplishment of the goals of public policy before establishing any independent public institutions or programs.[116]

This stipulation represented the logical end point of the Catholic theory of "subsidiarity" and the Catholic conception of corporatist democracy as it had developed since the beginning of the century. Indeed, Agnes Neuhaus had argued in 1921 for the insertion of just such a clause into the first paragraph of the original RJWG. At that time, her suggestion was rejected by the Ministry of the Interior on the grounds that "it cannot be the intention of the law to place private before public welfare."[117] By 1961, however, that was in fact precisely what the new version of the law was intended to do.

The Struggle in Parliament

Even the Protestant charities were somewhat taken aback by the Catholic position. Some Protestants strongly supported the principle of subsidiarity, but many were less committed to it than were Catholics. Manfred Müller, for example, wrote in *Sozialpädagogik* (the new title of *Evangelische Jugendhilfe*), "For us the principle of subsidiarity is not an ethical imperative."[118] And the Inner Mission and the Protestant youth groups issued a declaration in July 1959 in which they argued that only "objective factors"—that is, which organization could best perform the needed services—should decide whether private or public agencies should be responsible for a given program.[119]

Both the Gilde Soziale Arbeit and Workers' Welfare also supported this latter position; but while the Inner Mission was simply unenthusiastic, Workers' Welfare and the cities in particular were incensed by the new bill. In its concern for the rights and independence of the family and of the charities, they believed, the ministry had clearly failed to use the occasion of a reform of the law to promote actively the creation of programs with independent pedagogical functions that complemented the functioning of the family. The draft bills produced by the AGJJ and the government, Eyferth argued, failed to move beyond the old categories of problem children to the creation of a truly preventive child welfare system.[120] And in so doing, of course, they had passed up the opportunity to democratize the child welfare system, to create a system that would respond positively to the needs of the individual child. While Catholics argued that the charities were the indispensable repositories of ethical ideas and energies, Ludwig Preller argued that the only "ethical norm" that a public child welfare system absolutely must obey was that of "the welfare of the child and of all children."[121] And while Catholics worried about crippling self-reliance, those on the left argued, again, that citizens had social rights which the state was obligated to guarantee.

But beyond this failure, in the eyes of many on the left the bill's provisions constituted a positive threat to democratic institutions. Most prosaically, the requirement that the Youth Bureau support private institutions rather than create its own seemed to represent an outright abrogation of the financial sovereignty of the communal governments. But Workers' Welfare and the cities also held that democracy was learned and lived by the citizenry not in private associations—which were often elitist, exclusive, and undemocratic in their structure—but in the local, democratic, self-governing communities, the *Gemeinden*. The *Gemeinden* were not representatives of the power of the state but rather the fundamental cells of democratic life. "What is at stake," wrote one spokesman for municipal interests in 1961,

> is a fundamental question of democracy in the *Gemeinde* and therefore of democracy itself.
>
> Our democratic life in Germany must today once again find its starting point in the elementary democracy of the *Gemeinde*. . . .

It is not enough that people interest themselves in their private association and associational institutions. . . . That would mean the end of the ethical and state-political content of communal politics.[122]

And in a position paper of August 1958 Workers' Welfare argued that "democratization in child welfare means the strengthening of the idea of self-government, the waking of civic responsibility in the *Gemeinde*. Civic responsibility does not mean limitation [of participation] to certain recognized associations."[123] Real democratic participation, Workers' Welfare argued—as it had since the early 1920s—would be secured only by encouraging citizens (perhaps *trained* by the charities) to volunteer directly to serve in *public* child welfare agencies.

Finally, Workers' Welfare deplored the further "confessionalization" of child welfare that the bill represented. Lotte Lemke, among others, warned that dependence on the hierarchically structured churches and charities was a greater danger for democracy than dependence on democratically accountable public agencies; she believed that strengthening the role of the religious charities might in the end revoke the citizen's freedom of conscience and establish a de facto "state religion."[124] A number of critics on the left pointed out, too, that the charities had themselves become no less "bureaucratic" than the public agencies. But perhaps most fundamentally, some on the left explicitly rejected the Catholic conception of the relationship between democracy and "values." Walter Kutschbach, for example, observed that it was not true that the democratic state was ideologically neutral: for not only did it establish laws based on ethical principles, but also certain values—such as respect for human dignity, or democracy—were enshrined in the Fundamental Law. What is more, he held, again returning to an argument at least implicit in the Social Democratic and reform-pedagogical language of the 1920s, the most appropriate form of *Erziehung* for a democratic, pluralistic society (and moreover one in which received traditions were losing their persuasive power) was precisely *not* one that simply transmitted a given set of values but rather one that gave young people self-confidence and independence of mind—the freedom and the "capacity to form their own judgments."[125]

Since the Christian Democrats had an absolute majority in parliament, the debate in the Bundestag over the new law (which eventually, in the summer of 1960, was recast merely as a revision of certain paragraphs of the RJWG rather than a comprehensive overhaul of the system) amounted to an embittered exchange of recriminations. The SPD denounced the bill as an assault on the freedom of choice of those parents who did not wish to have their children raised as Christians; it warned that "confessionalization" would only divide, rather than unite, the nation's youth; and it accused the CDU of attempting to subject the municipalities "to a state dirig-

ism, to the total power of the state [*Staatsallmacht*]."[126] The FDP denounced the law for attempting to preserve the exclusive power of the charities by "preventing the initiative of the citizenry" in the democratic
Gemeinde, bringing about a "tyranny of the private associations," and
leaving the Youth Bureau "only the function of paymaster."[127] In contrast,
Deputy Even of the CDU scolded the SPD for being "unable to free your-
selves from the socialistic idea of the state spoon-feeding the citizen from
cradle to grave—while on our side stands the liberal ideal of a society in
which private initiative has precedence." The principle of subsidiarity
alone, the party held, preserved that "independent initiative and activity"
that formed the "most valuable capital of a society and a state that subscribe unconditionally to the ideal of freedom."[128]

In the end the new the Child Welfare Act (*Jugendwohlfahrtsgesetz,* or
JWG) was passed by the parliament by 212 votes to 157—with the Christian Democrats voting unanimously for the law, the Social Democrats
and the Free Democrats unanimously against it. A legal challenge lodged
with the Federal Constitutional Court (Bundesverfassungsgericht), on the
grounds that the law violated the constitution of local government, was rejected in 1967 (though the court ruled out the most aggressive interpretation of the obligation of the Youth Bureau to support the charities).

Left-leaning child welfare advocates and municipal administrators would
continue for the next three decades to denounce the law and call for its reform, arguing that it compromised the capacity of the Youth Bureaus to
provide universal child welfare services. But in fact, the complaints of those
disappointed by the new law were not entirely fair. It actually did accomplish a number of the goals set forth in the discussion of the RJWG
throughout the late 1950s. It helped to anchor the child's right to education
by generally requiring that the Youth Bureau "offer the necessary assistance
for the socialization of individual children according to their respective
pedagogical needs, in a timely and sufficient manner." Specifically, it required the Youth Bureau to establish institutions and programs for educational counseling, for the welfare of pregnant women, and for the support
of youth groups and political education; to support the enforcement of
morality legislation; and to support professional training. Material assistance to minors was finally transferred from the general Welfare Offices to
the Youth Bureaus. FEH was given a legal foundation.[129]

What enraged the opponents of the 1961 law was not that it ignored the
principles of "social pedagogy," but rather that it (like the RJWG itself) embraced a corporatist definition of democracy and the more conservative
variant of social pedagogy. It mandated a degree of state intervention that
would have horrified conservative Christians in the late nineteenth century;
but it did so in order to support, rather than supplant, existing social insti-

tutions such as the family and the charities. The law did not reject the idea of social management, then, but merely sought to impose a particular, cautious symbiosis between state and society, one in which mobilization and participation were not synonymous with majoritarianism and the expansion of the state. This compromise result may have been somewhat self-contradictory; but it was the logical outcome of an evolution—and struggle—begun as early as the 1890s.

Epilogue: The Reform of the JWG, 1961–1991

During the thirty years from 1961 to 1991, pressure for a further reform of the child welfare system was intense. In the context of the great democratic upheaval of the 1960s, a number of powerful groups (from quasi-syndicalist radical anticapitalist social workers through Workers' Welfare to left-liberal reform circles) consistently pressed for a further "democratization" of child welfare. Foremost among their demands were the abolition of the JWA and the corporatist structure of the Youth Bureau, the abolition of repressive programs such as correctional education, and a redefinition of programs and grounds for intervention which would encourage (or require) the Youth Bureau to respond flexibly to the specific needs of each individual child or "case" rather than in a routine fashion and only to those children who fell into particular categories.[130]

The SPD-FDP coalition which came to power in 1969 in fact passed such a law in the lower house of parliament in 1980; but the CDU and CSU defeated it in the upper house, which they controlled.[131] A new law, the Children and Young People's Welfare Act (Kinder- und Jugendhilfegesetz, or KJHG) was finally passed under the CDU-FDP government of Helmut Kohl in 1991. The debate over the new law, however, was in most of its essentials a rehearsal of that over the JWG in 1961, and the law in fact changed very little. The CDU remained committed to corporatist democracy and fundamentally opposed to the creation of a socialization role for the Youth Bureau independent of the family; and the deepening fiscal crisis—an important factor in the discussion since the first oil shock of 1973—in any case ruled out more ambitious schemes. In fact, the fiscal crisis had so trimmed the ambitions of local government by the 1980s that conflict between charities and municipalities, still sharp in the late 1960s, had become noticeably less intense.[132] The new law did abolish court-ordered correctional education, which had in any case virtually disappeared (only 1,250 children remained in court-ordered correctional education in 1985, in addition to 12,600 in FEH); but beyond that, it essentially merely recognized and sanctioned the more flexible and informal practices which had long since been adopted by the Youth Bureaus. (The BSHG also at last introduced a rather circumspect form of *Bewahrung,* which was then struck down by the federal Constitutional Court and replaced by an even more cautious procedure in 1974.)[133] It was this "notarial" function, as one commentator called it, which persuaded the SPD to vote for the law, despite arguments to the effect that, given the fact that Youth Bureaus around the country had long waiting lists for many counseling programs, the effort to "defend" the family against the state was anachronistic and amounted merely to "the creation of duties of parents to their children" rather than of "rights for minors."[134] To the surprise of the government, the bill was passed with almost as much unanimity as the original of 1922.

The fiscal crisis alone, however, does not explain the extraordinary longevity of the arrangements institutionalized in 1961. More fundamentally, the structure of child welfare policy established by the JWG has survived because it accomplishes the reconciliation of the two great traditions of German social reform, and of the cultures and social forces in which they were rooted. As we have seen, that structure was in fact already worked out—in theory—as early as 1918. It failed politically in the 1920s, virtually collapsed under the impact of the Great Depression, and was replaced for twelve disastrous years by a system which attempted to accomplish a similar reconciliation on the basis of authoritarian political principles and a monolithic ideological unity. After 1953 the corporatist democratic structure of child welfare proved viable because the war, fascism, and communism had annihilated the political extremes and because, unlike National Socialism, the compromises embodied in the institutional structure and ideology of the FRG did not create or permit a dynamic of radicalization, persecution, and aggression. It was also of critical importance, however, that psychotherapeutic counseling allowed public child welfare programs to avoid overly bitter conflicts with their targets, encouraged a democratic and therapeutic approach within both the progressive and the Christian camps, and provided a commonsense, "neutral" language in which, increasingly in the 1950s, problems of child welfare and child rearing were discussed by advocates of all persuasions.

In the structure established in 1961, the social-managerial ambition of progressive reform was reconciled with a definitive commitment to the familial social order defended by Christian culture—in large part through the mediation of "educational counseling" and the science of the soul. The progressive enthusiasm for bureaucratic organization and commitment to securing universal social rights was reconciled with voluntarism through the corporatist interpenetration of public and private welfare agencies. A liberal democratic legal order was combined with a Christian cultural agenda through the mechanism of institutions—established, for example, by the morality laws of the 1950s, or by the youth groups supported under the Youth Plans—designed to construct an essentially conservative cultural consensus around Christian values. Political democracy—again, in a particular sense—was reconciled with managerial authority and Christian bourgeois cultural hegemony through the mechanism of corporatist institutional structures. A nonauthoritarian, nonrepressive approach to problems of social and moral order was reconciled with authoritative (to use Ernst Ell's term) intervention and standards through programs designed to offer families and children assistance in achieving their own aims through integration into an industrial-capitalist and familial social order.

Postwar German child welfare programs thus achieved a balance between pragmatic, "scientific" social management and Christian culture; between democracy and bourgeois class power; between enthusiasm for the dynamism of the modern industrial economy and the determination to preserve the Christian familial social order. That balance was never an entirely happy one, and it was maintained in the face of a persistent challenge from Social Democracy and majoritarian democrats; but it did prove an extraordinarily durable solution to the fundamental political and social problems created by the process of industrialization, of social modernization.

Democracy, Fascism, and Social Policy

Perhaps the most striking thing about the history of child welfare policy in Germany since 1870 is the degree of continuity that characterizes it. The one hundred years between 1870 and 1970 saw four changes of regime, two devastating wars, and above all immense social and cultural transformations. In this context the more or less unbroken development of child welfare programs and of the discussion and debate surrounding them is quite extraordinary. Individual programs such as correctional education and public legal guardianship, institutions such as the Youth Bureau and the Juvenile Court, and organizations such as the DVAW/DVöpF, the AFET, the ADB, the DCV, and the Inner Mission, have all proven remarkably resilient. And the continuity of individual careers has been even more astonishing: as directors of private institutions or as professional bureaucrats, many of those active in child welfare were able to continue their careers, sometimes with brief interruptions, across two and even three changes of regime.

Most extraordinary of all has been the persistence of certain themes and arguments in the debate over child welfare policy. The grand trends in policy and thought have also persisted across regimes—thus, for example, the growing prominence of the idea of a "preventive" child welfare system from the 1900s onward; the growing commitment to the support and preservation of the family from at least the mid-1920s; the development of pedagogical counseling as a means of achieving both aims in the same period. And the terms of the debates over child welfare policy—in large part debates over the proper relationship between and among the state, the family, and the organizations of civil society—have also remained astonishingly stable, not changing greatly since Anna von Gierke commented at the beginning of the twentieth century that there was a danger that child care programs might create "a decline of parental responsibility, an increase in work by mothers outside the home, and the weakening of family ties."[1] Certainly these remarks would not have sounded out of place in the parliamentary debate of the 1950s (or, for that matter, in the 1980s).

Competing analyses of the development of family life have also remained virtually unchanged. The sense of moral and family crisis so central to the debate over the JWG in the late 1950s had a pedigree reaching back to the 1890s, even to the 1830s. And Hanns Eyferth's reflections on the dissolution of the traditional patriarchal family and on its inability to socialize children for life in a modern society would not have sounded unfamiliar to Gerhard Steuk in the late 1920s, or even to Wilhelm Polligkeit in 1905— and would be repeated in their essentials by critics of the KJHG in 1990. Even discussions of the institutional structure of child welfare programs— because they involved precisely these problems of the relationship of state to society and of the function and fate of the family in modern society— have remained surprisingly static. The municipalities' rejection of the corporatist structure of the Youth Bureau in the 1960s, for example, echoed their position in 1918. That structure itself, adopted formally in 1922 and in 1961, was prefigured as early as 1874 in the Inner Mission's demand that "all the actually existing moral forces" be given proper influence in the Community Orphans' Council (*Gemeindewaisenrat*); or in 1898 in Pastor Gustav von Rohden's proposal, in the context of the discussion of a new law on correctional education, for an "organization of all the pedagogically interested and competent forces in social life . . . furnished with official state authority and powers" to oversee the "whole system of socialization."[2]

Much historical work on the welfare state has interpreted such continuities as the product of an inherent "logic" of social policy, or of modernization itself. In the first place, optimistic assessments influenced by modernization theory have seen in the development of welfare programs a steady evolution (affecting the thinking of all groups, working class or middle class, religious or secular) toward greater social efficiency and increased democracy, from the authoritarian, niggardly, and punitive poor law of the nineteenth century to the ideal of universal well-being and social justice in the modern, democratic welfare state. T. H. Marshall first stated this view in 1950, arguing that the "social rights" guaranteed by the welfare state grew logically and naturally out of the civil and political rights won in the course of the eighteenth and nineteenth centuries; but there are echoes of such an interpretation in some of the literature into the 1980s as well.[3]

As we have seen, there is a great deal of truth in such arguments. There clearly *has* been a fit between the arguments of progressive child welfare reformers in favor of social mobilization, integration, and participation, and the democratic idea of citizenship; for one important goal of social policy has been to enable the less privileged to become active participants in economy, polity, and society. More specifically, progressives such as Pollig-keit, Spann, and Klumker, and Social Democrats in the 1920s and after the Second World War, *did* anchor their conception of social order (and na-tional power) in the idea of social rights—the "right of the child to educa-tion." Moreover, they developed an essentially democratic pedagogy to match this social program. And since the last war—or even since the turn of the century—citizens *have* also participated in the shaping of child welfare programs to an ever greater degree. On the one hand, the immense growth of the private charities—not only the Christian charities but also Workers' Welfare—and the creation of a corporatist structure of public child welfare programs has meant that an increasing number of people have been directly involved in shaping the specific practices and daily routines of public agen-cies. On the other, the professionalization of social work has broadened the social profile of those involved in caring work, and in the long term in-creased their numbers as well. Hugo Appelius's conception of the interpen-etration of state and society, elaborated in 1892 at the very inception of progressive child welfare programs, was not only programmatic but also prescient (see Chapter 1). Finally, since the turn of the century and again since World War II, the specific forms of intervention in child welfare have in fact become increasingly "democratic" and decreasingly coercive.

In such an optimistic assessment, Nazism must appear as an aberration, a departure from the smooth evolution of the German state. The discussion of late 1980s and early 1990s over whether the Nazi state can be character-ized as a "welfare state" at all derived in part from a desire to develop a more positive assessment of the welfare state after a quarter century of New Left and New Right assaults on it.[4] And in fact it would be easy to argue that the historical record proves that any regime that did not combine so-cial provision with democratic political forms was by nature unstable, that in the end the alternatives to the democratic welfare state did indeed prove to be nonviable. The coercive, authoritarian policies of the imperial govern-ment were clearly reaching a dead end by 1918; and National Socialism de-stroyed itself (and uncounted victims) partly because it attempted to com-bine social-managerial ambition with antidemocratic and racist principles and institutional forms.

But in fact since the late 1960s most historians who have addressed the question of continuities between pre-Nazi and Nazi social policy have come to very different, and much more damning, conclusions.

It would be easy, in the first place, to suggest that continuities are the product of sheer opportunism—of the astonishing willingness of a large number of activists and administrators, prominent or obscure, to serve al-most any master, which arose from their commitment to their own careers and their own projects. The sheer stamina of the Christian churches and

Christian culture also played a role, and some critics have detected in the survival of the private welfare organizations the stubborn persistence of the old regime, of the power of the Christian bourgeoisie in the age of democracy.[5] It is indeed hard not to be impressed by the staying power of Christian culture, which outlived and defeated the radical challenges of socialism, fascism, and secular social managerialism between 1900 and 1950, retaining its vitality, limiting and shaping public policy and state intervention—including child welfare policy—in crucial ways, and establishing a fundamentally conservative cultural hegemony after the Second World War. To a striking extent the history of the politics of child welfare policy is the history of the long struggle of German Catholicism to limit, contain, and guide public policy.

But as we have seen, much more than opportunistic adaptation to external political circumstances was involved in the evolution of child welfare policy and programs, which passed through crises that paralleled but did not entirely derive from those taking place in other institutional spheres. And despite very significant continuities, Christian ideas regarding child welfare policy actually changed substantially over time, and in particular came to have very different political meanings in different contexts. It would be a grave error to see the continued power of the Christian churches and Christian social teachings as merely a "survival," a "holdover" from the past; an adequate interpretation must account for these changes and for the continued relevance (the "modernity") of Christianity rather than focusing merely on the persistence of Christian culture.

The most persuasive "pessimistic" interpretations, therefore, begin instead from the fact that there were, in the thinking of both conservative and progressive child welfare advocates, themes that were also central to National Socialist child welfare policy. As Detlev Peukert pointed out, in many cases "National Socialist policy towards social outsiders rested on approaches . . . similar to those that had earlier been worked out by nonfascist policy-makers, academics and welfare workers"—and not coincidentally, for Nazism built very consciously on the progressive tradition.[6] More fundamentally, the progressives' fascination with national power and social efficiency, their often explicit imperialism, their tendency to view people as a resource to be exploited by the state, their devotion to scientific models and to "scientific" labeling and classification schemes, their enthusiasm for the diffusion (and political use) of information (or propaganda), their tendency toward a technocratic ideal of social management by experts, their ideal of universal participation in "national" economic and political life—all these make it impossible to overlook the genuine connections between National Socialism and early twentieth-century progressivism.

For all these reasons, it has been possible to construct extraordinarily pessimistic assessments of the development of the welfare state, and specifically of child welfare policy. Both Jacques Donzelot and Detlev Peukert, for example, interpret the development of child welfare policy as a process in which the life of individuals and of society as a whole was increasingly penetrated, shaped, and directed by laws, administrative agencies, social science, and the mechanisms and institutions of public economic, political, and cultural life.[7] While they appreciate the positive aspects of this process, and of modern society and the modern state, they are both preoccupied with its essentially negative consequences, with what Peukert calls the "pathological side-effects" of "progress," of "modernization."[8] They see in child welfare programs another instance of the creation of an iron cage of rationality, of the growing domination of social relations by cold, formal, and fundamentally inhumane legal rules, and of the subjection of people, their behavior, and even their psychic structure to constraining and oppressive norms fundamentally hostile to the irrationality, diversity, and vitality of human "life-worlds" (in Habermas' formulation). These processes created a new and more effectively enforced set of behavioral norms that stigmatized behaviors which did not fit into the "utopias of order" of the middle class, subjecting working-class people and families to ever more intrusive regulation. In Peukert's words, "the improvement of social provision and assistance was combined with an intensification of control mechanisms, a concentration of the system of sanctions, and a globalization of the dominant social norms of behavior."[9]

For Peukert, child welfare policy was a middle-class response to the emergence of a distinct sociology of working-class life and a subculture of working-class youth under the impact of industrialization. Because the industrial economy constantly reproduced the autonomy of working-class youth through factory labor, child welfare policy was doomed to a continual process of expansion and intensification of the effort to find a final solution to the problem of deviance. At the same time, because child welfare programs attempted to enforce "globally defined norms of virtue" which had little to do with the "personal or social needs" of working-class youths and children, ongoing and indeed intensifying conflict with their targets was inevitable. Thus, for Peukert the story of child welfare policy is a story of preprogrammed crisis produced by "the internal, structural pathologies of social assistance."[10]

Donzelot, by contrast, sees the development of child welfare as part of a broader process of social rationalization in which the middle class first recast its own child rearing practices, intensifying and extending pedagogical supervision within a now isolated, companionate nuclear family and thus raising their "investment" in their children in order to ensure their success in a more fluid social order, and then applied the same norms and principles to working-class families as well through the "invention of the social"— philanthropic organizations, protective legislation, medical norms, and eventually public social programs and social work. At the end of this process, "the family appears as though colonized. . . . A paradoxical result of the liberalization of the family, of the emergence of children's rights, of a rebalancing of the man-woman relationship: the more these rights are proclaimed, the more the stranglehold of a tutelary authority tightens around the poor family. In this system, family patriarchalism is destroyed at the cost of a patriarchy of the state."[11]

Both Peukert and Donzelot believe that the final result of the process of rationalization and disciplining which they describe is fascism. Although Peukert stressed that mass murder became possible only in the specific historical context of the depression, he wrote, "If the middle class could be understood as the normative class, which after the seizure of political power was able to define social norms, then there remained as options for the mastering of socially deviant behavior only the two . . . strategies of pedagogical normalization or eugenic exclusion."[12] While Peukert saw both these strategies as fundamentally objectionable, he did distinguish clearly between them. And yet, in light of his own implicit argument that "normalization" was doomed to failure by the logic of industrial capitalism, the reader is left to conclude that there was a necessary progression from the one to the other. By identifying the essential dynamic, the internal logic of welfare policy as disciplinarian and exclusionary, Peukert implied that the modern welfare state is in its *essence* potentially fascist—and indeed potentially homicidal, since the term "exclusion" *(Aussonderung)* inevitably brings the Nazis to mind. Donzelot makes this conclusion more explicit. He holds that there were two divergent strategies of bourgeois social reform in the early twentieth century, the one "nationalist and familialist," populationist and paternalist, sexually repressive and socially conservative, the other "socialist and individualist," neo-Malthusian, sexually permissive and feminist. But the end point of both was fundamentally the same: "Both implied an interventionist, coercive pole that welded them to one another," and the end product was either the "social fascism" of Vichy or the "social sector fascism" of postwar France.[13] Child welfare policy had a logic independent of specific programmatic variations, one that was, again, essentially fascist.

The critique of the welfare state which is implicit in these models must be considerably qualified. Above all, as both Peukert and Donzelot are quite aware, there is a certain tendency in such models toward a romanticization of preindustrial society, toward denial of selected social problems and social injustices, perhaps even toward neoliberal male supremacy. Power operated in and permeated preindustrial societies just as much as modern ones, though it may have been more decentralized and less regular or "rational." It is too easy simply to declare that the control mechanisms of the welfare state reduce personal freedom: we have to ask not only *how* free people were in pre-"rational" society, but also *who* was free, and free to do *what?* The social worker who removes a child from a family in which it is regularly beaten or raped or in which its labor is exploited to the detriment of its health, or who forces an illegitimate father to pay child support, is exercising a power of surveillance and intervention which limits the personal freedom of the parents but may well increase that of the child. *Some* people, in other words, may be in a very real sense *more* free in a society "disciplined" by social agencies.

Nevertheless, this study confirms the essential point of models such as Donzelot's and Peukert's. As we have seen, the expansion of child welfare programs in Germany has unmistakably been inspired by a yearning for social orderliness and discipline—and indeed often by an explicitly stated desire to prevent revolutionary upheaval. The improvement of social "services" has gone hand in hand with a progressive elaboration of coercive mechanisms and manipulative systems of reward and punishment, which limit personal freedom, often in invasive and seemingly arbitrary ways but also, more important, through the pervasive influence of rising standards of health, competence, and behavior for working-class parents and children. Whatever value one may assign to their impact, the programs I have examined—in addition to child labor legislation, mandatory public schooling, family support, housing law, criminal law, family law, and so on—have increasingly structured and constrained relations between adults and children, the public behavior of the young, and the choices made by families, subjecting them increasingly to rules and interventions. And it is clear that the application of rational economic and "scientific" (for example, biological) principles to human society lies at the root of the mass murder of "defectives" in Nazi Germany.

This study does not, however, confirm the equation of "social discipline" with fascism, much less mass murder. Fascism—in Germany, France, Italy, and elsewhere—was both more and something other than simple social interventionism. In theory as in practice it was a political order, an order of political institutions and behaviors; and it was also a set of ideas about politics and society and a set of (perceived) solutions to specific social and political problems. While National Socialism drew on established traditions and preserved many existing institutions, it is equally clear that Nazi policies were nevertheless qualitatively different from the policies of the 1920s or 1950s. The authoritarian and murderous potential of child welfare traditions could be realized only by a political system and a set of institutions based on principles very different from those that underlay the institutional structures and goals of the Empire or the Weimar Republic—or, for that matter, the Federal Republic. Specifically, of course, National Socialism explicitly and stridently rejected precisely the liberal and individualistic principles that had been central to the Weimar child welfare system. Despite all the similarities between the progressive agenda and that of the Nazis, there was this crucial difference: that the Nazis envisioned a "national community" *(Volksgemeinschaft)* founded on duty and self-sacrifice, whereas progressives before 1933 had more often envisioned one founded on rights and self-interest. While modern welfare states are "disciplined" societies, their political and intellectual underpinnings are simply not the same as those of fascist states. Nor is the global experience of living in a democratic welfare state anything like that of living in a totalitarian one (though many individual experiences, including contacts with social welfare bureaucracies, may be similar).

The model proposed in this study is one that is present in Peukert's work and became increasingly explicit in the discussion of National Socialism in the late 1980s and early 1990s: that the two "faces" of welfare policy, the humane and democratic and the homicidal and authoritarian, are complementary potentials of a single process. The progressive ideal of a rational, efficient, harmonious, productive, and powerful social order based on participation, as I argued in Chapter 3, implied a tendency not necessarily toward democracy but at least toward *mobilization,* toward expanding social, economic, and political *participation.* For that very reason, it also necessarily raised the question of what to do with those who could not participate, who could not be integrated into this organic structure—and thus opened the door to stigmatization, repression, bureaucratic authoritarianism, and institutionalized abuse. The establishment of standards for socialization that guaranteed the individual's capacity for participation meant that those who did not meet those standards became a "problem" to be addressed through scientific study and institutionalization or other forms—positive or repressive—of intervention. The history of correctional education gives a particularly striking example of this relationship: the idea of the isolation and "special treatment" of "abnormal" children grew not merely out of the lust for classification and the obsession with biology that characterized psychiatry, but also out of the program of prevention and even the "democratic" methods developed in correctional education.[14] In the context of economic and fiscal catastrophe, the elaboration of a vast system for the study, care, and/or control of the criminal, the delinquent, the mentally ill, the intellectually or physically handicapped, the "asocial," and so forth, which had seemed so essentially humane and rational before 1933, became the precondition for mass murder.

And yet obviously a study that takes 1961 rather than 1945 as its end point must come to grips with the fact that a homicidal "solution" to this "problem" was adopted only by the Nazi regime, and not by the Weimar state or the Federal Republic. Fascism and mass murder were possible outcomes of the progressive response to social change, to the emergence of industrial society; but they were clearly not the *only* possible ones. The postwar welfare state returned to the project, tendentially abandoned by

the Nazis, of rehabilitation and integration rather than of exclusion and extermination.

The explanation for the Nazis' drift toward mass murder lies not merely
in the inherent logic or "pathology" of social intervention but also and
specifically in the realm of *politics*, in the particular political organization
of welfare policy at the level of the state. It was the peculiar radicalizing dynamic of the Nazi regime that allowed the *potentially* murderous character
of social intervention to run increasingly out of control; and that dynamic
was inherent in the dictatorial structure of the Nazi regime and in its antiliberal ideology. By abandoning self-interest as the motor of integration
and virtually silencing public opinion—whether of "experts" or of citizens
at large—Nazism removed the governor on social intervention, on the activities and the thoughts of autocratic social engineers (as well as on those
of racists). This is why the T4 program, like the Holocaust as a whole, was
secret; why Protestant opponents attempted to persuade the regime to pro-
pose a euthanasia law, thereby subjecting the idea to public criticism; and
also why, in his extraordinary sermon condemning the Nazi euthanasia
program on August 3, 1941, Bishop Galen of Münster not only repeated
the episcopate's declaration one month earlier to the effect that the murder
of innocent people was forbidden by God's law, but also declared that "if it
is once allowed that people have the right to kill their 'unproductive' fellow
men" then in principle "the murder of each and all of us . . . is permitted
[as well]."[15] In the Federal Republic, a state committed to the rights as well
as the usefulness of human beings, and one constrained by a democratic
civil society and public opinion, no similar development was possible. It is
worth reminding ourselves that in nations where liberal political institutions were not abandoned—for example, in the United States, the United
Kingdom, or Australia and New Zealand—even very powerful traditions of
eugenic thought, imperialistic population policy, and biological determinism in psychiatry and penology did not give rise either to fascism or to
mass murder.[16]

If it was the structure of the Nazi regime and the principles on which it
was based that made the realization of the homicidal potentials of social intervention possible, then what explains the emergence of that structure and
those principles? What explains the shift among some child welfare advocates from a democratic and inclusive conception of social and political
"mobilization," of participation, to a totalitarian and exclusionary one?
This study has argued, in the first place, that the close association between
individual rights and state power or the public good in progressive thought
meant that this was not a particularly difficult transition. But much more
important, I have tried to explain the appeal of fascism in this particular
field not so much in terms of the autocratic attitudes of social managers—

although those attitudes certainly played a role—as in terms of the *politics* of child welfare, of the *conflicts* that social intervention created.

In the German case there was clearly no unified, monolithic group of welfare technocrats, working unopposed to construct the child welfare system. Instead, different groups of child welfare activists pursued very different and often conflicting reform agendas. They were guided by different conceptions of the social and cultural problems that needed to be solved, of the ultimate aims of welfare policy, and of how it should be organized and structured. Furthermore, whatever the ideas of those advocating state intervention, the history of child welfare policy is not merely the history of the imposition of programs and norms by elites, dominant classes, experts, and/or the state; there has often been, rather, a process of negotiation and struggle between policymakers and the targets of their policies.

These conflicts were the product of a mobilization of social and ideological communities that was an integral part of, and increasingly a reaction against, the interventionist response to social change. At the turn of the twentieth century, the expansion of private welfare organizations was actively pursued as an integral part of the construction of a new government of society; and by the 1920s those organizations were locked in a battle for the control of public welfare policies, while increasingly public opinion (often organized by the socialist movements) called particular aspects of those policies into question.

It is above all this complex struggle that explains the appeal of National Socialism—or at least the abandonment of democracy—among child welfare advocates at the beginning of the 1930s. Fascism emerged as a response to a specific crisis of democratic politics, and it was appealing precisely because it promised to resolve that crisis. Specifically, of course, many of those active in child welfare policy hoped that a National Socialist regime would serve their own interests and agendas. More generally, fascism appeared to offer a response to the fact that growing participation seemed to have created not harmony but irreconcilable political conflict; it appealed because it promised either to silence competing voices or to reconcile them through a higher synthesis.

Again, however, it must be remembered that the corporatism of the Weimar welfare system had been designed to achieve precisely such a reconciliation of competing groups and principles. That system failed in the 1920s; but after World War II it achieved an extraordinary stability and durability. If mass murder is not the only potential of social intervention, so also fascism is not the only solution to political and social conflict.

In each of the existing major interpretations it is the inflexibility and unidirectional "logic" of social forces, ideas, and institutional developments that is responsible for the extraordinary continuity characteristic of the development of welfare programs. Despite everything that happened in Germany between 1870 and 1970, fundamentally the *same* thing was always going on: the capitalist, Christian bourgeoisie was forever defeating its challengers; the logic of modernization was forever imposing growing social and political participation; the logic of social rationalization was forever imposing increased intervention and intensifying the "disciplining" of society; the growing social and political inclusion of the majority was forever intensifying the stigmatization and exclusion of the minority. And the whole system was forever rolling toward a predetermined goal: class tyranny, the democratic welfare state, the disciplinary society, mass murder.

Obviously, this study leads us to a different conclusion. What explains the survival of organizations, ideas, and individuals across changes of regime is precisely the flexibility of the great competing traditions and institutions of social reform. Despite wrenching political transformations, the fundamental building blocks of the modern German child welfare system—organizations, programs, institutions, the ideas that they embody or champion—have to a surprising degree remained the *same* precisely because the *different* potentials within them have been exploited to permit different combinations under different circumstances. Specifically, the great bourgeois reform traditions—Christian and progressive—have continued to champion essentially the same conceptions of the proper relationship between state and society; but these conceptions have proved compatible, at least rhetorically, with very different proposals for the organization—at the level of the state—of growing intervention and participation.

Thus, for example, the progressive ideal of mobilization and participation has been compatible with both democracy and fascism, and with both authoritarian and democratic pedagogy. Progressives such as Polligkeit and Webler have been able to shift very rapidly back and forth between the ideal of welfare *services* and the realization of individual *rights* by the state on the one hand, and the ideal of the state's power to use people for its own ends on the other—between the ideal of the "service state" *(Dienstleistungsstaat)* and that of the "power state" *(Machtsstaat)*. "Education for community" has been democratic in the 1920s and authoritarian in the 1930s. Progressive social-managerial ambition and the ideal of a harmonious, powerful national society *can* be social-liberal, and build on a model of an incipiently democratic, noncoercive system of rights, incentives, opportunities, empowerment, integration, and voluntary participation. But it can also be authoritarian and technocratic, building on the ideals of obedience, duty, and directed mobilization. The idea, for example, that children belong "not simply to their parents . . . but also to the state, which in its own interest should claim the right to supervise their raising and their well-being"[17] could be part of a social-liberal and humanitarian political program, as it surely was when advanced by the Child Protection Committee of the BDF in favor of child labor laws at the turn of the century; but it was also compatible with fascist ideology. The ideal of a preventive child welfare system was touted by the Nazis as a means of ensuring that there were sufficient recruits for the army, and by Social Democrats and left-liberals in the Federal Republic as essential to a democratic policy structure. The same progressive principles and programs were presented at different times as essential to the survival of the Weimar Republic and the rebuilding of German society during the debate around the RJWG in 1922; as a necessary ingredient of a successful fascist society at the time of the Nazi seizure of power; and then, once again, as fundamental to a democratic ordering of society after 1945.

Similarly, Christian pedagogical theory could be authoritarian and conservative in the Empire, and the Nazis could appeal to conservative Christian traditions in the early and mid-1930s; but Christians could also seek a reconciliation with the Weimar Republic on the basis of equally "traditional" Christian pedagogical ideas in the 1920s and argue in the 1950s that Christian pedagogy was essential to the stability of democracy. In the 1920s arguments to the effect that the state could not socialize children were part of the challenge to and the crisis of the democratic state, but in the 1950s they became part of the underpinnings of corporatist democracy. In the 1920s the Christian conservative critique of "massification" *(Vermassung)* was part of a larger criticism of modern, rational, democratic society; but in the 1950s it was part of a critique of "totalitarianism."[18] In the 1930s Christian anti-socialism was an important factor in the acceptance of fascism by many conservatives; by the 1950s, in very different political circumstances, it had become a central element in (corporatist) democratic discourse. In the 1930s the Christian opposition to a state that produced an "irresponsible, passive, and weak army of recipients of welfare benefits," as Heinz Sünker has pointed out,[19] was a part of the antidemocratic appeal; but in the 1950s it was part, again, of a corporatist *democratic* discourse.

The great exception, of course, has been socialism. Whatever its similarities with bourgeois social reform (in its approach to the poor, in its reception of eugenic thought, in its conception of welfare services), democratic socialism proved incompatible with fascism in a way that no "bourgeois" tradition did. There were no compromises with fascism in the Social Democratic camp; no major figures within the Social Democratic welfare establishment joined the Nazi regime, either as enthusiasts or in order to turn it to their own ends; there was no effort to reconcile the principles of Social Democratic welfare policy with those of National Socialism. Given the Social Democrats' commitment to democracy, that was impossible. As for the communists, they were banned both in the Third Reich and in the Federal Republic and made no significant contribution to either.

The point is not that the traditions of middle-class social reform were fundamentally corrupt, or that middle-class social reformers were somehow spineless opportunists. It is simply that political choices determine the boundaries and the potentials of social intervention.

Jugendpflege is a good example of the main point here. There is a clear continuity from "citizenship education" and the private *Jugendpflege* groups in the Empire through the Hitler Youth to "political education" and the Bundesjugendring in the Federal Republic—and of course also to the Freie Deutsche Jugend, the state youth organization in the German Democratic Republic. It has seemed imperative for those who dominate the modern German state to socialize or indoctrinate young people in ways appropriate to that state and fundamental to its legitimation, to mobilize them for constructive and active social and political participation—whatever form that state might take, whoever might dominate it, and whatever their values might be. This is not to suggest that Christian "youth cultivation" groups, the Hitler Youth, democratic youth organizations, and the communist Freie Deutsche Jugend are "the same." That is precisely *not* the point. What it *does* suggest, rather, is the extent to which a particular institution and a particular strategy can become part of very different political dynamics, and can take on very different meanings in different political contexts. The mobilization and integration of youth into the state appears to be an imperative of modern political development; but it can be accomplished in very different ways.

The specific form and content of efforts to guide the modern processes of political and social mobilization, in other words, *does* matter. What explains the political implications of social policies is not an inexorable logic inherent in policy agendas; it is rather the specific nature of the ideas that underlie them, and the political and social ideals they are intended to help realize. The use of "scientific" language, the concept of social rights, Christian authoritarianism, and so on all *could* form part of a fascist ideal of social policy; but they all *could* also form part of a democratic one. They created options and choices rather than only closing them off.

As I suggested briefly in Chapters 8 and 9, finally, the shift from biological determinism to psychoanalytic theory is particularly revealing in this respect. One is tempted to conclude that the choice of theories in each case (in the late 1920s and 1930s, and in the late 1940s and 1950s) was essentially guided by political principles. Detlev Peukert has written of the "genesis of the Final Solution from the spirit of science"; but it might be more accurate, for our purposes, to conclude that policymakers *choose* that "science" which is most congenial and useful to them.[20] Where social and political participation or citizenship was conceived in terms of duty, obedience, uniformity, and self-sacrifice, an exclusionary, punitive, and homicidal "science" was adopted; where it was conceived of in terms of rights, opportunities, diversity, and self-interest, a therapeutic and humanistic "science" was chosen. Again, it was political values, and not the inherent logic of rationalizing scientific language, that determined the potentials of social policy.

These conclusions are no grounds for complacency, however; and this study should not close with the suggestion that optimistic theories of modernization, which see democracy and social peace at the end of modern social development, are correct. In modern German child welfare policy, whether fascist or democratic, welfare programs and ideas were alternative responses to persistent, fundamental problems of modern social and political organization: the problem of securing the active participation of the population at large in the economy and the polity; that of achieving a stable relationship between the welfare programs that aim to achieve this first goal and their targets; and that of reconciling conflicting visions of social order among the ruling classes themselves. These problems are still very much with us; and there is no reason to think that the present dilemmas faced by Western societies and their governing classes could not generate solutions every bit as disastrous and self-destructive as fascism was. What is more, it does not seem impossible that the specific world-historical moment in which both fascism and modern democracy emerged has passed. It may be that the imperatives imposed by the process of industrialization are fading. If that is so, then it remains to be seen whether the democratic welfare state can survive in a deindustrializing society.

Notes

Introduction

1. The literature on "social control" is endless and varied in theoretical approach and interpretation: some particularly relevant examples are Anna Davin, "Imperialism and Motherhood," *History Workshop Journal* 4 (1978); Peter Gstettner, *Die Eroberung des Kindes durch die Wissenschaft* (Reinbek: Rowohlt, 1981); Jane Lewis, *The Politics of Motherhood* (London: Croom Helm, 1980); Philippe Meyer, *The Child and the State* (Cambridge: Cambridge University Press, 1983); and Anthony M. Platt, *The Child Savers* (Chicago: University of Chicago Press, 1969). There are compelling critiques in Robert van Kriecken, *Children and the State: Social Control and the Formation of Australian Child Welfare* (Sydney: Allen & Unwin, 1991); Eric C. Schreiner, *In the Web of Class: Delinquency and Reformers in Boston, 1810s–1930s* (New York: New York University Press, 1992); and John Sutton, *Stubborn Children* (Berkeley: University of California Press, 1988).
2. See, for example, Jacques Donzelot, *The Policing of Families* (New York: Pantheon, 1979); Detlev J. K. Peukert, *Grenzen der Sozialdisziplinierung: Aufstieg und Krise der deutschen Jugendfürsorge, 1878–1932* (Cologne: Bund, 1986); and, for the theoretical foundations, Michel Foucault, *The History of Sexuality*, vol. 1, *An Introduction* (1978; rpt. New York: Vintage, 1990).
3. Relevant examples are Linda Gordon, *Heroes of Their Own Lives* (London: Penguin, 1988); Young-Sun Hong, "Femininity as a Vocation," in *German Professions, 1800–1950*, ed. Geoffrey Cocks and Konrad Jarausch (New York: Oxford University Press, 1990); Molly Ladd-Taylor, *Mother-Work: Women, Child Welfare, and the State, 1890–1930* (Chicago: University of Illinois Press, 1994); Dietlinde Peters, *Mütterlichkeit im Kaiserreich* (Bielefeld: Kleine Verlag, 1984); and Christoph Sachße, *Mütterlichkeit als Beruf* (Frankfurt am Main: Suhrkamp, 1986).
4. See, for example, Peter Baldwin, *The Politics of Social Solidarity* (Cambridge: Cambridge University Press, 1990); Francis G. Castles, ed., *The Comparative*

History of Public Policy (Oxford: Polity, 1989); Gøsta Esping-Anderson, *The Three Worlds of Welfare Capitalism* (Oxford: Polity, 1990); Gerhard A. Ritter, *Der Sozialstaat* (Munich: R. Oldenbourg, 1989); and Sonya Michel and Seth Koven, "Womanly Duties: Maternalist Politics and the Origins of Welfare States in France, Germany, Great Britain, and the United States, 1880–1920," *American Historical Review* 95 (1990).

5. An important partial exception is the discussion—often implicit—of the relationship between gendered definitions of caring work and fascism: see, for example, Claudia Koonz, *Mothers in the Fatherland* (New York: St. Martin's, 1987); and Gisela Bock, "Antinatalism, Maternity, and Paternity in National Socialist Racism," in *Maternity and Gender Policies*, ed. Pat Thane and Gisela Bock (London: Routledge, 1991). Paula Baker, "The Domestication of American Politics," *American Historical Review* 89 (1984), addresses these issues obliquely.

6. See, for example, Ulrich Hermann and Jürgen Oelkers, eds., *Pädagogik im Nationalsozialismus* (Weinheim: Beltz, 1988); Carola Kuhlmann, *Erbkrank oder Erziehbar?* (Munich: Juventa, 1989); Hans Uwe Otto and Heinz Sünker, eds., *Soziale Arbeit und Faschismus* (Bielefeld: Karin Böllert KT-Verlag, 1986); Peukert, *Grenzen*; Paul Weindling, *Health, Race, and German Politics between National Unification and Nazism, 1870–1945* (New York: Cambridge University Press, 1989).

7. See Theda Skocpol et al., eds., *Bringing the State Back In* (New York: Cambridge University Press, 1985).

8. Geoff Eley has asked, "What Produces Fascism: Pre-Industrial Traditions or a Crisis of the Capitalist State?," in *From Unification to Nazism: Reinterpreting the German Past* (Boston: Allen & Unwin, 1986). There is an interesting discussion also in Rainer Zitelmann, "Die totalitäre Seite der Moderne," in *Nationalsozialismus und Modernisierung*, ed. Rainer Zitelmann and Michael Prinz (Darmstadt: Wissenschaftliche Buchgesellschaft, 1991).

1. The Inception of Modern Child Welfare Policy, 1840–1895

1. Quoted in Klaus Mollenhauer, *Die Ursprünge der Sozialpädagogik in der industriellen Gesellschaft* (Weinheim: Beltz, 1959), pp. 40–41.

2. Quoted ibid., p. 49.

3. "Übersicht der Entstehungszeit und der gegenwärtigen Anzahl der Rettungshäuser," *Fliegende Blätter* 25 (1868): 22–24.

4. Ibid., pp. 22–24.

5. Joseph Beeking, *Zeitfragen der Kinder- und Jugendfürsorge* (Freiburg: Caritas, 1927).

6. "Die Idioten-Anstalten Deutschlands und der Schweiz im Jahre 1895," *Zeitschrift für Kinderforschung* 1 (1896): 127.

7. Königliches Konsistorium der Provinz Preussen, "Die Verwilderung der Jugend: Aus der Provinz Preussen," *Fliegende Blätter* 33 (1876): 254–256.

8. Anton Kohler, *Die zunehmende Entsittlichung der Jugend in ihren Erscheinungen und Ursachen und die daraus erwachsende Aufgabe der Schule* (Freiburg: Herder, 1876), pp. 4–10.

9. Königliches Konsistorium, "Die Verwilderung," p. 255.

10. Kohler, *Die zunehmende Entsittlichung*, pp. 15, 22–23, 17–18.
11. Ibid., pp. 49–50.
12. Quoted in Florian Tennstedt, *Sozialgeschichte der Sozialpolitik in Deutschland vom 18. Jahrhundert bis zum Ersten Weltkrieg* (Göttingen: Vandenhoek & Ruprecht, 1981), p. 142.
13. Quoted in Rüdiger vom Bruch, ed., *"Weder Kommunismus noch Kapitalismus": Bürgerliche Sozialreform in Deutschland vom Vormärz bis zur Ära Adenauer* (Munich: Beck, 1985), p. 70.
14. Quoted Eckart Pankoke, *Sociale Bewegung-Sociale Frage-Sociale Politik: Grundfragen der deutschen "Socialwissenschaft" im 19. Jahrhundert.* (Stuttgart: Klett, 1970), p. 193.
15. R. Zelle, *Reform der Vormundschaftsgesetzgebung: Staats- oder Selbsthilfe?* (Berlin: Lüderitz, 1870).
16. Central-Ausschuss für Innere Mission, "Petition des Central-Ausschusses für Innere Mission an das preussische Abgeordneten-Haus, betreffend das Vormundschafts-Gesetz," *Fliegende Blätter* 31 (1874): p. 360.
17. Ibid., p. 149.
18. Deputy Wachler, in *Stenographische Berichte über die Verhandlungen des preussischen Hauses der Abgeordneten* (1878), 2:1069; *Stenographische Berichte über die Verhandlungen des preussischen Herrenhauses*, 1901, document 8, p. 35.
19. *Stenographische Berichte über die Verhandlungen des preussischen Hauses der Abgeordneten* (1878), 2:1440, 1496, 1068, 1444.
20. Ibid., 2:1629.
21. *Stenographische Berichte über die Verhandlungen des preussischen Herrenhauses* 439 (1901):31; and Martin Hennig, "Die Statistik der evangelischen Rettungshäuser Deutschlands," *Rettungshausbote* 17, nos. 10–11 (1897): 145–155.
22. Quoted in Detlev Peukert, *Grenzen der Sozialdisziplinierung: Aufstieg und Krise der deutschen Jugendfürsorge* (Cologne: Bund-Verlag, 1986), p. 120.
23. Quoted ibid., p. 126.
24. *Motive zum Entwurf eines Bürgerlichen Gesetzbuches für das Deutsche Reich*, vol. 4, *Familienrecht* (Berlin: J. Guttentag, 1888), p. 807.
25. Deutscher Verein für Armenpflege und Wohltätigkeit, *Schriften* 8 (1889): 59, and 9 (1890): 44.
26. On Appelius and the importance of the 1892 report, see Christine Dörner, *Erziehung durch Strafe: Die Geschichte des Jugendstrafvollzugs 1871–1945* (Weinheim: Juventa, 1991), pp. 35–41.
27. Hugo Appelius, *Die Behandlung jugendlicher Verbrecher und verwahrloster Kinder* (Berlin: J. Guttentag, 1892), pp. 200, 16.
28. Ibid., pp. 17, 18, 23–24, 25–28.
29. Ibid., pp. 19, 128, 37, 74.
30. Ibid., pp. 119–122, 35.
31. Ibid., p. 36.
32. Ibid., p. 69.
33. "Erläuterungen zum Entwurf eines Gesetzes betr. die Zwangserziehung verbrecherischer und verwahrloster Jugendlicher," ZSAM, Rep. 191, Preussisches Ministerium des Innern, no. 1995, fol. 271 (p. 3).

34. *Entwurf eines Bürgerlichen Gesetzbuches für das Deutsche Reich. Zweite Lesung. Nach den Beschlüssen der Redaktionskommission* (Berlin: J. Guttentag, 1895), pp. 491–492.
35. "Soziale Grundsätze," *Rettungshausbote* 17, no. 1 (1896): 9.
36. "Waisenerziehung und Vormundschaftswesen," *Fliegende Blätter* 337 (1880): 105.
37. Herbert Studders, *Das Taub'sche System der Ziehkinderüberwachung in Leipzig* (Berlin: Cotta, 1919), p. 49.
38. Max Taube, *Schutz der unehelichen Kinder in Leipzig: Eine Einrichtung zur Fürsorge ohne Findelhäuser* (Leipzig: Veit, 1893), p. 62.
39. Taube, *Schutz*, pp. 36–37.
40. Franz Pagel, *Der freiwillige Erziehungsbeirat für schulentlassene Waisen* (Berlin: Oehmigke, 1896), pp. 54, 13, 7–8.
41. Ibid., pp. 9–10.
42. Ibid., pp. 11, 58, 53.
43. Ibid., pp. 56, 57–58; for figures on "lost" wages, see p. 57.
44. See "Der freiwillige Erziehungsbeirat für schulentlassene Waisen," *Rettungshausbote* 19 (1899): pp. 164–166; and *Stenographische Berichte über die Verhandlungen der siebzehnten Jahresversammlung des deutschen Vereins für Armenpflege und Wohltätigkeit* (Leipzig: Duncker & Humblot, 1898), p. 58.
45. Pagel, *Der freiwillige Erziehungsbeirat*, p. 57.
46. Ibid., p. 51.
47. E. Mischler, "Ländliche Arbeitsverfassung und Vormundschaftswesen," *Zentralblatt* 2 (1910): 158.
48. Whereas 44 percent of Prussians under age eighteen lived in communities with under two thousand inhabitants in 1905, only 19 percent of children in correctional education in that year came from such communities. See Hans W. Gruhle, *Die Ursachen der jugendlichen Verwahrlosung und Kriminalität* (Berlin: Springer, 1912), p. 243.
49. Appelius, *Die Behandlung*, p. 25.
50. Ibid., pp. 150–151.
51. Quoted in vom Bruch, "*Weder Kommunismus noch Kapitalismus*," p. 134.

2. Competing Reform Conceptions in the 1890s

1. Ilka Riemann, "'Er mit der Waffe, sie mit Herz und Hand': Die Rolle der Frauenvereine in der Sozialpolitik, insbesondere die der Vaterländischen Frauenvereine," in *Frauenmacht in der Geschichte*, ed. Jutta Dalhoff, Uschi Frey, and Ingrid Schöll (Düsseldorf: Schwann, 1986), p. 351.
2. Emil Muensterberg, "Generalbericht über die Tätigkeit des Vereins in den fünfzehn Jahren seines Bestehens," in *Stenographischer Bericht über die Verhandlungen des sechzehnten Jahresversammlung des deutschen Vereins für Armenpflege und Wohltätigkeit am 24. und 25. September in Strassburg i. E.* (Leipzig: Duncker & Humblot, 1896), p. 1.
3. Kaplan Dr. Joseph Drammer, in *Fürsorge für Kinder und Jugendliche* (*Schriften der Centralstelle für Arbeiterwohlfahrtseinrichtungen*, vol. 4B) (Berlin: Heymanns, 1893), p. 133. On cities, see Klaus Tenfelde, "Großstadtjugend in Deutschland vor 1914: Eine historisch-demographische Annäherung," *Viertel-*

jahrsschrift für Wirtschafts- und Sozialgeschichte 69 (1982). On laboring youth, see Detlev Peukert, *Grenzen der Sozialdisziplinierung: Aufstieg und Krise der deutschen Jugendfürsorge, 1878–1932* (Cologne: Bund-Verlag, 1986), pp. 59–60. The number of workers under sixteen years of age rose from 155,642 in 1886 to 452,317 in 1908, and the number of those aged sixteen to twenty-one from 578,421 in 1892 to 1,174,880 in 1908.

4. For representative analyses, see *Fürsorge für die schulentlassene Jugend* (*Schriften der Centralstelle für Arbeiter-Wohlfahrtseinrichtungen,* vol. 19) (Berlin: Heymanns, 1900); Johannes Corvey, "Die heutige Arbeiterjugend und ihre Erziehung," *Arbeiterfreund* 28 (1890); and Klaus Saul's discussion in "'Der Kampf um die Jugend zwischen Volksschule und Kaserne.' Ein Beitrag zur 'Jugendpflege' im wilhelminischen Reich, 1890–1914," *Militärgeschichtliche Mitteilungen* 9 (1971): 97–143.

5. Carl von Massow, *Reform oder Revolution!* (Berlin: Otto Liebmann, 1895), p. 65.

6. See Klaus Wedekind, "Die Entstehung der Jugendpflege und ihre Ausgestaltung zu einem neuen Bereich öffentlicher Erziehung" (Diss. University of Cologne, 1971); Franz Josef Krafeld, *Geschichte der Jugendarbeit: Von den Anfängen bis zur Gegenwart* (Weinheim: Beltz, 1984); Saul, "Der Kampf um die Jugend"; John Gillis, *Youth and History* (New York: Academic Press, 1974), pp. 138–149; and Derek Linton, *"Who Has the Youth Has the Future": The Campaign to Save Young Workers in Imperial Germany* (Cambridge: Cambridge University Press, 1991).

7. *Stenographische Berichte über die Verhandlungen des preussischen Hauses der Abgeordneten* (1899), 2:1178, 1180 (Deputy Ernst).

8. "Der XV Kongress des Deutschen Vereins für Knabenhandarbeit," *Arbeiterfreund* 37 (1899): 422–427.

9. Quotes from the statutes of the EFB and the KDF in Dietlinde Peters, *Mütterlichkeit im Kaiserreich* (Bielefeld: Kleine Verlag, 1984), pp. 51–54.

10. See particularly Christoph Sachße, *Mütterlichkeit als Beruf: Sozialarbeit, Sozialreform und Frauenbewegung, 1871–1929* (Frankfurt: Suhrkamp, 1986), p. 117; Irene Stoehr, "'Organisierte Mütterlichkeit': Zur Politik der deutschen Frauenbewegung um 1900," in *Frauen Suchen Ihre Geschichte,* ed. Karin Hausen (Munich: Beck, 1983), pp. 224–225, 227; Barbara Brick and Christine Woesler, "Maschinerie und Mütterlichkeit," *Beiträge zur Feministischen Theorie und Praxis* 5 (1981); and, for a comparative perspective, see the essays in Seth Koven and Sonya Michel, eds., *Mothers of a New World: Maternalist Politics and the Origins of Welfare States* (New York: Routledge, 1993).

11. Wilhelm Baur, "Was sollen wir thun?," *Fliegende Blätter* 48 (1891): 6, 2.

12. Friedrich Bodelschwingh, "Was kann zur Pflege des christlichen Familienlebens geschehen," *Fliegende Blätter* 48 (1891): 35, 36.

13. Peukert, *Grenzen,* pp. 55–60.

14. The article, by "R.," is quoted in "Die Mordthat in Berlin," *Rettungshausbote* 17, no. 2 (1896): 24.

15. See *Stenographische Berichte über die Verhandlungen der . . . beiden Häuser des Landtages. Haus der Abgeordneten* (Berlin: W. Möser, 1899), 1:476, 3:2062.

16. Ibid., 1:501.

17. "Über die Verderbnis unserer Jugend," *Rettungshausbote* 17, no. 7 (1896): 110–112, 123–125.

18. Paul Felisch quoted in *Stenographische Berichte über die Verhandlungen der siebzehnten Jahresversammlung des Deutschen Vereins für Armenpflege und Wohltätigkeit* (Leipzig: Duncker & Humblot, 1898), p. 54.

19. Baur, "Was sollen wir thun?," pp. 1–11.

20. *Stenographische Berichte*, 2:1178, 1177.

21. Martin Hennig, *Der nächste Schritt in der Jugendfürsorge* (Berlin: Verlag des Ostdeutschen Jünglingsbundes, 1900), p. 6.

22. Von Massow, *Reform oder Revolution!*, p. 72.

23. Paul Scheven, "Die Gehe-Stiftung zu Dresden, eine Hochschule für staatsbürgerliche Erziehung," *Arbeiterfreund* 36 (1898): 180.

24. *Fürsorge für Kinder und Jugendliche*, pp. 144–145.

25. *Stenographischer Bericht*, pp. 70, 75.

26. Ibid., pp. 83, 78.

27. *Die für das Armenwesen wichtigsten Vorschriften des Bürgerlichen Gesetzbuches* (Leipzig: Duncker & Humblot, 1899), p. 78.

28. "Erläuterungen zum Entwurf eines Gesetzes betr. die Zwangserziehung," ZSAM, Rep. 191, no. 1995, fol. 279 (p. 19).

29. "Erörterungen über die Zwangserziehung der verwahrlosten Jugend (Verhandlungen des dritten Charitastages am 31. August 1898 zu Wiesbaden)," *Caritas* 4 (1899): 90, 36, 88, 33–34.

30. "Beschluss der preussischen Generalsynode," *Rettungshausbote* 18 (1898): 96–97.

31. Martin Hennig, "Die Statistik der evangelischen Rettungshäuser Deutschlands," *Rettungshausbote* 17, nos. 10–11 (1897): 150; idem, "Was können wir zur Bewahrung und christlichen Erziehung derjenigen sittlich gefährdeten Kinder thun welche vom Zwangserziehungsgesetz nicht erreicht werden?" *Rettungshausbote* 17, no. 8 (1897): 132, 133.

32. "Verhältnis der Rettungshäuser zum Staat," *Rettungshausbote* 16 (1895–96): 99.

33. *Motive zum dem Entwurfe eines Bürgerlichen Gesetzbuches für das Deutsche Reich,* vol. 4, *Familienrecht* (Berlin: J. Guttentag, 1888), p. 270.

34. Ibid., p. 1025.

35. See *Bericht der Reichstagskommission über den Entwurf eines Bürgerlichen Gesetzbuchs und Einführungsgesetzes* (Berlin: J. Guttentag, 1896), pp. 290–291.

36. Ibid., p. 781.

3. Expansion and Consolidation, 1900–1914

1. See *Stenographische Berichte über die Verhandlungen . . . des preussischen Landtages. Herrenhaus,* vol. 439 (1901), document 8, p. 26.

2. Martin Hennig, "Zum neuen Jahre," *Fliegende Blätter* 59 (1902): 3.

3. Carl von Massow, *Das preussische Fürsorgeerziehungsgesetz vom 2. Juli 1900 und die Mitwirkung der bürgerlichen Gesellschaft bei seiner Ausführung* (Berlin: Nicolaische Verlags-Buchhandlung, 1901), p. 3; Gustav von Rohden, "Von der prinzipiellen Tragweite des Fürsorge-Erziehungs-Gesetzes," *Jugend-*

fürsorge 2 (1901): 68; "Flugblatt herausgegeben von der Kommission für Kinderschutz," LAB, Helene-Lange Archiv, Film 51–236, 2.

4. Felix Paul Aschrott, "Das preussische FEG. in der Praxis," *Jugendfürsorge* 4 (1903): 129–136.

5. *Stenographische Berichte über die Verhandlungen des preussischen Landtages. Herrenhaus,* vol. 439 (1901), document 8, p. 31. See also, however, the Ministry of the Interior's *Votum* of December 21, 1895, ZSAM Rep. 191, no. 1995, fols. 110–115, p. 6, for an estimate of 180,000. Figures for 1914 from Franz Recke, "Die Durchführung der Fürsorgeerziehung in Preussen," *Concordia* 15 (1908): 1–6, 48–54. Detlev Peukert has published the relevant figures in *Grenzen der Sozialdisziplinierung* (Cologne: Bund-Verlag, 1986), p. 328.

6. See Heinrich Reicher, *Die Fürsorge für die verwahrloste Jugend,* pt. 3, vol. 1, *Die Theorie der Verwahrlosung und das System der Ersatzerziehung* (Vienna: Manz, 1908).

7. *Verhandlungen des ersten deutschen Jugendgerichtstages* (Berlin: Teubner, 1909), p. 56; *Verhandlungen des zweiten deutschen Jugendgerichtstages* (Berlin: Teubner, 1910), p. 6; and *Verhandlungen des Reichstages* 308 (1913): 1814–64.

8. See E. R. Mitchell, *European Historical Statistics* (New York: Columbia University Press, 1978), pp. 179–180, 300, 304; and K. D. Barkin, *The Controversy over German Industrialization, 1890–1902* (Chicago: Chicago University Press, 1970), pp. 110–111.

9. Fritz Klein, *Deutschland, 1897–1917* (Berlin: Verlag der Wissenschaften, 1977), p. 17.

10. Barkin, *The Controversy,* p. 13; Klein *Deutschland,* p. 19.

11. Barkin, *The Controversy,* pp. 116–117.

12. "23. ordentliche Hauptversammlung des Bergischen Vereins für Gemeinwohl," *Zentralblatt* 1 (1909): 188.

13. Quoted from the 1906–7 report of the DZJ, in Hedwig Kantorowicz, "Dr. jur. Frieda Duensing," *Zentralblatt* 12 (1920): 223.

14. *Stenographischer Bericht über die Verhandlungen der 25. Jahresversammlung des Deutschen Vereins für Armenpflege und Wohltätigkeit (Schriften des Deutschen Vereins,* no. 75) (Leipzig: Duncker & Humblot, 1905), pp. 24–25, 5.

15. See the report in BAK, Rep. R86 (Reichsgesundheitsamt), no. 2377.

16. *Schriften der Centralstelle für Arbeiter-Wohlfahrtseinrichtungen,* no. 17 (Berlin: Heymanns, 1900).

17. Verfügung des preussischen Ministeriums des Innern, January 14, 1905, BAK, Rep. R86, no. 2376.

18. Arthur Schlossmann, "Über die Organisation des Vereins für Säuglingsfürsorge im Regierungsbezirk Düsseldorf," *Concordia* 15 (1908): 239.

19. *Schriften der Centralstelle für Arbeiter-Wohlfahrtseinrichtungen,* no. 17 (Berlin: Heymanns, 1900), p. 72; *Schriften des Deutschen Vereins,* no. 75, p. 25.

20. This motivation is mentioned, for example, in Paul Weindling, *Health, Race, and German Politics between National Unification and Nazism* (Cambridge: Cambridge University Press, 1988), p. 205.

21. Arthur Keller, "Einheitsbestrebungen in der Säuglingsfürsorge," *Archiv für Volkswohlfahrt* 2 (1909): 593.

22. Max Seiffert, "Über die kulturelle und soziale Bedeutung der Kinder-sterblichkeit," reprinted from Alfred Lindheim, *Saluti Juventatutis* (Leipzig: Franz Deuticke, n.d.), SAD, Sächsisches Ministerium des Innern, no. 17219, fol. 168, pp. 77, 78.

23. Report of the Arbeitsausschuss des Komitees zur Errichtung einer Anstalt für die Bekämpfung der Säuglingssterblichkeit im Deutschen Reich, December 10, 1906, in BAK, Rep. R86, no. 2376.

24. Seiffert, "Über die kulturelle und soziale Bedeutung," pp. 75–76.

25. Ibid., p. 97.

26. Schlossmann, "Über die Organisation," p. 242. On Schlossmann, see Wein-dling, *Health, Race, and German politics,* pp. 200–202.

27. Helene Simon, "Die Abnahme der Geburtenrate," *Concordia* 14 (1907): 200.

28. Heinz Potthoff, "Die wirtschaftliche Rentabilität der Jugendfürsorge," *Zeit-schrift für Jugendwohlfahrt* 1 (1909): 207.

29. Hentig, "Jugendfürsorge und Staatsinteresse," *Zeitschrift für Jugendwohlfahrt* 1 (1909): 3–4.

30. Arthur Keller, "Ein Führer durch Deutschlands Fürsorgeeinrichtungen zum Schutze des Säuglings," *Zeitschrift für Säuglingsschutz* 3 (1911): 286.

31. Weindling, *Health, Race, and German Politics,* p. 175.

32. See Hildegard Böhme and Käthe Mende, *Jugendfürsorgevereine im Deutschen Reich* (Berlin: Zillessen, 1919).

33. See "11. Jahresbericht des Danziger Jugendfürsorge-Verbandes, 1911," GSAPKB, Rep. 84a, no. 10970, fol. 67. The fifty working members of the asso-ciation were slightly lower on the social scale: twenty of them were teachers. For a similar list from a western city, see "Jahresbericht der Harburger Zentrale für Jugendfürsorge, 1910," ibid., fols. 49–72.

34. *Verhandlungen des zweiten Jugendgerichtstages* (Berlin: Teubner, 1910), p. 6; "Erlass des Hessischen Justizministeriums," *Jugendfürsorge* 10 (1909): 243–244; "Eine allgemeine Verfügung des preussischen Justizministeriums vom 22. September 1909," *Zentralblatt* 1 (1909): 164–165; "Der Stand der Jugend-gerichtshilfe in Deutschland," *Zentralblatt* 2 (1910): 140; "Erlass des königi-lichen Bayrischen Staatsministeriums des Innern . . . vom 9. Dezember 1908," *Zentralblatt* 1 (1909): 71–72; "Gründung eines Bayerischen Landesausschusses für Jugendfürsorge," *Zentralblatt* 2 (1910): 117. Material on the Bavarian or-ganizations can be found in ADCV, Rep. CA VII, no. 230A.

35. "Jugendschutzverein Krefeld," *Zentralblatt* 2 (1910): 81; J. F. Landsberg, "Die Ausschüsse für Jugendfürsorge im Amtsgerichtsbezirk Lennep," *Zentralblatt* 1 (1909): 97–100.

36. *Denkschrift* of the Kaiserliches Gesundsheitsamt of December 29, 1906, and Saxon decree of April 29, 1907, SAD, Sächsisches Ministerium des Innern, no. 17219, fol. 8, 57–62; Bavarian decree of December 9, 1907, and Prussian de-cree of June 16, 1908, BAK, Rep. R86, no. 2376.

37. See Schlossmann,"Über die Organisation," and Regierungspräsident Düssel-dorf to the Landräte and Oberbürgermeister of the Regierungsbezirk, October 18, 1923, NRWHSAD, Regierung Düsseldorf, no. 33279. There are brief treat-ments in Rüdeger Baron and Rolf Landwehr, eds., *Geschichte der Sozialarbeit*

(Weinheim: Beltz, 1983); and Dietlinde Peters, *Mütterlichkeit im Kaiserreich* (Bielefeld: Kleine Verlag, 1987).

38. SAD, Sächsisches Ministerium des Innern, no. 17219, fol. 33.
39. Frieda Duensing, "Die Organisation der Jugendfürsorge," in *Schriften des Deutschen Vereins für Armenpflege und Wohltätigkeit* (Leipzig: Duncker & Humblot, 1910), p. 60.
40. Quoted in Frieda Duensing, "Zwei Verhandlungen über das preußische Fürsorgeerziehungsgesetz," *Die Frau* 14 (1906): 220.
41. Paul Köhne, *Kriminalität und sittliches Verhalten der Jugendlichen (Schriften der Gesellschaft für soziale Reform*, vol. 4, no. 2)(Jena: Gustav Fischer, 1910), p. 15.
42. Ibid., p. 20.
43. Franz von Liszt, "Die Kriminalität der Jugendlichen," *Jugendfürsorge* 2 (1901): 208.
44. *Verhandlungen des ersten deutschen Jugendgerichtstages* (Berlin: Teubner, 1909), pp. 47, 44, 45, 52–53.
45. See particularly Detlev J. K. Peukert, "The Genesis of the 'Final Solution' from the Spirit of Science," in *Reevaluating the Third Reich*, ed. Jane Caplan and Thomas Childers (New York: Holmes & Meier, 1993). For Social Democratic hopes that the scientific discovery of organic brain defects would lead to more rational treatment of reformatory inmates, see, for example, W.S., "Aus den Gemeinden: Groß-Berliner Rundschau," *KP* 6 (1907): 1224; and Gustav Major, "Die Statistik sagt's—und trotzdem ist's nicht wahr," *KP* 14 (1914): 648.
46. Pade, "Die Fürsorgeerziehung der Zigeunerkinder," *Zentralblatt* 4 (1912). Correctional education was commonly used against Sinti and Roma families; see, among others, Karola Frings and Frank Sparing, "'Tunlichst als erziehungsunfähig hinzustellen.' Zigeunerkinder und -jugendliche: Aus der Fürsorge in die Vernichtung," *Dachauer Hefte* 9 (1993): esp. 159–160.
47. Jens Paulsen, "Die Herrschaft der Schwachen und der Schutz der Starken in Deutschland," *Archiv für Rassen-und Gesellschaftsbiologie* 11 (1914).
48. Anne Taylor Allen, *Feminism and Motherhood in Germany, 1800–1914* (New Brunswick, N.J.: Rutgers University Press, 1987), p. 177. For similar arguments regarding infant welfare in Great Britain, see Anna Davin, "Imperialism and Motherhood," *History Workshop Journal* 4 (1978); and Jane Lewis, *The Politics of Motherhood* (London: Croom Helm, 1980).
49. *Schriften des Deutschen Vereins*, no. 75, p. 41; and decree of June 16, 1908, BAK, Rep. R86, no. 2376.
50. *Schriften der Centralstelle für Arbeiterwohlfahrtseinrichtungen*, no. 17 (Berlin: Heymanns, 1900), pp. 101–102.
51. Paul Köhne, "Die Stellung des Vormundes zur Mutter," *Schriften des Deutschen Vereins für Armenpflege und Wohltätigkeit* 81 (1907): 39.
52. See, for example, *Zur Frage der Berufsvormundschaft*, pt. 6, *Bericht der sechsten Tagung . . . 1911* (Dresden: O.V. Böhmert, 1912), p. 49. Agnes Neuhaus called this "cruelty toward reasonable unmarried mothers and against all mothers in general" (p. 57).
53. *Stenographische Berichte über die Verhandlungen des Hauses der Abgeordneten* (1912–13), 8:10801–8.

54. "Neue Wege auf dem Gebiet der Kinderfürsorge: Berufsvormundschaft und Berufspflegschaft," *Innere Mission* 5 (1910): 165–167; and *Schriften des Deutschen Vereins für Armenpflege und Wohltätigkeit,* no. 75 (Leipzig: Duncker und Humblot, 1905), p. 60.

55. Adolph Würtz, "Die Säuglingssterblichkeit und die Massregeln öffentlich-hygienischer Art, die zum Zwecke ihrer Herabsetzung genommen werden können," *Deutsche Vierteljahrsschrift für öffentliche Gesundheitspflege* 35 (1903): 390–424.

56. Eduard Dietrich, "Das Fürsorgewesen für Säuglinge," *Zeitschrift für Säuglingsfürsorge* 2 (1906): 28.

57. Franz Becker, "Die Organisation freiwilliger Liebestätigkeit auf dem Gebiete der Jugendfürsorge in ihrem Zusammenhange mit Vormundschaftsrichter und Jugendgericht," *Jugendfürsorge* 10 (1909): 706.

58. Ignaz Kaup, "Säuglingsfürsorgestellen," *Concordia* 14 (1907): 108; Gustav Tugendreich, "Bericht über die Säuglingsfürsorgestellen der Schmidt-Gallisch Stiftung in Berlin," *Zeitschrift für Säuglingsfürsorge* 4 (1910): 109.

59. See Anneliese Monat, *Sozialdemokratie und Wohlfahrtspflege* (Stuttgart: Kohlhammer, 1961), pp. 9–10, 25, 30, 33–34, 37; and, for example, R. Silberstein, "Die Aufgaben von Staat und Gemeinde bei der körperlichen Erziehung der Jugend," *KP* 6 (1906): 927, or "Ein Schritt zur Kinderfürsorge," *KP* 8 (1908): 1127. On the party congress of 1906, see "Beiträge zur Erziehungsfrage," *KP* 6 (1906): 921–945.

60. On the *Kinderschutzkommissionen,* see "Aus der Arbeit der Kinderschutzkommissionen," *KP* 11 (1911): 1100–1102; Louise Zietz, *Kinderarbeit, Kinderschutz, und die Kinderschutzkommissionen* (Berlin: Vorwärts/Paul Singer, 1912), esp. pp. 49–53; and Monat, *Sozialdemokratie,* pp. 38–39, 40, 27–28, 42.

61. Robert Behla, *Der Rückgang der allgemeinen Säuglingssterblichkeit in Preussen* (Berlin: Königliches preussisches statistisches Landesamt, 1911); Else Bachmann, "Zur Säuglingsfürsorge Gross-Berlins," *Concordia* 18 (1911): 93; and Joseph Ehler, "Erfolge der Säuglingsfürsorge in Freiburg im Breisgau," *Concordia* 18 (1911): 434.

62. Figures are summarized in Thomas Nipperdey, *Deutsche Geschichte, 1866–1918,* vol. 1, *Arbeitswelt und Bürgergeist* (Munich: Beck, 1990), p. 16.

63. Othmar Spann, *Die unehelichen Mündel des Vormundschaftsgerichts in Frankfurt am Main* (Dresden: O. V. Böhmert, 1909), pp. 102, 103.

64. Othmar Spann, *Die Stiefvaterfamilie unehelichen Ursprungs: Zugleich eine Studie zur Methodologie der Unehelichkeitsstatistik* (Berlin: Reimer, 1904), pp. 21, 29–30.

65. Hugo Neumann, "Die Unehelichen in der Säuglingsfürsorge," *Zeitschrift für Säuglingsfürsorge* 5 (1911): 288.

66. Preussisches Ministerium des Innern to the Regierungspräsidenten, July 13, 1900, GSAPKB, Rep. 84a, no. 5571, fol. 60.

67. See the list compiled by the Prussian Ministry of the Interior in 1918, "Landesgesetze über die Berufsvormundschaft," ZSAM, Rep. 191, no. 2366, fols. 359–392.

68. Franz Recke, "Der Siegeszug der öffentlichen Berufsvormundschaft," *Concordia* 18 (1911): 465–469.

69. "Zusammenstellung der in Preussen vorhandenen Berufsvormundschaften," ZSAM, Rep. 191, no. 2359, fols. 201–271; "Übersicht der Berufsvormundschaften im Deutschen Reiche (September 1913)," *Zentralblatt* 5 (1913): 130–141.

70. See, for example, Köhler, "Berufsvormundschaft und Reform des Vormundschaftsrechts," *Zentralblatt* 4 (1912): 49–56.

71. "Vierter deutscher Berufsvormündertag," *Zeitschrift für das Armenwesen* 10 (1909): 352.

72. *Schriften des Deutschen Vereins für Armenpflege und Wohltätigkeit*, no. 94 (Leipzig: Duncker & Humblot, 1910), pp. 34–54; "Ueber Kinderfürsorge," *KP* 9 (1909): 114; Monat, *Sozialdemokratie*, p. 33. The SPD did not develop its own concept for the organization of public child welfare.

73. *Schriften des Deutschen Vereins für Armenpflege und Wohltätigkeit*, no. 94 (Leipzig: Duncker & Humblot, 1910), p. 89.

74. *Schriften der Zentralstelle für Volkswohlfahrt*, no. 4 (Berlin: Heymanns, 1909), pp. 124, 155, 122.

75. Othmar Spann, "Die Erweiterung der Sozialpolitik durch die Berufsvormundschaft," *Archiv für Sozialwissenschaft und Sozialpolitik* 34 (1912): 560, 547.

76. Ibid., p. 549.

77. Paul Felisch, "Ein deutsches Jugendgesetz," *Deutsche Juristen-Zeitung* 17 (1912): 20.

78. Wilhelm Polligkeit, *Das Recht des Kindes auf Erziehung* (Dresden: Johannes Pässler, 1908), pp. 13–14.

79. Wilhelm Polligkeit, *Strafrechtsreform und Jugendfürsorge* (Langensalza: Hermann Beyer & Söhne, 1905), p. 10.

80. Polligkeit, *Das Recht*, pp. 28–31, 35.

81. Johannes Petersen, *Das Recht des Kindes auf Erziehung und dessen Verwirklichung* (Berlin: Deutsche Tageszeitung, 1912), pp. 12, 190, 8.

82. *Stenographische Berichte über die Verhandlungen des preussischen Hauses der Abgeordneten* (1912–1917), 8:10832.

83. Polligkeit, *Strafrechtsreform und Jugendfürsorge*, p. 8; Johannes Petersen, *Die öffentliche Fürsorge für die hilfsbedürftige Jugend* (Leipzig: Teubner, 1907), p. 87; Johannes Petersen/DZJ, *Jugendfürsorge* (Berlin: Heymanns, 1915), p. 1.

84. See Gerd Neises, ed., *Christian Jasper Klumker: Schriften zur Jugendhilfe und Fürsorge* (Frankfurt am Main: DVöpF, 1968); on Duensing, see Anne Taylor Allen, *Feminism and Motherhood in Germany, 1800–1914* (New Brunswick, N.J.: Rutgers University Press, 1991), pp. 219–228; on Polligkeit, see Carl Ludwig Krug von Nidda, *Wilhelm Polligkeit: Wegbereiter einer neuzeitlichen Fürsorge* (Berlin: Heymanns, 1961).

85. See especially Leonard Krieger, *The German Idea of Freedom* (Chicago: University of Chicago Press, 1957).

4. The Struggle over Child Welfare Policy, 1910–1914

1. *Deutsche Tageszeitung*, September 18, 1910, GSAPKB, Rep. 84a, no. 10968, fol. 225.

2. "Die Heranwachsenden," *Der Tag* August 13, 1910, GSAPKB, Rep. 84a, no. 10968, fol. 196.

3. "Woher kommt der Mangel an Autoritätsbewusstsein in unseren Tagen, beson-
   ders bei unserer Jugend, und wie ist sie zu bekämpfen?," *Fliegende Blätter* 62
   (1905): 96–106.

4. See F. Prinzing, "Eheliche und uneheliche Fruchtbarkeit und Aufwuchsziffer in
   Stadt und Land in Preussen," *Deutsche Medizinische Wochenschrift* (1918),
   reprinted in BAK, Rep. R86, no. 2383.

5. Arthur Schlossmann, "Die treibenden Kräfte," *Zeitschrift für Säuglingsfürsorge* 7 (1913): 185–186.

6. See particularly Jean Bornträger, *Der Geburtenrückgang in Deutschland. Seine
   Bewertung und Bekämpfung* (Würzburg: Curt Kabitzsch, 1913); the quotation
   is on p. 46. Bornträger also recommended more positive measures, however,
   such as tax benefits, housing schemes, a child allowance, and day care for large
   families, and a bachelor tax on single men.

7. Arthur Schlossmann, "Die Frage des Geburtenrückganges," *Zeitschrift für
   Säuglingsfürsorge* 8 (1914): 7.

8. *Jugendämter als Träger der öffentlichen Jugendfürsorge im Deutschen Reich*
   (Berlin: Heymanns, 1919), p. 143.

9. See Klaus Saul, "'Der Kampf um die Jugend zwischen Volksschule und
   Kaserne.' Ein Beitrag zur 'Jugendpflege' im wilhelminischen Reich, 1890–
   1914," *Militärgeschichtliche Mitteilungen* 9 (1971): 103–105. In 1908 socialist
   youth groups claimed 19,000 members, in 1913, 89,409; the Worker's Gymnastics Association claimed 20,874 members aged fourteen to seventeen in
   1908 and 32,358 in 1912.

10. *Votum* of the Kriegsminister, "Betreffend staatsbürgerliche Erziehung für die
    schulentlassene männliche Jugend," April 2, 1910, GSAPKB, Rep. 84a, no.
    10968, fol. 88–93, and app. 2, fol. 97.

11. *Votum* of the Ministerium der geistlichen usw. Angelegenheiten, July 15, 1910,
    GSAPKB, Rep. 84a, no. 10968, fol. 138.

12. *Nachtrag* of August 20 to Ministry of the Interior's *Votum* of August 11, 1911,
    ibid., fols. 187–189. See Georg Kerschensteiner, *Staatsbürgerliche Erziehung
    der Deutschen Jugend* (1900; rpt. Erfurt: Karl Villaret, 1909).

13. See "Sitzung des königlichen Staatsministeriums," September 19, 1910; and
    Votum of the Finanz-Minister, August 31, 1910, GSAPKB, Rep. 84a, no.
    10968, fols. 229–242, 201–204.

14. *Votum* of the Minister für Handel and Gewerbe, August 11, 1910, GSAPKB,
    Rep. 84a, no. 10968, fols. 165, 166.

15. *Votum* of the Finanz-Minister, August 31, 1910, ibid., fols. 201–204.

16. See "Sitzung des königlichen Staatsministeriums," September 19 and No-
    vember 15, 1910, ibid., fols. 229–242, 249–256.

17. Fuldaer Bischofskonferenz to Königliche Preussische Staatsregierung, No-
    vember 18, 1912, GSAPKB, Rep. 84a, no. 10974, fols. 106–110. The religious
    organizations eventually joined the Young Germany League in order to secure
    state subsidies. See Saul, "Der Kampf um die Jugend," pp. 118–123.

18. See Saul, "Der Kampf um die Jugend," p. 112. The church objected to the
    failure to provide for religious instruction—which the ministry regarded as di-
    visive and therefore dangerous—in these schools.

19. Johannes Trüper, "Zum Gesetz über die Zwangserziehung Minderjähriger in
    Preußen," *Zeitschrift für Kinderforschung* 5 (1900): 141. Trüper wanted com-

mittments placed in the hands of a council consisting not only of jurists but also of pedagogues, psychiatrists, clergy, and parents.

20. Oberlandesgerichtspräsident in Hamm, in "Auszug aus den Berichten der Oberlandesgerichtspräsidenten, betreffend Abänderung des Fürsorge-Erziehungs-Gesetzes," February 29, 1912, GSAPKB, Rep. 84a, no. 10986, fols. 24–34.

21. Max Taube, "Die Säuglingsfürsorge durch Staat, Gemeinde, und freie Liebestätigkeit," *Zeitschrift für Säuglingsfürsorge* 1 (1906): 32–33; Eduard Dietrich, "Das Fürsorgewesen für Säuglinge," *Zeitschrift für Säuglingsfürsorge* 2 (1908): 46; Arthur Schlossmann, "Zwei wichtige Fragen aus dem Gebiete der Säuglingsfürsorge," *Zeitschrift für Säuglingsfürsorge* 4 (1910): 235–236, 237.

22. *Stenographischer Bericht über die Verhandlungen der bayrischen Kammer der Abgeordneten . . . 14. Dezember 1907*, pp. 315–328, SAD, Sächsisches Ministerium des Innern, no. 17219, fols. 39–46.

23. Dr. Wichura, "Ethische Momente im Kampf gegen die Kindersterblichkeit," *Zeitschrift für Säuglingsfürsorge* 2 (1908): 291–292.

24. Marie Liedtki, "Noch einmal ethische Momente im Kampfe gegen die Kindersterblichkeit," *Zeitschrift für Säuglingsfürsorge* 3 (1909): 52–53.

25. See Frieda Duensing, "Zwei Verhandlungen über das preussische Fürsorgeerziehungsgesetz," *Die Frau* 14 (1906): 220–221; and Clemens Neisser, in Allgemeiner Fürsorgeerziehungstag, *Bericht über die Verhandlungen des Allgemeinen Fürsorge-Erziehungs-Tages am 11.–14. Juni 1906 zu Breslau* (Strausberg: Allgemeiner Fürsorgeerziehungstag, 1906).

26. Pastor Siebold, in *Bericht über die Verhandlungen des Allgemeinen Fürsorge-Eziehungs-Tages am 23.–27. Juni 1910 zu Rostock* (Berlin: Heymanns, 1910), p. 117.

27. Johannes Trüper, "Über das Zusammenwirken von Medizin und Pädagogik bei der Fürsorge für unsere abnormen Kinder," *Zeitschrift für Kinderforschung* 7 (1902): 102–103.

28. See "7. Generalversammlung des Bundes deutscher Frauenvereine," *Berliner Tageblatt*, October 9, 1906, ZSAP, Rep. 30.01, no. 1434.

29. Paul Natorp, "Über eine mögliche Umbildung der Familienerziehung in den arbeitenden Klassen," *Zeitschrift für Jugendwohlfahrt/Der Säemann* 1 (1910): 261.

30. Schwester von Tiele-Winkler, "Die Seele des Kindes," in *Frauen-Vormundschaft: Vorlesungen des ersten Lehrgangs über Vormundschaft und Waisenpflege für evangelische Frauen in der Königlichen Friedrich-Wilhelms-Universität zu Berlin vom 16. bis 18. April 1917* (Potsdam: Stiftungs-Verlag, 1917), pp. 20, 25.

31. Polykarp Niestroj, *Die Berufsvormundschaft und ihre Probleme* (Berlin: Gustav Ziemsen, 1913), p. 75.

32. *Stenographischer Bericht über die Verhandlungen der 27. Jahresversammlung des Deutschen Vereins für Armenpflege und Wohltätigkeit . . . 1907 (Schriften des Deutschen Vereins*, no. 83)(Leipzig: Duncker und Humblot, 1907), p. 43.

33. Ibid., p. 56. See also Niestroj, *Die Berufsvormundschaft*, p. 81.

34. "Weibliche Vormundschaft," *Neue Preussische Zeitung*, November 2, 1913, ZSAP, Rep. 30.01, no. 1434.

35. See *Zur Frage der Berufsvormundschaft . . . 1911* (Dresden: Böhmert, 1911), pp. 128. 130.

36. On the disappointment over the number of women guardians, see, for example, Allgemeiner Deutscher Frauenverein, "Frauen, übernehmt Vormundschaften!," and Verein für weibliche Vormundschaft, "Werdet Vormünderinnen!," both in ADCV, Rep. 319.4 (SKF), no. E IV 7,8, fasc. 1; on the Alliance, see Wilhelmine Mohr, "Die Frau in der Berufsvormundschaft und in den Jugendgerichten," *Vossische Zeitung* August 3, 1909, GSAPKB, Rep. 84a, no. 5571, fol. 165; "Zweiter Bericht über die Entwicklung und Tätigkeit des Vereins für weibliche Vormundschaft," ADCV, Rep. 221. Polykarp Niestroj reported in 1916 that the Berlin association had 1,454 wards in 1914; similar groups had 146 in Kiel in 1913, 72 in Munich in 1913, and so on. The KFV had 8,650 wards by 1921. See Polykarp Niestroj, "Fortschritte der Einzelvormundschaft," *Jugendwohl* 5 (1916): 11–13, and idem, "Fürsorgeverein für Mädchen, Frauen und Kinder," *Caritas* 1 (1922): 124–125.

37. See C. J. Klumker, "Die Organisation der Fürsorge für die hilfsbedürftige Jugend," in *Frauen-Vormundschaft*, p. 27.

38. Johannes Petersen, "Die Berufsvormundschaft in der Praxis," in C. J. Klumker and Johannes Petersen, *Berufsvormundschaft (Generalvormundschaft) (Schriften des Deutschen Vereins,* no. 81)(Leipzig: Duncker & Humblot, 1907), p. 23.

39. *Zur Frage der Berufsvormundschaft . . . 1914* (Dresden: Böhmert, 1914), p. 57.

40. Ibid., p. 57; Jenny Apolant, "Die Mitwirkung der Frau in der kommunalen Wohlfahrtspflege," *Die Frau* 23 (1915): p. 330.

41. On the history of social work as a profession, see Christof Sachße, *Mütterlichkeit als Beruf: Sozialarbeit, Sozialreform, und Frauenbewegung, 1871–1929* (Frankfurt: Suhrkamp, 1986), esp. pp. 145–146; Dietlinde Peters, *Mütterlichkeit im Kaiserreich: Die bürgerliche Frauenbewegung und der sozialen Beruf der Frau* (Bielefeld: Kleine Verlag, 1984); Young-Sun Hong, "Femininity as a Vocation: Gender and Class in the Professionalization of Social Work," in *The German Professions, 1800–1950,* ed. Geoffrey Cocks and Konrad Jarausch (New York: Oxford University Press, 1990).

42. See the report of Kneilmann, "Generalvormundschaft, Einzelvormundschaft und die Fürsorge für die bevormundete und gefährdete Jugend in der Stadt Dortmund," *Caritas* 9 (1906): 165–167, 188–190; "Der Deutsche Caritas und die Jugendfürsorge," ADCV, Rep. 171, fasc. 1; and Agnes Neuhaus quoted in *Zur Frage der Berufsvormundschaft . . . 1908* (Dreseden: Böhmert, 1908), pp. 90–91.

43. "Die Stellung der Katholiken zum Vormundschaftswesen," ADCV, Rep. CA VII, no. 70, fol. 188.

44. See Bernhard Wuermeling, "Einzelvormundschaft und Berufsvormundschaft, insbesondere städtische Sammelvormundschaft," reprinted from *Kommunalpolitische Blätter* 13 (1913), ZSAP, Rep. 30.01, no. 1430; "Caritasverband Berlin und die städtische Sammelvormundschaft," *Jugendwohl* 2 (1913): pp. 33–46.

45. Wuermeling, "Einzelvormundschaft und Berufsvormundschaft."

46. Friedrich, "Konferenz des 'evangelischen Erziehungsamts der Inneren Mission' in Weimar," *Zentralblatt* 5 (1913): 70.

47. *Stenographische Berichte über die Verhandlungen des preussischen Hauses der Abgeordneten* (1912–1917); 9:11566–77; and "Einzelvormundschaft und Berufsvormundschaft," p. 5.

48. "Die Stellung der Katholiken zur Vormundschaftsfrage," pp. 1–2.

49. See Hans-Joseph Wollasch, "Lorenz Werthmann (1858–1921)," in *Zeitgeschichte in Lebensbildern*, ed. Jürgen Aretz, Rudolf Morsey, and Anton Rauscher (Mainz: Grünewald, 1980), p. 86; "'Der an sich schöne Gedanke der Charitas' und die Geburtenwehen des Verbandes 1897," in *Caritas '88: Jahrbuch des Deutschen Caritasverbandes* (Freiburg: DCV, 1987).

50. On the KFV, see Andreas Wollasch, *Der Katholische Fürsorgeverein für Mädchen, Frauen und Kinder* (Freiburg: Lambertus, 1991).

51. Niestroj, *Die Berufsvormundschaft*, p. 33.

52. See Agnes Neuhaus, "Moderne Probleme der Jugendfürsorge," *Caritas* 16 (1911): 121–127; and Christian Bartels, "Der katholische Männer-Fürsorgeverein," *Jugendwohl* 2 (1913): 84–87.

53. Agnes Neuhaus, "Die Aufgaben der Fürsorge-Vereine," in *2 Vorträge* (Mönchen-Gladbach: Verlag der Zweigstelle des Katholischen Fürsorge-Vereins, 1906), p. 8.

54. Neuhaus, "Moderne Probleme," pp. 121–127.

55. See "Organisation der Jugendfürsorge," *Zentralblatt* 3 (1911): 174–175.

56. "Jahresbericht der Breslauer Zentrale für Jugendhilfe" (1909), GSAPKB, Rep. 84a, no. 10969, fols. 414–421; Sachße, *Mütterlichkeit als Beruf*, p. 91.

57. See Käthe Mende and Hildegard Böhme, *Die Jugendfürsorgevereine im Deutschen Reich* (Berlin: Zillessen, 1919).

58. *Stenographischer Bericht über die Verhandlungen der 30. Jahresversammlung des deutschen Vereins für Armenpflege und Wohltätigkeit (Schriften des Deutschen Vereins, no. 94)*(Leipzig: Duncker & Humblot, 1910), p. 56.

59. Natorp, "Über eine mögliche Umbildung," p. 260.

60. Johannes Petersen, "Gemeindewaisenrat und Jugendgericht," *Zentralblatt* 1 (1909): 28.

61. See, for example, Bernhard Wuermeling, in *Stenographische Berichte über die Verhandlungen des preussischen Hauses der Abgeordneten* (1912–1917), 9:11569.

62. See, for example, Franz Recke, "Die örtliche Organisation des Haltekinderwesens," *Zeitschrift für Säuglingsfürsorge* 4 (1912): 104; Frieda Duensing quoted in *Verhandlungen des ersten Jugendgerichtstages* (Berlin: Teubner, 1909), p. 63.

63. *Schriften des Deutschen Vereins*, no. 94, p. 73.

64. Quoted in Franz Recke, "Die örtliche Organisation," p. 129.

65. Figures from Detlev Peukert, *Grenzen der Sozialdisziplinierung: Aufstieg und Krise der deutschen Jugendfürsorge, 1878–1932* (Cologne: Bund, 1986), p. 330; *Rettungshausbote* 25 (1904–5): 5, and 29 (1908–9): 5.

66. For the entire discussion surrounding the problem, see *Stenographischer Bericht über die Verhandlungen der 23. Jahresversammlung des Deutschen Vereins für Armenpflege und Wohltätigkeit* (Berlin: Duncker & Humblot, 1903); and *Stenographische Berichte über die Verhandlungen des Preussischen Hauses der Abgeordneten*, (1903), 1:1146–70.

67. Franz Recke, "Die Durchführung der Fürsorgeerziehung in Preussen," *Concordia* 15 (1908): 1.

68. "Paragraph 1, Ziffer 1 preussisches Fürsorgeerziehungsgesetz. Begriff der Verwahrlosungsgefahr," *Zentralblatt* 2 (1910): 285–286.

69. See "Eine tieftraurige Nachricht," *Rettungshausbote* 26 (1906): 30; and "Die preussische Fürsorgeerziehung," *KP* 5 (1905): 867.

70. Wilhelm Backhausen, "Das Entweichen der Fürsorgezöglinge," *Zentralblatt* 2 (1911): 244–245.

71. *Bericht über die Verhandlungen des Allgemeinen Fürsorge-Erziehungs-Tages vom 24.–27. Juni 1912 zu Dresden* (Halle: Carl Marhold, 1912), p. 42.

72. Karl Neuendörfer, "Die gefährdete Jugend und die Ordnung in Staat, Gesellschaft und Kirche," *Jugendwohl* 14 (1925): 116.

73. *Bericht über die Verhandlungen des Allgemeinen Fürsorge-Erziehungs-Tages vom 24.–27. Juni 1912 zu Dresden* (Halle: Carl Morhold, 1912), p. 44.

74. Jean Ritzert, "Zur Frage der Fürsorgeerziehung," *KP* 11 (1911): 1526.

75. See *Bericht über die Verhandlungen des Allgemeinen Fürsorge-Erziehungstages . . . 1912*, p. 109; and Karl Zielke, "Strafe oder Erziehung?," *KP* 11 (1911): 1640.

76. *Bericht über die Verhandlungen des Allgemeinen Fürsorge-Erziehungs-Tages am 23.–27. Juni 1910 zu Rostock* (Berlin: Heymanns, 1910), p. 116.

77. Günter Dehn, "Großstadtjugend," *Ratgeber für Jugendvereinigungen* 8 (1914): 106, 98, 102–103.

78. Wilhelm Rhiel, "Die Vereinigung für katholische caritative Erziehungstätigkeit," *Jugendwohl* 1 (1912): 3.

79. *Bericht über die Verhandlungen des Allgemeinen Fürsorge-Erziehungs-Tages am 11.–14. Juni 1906 zu Breslau* (Strausberg: AFET, 1906), p. 101.

80. Otto Mönkemöller, "Die Strafe in der Fürsorgeerziehung," *Zeitschrift für Kinderforschung* 19 (1914): 152.

81. Herrenhaus, January 11, 1900, ZSAM, Rep. 191, no. 1997, fols. 259ff.

82. Karl Krohne, "Zur Frage der Abänderung des Gesetzes über die Fürsorgeerziehung Minderjähriger vom 2. Juli 1900," GSAPKB, Rep. 84a, no. 10985, fol. 252.

83. See Johannes Trüper, "Mieltschin," *Zeitschrift für Kinderforschung* 16 (1911): 129–142; idem, "Fürsorgeerziehung," *KP* 9 (1909): 1041–47.

84. Karl Zielke, "Strafe oder Erziehung?," *KP* 11 (1911): 1643; *Verhandlungen des Reichstages*, 286: 2901.

85. "Ein Schritt zur Kinderfürsorge," *KP* 8 (1908): 1124.

86. See Anneliese Monat, *Sozialdemokratie und Wohlfahrtspflege* (Stuttgart: Kohlhammer, 1961, p. 23; H. Borgman, "Das neue Verwaltungsgebäude der Berliner Wohlfahrtspflege," *KP* 10 (1910): 749; "Ein Schritt," sp. 1123; and Paul Hirsch, "Die Fürsorgeerziehung in Preussen," *KP* 11 (1911): 133.

87. See, for example, E. N., "Neuregelung der Fürsorgeerziehung in Sachsen," *KP* 8 (1908): 492–493; R. Silberstein, "Die Aufgaben von Staat und Gemeinde bei der körperlichen Erziehung der Jugend," *KP* 6 (1906): 927–930; Otto Uhlig, "Jugendfürsorge in Dresden," *KP* 6 (1906): 930–938; and Jean Ritzert, "Zur Frage der Fürsorgeerziehung Minderjähriger," *KP* 5 (1905): 129–133. The demands of Social Democratic critics are summarized in Monat, *Sozialdemokratie*, pp. 23, 26–27.

88. Trüper, "Mieltschin," p. 139; for his earlier criticism of the law, see Johannes Trüper, "Zum Gesetz über die Zwangserziehung Minderjähriger Personen," *Zeitschrift für Kinderforschung* 5 (1900).

89. "Unerhört" and "Das Unheil geht weiter," *Rettungshausbote* 32 (1911): 91–92.

90. "Vorwort," *Rettungshausbote* 31 (1911): 4.

91. Adalbert Gregor, "Zur Abgrenzung von Stufen moralischer Entwicklung und Verwahrlosung," *Zentralblatt* 9 (1917): 5–7; Gustav Major, "Die Statistik sagt's—und trotzdem ist's nicht wahr," *KP* 14 (1914): 648.

92. "Das neue Fürsorgegesetz im Königreich Sachsen," *Rettungshausbote* 28 (1908): 188; Blochwitz, "Soll das preussische Fürorgeerziehungsgesetz geändert werden?," *Innere Mission* 5 (1910): 321.

93. Hans Uellner, "Was sollen wir mit den sog. 'Unverbesserlichen' machen?," *Jugendfürsorge* 3 (1902): 525.

94. Ibid., p. 526.

95. Wilhelm Seiffert, "Allgemeine Fürsorgeerziehungstag (Rostock, 27. bis 30. Juni 1910)," *Zentralblatt* 2 (1910): 114–115, 124–126.

96. The petition is reprinted in "Antrag zum Preuss. Fürsorgeerziehungsgesetz," *Zentralblatt* 3 (1912): 238.

97. Draft of a decree, written in March 1912, GSAPKB, Rep. 84a, no. 10986, fols. 42–54 (quote on pp. 7–8).

98. C. J. Klumker, "Die Kriminalität der Jugendlichen," in Johannes Petersen/DZJ, *Jugendfürsorge* (Berlin: Heymanns, 1915), p. 127.

99. Buschmann, "Zur Praxis des Jugendgerichts Berlin-Mitte in Fürsorgeerziehungssachen," *Zentralblatt* 2 (1910): 67.

100. J. F. Landsberg, "Die Psychologie der normalen Jugendlichen," *Zentralblatt* 5 (1914): 219.

101. C. J. Klumker, "Das Hauptproblem in der Fürsorgeerziehung," *Zentralblatt* 5 (1914): 93–94.

102. See the quotes from Backhausen in "Missverständnis," *Rettungshausbote* 27 (1907): 89.

103. See Susanne Zeller, "Frieda Duensing und die Deutsche Zentrale für Jugendfürsorge Berlin," in *Mütterlichkeit als Profession? Lebensläufe deutscher Pädagoginnen in der ersten Hälfte dieses Jahrhunderts*, ed. Ilse Brehmer (Pfaffenweiler: Centaurus, 1990), p. 239.

104. E. N., "Fürsorgeerziehung im 'Jahrhundert des kindes'," *KP* 5 (1905): 535; "Von der Fürsorgeerziehung," *KP* 12 (1912): 1260.

105. Knaut, "Die Selbstverwaltung der älteren Fürsorgezöglinge," *Bericht über die Verhandlungen des Allgemeinen Fürsorge-Erziehungs-Tages . . . 1912*, p. 159.

106. F. W. Förster, "Autorität und Selbstregierung in der Leitung der Jugendlichen," *Zeitschrift für Kinderforschung* 20 (1915): 388. See also his speech before the AFET, reported in *Bericht über die Verhandlungen des Allgemeinen Fürsorge-Erziehungs-Tages vom 15. bis 17. Juni 1914 in Halle a. S.* (Berlin: Heymanns, 1914).

107. Förster, "Autorität," pp. 390–391.

108. Gertrud Bäumer, "Das Autoritätsproblem," *Zeitschrift dür Jugendwohlfahrtspflege/Der Säemann* 2 (1911): 261. Bäumer's liberal anti-Catholicism was cen-

tral to her thinking on this point; Förster, in contrast, was a convert to Catholicism.

109. Friedrich Zimmer, "Lebenserziehung," *Zeitschrift für Jugendwohlfahrt* 1 (1910): 392, 393.

110. Knaut, "Die Selbstverwaltung . . .," p. 159.

111. Förster, "Autorität und Selbstregierung," pp. 387, 394–395, 388.

112. Bäumer, "Autoritätsproblem," p. 257.

113. Förster, "Autorität und Selbstregierung," p. 399.

114. See, for example, Wilhelm Seiffert, "Konferenz der Deutschen Zentrale für Jugendfürsorge über Probleme der Fürsorgeerziehung," *Zentralblatt* 2 (1910): 20; and "Bemerkungen zu dem Erlab vom 25. Dezember 1910," ZSAM, Rep. 191, no. 2178, fol. 85.

5. Child Welfare Policy in the Great War, 1914–1918

1. J. F. Landsberg, "Krieg als Ursache und als Heilung von Verwahrlosung," *Zentralblatt* 6 (1914): 137–138.

2. F. Scherer, *Das Vaterland braucht den letzten Mann: Jugendnot und Jugendpflege im Kriege* (N.p.: Vereinigung für Knabenhandarbeit und Jugendpflege im Saargebiet, 1916), p. 6; Deutsches Archiv für Jugendwohlfahrt, "Die Folgen des Krieges für die Kinder in Deutschland" (1931), ADCV, Rep. 481.5, fasc. 3, p. 28.

3. Wilhelm Bloch, "Die Wirkung des Krieges auf die Jugendlichen," *Zentralblatt* 7 (1915): 38; Melchior von Borries, "Gegen die Verwahrlosung unserer Jugend," *Kreuz-Zeitung*, no. 660, December 28, 1915, ZSAM, Rep. 191, no. 2357, fol. 12.

4. Quote from "Die Kriegsverwahrlosung nach den Überweisungsakten schulentlassener Burschen," *Rheinische Fürsorgeerziehungsblatt* 17 (1919): 10.

5. "Erziehungshilfe der Bürgerschaft," *Rettungshausbote* 37 (1916): 174, 175.

6. "Nachweisungen über die Zahl der jugendlichen Personen, gegen welche in den ersten . . . zweiten . . . dritten . . . vierten Kalenderviertel ein Strafverfahren anhängig gemacht worden ist," ZSAM, Rep. 191, no. 2357, fols. 141ff. The national figures were 47,000 and 99,500; see Peter D. Stachura, *The Weimar Republic and the Younger Proletariat* (New York: St. Martin's, 1989).

7. Paul Felisch, *Wesen und Aufgaben der Jugendpolitik* (Berlin: Hermann Bousset, 1918), pp. 15, 24; Petition of November 8, 1918, to Regierungspräsident Oppeln, GSAPKB, Rep. 84a, no. 1016, fol. 1.

8. Gräfin Selma von der Gröben, "Freiheit," *Ratgeber für Jugendvereinigungen* 9 (1915): 191, 192.

9. See *Vorbericht* to the meeting of the Zentralstelle für Volkswohlfahrt, December 13, 1917, GSAPKB, Rep. 84a, no. 10972, fols. 252–270.

10. The Kammergericht concluded that "the danger of moral waywardness is . . . present when . . . the minor . . . is estranged from the Fatherland." "Zum Wesen deutscher Erziehung," *Zentralblatt* 9 (1917): 63–64. For a critical comment, see "Fürsorgeerziehung und Politik," *Zentralblatt* 9 (1917): 152–153.

11. "Unsere Kriegsjugendlichen," *Volkszeitung,* no. 209, April 23, 1916, ZSAM, Rep. 191, no. 2357.

12. Reports in RWHSA, Regierung Düsseldorf, no. 33120.

13. "Unsere Jugend im Kriege," *Rheinische Fürsorgeerziehungsblatt* 16 (1918): 45. One such was a decree of the Bundesrat which punished minors who worked late in bakeries, even if required to do so by their employers. See *Jahresbericht* of the Breslauer Zentrale für Jugendfürsorge, ADCV, Rep. CA VII, no. 229.

14. Zentralstelle für Volkswohlfahrt, *Zwang und Freiheit in der Jugendpflege* (Berlin: Heymanns, 1917), pp. 22–23.

15. Jaeger, in "Die VI. Jugendpflege-Konferenz der Zentralstelle für Volkswohlfahrt," *Ratgeber für Jugendvereinigungen* 9 (1915): 173–174.

16. "Vorbericht" to report of the meeting of the Zentralstelle für Jugendwohlfahrt, December 13, 1917, GSAPKB, Rep. 84a, no. 10972, fols. 252–270 (p. 19).

17. ZVW, *Zwang und Freiheit,* p. 189. The AFET was an important exception: it advocated retaining most restrictive measures after the end of the war. See "Beschlüsse des Allgemeinen Fürsorge-Erziehungstages (E.V.) (Angenommen in der Sitzung des Rechts-Ausschusses und des Vorstandes am 18. Juli 1917)," in *75 Jahre AFET: Erziehungshilfen und Gesellschaft,* ed. Martin Scherpner and Christian Schrapper (Hannover: AFET, 1981), 26–28.

18. See Pastor Thiele, "VI. Jugendpflege-Konferenz," p. 180.

19. Aloys Fischer, "Erziehungsziele nach dem Kriege," in *Zur Frage der Berufsvormundschaft 10: Berichte der zehnten Tagung Deutscher Berufsvormünder . . . , 1916* (Berlin: Heymanns, 1917), p. 82.

20. C. Weinbrenner, "Bevölkerungs-Fragen und -Aufgaben," *Zeitschrift für Säuglings- und Kleinkinderfürsorge* 10 (1918): 106.

21. K. Oldenburg, "Die deutsche Volkskraft und der Weltkrieg," in *Die Erhaltung und Mehrung der deutschen Volkskraft: Verhandlungen der 8. Konferenz der Zentralstelle für Volkswohlfahrt vom 26.–28. Oktober 1915* (Berlin: Heymanns, 1916, p. 21.

22. See Paul Weindling, *Health, Race, and German politics from Unification to Nazism, 1870–1945* (Cambridge: Cambridge University Press, 1989), pp. 288–290; Cornelie Usborne, *The Politics of the Body in Weimar Germany* (New York: Macmillan, 1992), pp. 17–19.

23. *Protokoll* of the meeting of the Zentral-Ausschuss of the DVAW, January 20, 1917, AIGM, no. 226.

24. "Aufsichtslose Kinder," *Germania,* no. 567, January 8, 1915, ZSAM, Rep. 191, no. 2357, fol. 10.

25. Heinrich Behm, "Geburtenrückgang und Volkssittlichkeit," *Zeitschrift für Bevölkerungspolitik und Säuglingsfürsorge* 10 (1918): 66, 83, 74–76.

26. Dr. Saalman, "Ein Beitrag zur Frage der Bevölkerungspolitik nach dem Kriege," *Zeitschrift für Bevölkerungspolitik und Säuglingsfürsorge* 10 (1918): 238, 233.

27. See, esp., Weindling, *Health, Race, and German Politics,* pp. 281–305; and Cornelie Usborne, "'Pregnancy Is the Woman's Active Service': Pronatalism in Germany during the First World War," in *The Upheaval of War: Family, Work, and Welfare in Europe, 1914–1918,* ed. Richard Wall and Jay Winter (Cambridge: Cambridge University Press, 1988), pp. 392–393.

28. See Kurt Blaum, "Die erste Etappe auf dem Wege der Bevölkerungspolitik," *Zentralblatt* 10 (1918): 106, 108.

29. Cornelie Usborne, *Politics of the Body*, p. 14.

30. Friedrich Zahn, "Deutsche Volkswirtschaft und Bevölkerungspolitik," in *Die Erhaltung und Mehrung der deutschen Volkskraft: Vorträge und Aussprachen gehalten bei der Tagung in München am 27. und 28. Mai 1918* (Munich: J. F. Lehmanns, 1918), p. 27.

31. Saalman, "Ein Beitrag," pp. 232, 233.

32. "Zweiter Teilbericht des 16. Ausschusses für Bevölkerungspolitik betreffend Schutz für Mutter und Kind," October 5, 1917, *Verhandlungen des Reichstages* 322:1831.

33. "Niederschrift über die im Ministerium des Innern am 9. Mai 1916 stattge-fundene kommissarische Beratungen, betreffend die Bekämpfung des Geburtenrückganges," GSAPKB, Rep. 84a, no. 437, fols. 4–10, p. 9.

34. Karl Böckenhoff, "Katholische Kirche und uneheliche Kinder. Ein theologisches Gutachten zur Stellungnahme des Caritasverbandes in seiner Eingabe an den Reichstag," *Caritas* 21 (1916): 312. *Caritas* noted, however, that many Catholics and Catholic organizations did support the petition. See "Die Reichsfürsorge für die unehelichen Kinder gefallener Kriegsteilnehmer," *Caritas* 21 (1916): 192.

35. Ibid., pp. 307–308, 312.

36. "Staatliche Kinderheime zur Lebensrettung unehelicher Kinder," *Zentralblatt* 9 (1918): 246.

37. Wilhelm Feld, "Steigerung der Wehrkraft oder Sittlichkeit?," *Hochland* 15 (1918): 453, 457.

38. *Die Erhaltung und Mehrung der deutschen Volkskraft* (Berlin: Heymanns, 1916), p. 141.

39. A. Hessenbach, "Wo steht die Bevölkerungspolitik?," in *Jugendfürsorge und Bevölkerungspolitik*, ed. Georg Lindermayr (Augsburg: Katholischer Jugendfürsorge-verein der Diözese Augsburg, 1918), p. 26.

40. "Zweiter Teilbericht des 16. Ausschusses," p. 1830.

41. For the discussion, see especially "Niederschrift über die am 8. April 1916 im Ministerium des Innern stattgefundene kommissarische Beratung, betr. Bekämpfung des Geburtenrückganges," ZSAM, Rep. 191, no. 2359, fols. 80–84, p. 8.

42. "Aufzeichnung über die kommissarische Beratung vom 24. Oktober 1918," GSAPKB, Rep. 84a, no. 437, fols. 113–118.

43. Feld, "Steigerung der Wehrkraft," p. 454.

44. "Niederschrift über die am 2. März im Ministerium des Innern stattgefundene kommissarische Beratung," GSAPKB, Rep. 84a, no. 437, fol. 81.

45. *Jugendämter als Träger der öffentlichen Jugendfürsorge im Deutschen Reich* (Berlin: Heymanns, 1919), pp. 30, 32; and *Zur Frage . . . 1917*, pp. 55–56.

46. *Zur Frage der Berufsvormundschaft . . . 1916*, pp. 87, 90, 91, 96, 90.

47. Burghardt, "Die reichsgesetzliche Regelung der Berufsvormundschaft," *Zentralblatt* 8 (1916): 47.

48. Deutsche Zentrale für Jugendfürsorge, *Gesamtbericht über die Tagung in Frankfurt am Main am 7., 8., und 9. Oktober 1915* (N.p., n.d.), esp. pp. 51, 53, 62, 105–107.

49. Ibid., pp. 44–45, 57, 62, 63.

50. Ibid., p. 67.

51. Ibid., pp. 86, 87.

52. *Zur Frage der Berufsvormundschaft . . . 1917*, (Berlin: Heymanns, 1919).

53. *Zur Frage der Berufsvormundschaft . . . 1916*, p. 97. Fischer's proposed solution, however, was merely to create advice clinics for parents.

54. Marie Baum, "Sozialhygienische Bevölkerungspolitik," from a speech to the 1916 conference of the BDF, in *Zeitschrift für Bevölkerungspolitik und Säuglingsfürsorge* 9 (1917): 330.

55. *Zur Frage der Berufsvormundschaft . . . 1917*, (Berlin: Heymanns, 1919), p. 64.

56. Christian Jasper Klumker, "Die Organisation der Fürsorge für die hilfsbedürftige Jugend," in *Frauen-Vormundschaft: Vorlesungen des ersten Lehrganges über Vormundschaft und Waisenpflege für evangelische Frauen . . . 16. bis 18. April 1917* (Potsdam: Stiftungs-Verlag, 1917), p. 29.

57. DST, *Denkschrift*, ZSAM, Rep. 191, no. 13222, fols. 451ff.

58. A first draft of the bill, dated July 12, 1917, was titled "Gesetz, betr. die Abänderung des Art. 77 un 78 des Ausführungsgesetzes zum BGB," see GSAPKB, Rep. 84a, no. 10972, fols. 10–51. Reactions to the bill from local government and judicial authorities are summarized in "Zusammenstellung des Inhalts der Berichte zur Begutachtung des Gesetzentwurfs über Jugendämter und Berufsvormundschaften" (Bl. 212–232). There is a report on the first consultation between the Ministry of the Interior and the charities and local government in "Verhandlung mit Sachverständigen" (Bl. 240–244), and a report from a Catholic perspective in "Besprechung des preussischen Gesetzentwurfs über Jugendämter und Berufsvormundschaft," ADCV, Rep. 212.

59. Buchberger, "Neuzeitlicher Säuglings- und Kleinkinderfürsorge," in Lindermayr, *Jugendfürsorge und Bevölkerungspolitik*, p. 19.

60. "Der neue preussische Jugendfürsorge-Gesetzentwurf," *Caritas* 23 (1918): 246.

61. Caritasverband für das katholische Deutschland, *Soll die Staatsaufsicht über die freie Wohlfahrtspflege in die Friedenszeit hinübergenommen werden?* (Freiburg: Caritasverband, 1917), p. 11.

62. "Besprechung des preussischen Gesetzentwurfs," pp. 5, 8, 10. The bill itself qualified these requirements with the word *tunlichst* (roughly, "if at all possible"); the DCV preferred *muss* (must). See Lamm, "Die Rücksichtsnahme auf das Bekenntnis im Jugendamts-Gesetz," *Zentralblatt* 10 (1918): 70–71.

63. Joseph Beeking, "Jugendämter," *Caritas* 23 (1918): 3.

64. "Jugendfürsorge-Ämter," *Rheinische Fürsorgeerziehungsblatt* 16 (1918): 6.

65. "Entwurf eines Jugendfürsorge-Gesetzes," *Zeitschrift für Bevölkerungspolitik und Säuglingsfürsorge* 10 (1918): 262.

66. Beeking, "Jugendämter," p. 181.

67. A. Feisenberger, "Einheit der Jugendfürsorge," *Zentralblatt* 9 (1918): 195.

68. See Young-Sun Hong, "The Contradictions of Modernization in the German Welfare State: Gender and the Politics of Welfare Reform in First World War Germany," *Social History* 17 (1992): 266–267; Marie-Elisabeth Lüders, *Das unbekannte Heer: Frauen kämpfen für Deutschland, 1914–1918* (Berlin: Verlag von E. S. Mittler & Sohn, 1936); and Christoph Sachße and Florian

Tennstedt, *Geschichte der Armenfürsorge in Deutschland*, vol. 2, *Fürsorge und Wohlfahrtspflege 1871–1929* (Stuttgart: Kohlhammer, 1988), pp. 56–64.

69. Abramczyk [secretary of DZJ] to Lorenz Werthmann [president of DCV], November 20, 1917, ADCV, Rep. CA VII, no. 61a; Paul Felisch to Justice Minister Peter Spahn, December 6, 1917, GSAPKB, Rep. 84a, no. 10972, fols. 168–169.

70. Constantin Noppel to "Herr Prälat [Werthmann]," November 17, 1917, ADCV, Rep. CA VII, no. 61a.

71. Constantin Noppel to Lorenz Werthman, January 17, 1918, ibid.

72. DVAW, *Jugendämter als Träger der öffentlichen Jugendfürsorge im Deutschen Reich* (Berlin: Heymanns, 1919), p. 172.

73. "Besprechung des preussichen Gesetzentwurfes über Jugendämter und Berufsvormundschaft," p. 4, ADCV, Rep. 212.

74. Unidentified draft of Neuhaus's declaration of intention not to boycott the National Child Welfare Conference, September 1918; and Agnes Neuhaus to Albert Lenné, October 19, 1918, ADCV, Rep. 319.4 (SKF), no. A II 5e, fasc. 1.

75. Early drafts of the law, of July 12 and October 31, 1917, are in GSAPKB, Rep. 84a, no. 10972, fols. 10–51 and 124–154. The draft presented to the parliament is printed in "Entwurf eines Jugendfürsorgegesetzes," *Zeitschrift für Bevölkerungspolitik und Säuglingsfürsorge* 10 (1918): 247–276.

76. *Zur Frage der Berufsvormundschaft*, vol. 11, p. 104.

77. Friedrich Siegmund-Schultze, "Wie kann die freie Liebestätigkeit zu einem vollen Erfolg der Jugendämter beitragen?," in *Jugendämter als Träger*, p. 161.

78. Else Wex, *Die Entwicklung der sozialen Fürsorge in Deutschland (1919–1927)* (Berlin: Heymanns, 1929), p. 17. Wex's assessment was overdramatic; as we have seen, the idea of building private organizations into public agencies was a very old one. The Inner Mission's petition of 1874 regarding the Orphans' Council created by the Prussian Vormundschaftsordnung supported the idea; and Franz Recke had suggested it at the 1910 DVAW meeting at which the idea of the Youth Bureau was launched. See *Schriften des Deutschen Vereins für Armenpflege und Wohltätigkeit*, no. 94 (Leipzig: Duncker & Humblot, 1910), p. 95. See also J. F. Landsberg, "Die Ausschüße für Jugendfürsorge im Amstgerichtsbezirk Lennep," *Zentralblatt* 1 (1909): 97, for an assessment of the advantages of combining public and private efforts. For a brief general discussion of corporatism in German history, see Volker Berghahn, "Corporatism in Germany in Historical Perspective," in *The Corporate State*, ed. Andrew Cox and Noel O'Sullivan (Aldershot: Edward Elgar, 1988).

79. *Zur Frage*, vol. 11, pp. 70–73, 74.

80. *Jugendämter als Träger*, pp. 18, 21.

81. Ibid., pp. 65, 163.

82. Ibid., p. 65.

83. Ibid., pp. 177–178.

84. Erzbischof von Köln to Justizminister Spahn, October 26, 1918, GSAPKB, Rep. 84a, no. 10972, fols. 485–486. The Protestant charities had already, in their own draft bill presented to the Prussian Ministry of the Interior on January 11, 1918, suggested the same measure.

85. See the draft of the bill written directly after the meeting of December 11, 1917, ZSAM, Rep. 191, no. 2366, fols. 78–88 (this draft was very similar to

that finally presented to the Landtag on July 9, 1918, which is in "Entwurf eines Gesetzes"); and "Zusammenstellung" of the bill and the decisions of the parliamentary committee, document no. 0202 of the Haus der Abgeordneten, 1916–1918, ZSAM, Rep. 191, no. 2367.

86. *Jugendämter als Träger,* p. 138.
87. Ibid., p. 149.
88. Petition of the Preussischer Städtetag to the Ministry of the Interior, October 30, 1918, ZSAM, Rep. 191, no. 2366, fols. 433–437. See also petitions of the Reichstädtebund, October 29, 1918, and of the Verband der grösseren preussischen Landgemeinden, November 2, 1918, ibid., fols. 430–431 and 439–440.
89. *Jugendämter als Träger,* p. 150.
90. Ibid., p. 96.
91. Finance Ministry to Ministry of the Interior, August 4, 1917, ZSAM, Rep. 191, no. 2359, fol. 159.

6. Revolution and the National Child Welfare Act, 1918–1924

1. "Die Stellung der privaten Fürsorge im neuen Staat," *Zentralblatt* 19 (1920): 210.
2. "Die Kommunalisierung der freien Liebesarbeit," *Die Kirchenfrage,* no. 254, April 13, 1920, ADW, CA/J 13.
3. Wilhelm Rhiel, "Zukünftige Aufgaben der caritativen Erziehung," *Jugendwohl* 8 (1919): 5.
4. Elizabeth Harvey, *Youth and the Welfare State in the Weimar Republic* (Oxford: Clarendon, 1993), p. 233.
5. Gottfried Schlegtendahl, "Der Kampf wider die konfessionelle Jugendfürsorge," *Rheinische Jugendfürsorgeblatt* 19 (1921): 21.
6. "Schreiben des Evangelischen Oberkirchenrats vom 19. Mai 1919 (Auszug aus der Urschrift in den Akten 232 des. C.A.)," ADW, CA/J 1, fols. 143–144.
7. On this continuity in personnel, see especially Cornelie Usborne, *The Politics of the Body in Weimar Germany* (New York: Macmillan, 1992), p. 34.
8. See Viktor Bode, "Sprechende Zahlen," *Hannoversche Kurier,* January 7, 1920; and Reichsernährungsminister, "Denkschrift über die Ernährungszustand der deutschen Kinder," August 19, 1921, ZSAP, Rep. 30.01, no. 1515, fols. 160–175.
9. Schumacher, "Die Fürsorgeerziehung unter der Einwirkung der Revolution," *Deutsche Tageszeitung,* March 31, 1921, ZSAP, Rep. 30.01, no. 1515, fol. 113.
10. Regierungspräsident Düsseldorf to Edelhoff in Düsseldorf's Kreisamt für Jugendpflege, February 15, 1922, RWHSA, Regierung Düsseldorf, no. 33123.
11. Rhiel, "Zukünftige Aufgaben," p. 5; Friedrich Siegmund-Schultze, in "Niederschrift über die Versammlung der Berliner Vereinigung für Jugendwohlfahrt am Donnerstag, den 10.11.1921," ADW, CA/J 2, fols. 585–588.
12. "Dritte Konferenz der Landesregierungen über Fragen der Jugendwohlfahrt im Reichsministerium des Innern am 5. April 1927," ZSAM, Rep. 191, no. 2382, fols. 202–255, pp. 5–6.
13. "Begründung" to the "Entwurf eines Reichsjugendwohlfahrtsgesetzes," *Verhandlungen des Reichstages,* vol. 322, document no. 1666, p. 19.

14. On eugenics in the Weimar period, see particularly Paul Weindling, *Health, Race, and German Politics between National Unification and Nazism, 1870–1945* (Cambridge: Cambridge University Press, 1989), pp. 399–430; Usborne, *Politics of the Body*, pp. 34–38, 133–139; and Jürgen Reyer, *Alte Eugenik und Wohlfahrtspflege: Entwertung und Funktionalisierung der Fürsorge vom Ende des 19. Jahrhunderts bis zur Gegenwart* (Freiburg: Lambertus, 1992), esp. pp. 81–157.

15. See Alfons Labisch, *Homo Hygienicus: Gesundheit und Medizin in der Neuzeit* (Frankfurt am Main: Campus, 1992), p. 203.

16. There were four municipal Health Bureaus in 1914; sixty were established between 1919 and 1929. In addition, there were a number of county Health Bureaus—twenty-eight by 1923. See Christoph Sachße, *Mütterlichkeit als Beruf: Sozialarbeit, Sozialreform und Frauenbewegung, 1871–1929* (Frankfurt am Main: Suhrkamp, 1986), pp. 70, 322. For a good brief discussion of health policy in the Weimar period, see Christoph Sachße and Florian Tennstedt, *Geschichte der Armenfürsorge in Deutschland*, vol. 2, *Fürsorge und Wohlfahrtspflege, 1871–1929* (Stuttgart: Kohlhammer, 1988), pp. 114–138.

17. On the distinction between these concepts, see Weindling, *Health, Race, and German Politics*, pp. 317, 319, 333–335; Harvey, *Youth and the Welfare State*, p. 162; Sheila Faith Weiss, "Die Rassenhygienische Bewegung in Deutschland, 1904–1933," in *Der Wert des Menschen: Medizin in Deutschland, 1918–1945*, ed. Christian Pross and Götz Aly (Berlin: Hentrich, 1989); and Sachße and Tennstedt, *Geschichte*, p. 124. For a more pessimistic assessment, see Labisch, *Homo Hygienicus*, esp. pp. 195–208, 215–216.

18. See Usborne, *Politics of the Body*, pp. 43–53.

19. See esp. Weindling, *Health, Race, and German Politics*, pp. 409–424, 426–430.

20. Sachße and Tennstedt, *Geschichte*, p. 120.

21. See Richard J. Evans, *The Feminist Movement in Germany, 1894–1933* (London: SAGE, 1976), pp. 241–245.

22. See Christoph Sachße, "Social Mothers: The Bourgeois Women's Movement and German Welfare State Formation, 1890–1929," in *Mothers of a New World: Maternalist Politics and the Origins of Welfare States*, ed. Seth Koven and Sonya Michel (New York: Routledge, 1993), p. 153.

23. Ibid., p. 152; and Sachße, *Mütterlichkeit als Beruf*, p. 290.

24. See Young-Sun Hong, "Gender and Rationalization in the Making of the Weimar Welfare System," paper presented to the American Historical Association, Chicago, January 1995.

25. See Helene Weber, "Zur Soziologie der Jugend," in *Grundfragen der Jugendwohlfahrtspflege* (Münster: Aschendorffsche Verlagsbuchhandlung, 1932), p. 23; and Jürgen Reulecke, "Jugend und 'Junge Generation' in der Gesellschaft der Zwischenkriegszeit," in *Handbuch der deutschen Bildungsgeschichte*, vol. 5, *1918–1945*, ed. Dieter Langewiesche and Heinz-Elmar Tenorth (Munich: C. H. Beck, 1989), p. 100. On the youth movements and social policy, see Manfred Zwerschke, *Jugendverbände und Sozialpolitik: Zur Geschichte der deutschen Jugendverbände* (Munich: Juventa, 1963).

26. Hedwig Wachenheim, "Der Vorrang der öffentlichen Wohlfahrtspflege. Grundsätzliches zur Krise in der rheinischen Jugendwohlfahrtspflege," *Arbeiterwohlfahrt* 1 (1926): 67.

27. See, for example, Christian Jasper Klumker, "Fürsorgewesen und Reichsverfassung," *Zentralblatt* 10 (1919): 217.

28. Sachße and Tennstedt, *Geschichte*, p. 86.

29. Schulz, "Uber die Notwendigkeit einer planmässigen geistigen und sittlichen Jugendpflegearbeit," probably early April 1925, RWHSA, Regierung Düsseldorf, no. 33120; "Jugend und Sexualität," *Zentralblatt* 24 (1932): 208.

30. See Dr. J. F., "Die Ehe ein Jazz," *Jugendrettung* 9 (1929): 164.

31. Karl Brunner, "Die Jugendlichen im Lichtspielgesetz," *Zentralblatt* 12 (1920): 68–70.

32. See Lynn Abrams, "From Control to Commercialization: The Triumph of Mass Entertainment in Germany, 1900–1925?," *German History* 8 (1990): 282.

33. On the SPD's position, see ibid., and Usborne, *Politics of the Body*, pp. 79–80.

34. Quoted in Detlev Peukert, *Grenzen der Sozialdisziplinierung* (Cologne: Bund-Verlag, 1986), p. 183.

35. Robert von Erdberg, "Das Gesetz zur Bewahrung der Jugend vor Schund- und Schmutzschriften," *Erziehung* 2 (1927): 165–166.

36. Klaus Petersen, "The Harmful Publications (Young Persons) Act of 1926: Literary Censorship and the Politics of Morality in the Weimar Republic," *German Studies Review* 15 (1992): 505.

37. Abrams, "From Control to Commercialization," p. 285.

38. Ina Neuendörfer, "Die Familie und das sozialistische Erziehungsprogramm," *Jugendwohl* 9 (1921): 45.

39. See Christiane Eifert, *Frauenpolitik und Wohlfahrtspflege: Zur Geschichte der sozialdemokratischen "Arbeiterwohlfahrt"* (Frankfurt am Main: Campus, 1993); Karen Hagemann, *Frauenalltag und Männerpolitik: Alltagsleben und gesellschaftliches Handeln von Arbeiterfrauen in der Weimarer Republik* (Bonn: Dietz, 1990), esp. pp. 600–632; Elizabeth Harvey, *Youth Welfare and Social Democracy in Weimar Germany: The Work of Walter Friedländer* (New Alyth, Scotland: Lochee Publications, 1987), chap. 5; and Anneliese Monat, *Sozialdemokratie und Wohlfahrtspflege: Ein Beitrag zur Entstehungsgeschichte der Arbeiter wohl falart* (Stuttgart: Kohlhammer, 1961).

40. Gottfried Schlegtendahl, "Der Kampf wider die konfessionelle Jugendfürsorge," *Rheinische Fürsorgeerziehungs-Blatt* 19 (1921): 21.

41. See "4. Konferenz der Landesregierungen über Fragen der Jugend Wohlfahrt im Reichsministerium des Innern am 15. und 16. Juni 1928," ZSAP, 30.01, no. 1517. Otto Ohl's remarks in "Aussprache nach dem Referat von Pastor Ohl," ADW, CA/J 78; Hagemann, *Frauenalltag*, pp. 608–609; and Eifert, *Frauenpolitik*, pp. 34, 55–56.

42. "Bericht über die Besprechung der Kommission zur Vorbereitung für die Ausführungsbestimmungen des Reichsjugendwohlfahrtsgesetzes . . . 21.8.1922," ADW, CA/J 2, fols. 282–283.

43. See Viktor Fadrus, "Die Kinderfreundebewegung in Österreich und Deutschland (Schluß)," *Erziehung* 5 (1930): 294–301; and Renate Wolter-Brandecker, *Sie kamen aus der dumpfen Stadt: Arbeiterkindheit und Kinderfreundebewegung in Frankfurt am Main, 1919–1933* (Bonn: Sozialistische Jugend Deutschlands—Die Falken, 1982).

44. *Der Helfer: Mitteilungsblatt des Reichsverbandes für Dissidentische Fürsorge* (April 1931), ADW, CA/J 78.

45. See *Der Rote Helfer* 2, no. 8 (August 1926): 8; and "Organisations-Richtlinien der RHD," *Der Rote Helfer* 3, no. 1 (January 1927).

46. See Ernst Schellenberg, "'Arso' und Jugendwohlfahrt," *Proletarische Sozialpolitik* 3 (1930): esp. 377; Martha Arendsee, "Ausschaltung konfessioneller Gesichtspunkte bei Fürsorgemaßnahmen," *Proletarische Sozialpolitik* 1 (1928): 53; August Brandt, "Zwischenbilanz der Fürsorgeerziehungs-Kampagne der IAH," *Proletarische Sozialpolitik* 2 (1929): esp. 180–181.

47. See Daniel R. Borg, *The Old-Prussian Church and the Weimar Republic: A Study in Political Adjustment, 1917–1927* (Hanover, N.H.: University Press of New England, 1984), pp. 123–167 (quotation p. 123).

48. Magdalene von Tiling, in "Roh-Protokoll der Diskussion von Dr. Stahl über 'Religiöse Erziehung in der Jugendwohlfahrt,'" ADW, CA/J 78.

49. Gustav Radbruch, quoted in Christa Hasenclever, *Jugendhilfe und Jugendgesetzgebung seit 1900* (Göttingen: Vandenhoeck & Ruprecht, 1978), p. 89.

50. Wilhelm Stern, commentary on a decision of the Oberlandesgericht Berlin, in the "Rechtssprechung" section of *Juristische Wochenschrift* 53, nos. 21–22 (1924): 1779.

51. Cited in Harvey, *Youth and the Welfare State*, p. 219.

52. For good discussions, see Georg Lilienthal, "The Illegitimacy Question in Germany, 1900–1945: Areas of Tension in Social and Population Policy," *Continuity and Change* 5, no. 2 (1990); and Andreas Wollasch, *Der katholische Fürsorgeverein für Mädchen, Frauen und Kinder* (Freiburg: Lambertus, 1991), pp. 174–193. A report on the status of the debate in parliamentary committee in 1931 is found in ZSAP, Rep. 30.01, no. 1417, fols. 173–175 (Reichsjustizministerium to Reichskanzler, February 18, 1931).

53. See Reichsministerium des Innern to Prussian Justizministerium, April 22, 1919, GSAPKB, Rep. 84a, Nr. 1016, fols. 22–24.

54. One recent student has remarked that the SPD "did no more than echo and amplify long-standing reform demands" in the early 1920s. See Harvey, *Youth Welfare and Social Democracy*, p. 24.

55. "Aufzeichnung über das Ergebnis der am 5. Mai 1919 im Reichsministerium des Innern abgehaltenen kommissarischen Beratung über die reichsrechtliche Regelung der Jugendwohlfahrt," GSAPKB, Rep. 84a, no. 1016, fols. 30–36.

56. Ibid., fols. 30–36

57. See comments of von Schütz of the Prussian Ministry of the Interior, in "Aufzeichnung über das Ergebnis der am 9. Juni 1919 im Reichsministerium des Innern abgehaltenen Beratung des Unterausschusses für das Reichsjugendwohlfahrtsgesetzes," GSAPKB, Rep. 84a, no. 1016, fol. 96.

58. See Benedict Kreutz to Deutscher Caritasverband, n.d. (perhaps mid-March 1920), ADCV, Rep. CA VII, no. 61a.

59. See report of the Saxon envoy to the national government in Berlin, February 6, 1920, SAD, Sächsische Gesandtschaft Berlin, no. 908. For reports on meetings with representatives of the states, see GSAPKB, Rep. 84a, no. 1016, fols. 147–151, 154–157, 158–162, 164–171, 175–184.

60. The bill actually submitted to the lower house differed considerably from that passed by the upper; owing to a dispute over finances, the government decided to submit the bill it had submitted to the Reichsrat in parallel with the revised

version passed by that body. The petitions presented by the various states are summarized in "Zusammenstellung der Reichsratsanträge zum Reichsjugend-wohlfahrtsgesetz," ZSAM, Rep. 191, no. 2378, fols. 233–252.

61. See Constantin Noppel to Arthur Hugo Klieber, July 2, 1919, ADCV, Rep. CA 7, no. 61a; and Deutsche Zentrale für Jugendfürsorge to Deutscher Caritasver-band, May 19, 1920, ibid.

62. For a rather confused record of the proceedings, see DVöpF, *Materialien zum Reichsgesetz für Jugendwohlfahrt* (Frankfurt am Main: DVöpF, 1961).

63. "Denkschrift zum Entwurf eines Reichsjugendwohlfahrtsgesetzes vom Stand-punkt der Berufsvormundschaft. Herausgegeben vom Verein der Berufsvor-münder Groß-Berlins und der Provinz Brandenburg," April 12, 1921, HASK, Bestand 1070 (Nachlaß Marx), no. 217.

64. Hanna Hellinger, "Statistisches über Vorbildung, Einkommen und Tätigkeit der Berufsvormünder," *Zentralblatt* 13 (1921): 42–43.

65. See Wilhelm Polligkeit and Hilde Eiserhardt, *Denkschrift zum Reichsjugend-wohlfahrtsgesetz* (Frankfurt, 1921), pp. 5, 12–13.

66. "Die Vormundschaftsfrage," *Germania*, July 28, 1921. For a similar view, see Franz Velder to DCV, December 9, 1920, ADCV, Rep. CA VII, no. 61c.

67. See Hans Engelmann, "Mit welcher Amtsstelle sind am zweckmäßigsten die Ju-gendämter zu verbinden?," *Caritas* 24 (1919): 198; and "Das Jugendfürsorge-gesetz," *Rheinische Fürsorgeerziehungsblatt* 17 (1919): 21. The southern state of Baden had plans to create just such a system as early as 1918; see Ministeri-alrat Ritter, in *Jugendämter als Träger der öffentlichen Jugendfürsorge im Deutschen Reich* (Berlin: Heymanns, 1919), pp. 78–79.

68. See "Zum Reichsjugendwohlfahrtsgesetz: Ergebnis der Beratung des Badischen Landesausschusses für Jugendfürsorge unter dem Vorsitz des Justizminis-teriums," n.d. (probably January or early February 1920, ADCV, Rep. CA VII, no. 61f; and "Zur Frage der Jugendämter," *Zentralblatt* 10 (1919): 251.

69. See DCV to Constantin Noppel, June 23, 1921, ADCV, Rep. CA 7, no. 61c; and Joseph Beeking to "Die Mitglieder des Zentralauschusses für kathol-ische Jugendfürsorge," July 8, 1921, ADCV, Rep. 319.4 (SKF), no. A II.5o, fasc. 1.

70. Hans Engelmann to DCV, August 8, 1921, ADCV, Rep. CA VII, no. 61c.

71. Quoted in Florentine Rickmers, "Agnes Neuhaus—Leben und Werk," *Jugend-wohl* 3 (1950): 34.

72. Ibid., pp. 22–23.

73. Deutscher Caritasverband, *Denkschrift zum Entwurf eines Reichs-Jugend-wohlfahrtsgesetz* (Freiburg: DCV, 1920). A record of the meeting's resolutions is contained in Hans Engelmann's report of July 15, 1920, ADCV, Rep. CA VII, no. 61a.

74. "Protokoll der Beratungen der Caritaskommission zum Reichsjugendwohl-fahrtsgesetzentwurf . . . am 9. und 10. Dezember 1921 in Dortmund im Josefi-nenstift," pp. 9–17, ADCV, Rep. 319.4 (SKF), no. E II.6, fasc. 1; "Sitzung der Caritaskommission zur Beratung des Entwurfs zum Reichsjugend-Wohlfahrts-gesetz am 5., 6., und 7. März in Koblenz," ADCV, Rep. CA VII, no. 61d, p. 46.

75. "Sitzung," pp. 32, 45.

76. Constantin Noppel to DCV, November 4, 1920, ADCV, Rep. CA VII, no. 61c.

77. Adolf Kardinal Bertram, Fürstbischof von Breslau, "Zum Entwurf des Reichs-jugendwohlfahrtsgesetzes," letter to Wilhelm Marx, May 20, 1920, ADCV, Rep. CA VII, no. 61d.

78. "Gegenentwurf zu einem Reichsjugendamts-Gesetz," ADCV, Rep. CA VII, no. 61b.

79. See draft of "Gutachten zu dem Entwurf eines Reichsjugendwohlfahrtsgesetzes, erstellt vom Deutschen Verein durch seinen Fachausschuss für öffentliche Jugendfürsorge," ADCV, Rep. CA VII, no. 61b.

80. See the resolution of the Innere Mission's "Kommission zur Beratung des Entwurfs eines Reichsjugendwohlfahrtsgesetzes" of April, 19, 1921, ADW, CA/J 5, fols. 41–43; "Protokoll der Besprechung über das Reichs-Jugendwohlfahrtsgesetz. 1. Juni 1920, 4 Uhr," ibid., fols. 10–13; "(Entwurf zu Pkt. 3 der Tagesordnung der Sitzung vom 10.V.1921): Antrag an den 29. Reichstagsausschuss," ADW, CA/J 3; Constantin Noppel to Deutscher Caritasverband, Fachausschuss für Jugendfürsorge, June 20, 1921, ADCV, Rep. CA VII, no. 61c.

81. The different versions of the bill are reprinted in *Verhandlungen des Reichstages*, vol. 366, document 1666; vol. 372, document 3959. See also the report on the changes made in committee, in "Zusammenstellung des Entwurfs eines Reichsjugendwohlfahrtsgesetzes . . . (Nr. 1666 der Drucksachen) mit den Beschlüssen des 29. Ausschusses in 1. Lesung," ZSAP, Rep. 30.01, no. 1374.

82. *Verhandlungen des Reichstages*, 355 (1922): 7787, 7802, 7788.

83. See Wilhem Polligkeit, *Landesrechtliche Ausführungsbestimmung zum Reichs-Jugendwohlfahrtsgesetz* (Berlin: Heymanns, 1930), for a good summary.

84. *Sitzungsberichte des preussischen Landtages. Anlagen,* (1924) 13:8146 (report of the parliamentary committee on the law).

85. Hans Engelmann, "Bemerkungen zu dem neuen Entwurf des preussischen Ausführungsgesetzes zum RJWG," May 1923, ADCV, Rep. 319.4 (SKF), no. E II.6, fasc. 2.

86. For the cities' perspective, see the relevant documents in LAB, Rep. 142, no. 4356.

87. Neuhaus quoted in Wollasch, *Der Katholische Fürsorgeverein,* p. 127; Schl[egtendahl], "Das Reichsjugendwohlfahrtsgesetz," *Rheinischer Fürsorge-Erziehungsblatt* 21, no. 1 (1923): 6.

88. "Protokoll der Sitzung des Fachausschusses für Jugendfürsorge zusammen mit dem Fachausschuss für Kleinkinderfürsorge am 8. November 1922 . . . in Köln," ADCV, Rep. 319.4 (SKF), no. A II.5o, fasc. 1; "Richtlinien betr. Reichsjugendwohlfahrtsgesetz," *Caritas* 4 (1925): 31.

89. See Wollasch, *Der katholische Fürsorgeverein,* p. 147.

90. "Leitsätze des C. A. für die Besprechung am 25. August 1922 im Evangel. Oberkirchenrat"; "Auszug aus dem Rundschreiben des Evangelischen Reichs-Erziehungs-Vereins vom 9. Januar 1923"; and "Welche organisatorische Aufgaben stellt das Reichsjugendwohlfahrtsgesetz der evangelischen Kirche?," all in ADW, CA/J 6, fols. 2–4, 5–8, 12–18.

91. Heinrich Webler, "Bericht über die Tagung des Archivs Deutscher Berufsvormünder vom 21.–23. August 1924 in Chemnitz," *Zentralblatt* 16 (1924): 189. For the speech, see Immanuel Fischer, "Das Jugendamt als Erziehungsamt," in

Das Jugendamt am Scheideweg: Behördengeist und Erziehung, ed C. J. Klumker (n.d., n.p., [1925]), pp. 12–14.

92. Joseph Beeking, "Die Grundsätzliche Stellung der freien Liebestätigkeit im Reichsgesetz für Jugendwohlfahrt," in *Das Reichsgesetz für Jugendwohlfahrt und die Caritas*, ed. Joseph Beeking (Freiburg: Caritasverlag, 1925), p. 84.

93. Agnes Neuhaus to Joseph Beeking, January 5, 1924, ADCV, Rep. 319.4 (SKF), no. E II.6, fasc. 1.

94. *Schriften des Deutschen Vereins für öffentliche und private Fürsorge* (Berlin: Heymanns, 1924), 3:128.

95. Ibid., 3:112–113.

96. See, for example, Solingen to Regierungspräsident Düsseldorf, November 26, 1920, RWHSA, Regierung Düsseldorf, no. 33123.

97. See Deutscher Städtetag and Verband preussischer Landkreisen to Reichsrat, February 9, 1921, ZSAM, Rep. 191, no. 2381, fols. 151–162; Verband der preussischen Landkreise, *Eingabe* to 29th Reichstagsausschuss, April 12, 1921, ibid., fols. 171–179; and Deutscher Städtetag, *Eingabe* to 29th Ausschuss des Reichstages, April 8, 1921, ibid.

98. "2. Eingabe des Deutschen Städtetags," February 23, 1922, and *Eingabe* of the Verband preussischer Landkreise to the Center party fraction of the Reichstag, March 29, 1922, HASK, Rep. 1070, no. 217.

99. See Constantin Noppel's incisive report, Noppel to DCV, December 17, 1923, ADCV, Rep. CA VII, no. 61d. Both the national minister of the interior (Karl Jarres) and the finance minister (Hans Luther) were close to municipal interests, the latter having been executive secretary and then director of the DST.

100. See the DST's *Eingabe* of November 10, 1923, LAB, Rep. 142, no. 4357, reported in "Stellungnahme des Deutschen Städtetages zum Reichsjugendwohlfahrtsgesetz," *Zentralblatt* 15 (1923): 171–172.

101. See DST to Reichs-Finanz-Minister, November 19, 1923, and DST to Karl Jarres, November 20, 1023, both in LAB, Rep. 142, no. 4357; Prussian Ministerium des Innern to Prussian Finanzministerium, December 4, 1923, ZSAM, Rep. 191, no. 2379, fol. 206; Reichsfinanzministerium to Reichskanzlei, January 5, 1924, BAK, Rep. R43, no. I/784, vol. 1, fols. 219–220; Prussian Finanzministerium to Prussian Ministerium für Volkswohlfahrt, February 26, 1923, and March 3, 1923, and to Prussian Ministerpräsident, December 21, 1923, ZSAM, Rep. 191, no. 2379, fols. 124, 129–130, and 22.

102. For the whole debate surrounding the emergency decree, see "Eingabe des Deutschen Vereins für öffentliche und private Fürsorge, zu Händen von Herrn Staatssekretär Schulz," November 5, 1923, LAB, Rep. 142, no. 4357; "Abänderungsvorschläge für den Vollzug des Reichsgesetzes für Jugend-Wohlfahrt," ADCV, Rep. CA VII, no. 61d; "Niederschrift über die Beratung vom 8. Dezember 1923 in Berlin . . . über die Frage des Vollzugs des R.J.W.G.," ZSAM, Rep. 191, no. 2379, fols. 209–221; *Eingabe* of DST to Reichsministerium des Innern, December 18, 1923, LAB, Rep. 142, no. 4357; "Auszug aus dem Protokoll der Sitzung des Reichsministeriums vom 6. Februar 1924," BAK, Rep. R43, no. I/784, vol. 1, fols. 237–238; "Entwurf einer Verordnung über das Inkrafttreten des Reichsgesetzes für Jugendwohlfahrt" and "Reichsratsausschüsse III, V, und VII: Entwurf einer Verordnung," Feb-

ruary 7, 1924, ZSAM, Rep. 191, no. 2379, folio 265 and 248; Benedikt Kreutz to Reichskanzler Wilhelm Marx, December 20, 1923, ADCV, Rep. CA VII, no. 61d; Centralausschuss für Innere Mission to Reichsjustizministerium, January 18, 1924, ZSAP, Rep. 30.01, no. 1520; "Protokoll d. C.A.f.I.M. 8 Januar 1924," ADW, CA/J 18; and Becker, "Verordnung über das Inkrafttreten des Reichsgesetzes für Jugendwohlfahrt vom 14. Februar 1924," *Zentralblatt* 15 (1924): 229–232.

103. *Schriften des Deutschen Vereins,* n.s., 3 (1924): 112–113.
104. "Sitzung der Caritaskommission zur Beratung des Entwurfs zum Reichsjugend-Wohlfahrtsgesetz am 5., 6., und 7. März in Koblenz," p. 2, ADCV, Rep. CA VII, no. 61d.

7. Child Welfare, Bureaucracy, and "Cultural War," 1924–1929

1. See Marie Baum, *Familienfürsorge: Eine Studie* (Karlsruhe: G. Braun, 1928), esp. p. 36.
2. Aloys Fischer, "Familie und Gesellschaft," in *Familie und Fürsorge,* ed. Wilhelm Polligkeit (Langensalza: Hermann Beyer & Söhne, 1927), pp. 11, 12, 16, 18–19.
3. Gottlieb Storck, "Erziehungshilfe in der Familie als Massnahme der Jugendfürsorge," in Polligkeit, *Familie und Fürsorge,* p. 114. For other examples (Wilhelm Polligkeit, Alice Salomon), see Christoph Sachße and Florian Tennstedt, *Der Wohlfahrtsstaat im Nationalsozialismus: Geschichte der Armenfürsorge in Deutschland,* vol. 3 (Stuttgart: Kohlhammer, 1992), p. 46.
4. Hermann Nohl, "Die pädagogische Idee in der öffentlichen Jugendhilfe," *Zentralblatt* 20 (1928): 1.
5. Wilhelm Hertz, "Sorgen des Jugendamts," *Zentralblatt* 19 (1927): 199–200.
6. Hermann Nohl, "Die Sozialpädagogik in der Wohlfahrtspflege," *Zentralblatt* 18 (1926): 89; idem, "Die pädagogische Idee," p. 1.
7. Nohl, "Die pädagogische Idee," p. 14.
8. Gertrud Bäumer, "Die sozialpädagogische Aufgabe in der Jugendwohlfahrtspflege," *Schriften des Deutschen Vereins für öffentliche und private Fürsorge,* n.s., (Karlsruhe: G. Braun, 1931), 15:64.
9. Gerhard Steuk, "Die Familie das sozialpädagogische Ziel der Wohlfahrtspflege? Eine soziologische Skizze," *Freie Wohlfahrtspflege* 2 (1928): 105, 109, 111.
10. *Die öffentliche Fürsorge im Deutschen Reich in den Rechnungsjahren, 1927–1931 (Statistik des Deutschen Reiches,* vol. 421) (Berlin: Reimar Hobbing, 1933), p. 237. Of 993 Youth Bureaus reporting, 973 were directed by men.
11. Stuttgarter Jugendsekretariat to Centralausschuss für Innere Mission, July 13, 1928, ADW, CA/J 8; Immanuel Fischer, "Die heutige Lage der Jugendämter," *Zentralblatt* 19 (1928): 309–310.
12. *Die öffentliche Fürsorge,* p. 237.
13. Gottlob Binder, "Jugendpflege und Jugendamt," *Zentralblatt* 17 (1925): 189.
14. Immanuel Fischer, "Das Jugendamt als Erziehungsamt," in *Das Jugendamt am Scheideweg: Behördengeist und Erziehung,* ed. C. J. Klumker (n.d., n.p.

[1925]), p. 3; "4. Konferenz der Landesregierungen über Fragen der Jugend-wohlfahrt im Reichsministerium des Innern am 15. und 16. Juni 1928," p. 30, ZSAP, Rep. 30.01, no. 1517, fols. 246–297.

15. Otto Wehn, "Erziehung in der Jugendfürsorge," *Zentralblatt* 20 (1925): 116.

16. Heinrich Webler, "Von den Aufgaben des Zentralblattes," *Zentralblatt* 19 (1927): 2.

17. C. J. Klumker, "Woran krankt die deutsche Fürsorge der Gegenwart?," *Concordia* 5 (1930–31): 342; idem, "Die Aussichten der Jugendwohlfahrtspflege im Augenblick," reprinted from *Blätter des Deutschen Roten Kreuzes*, November 1930, pp. 1, 4.

18. Hedwig Wachenheim, review of Klumker's article, in *Arbeiterwohlfahrt* 6 (1931): 56–57.

19. Quoted in Young-Sun Hong, "Gender and Rationalization in the Making of the Weimar Welfare System," paper presented to the American Historical Association, Chicago, January 1995.

20. Deutscher Verband der Sozialbeamtinnen, ed., *10 Jahre soziale Berufsarbeit* (Berlin: F. A. Herbig, 1926), p. 12.

21. Christiane Eifert, *Frauenpolitik und Wohlfahrtspflege: Zur Geschichte der sozialdemokratischen "Arbeiterwohlfahrt"* (Frankfurt am Main: Campus, 1993), p. 647; Christoph Sachße and Florian Tennstedt, *Geschichte des Armenfürsorge in Deutschland*, vol. 2, *Fürsorge und Wohlfahrtspflege, 1871–1929* (Stuttgart: Kohlhammer, 1988), p. 170.

22. Pastor Lilge, Evangelischer Landeswohlfahrtsdienst Hannover, Abteilung Jugendfürsorge, to EREV, January 26, 1925, ADW, CA/J 2.

23. Pastor Niemöller, "Die Auswirkungen des [Paragraph] 5 R.F.V. und der [Paragraphen] 6, 9, und 11 RJWG auf die Zusammenarbeit von evang. Liebestätigkeit u. öffentl. Fürsorge," (dated in pencil "Anfang 1926"), ADW, CA/J 2.

24. Amman, "Die Wiederherstellung des [Paragraph] 9 R.J.W.G. vom verwaltungsrechtlichen und fürsorgerischen Standpunkt aus," in "Deutscher Verein für öffentliche und private Fürsorge. . . . Fachauschuss für Jugendfürsorge," p. 30.

25. "4. Konferenz der Landesregierungen."

26. Maria Kiene, "Neue Gefahren in der katholischen Jugendfürsorge," in "Sitzung des Fachausschusses für Kinder- und Jugendfürsorge am 29. März 1927, Fulda," ADCV, Rep. DK, no. 113.3 I, II.

27. See Wilhelm Hertz, "Freie und amtliche Jugendwohlfahrt: Versuch einer grundsätzlichen Ausgleichung," p. 3, ADCV, Rep. 481.5, fasc. 3.

28. "4. Konferenz der Landesregierungen," pp. 31–32.

29. "Protokoll über die Sitzung des Fachausschusses für Wohlfahrtspflege und Jugendwohlfahrtspflege beim Deutschen Roten Kreuz am 22. und 23. Oktober 1926," ZSAP, Rep. 30.01, no. 1414, fols. 425–451.

30. Adolf Stahl, in report on a "Geschäftsführerkonferenz am 27./28.8.26 in Düsseldorf," ADW, CA/J 13.

31. Friedrich Grüneisen, in "Protokoll über die Sitzung des Fachausschusses für Wohlfahrtspflege und Jugendwohlfahrtspflege beim Deutschen Roten Kreuz am 22. und 23. Oktober 1926," p. 4, ZSAP, Rep. 30.01, no. 1414, fols. 425–451.

32. Joseph Beeking, "Gefahren in der gegenwärtigen Entwicklung der Kinder- und Jugendfürsorge," *Jugendwohl* 15 (1926): 89. On Workers' Welfare's problems with the Youth Bureaus, see Eifert, *Frauenpolitik,* pp. 60–61.

33. Joseph Gillmann, "Methodik in der Zusammenarbeit der Caritas und der Jugendwohlfahrtsbehörden," *Jugendwohl* 17 (1928): 17; Joseph Beeking, in "Deutscher Verein für öffentliche und private Fürsorge, Kommission zur Vorbereitung einer Konferenz über das Zusammenarbeiten der öffentlichen und der freien Wohlfahrtspflege. Niederschrift über die Verhandlungen vom 6. und 7. August 1925 in Heidelberg," p. 36, ADCV, Rep. 319.4 (SKF), no. A II.12b, fasc. 2.

34. See "Sitzung der Reichsverbände," p. 24; DZJ to Minister für Volkswohlfahrt, June 14, 1928, ADCV, Rep. 319.4 (SKF), no. E I.5, fasc. 2.

35. See the comments of Gertrud Bäumer (in the national Ministry of the Interior) and Anna Maier (in the Prussian Ministry of Welfare) in "Deutscher Verein für öffentliche und private Fürsorge . . . Niederschrift über die Verhandlungen des Fachausschusses für Jugendfürsorge am 21.4.1925 in Eisenach," pp. 45, 47, ADW, C IVf.

36. See Martha Krueger, "Gesamtstatistik der deutschen freien Wohlfahrtspflege," *Freie Wohlfahrtspflege* 4 (1929): 1–12.

37. [KFV], *1900–1950: Katholische Fürsorge-Arbeit in 50 Jahren* (Dortmund: Zentrale des KFV, 1950), pp. 13–14.

38. For the Inner Mission, see Jochen-Christoph Kaiser, *Sozialer Protestantismus im 20. Jahrhundert: Beiträge zur Geschichte der Inneren Mission, 1914–1945* (Munich: R. Oldenbourg, 1989), esp. pp. 80–89, 96, 445; for the DCV, see Erwin Gatz, "Caritas und sozialen Diensten," in *Der soziale und politische Katholizismus,* ed. Anton Rauscher (Munich: G. Olzog, 1982).

39. Michael Phayer, *Protestant and Catholic Women in Nazi Germany* (Detroit: Wayne State University Press, 1990), p. 26.

40. See "Der Stand der Durchführung des Reichsgesetzes für Jugendwohlfahrt und der Organization der Jugendämter," *Verhandlungen des Reichstages* (1927), document no. 52, app. 3 (January 22, 1927), p. 28.

41. See Benno Hafeneger, *Jugendarbeit als Beruf: Geschichte einer Profession in Deutschland* (Opladen: Westdeutscher Verlag, 1992), pp. 58–60 (figures p. 59).

42. Maria Kiene, "Gegenwärtige Gefahren auf dem Gebiete der Kinderfürsorge," in *Zeitfragen der Kinder- und Jugendfürsorge,* ed. Joseph Beeking (Freiburg: Caritasverlag, 1927), pp. 12, 13, 18.

43. Pastor Eggebrecht, "Kirche und Jugendamt in der Provinz Sachsen," *Evangelische Jugenddienst* 4, nos. 10–11 (1926): 162.

44. Wilhelm Backhausen, "Evangelische Erziehung und öffentliche Jugendpflege," *Innere Mission* 17 (1922): 17, 18.

45. For good general discussions, see Klaus Scholder, *Die Kirchen und das Dritte Reich,* vol. 1 (Frankfurt am Main: Ullstein, 1977), chap. 3; and Franz G. M. Feige, *The Varieties of Protestantism in Nazi Germany: Five Theological Positions* (New York: Edwin Mellen, 1990).

46. Ruhnke, "Die rechtliche Stellung des Jugendamtes zu seinem Einrichtungen und die sich hieraus ergebenden Folgerungen für die ev. Jugendwohlfahrtsarbeit," *Evangelische Jugendhilfe* 7 (1931): 301.

47. "Bericht von Pastor Beutel in der Sitzung des Centralausschusses für Innere Mission am Mittwoch, den 12. Nov. 1924," ADW, CA/J 13.

48. Joachim Beckmann, "Die Grundlagen der evangelischen Jugendfürsorge: 2. Kapitel," *Evangelische Jugendhilfe* 4 (1928): 271–272.

49. Joseph Beeking, "Gefahren in der gegenwärtigen Entwicklung der Kinder- und Jugendfürsorge," *Jugendwohl* 15 (1926): 91.

50. "Auszug aus dem Bericht der Sitzung des C.A. am 9. und 10. November 1926: 'Die religiöse Erziehung in der Jugendfürsorge,'" ADW, CA/J 78.

51. Otto Wehn, "Die Wurzeln erziehlichen Wirkens in der Jugendfürsorge," *Zentralblatt* 18 (1927): 124, 125.

52. "Grundlagen und Ziele des Zusammenwirkens der verschiedenen Richtungen in der freien Wohlfahrtspflege untereinander und im Verhältnis zur öffentlichen Fürsorge" (dated in pencil 1925), ADW, CA/J 13.

53. Karl Vossen, "Probleme der Zusammenarbeit von öffentliche und private Jugendfürsorge," in Beeking, *Zeitfragen,* p. 27. For a blistering critique of this theory, see Hermann Nohl, "Weltanschauung und Erziehung," in his *Ausgewählte pädagoische Schriften* (1931; rpt. Paderborn: Schöningh, 1967).

54. Karl Neuendörfer, "Die gefährdete Jugend und die Ordnung in Staat, Gesellschaft, und Kirche," *Jugendwohl* 14 (1925): 121–122.

55. Eggebrecht, "Kirche und Jugendamt," p. 162.

56. Beckmann, "Die Grundlagen der evangelischen Jugendfürsorge," p. 269.

57. "Bei der Geschäftsführerkonferenz Düsseldorf 27.8.26: Die Sicherstellung der religiösen Erziehung in der Jugendfürsorge," p. 11, ADW, CA/J 78.

58. See Karl Vossen, "Probleme der Zusammenarbeit von öffentliche und private Jugendfürsorge," in Beeking, *Zeitfragen,* pp. 24–37; idem, "Die heutige Lage der Jugendämter," *Zentralblatt* 20 (1926): 5–6; and Alois Braekling, "Die Arbeiterwohlfahrt und die Caritas," *Caritas* 5 (1926): 131.

59. Fischer, "Zur heutigen Lage," pp. 313–314.

60. Albert Graf, "Die Dienstanweisungen für Ortsjugendräte und Ortsjugendhelfer im Freistaat Baden," *Arbeiterwohlfahrt* 2 (1927): p. 749.

61. Erich Weniger, "Die Gegensätze in der modernen Fürsorgeerziehung," *Erziehung* 1 (1926): 351.

62. Aloys Fischer, "Unsere Zeit und die Mission der Pädagogik," *Erziehung* 1 (1926): 2.

63. Wehn, "Die Wurzeln," p. 123.

64. See, in Deutscher Verein für öffentliche und private Fürsorge, Kommission zur Vorbereitung einer Konferenz über das Zusammenarbeiten der öffentlichen und der freien Wohlfahrtspflege, "Niederschrift über die Verhandlungen vom 22. April 1925 in Eisenach," ADCV, Rep. 461.055, folder 3, Carl Neinhaus, "Versuch zu einer ideellen Grundlegung der öffentlichen Wohlfahrtspflege," pp. 3–4, 12, 10.

65. See, in Deutscher Verein für öffentliche und private Fürsorge, Kommission zur Vorbereitung einer Konferenz über das Zusammenarbeiten der öffentlichen und freien Wohlfahrtspflege, "Niederschrift über die Verhandlungen vom 6. und 7. August 1925 in Heidelberg," ADCV, Rep. 319.4 (SKF), no. A II, 12b, fasc. 2, Otto Ohl, "Grundlagen und Ziele des Zusammenarbeitens von öffentlicher und freier Wohlfahrtspflege in der Jugendwohlfahrtspflege," pp. 11–14. Nor is

this the only instance of an appeal to racist or biologistic notions in the face of the frustrations of the late 1920s. There was a similar development in social work, where some female social workers resorted increasingly to a mystico-biologistic concept of women's innate motherliness as an ideological response to their own marginalization and subordination to male bureaucrats. See Hong, "Gender and Rationalization."

66. "Niederschrift über die Verhandlungen . . . in Eisenach," discussion, pp. 27.1.

67. "Niederschrift über die Verhandlungen . . . in Heidelberg," pp. 19, 32, 52, 84.

68. "Niederschrift üder die Verhandlungen . . in Eisenach," p. 9.

69. Paula Kurgass, "Gefährdetenfürsorge?," *Arbeiterwohlfahrt* 3 (1928): 728–29.

70. Landesgerichtspräsident Dortmund to Oberlandesgerichtspräsident der Rheinprovinz, July 9, 1925, GSAPKB, Rep. 84a, no. 1018, fol. 264.

71. "Die Fonds des Reichsarbeitsministeriums," *Arbeiterwohlfahrt* 1 (1926): 85–86.

72. Hedwig Wachenheim, "Der Vorrang der öffentlichen Wohlfahrtspflege. Grundsätzliches zur Krisis in der rheinischen Jugendwohlfahrtspflege," *Arbeiterwohlfahrt* 1 (1926): 67.

73. Rudolf Schlosser, "Über sozialistische Erziehung," *Arbeiterwohlfahrt* 1 (1926): 167.

74. See Eifert, *Frauenpolitik*, p. 56.

75. Bgm., "Entwicklung und Ziel der Kinderfreundebewegung," *Jugendrettung* 9 (1929): 134. See also Konrad Algermissen, *Sozialistische und christliche Kinderfreundebewegung* (Hannover: Joseph Giesel, 1931).

76. Otto Ohl, in Deutscher Verein für öffentliche und private Fürsorge. Kommission zur Vorbereitung einer Konferenz über das Zusammenarbeiten der öffentlichen und privaten Wohlfahrtspflege, "Niederschrift über die Verhandlungen . . . vom 11. und 12. Juni 1926 in Eisenach," p. 17, ADCV, Rep. 319.4 (SKF), no. A II.12b, fasc. 2.

77. R. Görlinger, "Die Krise in der rheinischen Jugendwohlfahrtspflege," *Arbeiterwohlfahrt* 1 (1926): 33; see also "Zur Frage der Übertragung jugendämtlicher Aufgaben an Vereine und Einzelpersonen," *Jugendwohl* 16 (1927): 81–83; and Joachim Beckmann, "Arbeiterwohlfahrt und Jugendfürsorge: Richtlinien für eine Aussprache über das Problem" (n.d. [1928?]), ADW, CA/J 78.

78. Rudolf Schlosser, "Sozialistische Erziehung," presentation to the DVöpF's Kommission zur Vorbereitung, ADCV, Rep. 461.055, folder 3. See also Walter Friedländer, "Die Rechtsgrundlage der Zuständigkeit in der freien Wohlfahrtspflege," *Arbeiterwohlfahrt* 1 (1926): 99–100.

79. Hedwig Wachenheim, "Kulturkampf gegen den Sozialismus?," *Die Gemeinde* 3 (1926): esp. 546.

80. "Niederschrift über die Verhandlungen . . . 11. und 12. Juni 1926 in Eisenach," p. 41, 13–14.

81. Ibid., pp. 71, 70, 36.

82. For Ohl, see "Bei der Geschäftsführerkonferenz Düsseldorf," and "Niederschrift über die Sitzung des Ausschusses für offene Jugendfürsorge in Neuwied. . . vom 21.–23. November 1927," ADW, EREV 11; for Niemöller, see "Aussprache nach dem Referat von Pastor Lic. Ohl," ADW, CA/J 78.

83. Otto Ohl to Adolph Stahl, June 14, 1926, ADW, CA/J 78.

84. "Essen, Franz-Saleshaus, 5.4.1929" [in pencil, "Fachausschuss für Jugendfürsorge?"], ADCV, Rep. 319.4 (SKF), no. A II.5o, fasc. 1; "Niederschrift über die Sitzung des Ausschusses für offene Jugendfürsorge am 23. und 24. April 1928," ADW, EREV 11.
85. Walter Friedländer, "Anstaltsdisziplin auf dem AFET," *Arbeiterwohlfahrt* 1 (1926): 76.
86. Karl Mennicke, "Zum Problem des erziehlichen Wirkens in der Jugendfürsorge," *Zentralblatt* 20 (1928): 36.
87. Walter Hoffmann, "Die Fürsorgeerziehung in ihren Beziehungen zur modernen Pädagogik, Psychologie, und Soziologie," in *Die Fürsorgeerziehung in ihren Beziehungen zur modernen Pädagogik, Psychologie, und Soziologie. Berufsprobleme der Fürsorgeerziehung. Bericht über die Tagung des Allgemeinen Fürsorge-erziehungstages in Hamburg, 22. bis 24. September 1927* (Hannover-Kleefeld: Stefansstift, [1927]), p. 23.
88. Karl Mennicke, "Zum Problem des erziehlichen Wirkens," p. 37.
89. Wilhelm Paulsen, "Freie Erziehung, freie Erzieher," *Erziehung* 3 (1928): 537, 541.
90. "Niederschrift über die Verhandlungen . . . 11. und 12. Juni 1926 in Eisenach," p. 29 (Polligkeit paraphrasing Storck); Nohl, "Weltanschauung und Erziehung," p. 64.
91. "Signale: Revolution der Sexualethik," *Jugendrettung* 9 (1929): 34.
92. Walter Hoffmann, "Die Fürsorgeerziehung in ihren Beziehungen," p. 7; Isemann quoted in Ruth van der Leyen, "Zeitgemäße Ausgestaltung der Heim und Anstaltserziehung," *Zeitschrift für Kinderforschung* 28 (1923): 209..
93. W., "Kollektivismus," *Jugendwohl* 20 (1931): 295–296.
94. Alfred Fritz, "Zur Fürsorgeerziehung der Inneren Mission," *Erziehung* 5 (1930): 358.
95. Quoted in Gottfried Schlegtendahl, "VII. Tagung des Allgemeinen Fürsorgeerziehungstages in Köln am 19. Mai 1921," *Zentralblatt* 13 (1921): 62.
96. Otto Flug, "Der allgemeine Fürsorgeerziehungstag," *Erziehung* 3 (1928): 254.
97. Erich Weniger, "Die Gegensätze in der modernen Fürsorgeerziehung," *Erziehung* 1 (1925): 269.
98. See Carola Kuhlmann, *Erbkrank oder Erziehbar? Jugendhilfe als Vorsorge und Aussonderung in der Fürsorgeeziehung in Westfalen von 1933–1945* (Weinheim: Juventa, 1989), p. 30.
99. See Andreas Wollasch, *Der Katholische Fürsorgeverein für Mädchen, Frauen und Kinder* (Freiburg: Lambertus, 1991), pp. 253–255.
100. Karl Wilker, *Der Lindenhof: Werden und Wollen* (Heilbronn am Neckar: Lichtkampf-Verlag Hanns Altermann, 1921).
101. "Tagung des Hauptausschusses des Allgemeinen Fürsorgeerziehungstages in Hildesheim am 23. und 24. September 1926," *Zentralblatt* 18 (1926): 243.
102. Wilhelm Hertz, "Nachklänge vom AFET in Hildesheim," *Zentralblatt* 18 (1926): 245.
103. Otto Flug, "Der Allgemeine Fürsorgeerziehungstag," *Erziehung* 3 (1928): 255.
104. See Christian Schrapper and Martin Scherpner, *75 Jahre AFET* (Hannover: AFET, 1987), pp. 48–53.

105. Gustav von Mann, "Um die Zukunft unserer Anstalten," *Jugendwohl* 19 (1930): 2.

106. Landesjugendamt Berlin, *Fünf Jahre Landesjugendamt Berlin: Arbeit an der Jugend einer Millionenstadt* (n.d., n.p. [Berlin: Landesjugendamt Berlin, 1925?]), p. 27.

107. This list is taken from Jacob Hein, "Kampf dem Fürsorgeerziehungsskandal!," *Proletarische Sozialpolitik* 4 (1931): 240. It is most probably incomplete.

108. See Knaut, "Die Vorgänge im Landerziehungsheim Scheuen," *Zentralblatt* 22 (1930): 46–50; Gustav Peukert, *Grenzen der Sozialdisziplinierung: Aufstieg und Krise der dentschen Jugendfürsorge, 1878–1932* (Cologne: Bund, 1986), pp. 243–244; Heinrich Webler, "Neue Anstaltsprozesse," *Zentralblatt* 24 (1932): 58–59; Egon Behnke, "Der Waldhof-Prozess in Templin," *Zentralblatt* 24 (1932): 153–162; Erna Gysi, "Prozeß Waldhof-Templin oder Prügel als Weltanschauung," *Proletarische Sozialpolitik* 5 (1932); Curt Bondy, "Kritisches zur Fürsorgeerziehung," *Zentralblatt* 22 (1930): 148.

109. Landrat Soest to Landesgerichtspräsident Dortmund, June 2, 1927, ZSAM, rep. 191, no. 2019, fol. 217–219.

110. Leo Pelle, "Können die Jugendämter noch Anträge auf Fürsorgeerziehung stellen?," *Zentralblatt* 23 (1930): 210–212.

111. Adalbert Gregor and Else Voigtländer, *Die Verwahrlosung: ihre klinischpsychologische Bewertung und ihre Bekämpfung. Für Pädagogen, Ärzte, und Richter* (Berlin: S. Karger, 1918); Peukert, *Grenzen*, p. 250.

112. Quoted in Peukert, *Grenzen*, p. 248.

113. Ruth Van der Leyen, "Wege und Aufgaben der Psychopathenfürsorge," *Zeitschrift für Kinderforschung* 28 (1923): 39.

114. On *Psychopathenfürsorge*, see the brief discussion in Paul Weindling, *Health, Race, and German Politics between National Unification and Nazism, 1870–1945* (Cambridge: Cambridge University Press, 1988), pp. 381–383 (figures p. 382).

115. For a good discussion, see Peukert, *Grenzen*, pp. 248–252.

116. See Otto Mönkemöller, "Die Sonderbehandlung der schwersterziehbaren Fürsorgezöglinge und der Geschlechtskranken innerhalb der Anstalt," *Verhandlungen der Tagung des Allgemeinen Deutschen Fürsorge-Erziehungs-Tages zu Dresden am 12. und 13. Oktober 1925* (Hannover: Stefansstift [1925]), and Klumker's comment, p. 43.

117. Rudolf Hartmann in *Die Fürsorgeerziehung in ihren Beziehungen*, pp. 25–26.

118. Walter Hoffmann in *Die Fürsorgeerziehung in ihren Beziehungen*, p. 9.

119. Mönkemöller, "Die Sonderbehandlung," pp. 4–5.

120. *Die öffentliche Fürsorge im Deutschen Reich*, p. 246.

121. See "Zahl der gestellten Anträge betr. Freiwillige Erziehungshilfe (FEH) und Zahl der Überweisungen in Fürsorgeerziehung (FE) in den Regierungsbezirken auf 100,000 Einwohner," "Zahl der gestellten Anträge betr. Freiwillige Erziehungshilfe (FE) und Zahl der Überweisungen in Fürsorgeerziehung (FE) in Stadt- und Land-kreisen auf 100,000 Einwohnern," and "Der Stand der Freiwilligen Erziehungshilfe in der Rheinprovinz," all in ADCV, Rep. 319.4 (SKF), no. E II.12a, fasc. 1.

122. See Anne Marie Kadauke-List, "Erziehungsberatungsstellen im Nationalso-zialismus," in *Erinnerungen einer Profession: Erziehungsberatung, Jugend-hilfe und Nationalsozialismus,* ed. Renate Cogoy, Irene Kluge, and Brigitte Meckler (Munster: VOTUM, 1989), p. 153.

123. Lene Mann, "Zur Krisis der Jugendämter," *Zentralblatt* 20 (1928): 240. For a similar view, see Ruth van der Leyen, "Die Gefährdung der vorbeugenden Erziehungsfürsorge," *Zentralblatt* 22 (1930): 41–45.

124. Franz Becker, "Erziehungshilfe durch geschlossene Fürsorge," in *Der Erzieh-ungsgedanke im modernen Jugendrecht,* ed. Ludwig Clostermann (Düsseldorf: Landesjugendamt der Rheinnprovinz, 1927), p. 73.

125. See Peukert, *Grenzen,* p. 349; and "Statistik über die Fürsorgeerziehung in Preussen für das Rechnungsjahr 1931," ZSAP, Rep. 30.01, no. 1518, fols. 185–194.

126. Walter Friedländer and Earl Dewey Meyers, *Child Welfare in Germany before and after Nazism* (Chicago: University of Chicago Press, 1940), p. 137.

127. "Die Belegung der Fürsorgeerziehungs-Anstalten," *Wohlfahrtspflege in der Rheinprovinz* 5 (1929): 173.

128. For these figures, see Elizabeth Harvey, *Youth and the Welfare State in the Weimar Republic* (Oxford: Oxford University Press, 1993), p. 240.

129. Prussian Ministerium für Volkswohlfahrt, *Erlass* of February 10, 1923, ADW, EREV 100; *Evangelische Jugendhilfe* 5, no. 8 (1929): 259–260; and Heinrich Webler, "Prügelstrafen und Beschwerderecht in den FE-Anstalten," *Zentral-blatt* 21 (1929): 234.

130. There is a particularly clear argument in Gregor, "Über zeitgemäße Gestaltung der Fürsorge erziehungsanstalten," *Zeitschrift für Kinderforschung* 28 (1923), pp. 51–53.

131. See "Zusammenkunft der Freien Vereinigung grobstädtischer Jugendämter in Köln . . . am 28. Mai 1925," LAB, Rep. 142 (DST), no. StB 2850; Hans Maier, "Brauchen wir noch Fürsorgeerziehung?," *Arbeiterwohlfahrt* 1 (1926): 129–133; Walter Friedländer, "Abänderungsvorschläge zur Fürsorgeerzieh-ung," *Zentralblatt* 21 (1929): 386–389; Adolf Grabowsky, "Die fünfte Tagung Deutscher Berufsvormünder," *Zentralblatt* 2 (1910): 197.

132. Petto, in "Niederschrift über die Sitzung der Kommission über die Fragen der Schwererziehbarkeit in Limburg a.d. Lahn, 28.10.1931," ADCV, Rep. 319.4 (SKF), no. A II.5o, fasc. 2.

133. Pfarrer A. Wendelin, "Kritisches zur Fürsorgeerziehung," *Zentralblatt* 22 (1930): 272.

134. Helmuth Schreiner, "Die Krisis der Fürsorgeerziehung," *Innere Mission* 24 (1929): 57.

8. The Great Depression and National Socialism, 1930–1945

1. Christa Hasenclever, *Jugendhilfe und Jugendgesetzgebung seit 1900* (Göt-tingen: Vandenhoeck & Rupprecht, 1978), p. 124; "Notprogramme der Ju-gendfürsorge," *Zentralblatt* 23 (1931): 385; Heinrich Webler, "Jugendfür-sorge im Chaos," *Zentralblatt* 24 (1932): 1; and P. Hoffmann, "Die Not der ländliche Jugendhilfe," *Zentralblatt* 22 (1930): 293.

2. Quoted in Elizabeth Harvey, "Die Jugendfürsorge in der Endphase der Weimarer Republic," in *Sozialarbeit im Faschismus,* ed. Hans-Uwe Otto and Heinz Sünker (Bielefeld: Böllert KT-Verlag, 1986), p. 296.

3. For figures, see ibid., p. 299, and Detlev Peukert, *Grenzen der Sozialdisziplinierung* (Cologne: Bund-Verlag, 1986), p. 258.

4. See "Forderungen des Kampfausschußes gegen Fürsorgeerziehung," *Proletarische Sozialpolitik* 4 (1931): esp. 372–374; Ernst Schellenberg, "Fürsorgeerziehung und Proletariat," *Proletarische Sozialpolitik* 4 (1931): esp. 88–89.

5. See Peukert, *Grenzen,* p. 259. The background to the emergency decrees of November 1932 is discussed in detail in Hasenclever, *Jugendhilfe,* p. 117; Peukert, *Grenzen,* pp. 255–260; Harvey, "Die Jugendfürsorge," pp. 296–308.

6. See "Statistik über die Fürsorgeerziehung in Preussen für das Rechnungsjahr 1932," reprinted from *Zeitschrift des Preussischen Statistischen Landesamts,* ZSAP, Rep. 30.01, no. 1518, fols. 208–216.

7. Figures from Rolf Landwehr, "Funktionswandel der Fürsorge vom Ersten Weltkrieg bis zum Ende der Weimarer Republik," in *Geschichte der Sozialarbeit: Hauptlinien ihrer Entwicklung im 19. und 20. Jahrhundert,* ed. Rolf Landwehr and Rüdiger Baron (Weinheim: Beltz, 1983), pp. 134, 137; Hasenclever, *Jugendhilfe,* p. 120; and Peter D. Stachura, *The Weimar Republic and the Younger Proletariat: An Economic and Social Analysis* (London: Macmillan, 1989), pp. 115–119, 131.

8. On all these programs, see Elizabeth Harvey, *Youth and the Welfare State in the Weimar Republic* (Oxford: Clarendon, 1993), pp. 122–151 (figures pp. 122, 143).

9. "Vorbericht für die Tagung des Fachausschusses für Kinder- und Jugendfürsorge im Deutschen Caritasverband, Würzburg 7. und 8. Juni 1932," ADCV, Rep. 319.4 (SKF), no. A II.50, fasc. 2.

10. On the growing appeal—and increasingly punitive spirit—of eugenics during the depression, see Paul Weindling, *Health, Race, and German Politics between National Unification and Nazism, 1870–1845* (Cambridge: Cambridge University Press, 1989), esp. pp. 444, 578; and—more skeptically—Cornelie Usborne, *The Politics of the Body in Weimar Germany* (New York: Macmillan, 1992), pp. 134–139.

11. Quoted in Jochen-Christoph Kaiser, "Diakonie und Eugenik im 'Dritten Reich': Grundzüge der Entwicklung 1933–1945," in *Kirche und Nationalsozialismus,* ed. Wolfgang Stegemann (Stuttgart: Kohlhammer, 1990), p. 121.

12. See Heidemarie Lauterer-Pirner, "Eugenik und freie Wohlfahrtspflege: Die Geschichte einer Folgenschweren Beziehung (1900–1931)," *Diakonie* 5 (1991): 300; Sabine Schleiermacher, "Die Innere Mission und ihr bevölkerungspolitisches Programm," in *Der Griff nach der Bevölkerung,* ed. Heidrun Kaupen-Haas (Nördlingen: Greno, 1986); and idem, "Der Centralausschuß für die Innere Mission und die Eugenik am Vorabend des 'Dritten Reiches,'" in *Diakonie im Dritten Reich: Neuere Ergebnisse zeitgeschichtlicher Forschung,* ed. Theodor Strohm and Jörg Thierfelder (Heidelberg: Heidelberger Verlagsanstalt, 1990).

13. Quoted in Ernst Klee, *"Die SA Jesu Christi": Die Kirchen im Banne Hitlers* (Frankfurt am Main: Fischer 1989), p. 88.

14. See Paul Weindling, "Eugenics and the Welfare State During the Weimar Republic," in *The State and Social Change in Germany, 1880–1980,* ed. W. R. Lee and Eve Rosenhaft (New York: Berg, 1990), esp. p. 157; Klee, *"Die SA Jesu Christi,"* pp. 99–100; and, on Mayer, Hans-Josef Wollasch, "War der katholische Priester und Eugeniker Joseph Mayer ein Wegbereiter der NS-Euthanasie?," in *Caritas '91: Jahrbuch des Deutschen Caritasverbandes,* ed. DCV (Freiburg: DCV, 1990).

15. Quoted in Hans-Josef Wollasch, *Der Katholische Fürsorgeverein für Mädchen, Frauen und Kinder* (Freiburg: Lambertus, 1991), p. 209.

16. See Harvey, *Youth and the Welfare State,* pp. 310, 211, 261–262. Whereas three quarters of prison sentences imposed by juvenile courts were suspended in 1925–1930, that rate fell to 70 percent in 1931 and 67 percent in 1932 (p. 213).

17. Ibid., pp. 269–271, 141.

18. Max Havenstein, "Weichlichkeiten in der modernen Erziehung," *Erziehung* 5 (1930): 161, 162, 163.

19. Werner Villinger, "Die Grenzen der Erziehbarkeit und ihre Erweiterung," in *Bericht über den vierten Kongres für Heilpädagogik, 11.–15. April 1928,* ed. Erwin Lesch (Berlin: Springer, 1928), pp. 246–247.

20. This was a development foreshadowed in some of the works of "reform" pedagogues in the late 1920s; see Wilhelm Flitner, "Reformpädagogik," in *Kulturkritik und Jugendkult,* ed. Walter Rüegg (Frankfurt am Main: Vittorio Klostermann, 1974), esp. p. 143.

21. Alfred Fritz, "Pädagogische Bewegung oder Pädagogische Reaktion?," *Evangelische Jugendhilfe* 8 (1932): 306–307; Alfred Fritz to Johannes Wolff, ADW, EREV 98, cited in Carola Kuhlmann, *Erbkrank oder Erziehbar? Jugendhilfe als Vorsorge und Aussonderung in der Fürsorgeerziehung in Westfalen von 1933–1945* (Weinheim: Juventa, 1989), p. 40.

22. Hermann Herrigel, "Autorität: Bemerkungen zu Gogarten's Schrift 'Wider die Ächtung der Autorität,'" *Erziehung* 6 (1931): 429.

23. See particularly Heinz Hürten, "Der katholische Episkopat nach dem Reichskonkordat," in *Kirchen in der Diktatur,* ed. Günther Heydemann and Lothar Kettenacker (Göttingen: Vandenhoeck & Ruprecht, 1993).

24. See Jochen-Christoph Kaiser, "NS-Volkswohlfahrt und freie Wohlfahrtspflege," in *Politische Formierung und soziale Erziehung im Nationalsozialismus,* ed. Hans-Uwe Otto and Heinz Sünker (Frankfurt am Main: Suhrkamp, 1992), pp. 90, 101.

25. See Heinz Sünker, "Soziale Arbeit im Nationalsozialismus: 'Endlösung der sozialen Frage'?," *Neue Praxis* 20 (1990): 356.

26. On the relationship between National Socialism and the Inner Mission, see Jochen-Christoph Kaiser, *Sozialer Protestantismus im 20. Jahrhundert: Beträge zur Geschichte der Inneren Mission, 1914–1945* (Munich: R. Oldenbourg, 1989); on the Protestant Women's Auxiliary, see Michael Phayer, *Protestant and Catholic Women in Nazi Germany* (Detroit: Wayne State University Press, 1990), chap. 2; on the response of the churches to sterilization specifically, see the summary by Claudia Koonz in "Eugenics, Gender, and Ethics in Nazi Germany: The Debate about Involuntary Sterilization, 1933–1936," in *Reevalu-*

ating the Third Reich, ed. Thomas Childers and Jane Caplan (New York: Holmes & Meier, 1993); and idem, "Ethical Dilemmas and Nazi Eugenics: Single-Issue Dissent in Religious Contexts," *Journal of Modern History* 64 (1992). On the response of Protestant day care workers, see Manfred Heinemann, "Evangelische Kindergärten im Nationalsozialismus: Von den Illusionen zum Abwehrkampf," in *Erziehung und Schule im Dritten Reich,* pt. 1, *Kindergarten, Schule, Jugend, Berufserziehung,* ed. Manfred Heinemann (Stuttgart: Klett-Cotta, 1980), esp. pp. 60–61.

27. Quoted in Günter Brakelmann, "Hoffnungen und Illusionen evangelischer Prediger zu Beginn des Dritten Reiches: gottesdienstliche Feiern aus politischen Anlässen," in *Die Reihen fast geschlossen: Beiträge zur Geschichte des Alltags unterm nationalsozialismus,* ed. Detlev Peukert and Jürgen Reulecke (Wuppertal: Hammer, 1981), p. 132.

28. Quoted in Ernst Klee, *"Die SA Jesu Christi": Die Kirchen im Banne Hitlers* (Frankfurt am Main: Fischer, 1989), p. 33.

29. Horst Schirmacher quoted ibid., p. 57; D. Engelke, "Freudiges Erziehen im starken Staat," *Evangelische Jugendhilfe* 10 (1934): 159.

30. See Rudolf Kraus, "Die Fürsorgeerziehung im dritten Reich (1933–1945)," *Archiv für Wissenschaft und Praxis der sozialen Arbeit* 5 (1974): 186, 204; and Eckhard Hansen, *Wohlfahrtspolitik im NS-Staat: Motivationen, Konflikte und Machtstrukturen im "Sozialismus der Tat" des Dritten Reiches* (Bremen: Maro Verlag, 1991), p. 245.

31. "Statistik über die Fürsorgeerziehung in Preussen für das Rechnungsjahr 1931," ZSAP, Rep. 30.01, no. 1518, fol. 181; and "Statistik über die Fürsorgeerziehung in Preussen für das Rechnungsjahr 1939," BAK, Rep. R 22, no. 1915, fol. 393.

32. Quoted in Kuhlmann, *Erbkrank oder Erziehbar,* p. 61.

33. Quoted in Wollasch, *Der Katholische Fürsorgeverein,* p. 258.

34. Alfred Fritz, "Evangelische Jugendfürsorge in der nationalen Umwälzung," *Evangelische Jugendhilfe* 9 (1933): 74; Ina Hundinger, "Arbeitsbericht des Evangelischen Reichs-Erziehungs-Verbandes eV. für die Zeit vom 1. April 1932 bis 31. März 1933," *Evangelische Jugendhilfe* 9 (1933): 102.

35. Johannes Wolff, "Welche Aufgaben hat die freie Jugendhilfe im nationalsozialistischen Staat?," *Evangelische Jugendhilfe* 10 (1934): 83.

36. "Zusammenwirkung von öffentlicher und freier Wohlfahrtspflege," *Evangelische Jugendhilfe* 9 (1933): 141–142; also reproduced in *Zentralblatt* 25 (1933): 133–134.

37. See "Niederschrift über die Sitzung der Sachverständigenkommission zur Beratung der Neugestaltung der Jugendwohlfahrtspflege am 12. und 13. August 1933 in Berlin"; the untitled response to the DVöpF's paper, dated June 23, 1933; and Gustav von Mann, "Gedanken zur Reform des Reichsjugendwohlfahrtsgesetzes," all in ADCV, Rep. 319.4 (SKF), no. E II.6, fasc. 3.

38. Elisabeth Zillken to Agnes Neuhaus, August 15, 1933, ADCV, Rep. 319.4 (SKF), no. E II.6, fasc. 3.

39. See Zengerling to DVöpF, August 15, 1933; and "Vorschläge des Deutschen Gemeindetages für die Schaffung eines Reichsjugendgesetzes (Reform des RJWG)," both in ADCV, Rep. 319.4 (SKF), no. E II.6, fasc. 4.

40. Ina Hundinger, "Umgestaltung des Reichsjugendwohlfahrtsgesetzes," *Evangelische Jugendhilfe* 9 (1933): 291, 293.
41. See Ute Frevert, *Women in German History: From Bourgeois Emancipation to Sexual Liberation* (New York: Berg/St. Martin's, 1989), pp. 230–233.
42. Quoted in Schleiermacher, "Der Centralauschuß für die Innere Mission," p. 73.
43. On Polligkeit's response to the seizure of power, see Christoph Sachße and Florian Tennstedt, *Der Wohlfahrtsstaat im Nationalsozialismus: Geschichte der Armenfuursorge in Deutschland*, vol. 3 (Stuttgart: Kohlhammer, 1992), pp. 133, 147–148.
44. DVöpF, "Jugendwohlfahrtspflege im künftigen Gesamtsystem der Jugenderziehung (Entwurf)," June 24, 1933, p. 1, ADCV, Rep. CA VII, no. 61f, pp. 3, 9, 5–6.
45. Heinrich Webler, "Familie und Erziehung im Recht," *Deutsches Recht* 5, no. 4 (1935): 89, 90.
46. Gustav von Mann, "Erziehungsrecht," *Jugendwohl* 24 (1935): 65–67.
47. See Hansen, *Wohlfahrtspolitik im NS-Staat*, pp. 19–20.
48. See "Statistik über das Hilfswerk Mutter und Kind," reprinted in Herwart Vorländer, *Die NSV: Darstellung und Dokumentation einer nationalsozialistischen Organisation* (Boppard: Harald Boldt, 1988), p. 267.
49. Ibid., pp. 266–267. On Nazi EB, see Frieda Ott, "Die Erziehungsberatungsstelle des Stadtjugendamts Karlsruhe i. B.," *Zentralblatt* 27 (1935); and Paul Thomas, "Erziehungsberatung," *Zentralblatt* 27 (1935).
50. See Anne Marie Kadauke-List, "Erziehungsberatungsstellen im Nationalsozialismus," in *Erinnerungen einer Profession: Erziehungsberatung, Jugendhilfe und Nationalsozialismus*, ed. Renate Cogoy, Irene Kluge, and Brigitte Meckler (Münster: VOTUM, 1989), esp. pp. 184–187; and Hildegard Hetzer, "Die Erziehungsberatung als Mittel der NSV-Jugendhilfe," *Zentralblatt* 32 (1940).
51. Quoted in Kuhlmann, *Erbkrank oder Erziehbar?*, p. 181.
52. See "Stellungnahme der NSV. zur Reform des RJWG," ADCV, Rep. 319.4 (SKF), no. E II.6, fasc. 4; "Ergebnis einer Rundfrage des AFET zur Frage der Abänderung der die Fürsorgeerziehung betreffenden Bestimmungen," September 1933, BAK, Rep. R 36, no. 1953, p. 12; Heinrich Pohlmann, "Plan einer künftigen reichseinheitlichen Fürsorgeerziehung," *Nationalsozialistischer Volksdienst* 5 (1938); Alfred Späth, "Wie lange soll die Anstaltserziehung für einen normalen Jugendlichen dauern?," *Zentralblatt* 28 (1936); idem, "Anstaltserziehung und Elternhaus," *Zentralblatt* 29 (1937); Leo Pelle, "Zur Frage der vorbeugenden Fürsorgeerziehung," *Zentralblatt* 29 (1938); Kotthaus, "Die Arbeit der Jugendheimstätten der NSW," *Nationalsozialistischer Volksdienst* 7 (1940). Sachße and Tennstedt, *Der Wohlfahrtsstaat*, hold that there were only fifteen *Jugendheimstätten* by 1939 (p. 164); Kuhlmann, *Erbkrank oder Erziehbar?*, counts thirty-one by 1937 (p. 184). FEH was given formal legal basis by a *Runderlass* of the national Ministry of the Interior, August 25, 1943; see BAK, Rep. B 153, no. 108. fol. 384.
53. See Hans-Uwe Otto and Heinz Sünker, "Volksgemeinschaft als Formierungsideologie des Nationalsozialismus. Zu Genesis und Geltung von 'Volkspflege'," in Otto and Sünker, *Politische Formierung und soziale Erziehung*, p. 70.
54. At the 1921 conference of Workers' Welfare, for example, Helene Simon had spoken of the need for a "supreme guardianship by the state" to ensure that the

family performed its "social duty" and of the individual's "duty" to work. See Christiane Eifert, *Frauenpolitik und Wohlfahrtspflege: Zur Geschichte der sozialdemokratischen "Arbeiterwohlfahrt"* (Frankfurt am Main: Campus, 1993), pp. 41–43.

55. Erich Hilgenfeldt, "Aufgaben der NS.-Volkswohlfahrt," *Nationalsozialistischer Volksdienst* 1 (1933): 5.

56. Quoted in Stefan Schnurr, "Die nationalsozialistische Funktionalisierung sozialer Arbeit: Zur Kontinuität und Diskontinuität der Praxis sozialer Berufe," in Otto and Sünker, *Politische Formierung und soziale Erziehung,* p. 118.

57. See Peukert, *Grenzen,* pp. 274–291. *Bewahrung* was introduced independently in the Rhineland, Berlin, Hamburg, Hannover, Baden, and Thuringia after 1934.

58. For the history of the NSV, see Vorländer, *Die NSV* (figures on the *Winterhilfswerk,* pp. 101–102; relations with other Nazi organizations, pp. 65, 69, 99, 103–104).

59. The Central Welfare Organization of the German Jews continued to operate outside the Reichsgemeinschaft.

60. See Claudia Koonz, *Mothers in the Fatherland* (New York: St. Martin's, 1987), p. 183. On the close relationship between the NSV and the NSF, see Jill Stephenson, *The Nazi Organization of Women* (London: Croom Helm, 1981), esp. pp. 104–105.

61. Reproduced in Vörlander, *Die NSV,* p. 199.

62. "Die Hilfswerke 1936/37," *Nationalsozialistischer Volksdienst* 4 (1937): 109.

63. "Stellungnahme der NSV. zur Reform des RJWG.," September 12, 1933, ADCV, Rep. 319.4 (SKF), no. E II.6, fasc. 4.

64. "Niederschrift der Sitzung der Kommission zum R.J.W.G. am 15. September 1933," ADCV, Rep. 319.4 (SKF), no. E II.6, fasc. 4.

65. "Niederschrift über die Sitzung der Sachverständigen-Kommission zur Beratung der Neugestaltung der Jugendwohlfahrtspflege am 12. und 13. August 1933," p. 6, ADCV, Rep. 319.4 (SKF), no. E II.6, fasc. 3.

66. "2. Entwurf der Reichsgemeinschaft der freien Wohlfahrtspflege Deutschlands zum 'Allgemeinen Teil' des Reichsjugendgesetzes," ADCV, Rep. 319.4 (SKF), no. E II.6, fasc. 3. For Catholic concerns regarding this omission, see "Bericht über die Sitzung über das Reichsjugendgesetz in Berlin, Dezember 1933," ibid.

67. Reichsgemeinschaft der freien Wohlfahrtspflege, "Entwurf eines Reichsjugendgesetzes," January 3, 1934, ADCV, Rep. 319.4 (SKF), no. E II.6, fasc. 4.

68. See Phayer, *Protestant and Catholic Women,* chap. 5; "Besprechung über Fragen der Jugendfürsorge am 25. August 1933 in Freiburg im Breisgau," ADCV, Rep. 319.4 (SKF), no. E II.6, fasc. 3; and Hansen, *Wohlfahrtspolitik,* pp. 71–72.

69. The Catholic youth organizations were destroyed in 1939; see Barbara Schellenberger, *Katholische Jugend und Drittes Reich* (Mainz: Matthias Grünewald, 1975).

70. The literature on the "church struggle" is vast. See particularly Kurt Meier, *Der evangelische Kirchenkampf,* 3 vols. (Göttingen: Vandenhoeck & Ruprecht,

1976–1984); and idem, *Kreuz und Hakenkreuz: Die evangelische Kirche im Dritten Reich* (Munich: DTV, 1992).

71. See Kuhlmann, *Erbkrank oder Erziehbar?*, pp. 112–113.
72. For Nazi attacks on the family, see particularly Koonz, *Mothers*, pp. 178, 208–212.
73. Gustav von Mann to Adolf Cardinal Bertram, January 12, 1934, ADCV, Rep. 319.4 (SKF), no. E II.6, fasc. 3.
74. Otto Hipp, "Jugendwohlfahrt, Elternrecht, und neuer Staat," *Jugendwohl* 22 (1933): 283.
75. Anna Zillken, "Staatsbürgerliche Erziehung," *Jugendwohl* 22 (1933): p. 230.
76. Elisabeth Zillken, "Die Familie als Träger der Erziehung und die Grenzen ihrer Rechte und Pflichten," *Jugendwohl* 22 (1933): 241–253.
77. Hans Wollasch, "Die Erziehung in der Wende zur Nation," *Jugenwohl* 22 (1933): 174.
78. Phayer, *Protestant and Catholic Women*, pp. 121, 176; and [KFV], *1900–1950: Katholische Fürsorge-Arbeit in 50 Jahren* (Dortmund: Zentrale des KFV, 1950), pp. 13–14.
79. Ina Hundinger, "Arbeitsbericht des Evangelischen Reichs-Erziehungs-Verbandes für die Zeit vom 1. April 1933 bis 31. März 1934," *Evangelische Jugendhilfe* 10 (1934): 106; Fritz Trost, "Evangelische Erziehung im nationalsozialistischen Staat," *Evangelische Jugendhilfe* 10 (1934): 130. Trost also insisted, however, that resistance to the new state's measures was un-Christian.
80. On relations between the Christian churches and the Nazi regime, see Robert P. Eriksen, "A Radical Minority: Resistance in the German Protestant Church," and Donald Dietrich, "Catholic Resistance to Biological and Racist Eugenics in the Third Reich," both in *Germans against Nazism*, ed. Francis R. Nicosia and Lawrence D. Stokes (New York: Berk, 1990); E. C. Helmreich, *The German Churches under Hitler* (Detroit: Wayne State University Press, 1979); and Klaus Scholder, *Die Kirchen und das Dritte Reich* (Frankfurt am Main: Ullstein, 1977).
81. Some 5 percent of reformatory inmates were sterilized each year in 1934 and 1935, after which figures were not published (Kraus, "Fürsorgeerziehung," pp. 208–209). Earl Dewey Meyers and Walter Friedländer report that 3.2 percent were sterilized in 1935–36; see their *Child Welfare in Germany before and after Nazism* (Chicago: University of Chicago Press, 1940), p. 132.
82. On Catholic responses to the sterilization laws, see Koonz, "Eugenics, Gender, and Ethics," pp. 72–76; Dirk Blasius, "Psychiatrischer Alltag im Nationalsozialismus," in Peukert and Reulecke, *Die Reihen*, esp. pp. 373–374; and Hans-Josef Wollasch, "Kirchliche Reaktionen auf das 'Gesetz zur Verhütung erbkranken Nachwuchses' vom Jahre 1933," in Hans-Josef Wollasch, *Beiträge zur Geschichte der Deutschen Caritas in der Zeit der Weltkriege: Zum 100. Geburtstag von Benedikt Kreutz (1879–1949)* (Freiburg: DCV, 1978). For Protestant views, see especially Schleiermacher, "Die Innere Mission" and "Der Centralausschuß für die Innere Mission," and Klee, *"Die SA Jesu Christi,"* pp. 91–93.
83. See the remarks of Justice Minister Hans Frank in "Akademie für deutsches Recht: Familienrechtsausschuß. Sitzung vom 13. Juli 1937, 'Vorschlag des Fa-

milienrechtsausschußes zum Recht der Ehelichkeit und Unehelichkeit von Kindern,'" BAK, Rep. R61, no. 169 (p. 171); "Das Blut ist stärker als Paragraphen," *Der SA-Mann*, August 14, 1937, p. 4, ADCV, Rep. 230.71; and Frevert, *Women in German History*, p. 238.

84. Quoted in Jochen-Christoph Kaiser, "NS-Volkswohlfahrt und freie Wohlfahrtspflege im 'Dritten Reich,'" in Otto and Sünker, *Politische Formierung und soziale Erziehung*, p. 85.

85. NSDAP Hauptamt für Volkswohlfahrt, Amt für Wohlfahrtsplege und Jugendhilfe, "Betr.: Deutsche Zentrale für freie Jugendwohlfahrt: Zusammenarbeit in der freien Jugendhilfe," December 2, 1935, ADCV, Rep 481.5, fasc. 5; and Gustav von Mann to Benedict Kreutz, October 29, 1935, ibid., fasc. 4. The local organs of the party would also review the political reliability of all volunteers and foster families.

86. See Vorländer, *Die NSV*, pp. 293–294; Hansen, *Wohlfahrtspflege*, p. 248.

87. See "Niederschrift über die Sitzung des Sachverständigen-Ausschusses über Fragen der Kinder und Jugendfürsorge am 11. und 12. November 1938," ADCV, Rep. 319.4 (SKF), no. A II.5o, fasc. 2.

88. Ina Hundinger, "Arbeitsbericht des Evangelischen Reichs-Erziehungs-Verbandes für die Zeit vom 1. April 1934 bis 31. März 1935," *Evangelische Jugendhilfe* 11 (1935): 122.

89. H. Edwards, "Lebensgesetze der Veste Deutschland: Schicksalsgemeinschaft oder Organisationschaos," *Nationalsozialistischer Volksdienst* 4 (1937): 122; Heinz Vagt, "Heimerziehung," *Zentralblatt* 29 (1937): 265–266.

90. See Phayer, *Protestant and Catholic Women*, pp. 258, 190; and Rainer Bookhagen, "Evangelische Kinderpflege im Nationalsozialismus—Die Kriesenjahre 1939–1941," in *Diakonie im "Dritten Reich": Neuere Ergebnisse zeitgeschichtlicher Forschung*, ed. Theodor Strohm and Jörg Thierfelder (Heidelberg: Heidelberger Verlagsanstalt, 1990).

91. Reichsminister des Innern to Reichsminister der Justiz, December 22, 1938, BAK, Rep. R 22, no. 1915, fol. 229; and "Niederschrift über die Sitzung des Sachverständigen-Ausschusses über Fragen der Kinder und Jugendfürsorge am 11. und 12. November 1938," ADCV, Rep. 319.4 (SKF), no. A II.5o, fasc. 2.

92. Alfred Fritz, "Zur Jahreswende," *Evangelische Jugendhilfe* 13 (1937): 3.

93. On the survival of the charities, see Wollasch, *Der Katholische Fürsorgeverein*, pp. 293, 310, 313–314.

94. Reichsministerium des Innern to Reichsministerium der Justiz, October 18, 1939, BAK, Rep. R 22, no. 1915, fols. 306–310.

95. Quoted ibid., p. 17.

96. See, for example, Götz Aly, "Der Mord an behinderten Kindern zwischen 1939 und 1945," in *Heilen und Vernichten im Mustergau Hamburg: Bevölkerungs und Gesundheitspolitik im Dritten Reich,* ed. Angelika Ebbingahus, Heidrun Kaupen-Haas, and Karl Heinz Roth (Hamburg: Konkret Literatur, 1984); and Robert Proctor, *Racial Hygiene: Medicine under the Nazis* (Cambridge, Mass.: Harvard University Press, 1988), pp. 185–188.

97. See Hans-Josef Wollasch, "Caritas und Euthanasie im Dritten Reich: Staatliche Lebensvernichtung in katholischen Heil- und Pflege-Anstalten 1936 bis 1945," in Wollasch, *Beiträge*, p. 222. On Christian responses to the "euthanasia" pro-

gram generally, see Martin Höllen, "Episkopat und T4," in *Aktion T4, 1939–1945: Die "Euthanasie"-Zentrale in der Tiergartenstraße 4*, ed. Götz Aly (Berlin: Hentrich, 1987); Kurt Nowak, *"Euthanasie" und Sterilisierung im "Dritten Reich"* (Göttinger: Vandenhock und Ruprecht, 1984), and idem, "Sterilisation, Krankenmord, und Innere Mission im 'Dritten Reich,'" in *Medizin unterm Hakenkreuz*, ed. Achim Thom and Genadij I. Caregorodcev (Berlin: Volk und Gesundheit, 1989); Ernst Klee, *"Euthanasie" im NS-Staat* (Frankfurt: Fischer, 1983), esp. pp. 200–219 and 317–340; and Sabine Schleiermacher, "Der Centralausschuß für die Innere Mission und die Eugenik am Vorabend des 'Dritten Reich,'" in *Diakonie im Dritten Reich: Neuere Ergebnisse Zeitgeschichtlicher Forschung*, ed. Theodor Strohm and Jörg Thierfelder (Heidelberg: Heidelberger Verlagsanstalt, 1990).

98. Martini, quoted in Emilija Mitrovic, "Fürsorgerinnen im Nationalsozialismus: Hilfe zur Aussonderung," in *Opfer und Täterinnen: Frauenbiographien im Nationalsozialismus*, ed. Angelika Ebbinghaus (Nördlingen: Delphi/Greno, 1987), p. 31.

99. See Kuhlmann, *Erbkrank oder Erziehbar?*, p. 153.

100. "Wer war das—'Stadt-Jugendamtmann'?," *Die Hitler-Jugend*, July 17, 1937, clipping in BAK, Rep. R 36, no. 1402.

101. See Hermann Hübner, "Grundsätzliches zur Zusammenarbeit zwischen Jugendamt und NSV-Jugendhilfe," *Zentralblatt* 27 (1936): esp. 386, 388. On the issue of political reliability, see, for example, the comments in "Niederschrift über die Besprechung über '*Erziehungsfürsorge*' im Deutschen Verein für öffentliche und private Fürsorge am 26.6.1939," BAK, Rep. R 36, no. 1407.

102. See Staatssekretär Pfundter of the Reichsministerium des Innern to Reichskanzlei, January 20, 1939, and Reichsminister des Innern to Stellvertreter des Führers, March 10, 1939, both reproduced in Vorländer, *Die NSV*, p. 148; Bormann quoted in Hansen, *Wohlfahrtspflege*, p. 137.

103. Position paper of the Deutsche Gemeindetag, March 3, 1939, reproduced ibid., p. 366; Sachße and Tennstedt, *Der Wohlfahrtsstaat*, p. 161.

104. "Niederschrift über die Besprechung."

105. See "Aufzeichnung über die Beratungen zwischen Vertretern preussischer Fürsorgeerziehungsbehörden über die Zusammenarbeit zwischen Fürsorgeerziehungsbehörde und NSV-Jugendhilfe," September 9, 1941, BAK, Rep. R36, no. 1996.

106. See Earl Dewey Meyers and Walter Friedländer, *Child Welfare in Germany before and after Nazism* (Chicago: University of Chicago Press, 1940), pp. 240–241; and "Lebensuntüchtigkeit bedeutet Verwahrlosung," *Nationalsozialistischer Volksdienst* 4 (1937): 119–120.

107. Reproduced in Vorländer, *Die NSV*, pp. 198–200 (quotes p. 199).

108. "Ausschnitt aus der Niederschrift über die Verhandlungen der Arbeitsgemeinschaft der preußischen Fürsorgeerziehungsdezernenten am 28. Juni 1934 in Berlin" (pp. 12–13), BAK, Rep. R36, no. 1953.

109. Hilgenfeldt, "Aufgaben," p. 5.

110. There is a particularly clear discussion of this point in Sachße and Tennstedt, *Der Wohfahrtsstaat*, pp. 50–53.

111. See Analiese Ohland, "Ist Fürsorgeerziehung Minderwertigenfürsorge oder volksaufbauende Erziehungsarbeit?," *Zentralblatt* 26 (1934); and Kuhlmann, *Erbkrank oder Erziehbar?*, pp. 82–88, 129–130.

112. Walter Baumeister, "Ist ein Bewahrungsgesetz notwendig?," *Caritas* 39 (1934): 183.

113. See the discussion in Jürgen Blankow, "'Fürsorgliche Bewahrung'—Kontinuitäten und Diskontinuitäten in der Bewahrung 'Asozialer,'" in Cogoy, Kluge, and Meckler, *Erinnerungen einer Profession*, esp. pp. 133–135.

114. Gertrud Bäumer, "Der Sinn der Wohlfahrtspflege und die Frauenarbeit," *Die Frau* 42 (1935): 329–330.

115. See Vorländer, *Die NSV*, pp. 106–107; Sachße and Tennstedt, *Der Wohlfahrtsstaat*, p. 107; Dietrich Kühn, "Entwicklung des Jugend- und Gesundheitsamts im Nationalsozialismus," *Neue Praxis* 16 (1986); Hasenclever, *Jugendhilfe*, p. 131. And for an interesting discussion of one important aspect of the Health Bureaus' work, see Gabriele Czarnowski, *Das kontrollierte Paar: Ehe- und Sexualpolitik im Nationalsozialismus* (Weinheim: Deutscher Studien Verlag, 1991), esp. chap. 5.

116. Hermann Hübner, "Grundsätzliches zur Zusammenarbeit zwischen Jugendamt und NSV-Jugendhilfe," *Zentralblatt* 27 (1936): 391; Hansen, Wohlfahrtspflege, p. 150.

117. Hildegard Villnow, "Aufgabe und Bedeutung der NSV-Kindergarten," *Nationalsozialistischer Volksdienst* 3 (1935): 38.

118. See E. Schott, "Verstärkter Einsatz der NSV-Erziehungsberatung," *Nationalsozialistischer Volksdienst* 7 (1940).

119. See, among others, Paul Weindling, "Die preussische Medizinalverwaltung und die 'Rassenhygiene' 1905–1933," in *Medizin im Faschismus: Symposium über das Schicksal der Medizin in der Zeit des Faschismus 1933–1945*, ed. Achim Thom and Horst Spaar (Berlin: Volk und Gesundheit, 1985), p. 55. For an opposing view to Weindling's, see Gisela Bock, *Zwangs-sterilisation im Nationalsozialismus* (Opladen: Westdeutscher Verlag, 1986), esp. pp. 30, 54, 71.

120. See Peter Dudek, "Nationalsozialistische Jugendpolitik und Arbeitserziehung: Das Arbeitslager als Instrument sozialer Disziplinierung," in Otto and Sünker, *Politische Formierung und soziale Erziehung* (by 1938 the program still did not exceed the FAD of 1932 in size); and Jürgen Schiedeck and Martin Stahlmann, "Die Inszenierung 'totalen Erlebens': Lagererziehung im Nationalsozialismus," in Otto and Sünker, *Politische Formierung und soziale Erziehung*.

121. See Bechert and Cornelius in "Aus der Rechtsabteilung-Reichsleitung der NSDAP," *Deutsches Recht* 4, no. 17 (January 1935).

122. See "Das Blut ist stärker als Paragraphen," *Der SA-Mann*, August 14, 1937, p. 4, ADCV, Rep. 230.71.

123. Erich Hilgenfeldt, "Vom Sinn und Ziel nationalsozialistischer Volkswohlfahrtsarbeit," *Nationalsozialistischer Volksdienst* 6 (1939): 1.

124. Bookhagen, "Evangelische Kinderpflege," p. 104; see also Heinemann, "Evangelische Kindergärten," esp. pp. 70–87.

125. See Vorländer, Die NSV, pp. 150–153, 157–160; and Keßler, "Kindergarten und Recht," *NS-Volksdienst* 9 (1942): 186. For a contrasting view, see Carl Maria Fernkorn, "Kindergarten und Recht," *NS-Volksdienst* 9 (1942): 248–253.

126. Vorländer, *Die NSV*, pp. 154–157, 469.
127. See Hansen, *Wohlfahrtspflege*, pp. 261–262.
128. "Niederschrift über die Sitzung des Sachverständigen-Ausschusses über Fragen der Kinder- und Jugendfürsorge am 11. und 12. November 1938," ADCV, Rep. 319.4 (SKF), no. A II.5o, fasc. 2. There is a good brief discussion of the escalation of crime and repression during the war in Jörg Wolff, *Jugendliche vor Gericht im Dritten Reich: Nationalsozialistische Jugendstrafrechtspolitik und Justizalltag* (Munich: C. H. Beck, 1992), pp. 28–34.
129. For the history of these gangs and upper-class "Swing Youth," see Detlev Peukert, "Youth in the Third Reich," in *Life in the Third Reich*, ed. Richard Bessel (Oxford: Oxford University Press, 1987); idem, *Inside Nazi Germany* (New Haven: Yale University Press, 1987), pp. 145–175; and Wilfried Breyvogel, ed., *Piraten, Swings, und Junge Garde: Jugendwiderstand im Nationalsozialismus* (Bonn: Dietz, 1991).
130. "Ist das uneheliche Kind minderwertig?," from *Der SA-Mann*, August 7, 1937, p. 4, ADCV, Rep. 230.71.
131. See Kuhlmann, *Erbkrank oder Erziehbar*, p. 197.
132. On all these measures, see Hansen, *Wohlfahrtspflege*, pp. 281–282.
133. See Christine Dörner, *Erziehung durch Strafe: Die Geschichte des Jugendstrafvollzugs 1871–1945* (Weinheim: Juventa, 1991), esp. pp. 157–171; Kuhlmann, *Erbkrank oder Erziehbar?*, pp. 201–202; Hasenclever, *Jugendhilfe*, pp. 148–153; Peukert, *Grenzen*, pp. 282–284; Elizabeth Harvey, *Youth and the Welfare State*, pp. 288–291; Martin Guse, Andreas Kohrs, and Friedhelm Vahsen, "Das Jugendlager Moringen—Ein Jugendkonzentrationslager," in Otto and Sünker, *Sozialarbeit*; and Detlev J. K. Peukert, "Arbeitslager und Jugend-KZ: Die 'Behandlung Gemeinschaftsfremder' im Dritten Reich," in Peukert and Reulecke, *Die Reihen*.
134. See Aly, "Medizin gegen Unbrauchbare," p. 31.
135. See Benno Müller-Hill, *Murderous Science* (Oxford: Oxford University Press, 1988), pp. 31, 41; Paul Weindling, "Eugenics and the Welfare State during the Weimar Republic," in *The State and Social Change in Germany, 1880–1980*, ed. W. R. Lee and Eve Rosenhaft (New York: Berg, 1990), p. 150; Klee, "Die SA Jesu Christi," pp. 91–92, 96, and *Euthanasie im NS-Staat*, p. 205. According to Klee (*Euthanasie*, p. 205), Villinger appears to have participated more to sabotage than to assist in the program ("eher sabotierend gearbeitet").
136. See Karola Fings and Frank Sparing, "'Tunlichst als erziehungsunfähig hinzustellen'. Zigeunerkinder und- jugendliche: Aus der Fürsorge in die Vernichtung," *Dachauer Hefte* 9 (1993).

9. Child Welfare Policy in the Federal Republic, 1945–1961

1. These data come from Eckart Hansen, *Wohlfahrtspolitik im NS-Staat* (Bremen: MaroVerlag, 1991), pp. 388, 400–401, 405, 420, 422, 423; Ernst Klee, *"Die SA Jesu Christi": Die Kirchen im Banne Hitlers* (Frankfurt am Main: Fischer, 1989), p. 67.
2. Walter Becker, "Rebellionen der Jugend," *Recht der Jugend* 9 (1961): 137.
3. On developments within the Protestant churches, see Klaus Scholder, *Die Kirchen und das Dritte Reich* (Frankfurt am Main: Ullstein, 1977); Frederic

Spott, *The Churches and Politics in Germany* (Middletown, Conn.: Wesleyan University Press, 1973), esp. pp. 9–12 and chap. 5; Andreas Permien, *Protestantismus und Wiederbewaffnung, 1950–1955* (Cologne: Rheinland, 1994); Ewald Hein-Janke, *Protestantismus und Faschismus nach der Katastrophe (1945– 1949)* (Stuttgart: Alektor, 1982); and Clemens Vollnhals, "Die evangelische Kirche zwischen Traditionswahrung und Neuorientierung," in *Von Stalingrad zur Währungsreform: Zur Sozialgeschichte des Umbruchs in Deutschland,* ed. Martin Broszat et al. (Munich: Oldenbourg, 1990).

4. See Christiane Eifert, *Frauenpolitik und Wohlfahrtspflege: Zur Geschichte der sozialdemokratischen "Arbeiterwohlfahrt"* (Frankfurt am Main: Campus, 1993), pp. 210, 214.

5. Quoted in Richard Haar, "Zur Entwicklung der Arbeiterwohlfahrt nach 1945," in *Arbeiterwohlfahrt: Verband für soziale Arbeit—Geschichte, Selbstverständnis, Arbeitsfelder, Daten,* ed. Heinz Niedrig et al. (Wiesbaden: Wirtschaftsverlag, 1985), p. 41.

6. Quoted in Eifert, *Frauenpolitik,* p. 224.

7. Haar, "Zur Entwicklung," p. 42. Haar also stressed the demoralization created by the unrelenting conservatism of the new Federal Republic, the failure of denazification, and the cold war.

8. Willi Eichler, quoted in Eifert, *Frauenpolitik,* p. 222.

9. Hermann Glaser, *Kleine Kulturgeschichte der Bundesrepublik Deutschland* (Bonn: Carl Hanser, 1991), pp. 72–73.

10. Robert Scholl, "Die Erziehungsberatungsstelle als gemeinsame Einrichtung von Jugend- und Schulamt," *Zentralblatt* 39 (1952): 142.

11. See Ute Frevert, *Women in German History: From Bourgeois Emancipation to Sexual Liberation* (New York: Berg/St. Martin's, 1989), p. 256.

12. Christa Hasenclever, *Jugendhilfe und Jugendgesetzgebung seit 1900* (Göttingen: Vandenhoeck & Rupprecht, 1978), p. 160.

13. See Benno Hafeneger, *Alle Arbeit für Deutschland: Arbeit, Jugendarbeit und Erziehung in der Weimarer Republik, unter dem Nationalsozialismus und in der Nachkriegszeit* (Cologne: Bund, 1988), esp. chap. 5.

14. *Statistisches Jahrbuch der Bundesrepublik Deutschland* (Stuttgart: Kohlhammer, 1957), p. 52 (illegitimacy); "Geschlechtskrankheiten bei Jugendlichen," *Jugendwohl* 30 (1949): 59; "Das Problem der unehelichen Besatzungskinder," from *Nachrichtendienst* of April 1952, BAK, Rep. B 153, no. 108; "Kinder ohne Väter," *Jugendwohl* 30 (1949): 129; Hans Wollasch, "Querschnitt durch die Nachkriegskriminalität," *Jugendwohl* 31 (1950) (citing a 500 percent rise in juvenile delinquency from 1938 to 1946); Annette Baudert, "Erziehungshilfe für vaterlose Kinder," *Unsere Jugend* 2 (1950); Oskar Hammelsbeck, "Sexualkrise und erzieherische Verantwortung," *Die Sammlung* 6 (1951): 282. See also David F. Smith, "Juvenile Delinquency in the British Zone of Germany, 1945–1951," *German History* 12 (1994).

15. Gustav von Mann, "Die gegenwärtige Jugendgefährdung," *Jugendwohl* 29 (1948): 18.

16. "Zur Jugendverwahrlosung," *Rundbrief der Referate Kinder- und Jugendfürsorge am Deutschen Caritasverband* (February 1946), p. 46.

17. Walter Cimbal, "Aufbau der Nachkriegsjugend," *Jugendwohl* 29 (1948): 11–17; "Öffentliche Erziehung—Freiwillige Erziehungshilfe und Fürsorgeerziehung," *Neues Beginnen* 8 (1953): 6. For similar remarks, see Hermann Nohl, "Die geistige Lage im gegenwärtigen Deutschland," *Die Sammlung* 2 (1947): p. 603.

18. There is a particularly useful critical discussion in two works by Robert G. Moeller: "Reconstructing the Family in Reconstruction Germany: Women and Social Policy in the Federal Republic, 1949–1955," *Feminist Studies* 15 (1989), and *Protecting Motherhood: Women and the Family in the Politics of Postwar West Germany* (Berkeley: University of California Press, 1993). See also Astrid Joosten, *Die Frau, das "segenspendende Herz der Familie": Familienpolitik und Frauenpolitik in der Ära Adenauer* (Pfaffenweiler: Centaurus, 1990); and Ursula Münch, *Familienpolitik in der Bundesrepublik Deutschland: Maßnahmen, Defizite, Organisation familienpolitischer Staatstätigkeit* (Freiburg: Lambertus, 1990). For a summary of contemporary views on the importance of the family, see Helmut Schelsky, *Die skeptische Generation* (Düsseldorf: Diederichs, 1957), pp. 135–138.

19. See Ingrid Langer, "Die Mohrinnen haben ihre Schuldigkeit getan.... Staatlich-moralische Aufrüstung der Familien," in *Die fünfziger Jahre: Beiträge zu Politik und Kultur,* ed. Dieter Bänsch (Tübingen: G. Narr, 1985), pp. 121–122, 124.

20. The total between 1950 and 1956 was 220 million marks. See "Die Jugenddebatte im Bundestag," *Jugendwohl* 37 (1956).

21. "Empfehlungen der Arbeitsgemeinschaft für Jugendpflege und Jugendfürsorge zur Behebung der Jugendberufsnot" [1951], BAK, Rep. B 153, no. 133, fols. 516–528.

22. Fr. Söhlmann, "Über die dringende Reform des Reichsjugendwohlfahrtsgesetzes," *Zentralblatt* 39, no. 4 (1952): 135.

23. On the question of vocational training, apprenticeships, and housing, see Mark Roseman, "The Organic Society and the 'Massenmenschen': Integrating Young Labour in the Ruhr Mines, 1945–1958," *German History* 8 (1990); on the Mutterschutzgesetz, see Robert G. Moeller, "Protecting Mother's Work: From Production to Reproduction in Potwar West Germany," *Journal of Social History* 22 (1989).

24. "Tagung der Arbeitsgemeinschaft der Länderreferenten für den Bundesjugendplan am 29./30.6.1951," in BAK, Rep. B 153, no. 136, fols. 36–41.

25. "Die Jugenddebatte im Bundestag," *Jugendwohl* 37 (1958).

26. "Die Rede des Bundesministers des Innern Gerhard Schröder vor dem Kuratorium für Jugendfragen am 14. Dezember 1954 in Bonn," BAK, Rep. B 153, no. 132, fols. 503–509.

27. "AFET: Bericht über die Fachberatung in Mannheim vom 19.–21.3.1950," *Zentralblatt* 37 (1950): 98.

28. Elisabeth Bamberger quoted in "Protokoll der Sitzung des Fachausschusses für Jugendrecht der Arbeitsgemeinschaft für Jugendpflege und Jugendfürsorge am 10./11.10.1951," ADCV, Rep. 481.045 I, fasc. 1949–1951.

29. "Der Allgemeine Fürsorge-Erziehungs-Tag 1950," *Unsere Jugend* 2 (1950): 161–166.

30. *Statistisches Handbuch für die Bundesrepublik Deutschland* 1962 (Stuttgart: Kohlhammer, 1962); Gustav von Mann, "Wandlungen in der Fürsorgeerziehung," *Unsere Jugend* 8 (1955): 343.

31. Walter Becker, "Die öffentliche Jugendhilfe im Berichtsjahr 1958/1959," *Jugendwohl* 41 (1960): 104–108.

32. Andreas Mehringer, "Reform der Anstalt," *Unsere Jugend* 1, no. 1 (1949): 13–15.

33. Figures from *Statistisches Handbuch für das Deutsche Reich* (1940) (Berlin: Reimar Hobbing, 1940); and *Statistisches Handbuch für die Bundesrepublik Deutschland* (Stuttgart: Kohlhammer, 1954, 1956, 1958, 1963, 1972).

34. See *Rundbrief der Referate Kinder- und Jugendfürsorge am Deutschen Caritasverband* (February 1946), pp. 14–16; "Denkschrift des Deutschen Vereins für öffentliche und private Fürsorge, betreffend eine Novelle zum Reichsjugendwohlfahrtsgesetz," ADCV, Rep. 481.045 Ib; "Die Grundgedanken der RJWG-Reform," in *Nachrichtendienst* 2 (1950): 25–29; "Denkschrift für die Vorbereitung einer Reform des Jugendwohlfahrtsrechts," *Nachrichtendienst* 6 (1950): 125–137.

35. "Grundgedanken," p. 28.

36. The officials of the Youth Bureau were to have nonvoting seats in the JWA. See "Aktennotiz. Betr. Sitzung des Jugendwohlfahrtsausschusses am 17.1.1950," BAK, Rep. B 153, no. 111, folio 112–117; AGJJ, "Stellungnahme zu dem Regierungsentwurf eines Gesetzes zur Änderung des RJWG vom 22 Juli 1952," ADW, CAW 118, no. 723, fols. 340–342; and Centralausschuss für Innere Mission, "Stellungnahme," ADW, CAW 118, no. 723, fols. 383–385.

37. "Stellungnahme des Central-Ausschuss für die Innere Mission der Deutschen Evangelischen Kirche zum Entwurf eines Gesetzes über Jugendpflege in Hessen," September 9, 1949, ADCV, Rep. 319.4 (SKF), no. E II.9a, fasc. 1. For the Catholic position, see Gustav von Mann, "Das Jugendamt neuer Ordnung," *Jugendwohl* 34 (1953): 70.

38. Hasenclever, *Jugendhilfe*, p. 187.

39. Erna Maraun, "Aus der Jugendförderungsarbeit in Berlin," *Unsere Jugend* 2 (1950): 417–422.

40. For an early attempt to introduce extensive EB at the socialist-dominated Youth Bureau in Prenzlauer Berg, Berlin, see Elizabeth Harvey, *Youth Welfare and Social Democracy in Weimar Germany: The Work of Walter Friedländer* (New Alyth, Perthshire: Lochee Publications, 1987). On the complicated development of psychotherapy under the Nazis, see Geoffrey Cocks, *Psychotherapy in the Third Reich: The Göring Institute* (New York: Oxford University Press, 1985).

41. Magistrat von Groß-Berlin, Hauptjugendamt, to Bundesministerium des Innern, August 24, 1950, BAK, Rep. B 153, no. 109, fols. 172–173.

42. A good example of doubts regarding the prevalence of organic brain defects is Adolf Busemann, "Scheinbarer Schwachsinn," *Jugendwohl* 31 (1952): 173–175. For an important and influential exception (Hermann Stutte of the AFET), see Jürgen Blankow, "'Fürsorgliche Bewahrung'—Kontinuitäten und Diskontinuitäten in der Bewahrung 'Asozialer,'" in *Erinnerungen einer Profession: Erziehungsberatung, Jugendhilfe und Nationalsozialismus,* ed. Renate Cogoy, Irene Kluge, and Brigitte Meckler (Münster: VOTUM, 1989), p. 138.

43. Magistrat von Groß-Berlin, Hauptjugendamt, to Bundesministerium des Innern, August 24, 1950, BAK, Rep. B 153, no. 109, fols. 172–173.

44. See Jürgen Blankow, "'Fürsorgliche Bewahrung,'" p. 139.

45. Magistrat von Groß-Berlin, Hauptjugendamt, to Bundesministerium des Innern, August 24, 1950, BAK, Rep. B 153, no. 109, fols. 172–173.

46. "Beiträge zur praktischen Jugendhilfe in Hessen. Heft 1: Erziehungsberatung und Heimerziehung," BAK, Rep. B 153, no. 108, fols. 406–430. The AFET also supported widespread EB; see "AFET fordert Erziehungsberatungsstellen," *Jugendwohl* 30 (1950): 143.

47. "Bundeseinheitliche Richtlinien für Erziehungsberatung," *Unsere Jugend* 6 (1954).

48. Hasenclever, *Jugendhilfe,* p. 320; Becker, "Die öffentliche Jugendhilfe," pp. 104–108. In 1959 there would have been about 11 million children aged five to nineteen in West Germany.

49. Ruth Feistkorn-Wacker, "Die Schuld der Eltern," *Unsere Jugend* 3 (1951): 202.

50. "Beiträge zur praktischen Jugendhilfe in Hessen," pp. 13–17. The other major sources of referrals were the Youth Bureaus (about a third) and the schools (about a fifth).

51. Rudolf Gunzert, *Organisation und Tätigkeit der Jugendämter in der Bundesrepublik Deutschland und West-Berlin 1957/1958* (Frankfurt: Institut für Sozialforschung, 1959), p. 5.

52. Ibid., table 42; and Hans Nootbar, "Sozialarbeit und Sozialpädagogik in der Bundesrepublik 1949–1962," in *Geschichte der Sozialarbeit: Hauptlinien ihrer Entwicklung im 19. und 20. Jahrhundert,* ed. Rolf Landwehr and Rüdeger Baron (Weinheim: Beltz, 1983), pp. 278, 279.

53. Gunzert, *Organisation,* table 28; and Nootbar, "Sozialarbeit und Sozialpädagogik," p. 279.

54. Max Würfflein, "Das Jugendamt—Selbst ein Stiefkind," *Unsere Jugend* 5 (1953): 140.

55. See, for example, "Überlegungen zu einem neuen Jugendhilfegesetz: A. Grundfragen an ein neues Jugendhilfegesetz," *Neues Beginnen* 11 (1958): 3; Elisabeth Bamberger, "Inwieweit wird das geltende Jugendwohlfahrtsrecht dem jungen Menschen in unserer Zeit gerecht?," *Mittelungen der Arbeitsgemeinschaft für Jugendpflege und Jugendfürsorge* 25 (July 1958): 11.

56. See Hanns Eyferth, "Restauration des Jugendamtes genügt nicht!," *Unsere Jugend* 4 (1952): 405, 404.

57. Christa Hasenclever, "Jugendwohlfahrt als gesellschaftliche Verpflichtung," *Neues Beginnen* 3 (1953): 6. Hasenclever was arguing for the restoration of paragraph 4 of the RJWG, but the same argument was advanced in the later reform as well.

58. Hanns Eyferth, "Psychologische Erkenntnisse und gewandelte pädagogische Einsichten," *Mittelungen der Arbeitsgemeinschaft für Jugendpflege und Jugendfürsorge* 25 (July 1958): 9.

59. Ernst Bornemann, "Erziehungsberatung in soziologischer Sicht," *Unsere Jugend* 9 (1957): 439.

60. Gerhard Wurzbacher, "Die Jugend in der Gesellschaft nach dem ersten Weltkrieg und heute," *Mitteilungen der Arbeitsgemeinschaft für Jugendpflege und Jugendfürsorge* 25 (July 1958): 1–3.

61. Eyferth, "Psychologische Erkenntnisse," p. 8.

62. Lotte Lemke, "Die freie Wohlfahrtspflege in den Wandlungen unserer Zeit," *Neues Beginnen* 12 (1957): 178.

63. Friedrich Rothe, "Gedanken zu einem Jugendhilfegesetz," *Unsere Jugend* 7 (1955): 385.

64. "Aufbau unseres Jugendwohlfahrtsrechts," ADCV, Rep. 319.4 (SKF), no. E II.7, fasc. 4.

65. Helmut Schelsky, *Die skeptische Generation* (Düsseldorf: Eugen Diederichs, 1957).

66. "Deutscher Fürsorgetag 1953," *Zentralblatt* 40 (1953): 251.

67. Heinz Fleckenstein, "Sittliche und religiöse Persönlichkeitsbildung und die heutige Gefährdung," *Jugendwohl* 34 (1953): 90–92.

68. Franz Prinz, "Die Jugendleiterin und Kindergärtnerin in der Situation der Zeit," *Jugendwohl* 34 (1953): 265–269. For a similar Protestant view, see Willy Lauk, "Grundlinien evangelischer Pädagogik," *Evangelische Jugendhilfe* 77 (1957): 68.

69. Fleckenstein, "Sittliche und religiöse Persönlichkeitsbildung," p. 93.

70. See Heide Fehrenbach, "The Fight for the 'Christian West': German Film Control, the Churches, and the Reconstruction of Civil Society in the Early Bonn Republic," *German Studies Review* 14 (1991).

71. "Wahrung der sittlichen Freiheit," *Jugendwohl* 34 (1953): 21–22.

72. "Vermerk über die Sitzung der Jugend- und Gefährdeten-Fürsorge der Diözese Trier in Verbindung mit dem Katholischen Fürsorgeverein, Dortmund, am 30. Juli 1952 in Trier," BAK, Rep. B 153, no. 108, fols. 127–130.

73. See "Grundsätze der Freiwilligen Filmselbstkontrolle der Filmwirtschaft," BAK, Rep. B 153, no. 108, fol. 357.

74. Unidentified [DCV?] "Stellungnahme zum Jugendschutzgesetz," ADCV, Rep. 232.20, fasc. 0. For the best exposition of the theory of *Jugendschutz,* see Walter Becker, *Kleines Handbuch des Jugendschutzes* (Berlin: Hermann Luchterhand, 1963).

75. Walter Becker, "Schutzbedürftige Jugend im Wandel der Gesellschaft," *Unsere Jugend* 8 (1956): 151.

76. Friedrich Rothe, "Die anstehenden Aufgaben des Bundes auf dem Gebiet der Jugendgesetzgebung," *Unsere Jugend* 10 (1958): 7.

77. Becker, "Schutzbedürftige Jugend," p. 148.

78. "Warum geht die Jugend ins Kino?," *Jugendwohl* 32 (1951): 298–299.

79. Quoted in Paul Ascher, "Revolution der Jugend?," *Unsere Jugend* 10 (1958): 184. For a contrasting view, see Walter Gerson, "Das Geltungsbetrieb als pädagogisches Problem," *Die Sammlung* 11 (1956): esp. 259.

80. Fleckenstein, "Sittliche und religiöse Persönlichkeitsbildung," p. 95.

81. Ernst Ell, "Zwang oder Freiheit in der Erziehung," *Jugendwohl* 38 (1957): 96.

82. Ernst Ell, "Die Problematik der Erziehung junger Menschen," *Jugendwohl* 38 (1957): 267; and idem, "Der Gehorsam in der Krise der Zeit," *Jugendwohl* 42 (1961): 281.

83. Wolfgang Fischer, "Erziehung um der Freiheit der Menschen willen," *Evangelische Jugendhilfe* 78 (1958): 97.
84. Franz-Josef Wehnes, "Das Kind in der heutigen Verbrauchergesellschaft," *Jugendwohl* 40 (1959): 243–244.
85. Andreas Mehringer, "Über moderne und mißverstandene 'moderne' Erziehung," *Unsere Jugend* 7 (1955): 487, 488, 489, 491, 493.
86. Gerhard Fangmeier, "Verträgt sich heutige Menschenführung mit Strafe?," *Evangelische Jugendhilfe* 73 (1953): 43.
87. See Hans Wollasch, "Tiefenpsychologie in der Sicht katholischer Erziehung," *Jugendwohl* 34 (1953): 306–307.
88. Waltraud Krützfeld-Eckhard, "Für und gegen die Technik sozialer Arbeit," *Evangelische Jugendhilfe* 75 (1955): 45, 49.
89. Karl Janssen, "Freiheit und Bindung als grundsätzliche Frage der Sozialpädagogik," *Evangelische* Jugendhilfe 73 (1953): 98.
90. "Bundeseinheitliche Richtlinien," p. 273.
91. Kurt Nachbauer, "Umfassende Jugendhilfe: Gedanken über einen Zehnjahresweg," *Jugendwohl* 37 (1956): 5, 6.
92. "Niederschrift über die Sitzung des Fachausschusses für Kinder- und Jugendfürsorge am 26. und 27. September 1950 in Münster i. Westfalen," pp. 8 and 10, ADCV, Rep. 319.4 (SKF), no. A II.5o, fasc. 3.
93. "Fachausschuss des Deutschen Vereins für öffentliche und private Fürsorge und der Arbeitsgemeinschaft für Jugendpflege und Jugendfürsorge, Sitzung 8.12. 1949," p. 17, BAK, Rep. B 153, no. 111, fols. 40–54.
94. Gustav von Mann, "Anwalt der Jugend," *Jugendwohl* 34 (1953): 5.
95. "Stellungnahme zu dem Entwurf eines Gesetzes zur Änderung von Vorschriften des Reichsjugend-Wohlfahrts-Gesetzes," BAK, Rep. B 153, no. 111, fols. 136–139.
96. See "Novelle zum RJWG," *Informationsdienst* of the Bund der deutschen katholischen Jugend, December 22, 1952, BAK, Rep. B 153, no. 111, fols. 163–167.
97. *Verhandlungen des Bundestages,* I. Wahlperiode 1949, document no. 3641, "Entwurf eines Gesetzes zur Änderung von Vorschriften des Reichsjugendwohlfahrtsgesetzes"; and President of the Deutscher Bundestag, to Bundesministerium des Innern, June 19, 1953, app. 1 to Rothe, "Vermerk, Betr.: Grundgedanken eines neuen Jugendhilfegesetzes," ADCV, Rep. 481.045 Ib.
98. Bamberger, "Inwieweit wird das geltende Jugendwohlfahrtsrecht dem jungen Menschen in unserer Zeit gerecht?" *Mitteilungen der AGJJ* 25 (1958): 14.
99. Ibid., pp. 11, 12.
100. Gustav von Mann, "Anwalt der Jugend," *Jugendwohl* 34 (1953): 3.
101. A good example is J. David, S.J., "Unersetzliche Bedeutung der Familie für Leben und Formung des jungen Menschen—heute," *Grundfragen des Jugendhilferechts* (Berlin: Heymanns, 1962).
102. Toni Thurnreit, "Vorrang der behördlichen Jugendpflege?," *Jugendwohl* 40 (1959): 209.
103. There is a particularly clear discussion in Walter Kutschbach, "Streitobjekt Jugendhilfe," *Recht der Jugend* 9 (1961): 145–146.
104. Ibid., p. 4.

105. Elisabeth Zillken to Friedrich Rothe, March 18, 1958, ADCV, Rep. 319.4 (SKF), no. E II.7, fasc. 4; Friedrich Rothe, "Gedanken zu einem Jugendhilfegesetz," pp. 1, 2, 15, ADCV, Rep. 319.4 (SKF), no. E II.7, fasc. 4.

106. Friedrich Rothe, "Nochmals: das Subsidiaritätsprinzip in der Jugendarbeit der Gemeinden," reprinted from *Kommunalpolitische Blätter* 18 (1953) in ADW, CA-West 118, no. 723, fols. 146–149 (quotation p. 7).

107. Quoted in Kerstin Bast and Ilona Ostner, "Ehe und Familie in der Sozialpolitik der DDR und BRD—ein Vergleich," in *Sozialpolitik im Prozeß der deutschen Vereinigung*, ed. Winfried Schähl (Frankfurt am Main: Campus, 1992), p. 251.

108. Hugo Möller, "Massengesellschaft und Du-Vergessenheit," *Die Sammlung* 9 (1954): 575; Alexander Rüstow, "Wohlfahrtsstaat oder Selbstverantwortung?," *Die Sammlung* 11 (1956): 370.

109. *Verhandlungen des Deutschen Bundestages, Stenographische Berichte*, 49: 9505.

110. M, "Aus der Arbeit des Katholischen Fürsorgevereins," *Jugendwohl* 34 (1953): 458.

111. Lotte Lemke, "Die freie Wohlfahrtspflege in den Wandlungen unserer Zeit," *Neues Beginnen* (1957): 179. Figures from Lotte Lemke, "Die Arbeiterwohlfahrt—Situation, Grundlagen, Ziel," *Neues Beginnen* (October 1951): 1.

112. Elisabeth Bamberger, "Ein Streitgespräch," *Unsere Jugend* 8 (1956).

113. Elisabeth Bamberger and Gustav von Mann, "Vorschläge für ein neues Jugendwohlfahrtsgesetz," *Mitteilungen der Arbeitsgemeinschaft für Jugendpflege und Jugendfürsorge* 24 (April 1958): 2–4.

114. "Ergebnisprotokoll über die Sitzung der Sonderkomission Jugendrecht in Königstein vom 20.-25.1.1958," and "Ergebnisprotokoll über die 2. Sitzung der Sonderkomission Jugendrecht in Stuttgart-Degerloch vom 18.–21.3. 1958," both in ADCV, Rep. 319.4 (SKF), no. E II.7, fasc. 4.

115. On Wuermeling, see Spott, *Churches and Politics*, pp. 282–283.

116. Drafts were produced in October 1958; in March, May, June, and August 1959; and in January and February 1960. All the drafts can be found in ADCV, Rep. 232.20, fascs. 1, 2, and 3.

117. Quoted in Andreas Wollasch, *Der Katholische Fürsorgeverein für Mädchen, Frauen und Kinder* (Freiburg: Lambertus, 1991), p. 134.

118. Manfred Müller, "Eine neue Novelle zum Reichsjugendwohlfahrtsgesetz," *Sozialpädagogik* 3 (1961): 81.

119. Innere Mission der Evangelischen Kirche in Deutschland and Jugendkammer der Evangelischen Kirche in Deutschland, "Anmerkungen zu dem Vorentwurf eines Jugendhilfegesetzes," ADCV, Rep. 319.4 (SKF), no. E II.7, fasc. 3.

120. "Überlegungen zu einen neuen Jugendhilfegesetz," *Neues Beginnen* (1958): 169.

121. "Subsidiarität—ein Prüfstein der Demokratie?," *Neues Beginnen* (1956): 170.

122. Paul Neuermann, "Jugendhilfe—Aufgabe der Gemeinde? Das Gesetz ist ein Misstrauensvotum gegen die Städte," *Welt*, June 16–17, 1961, ADCV, Rep. 319.4 (SKF), no. E II.7, fasc. 4.

123. Hasenclever, "Öffentliche Erziehungshilfe im Umbruch?," p. 3.

124. Lemke, "Die freie Wohlfahrtspflege," p. 180. See also Christa Hasenclever, "Probleme der Reform des Jugendhilferechts—Stellungnahme der Arbeiterwohlfahrt," *Neues Beginnen* 10 (1959): 147; Erdmuthe Falkenberg, "Zur Subsidiarität der öffentlichen Jugendhilfe," *Zentralblatt* 46 (1959): 315–316; and "Überlegungen," p. 163.

125. Walter Kutschbach, "Streitobjekt Jugendhilfe," *Recht der Jugend* 9 (1961): 146–147.

126. *Verhandlungen des Deutschen Bundestages, 3. Wahlperiode, Stenographische Berichte,* 49:9504, 9505, 9509, 9514.

127. "Jugendwohlfahrtsnovelle im Bundestag," *Jugendwohl* 42 (1962): 96.

128. *Verhandlungen des Deutschen Bundestages,* p. 9541; ibid., p. 9507 (Deputy Rommerskirchen).

129. For the new law, see Bundesgesetzblatt 1, August 16, 1961, pp. 1193–1205. The law also made several minor changes in other sections of the RJWG—for example, raising the age to which foster children were under the oversight of the Youth Bureau, rechristening protective supervision "educational assistance," and introducing oversight over the reformatories by the State Youth Bureaus.

130. See, for example, Arbeiterwohlfahrt Bundesverband e.V., *Vorschläge für ein Erweitertes Jugendhilferecht* (Bonn: Arbeiterwohlfahrt, 1970), pp. 17, 20, calling for the abandonment of the style of "thinking of the old authoritarian administrative state" in favor of that of the "service state." See also AGJJ and Fachhochschule für Sozialarbeit und Sozialpädagogik, Berlin, *60 Jahre Gesetz für Jugendwohlfahrt, 1922–1982: Dokumentation einer Tagung am 15. Oktober 1982 in Berlin* (Berlin: AGJJ, 1983). For an excellent example and compendium of criticisms of the JWG and the Youth Bureaus in the 1960s, see Elke Fluk, *Jugendamt und Jugendhilfe im Spiegel der Fachliteratur—Analyse und Kritik der Diskussion 1950–1970* (Munich: Deutsches Jugendinstitut, 1972).

131. For the CDU's arguments against the law, see Reinhard Wiesner, "Der mühsame Weg zu einem neuen Jugendhilfegesetz," *Recht der Jugend und des Bildungswesens* 38 (1990): 117.

132. Hubertus Junge, "Das neue Kinder- und Jugendhilfegesetz," *Caritas '91: Jahrbuch des Deutschen Caritasverbandes* (Freiburg: DCV, 1990), p. 86.

133. Monika Pankoke-Schenk, "Agnes Neuhaus (1854–1944)," in *Zeitgeschichte in Lebensbildern,* ed. Rudolf Morsey et al. (Mainz: Grünewald, 1980), 4:139.

134. See Johannes Münder, "Das neue Kinder- und Jugendhilfegesetz," *Neue Praxis* 20 (1990): 348, 351, 352.

Conclusion

1. Quoted in Anne Taylor Allen, *Feminism and Motherhood in Germany, 1800–1914* (New Brunswick, N.J.: Rutgers University Press, 1991), p. 218.

2. "Petition des Centralausschusses für Innere Mission an das preussische Abgeordneten-Haus, betreffend das Vormundschafts-Gesetz," *Fliegende Blätter* 31 (1874): 360; Gustav von Rohden, "Bedeutung der Rettungshäuser für das öffentliche Leben," *Fliegende Blätter* 55 (1898): 272–275.

3. See, for example, T. H. Marshall, *Citizenship and Social Class* (Cambridge: Cambridge University Press, 1950); idem, *Social Policy in the Twentieth Century* (London: Hutchinson, 1967); Reinhard Bendix, *Work and Authority in Industry* (New York: Wiley, 1956); Peter Flora and Jens Alber, "Modernization, Democratization, and the Development of Welfare States in Western Europe," in *The Development of Welfare States in Europe and America,* ed. Peter Flora and Arnold J. Heidenheimer (New Brunswick, N.J.: Transaction, 1982); and Herbert Ehrenberg and Anke Fuchs, *Sozialstaat und Freiheit: Von der Zukunft des Sozialstaats* (Frankfurt: Suhrkamp, 1980). For child welfare, see, for example, Hans Scherpner, *Geschichte der Jugendfürsorge,* ed. Hanna Scherpner (Göttingen: Vandenhoeck & Ruprecht, 1969).

4. See Jochen-Christoph Kaiser, "NS-Volkswohlfahrt und freie Wohlfahrtspflege im Dritten Reich," in *Politische Formierung und soziale Erziehung im Nationalsozialismus,* ed. Hans-Uwe Otto and Heinz Sünker (Frankfurt am Main: Suhrkamp, 1992), pp. 78–80; H.-U. Otto and H. Sünker, "Volksgemeinschaft als Formierungsideologie des Nationalsozialismus. Zur Genesis und Geltung von 'Volkspflege,'" ibid., p. 65.

5. See, for example, Rudolph Bauer, ed., *Die Liebe Not: Zur historischen Kontinuität der "Freien Wohlfahrtspflege"* (Weinheim & Basel: Belt, 1984).

6. Detlev J. K. Peukert, *Inside Nazi Germany: Conformity, Opposition, and Racism in Everyday Life,* trans. Richard Deveson (New Haven: Yale University Press, 1987), p. 213.

7. See Detlev J. K. Peukert, *Grenzen der Sozialdisziplinierung: Aufstieg und Krise der deutschen Jugendfürsorge, 1878–1932* (Cologne: Bund Verlag, 1986); Jacques Donzelot, *The Policy of Families* (New York: Pantheon, 1979).

8. Peukert, *Grenzen,* p. 18.

9. Ibid., p. 23; for Peukert's term *Ordnungsutopien,* see p. 19.

10. Ibid., pp. 22, 21.

11. Donzelot, *Policing,* p. 103.

12. Peukert, *Grenzen,* p. 77.

13. Donzelot, *Policing,* pp. 174–175, 187.

14. See, among others, Michael Prinz, "Wohlfahrtsstaat, Modernisierung und Nationalsozialismus. Thesen zu ihrem Verhältnis," in *Soziale Arbeit und Faschismus,* ed. Hans-Uwe Otto and Heinz Sünker (Frankfurt am Main: Suhrkamp, 1989); and Hans-Uwe Otto and Heinz Sünker, "Volksgemeinschaft als Formierungsideologie des Nationalsozialismus. Zu Genesis und Geltung von 'Volkspflege'," in *Politische Formierung und soziale Erziehung im Nationalsozialismus,* ed. Otto and Sünker (Frankfurt am Main: Suhrkamp, 1992).

15. Quoted in Ernst Klee, *"Euthanasie" im NS-Staat: Die "Vernichtung lebensunwerten Lebens"* (Frankfurt am Main: Fischer, 1983), p. 335.

16. Paul Weindling, while he convincingly demonstrates the authoritarian potentials of scientific "medicalization" and the professionalization of medicine, presents a particularly nuanced picture, and one that suggests the extent to which the outcome of these processes in Germany was the product of particular political and social circumstances. See Paul Weindling, *Health, Race, and German Politics between National Unification and Nazism* (Cambridge: Cambridge University Press, 1989), esp. pp. 184, 226, 398, 470–477, 493–497, 574.

17. "Petition des Bundes Deutscher Frauenvereine zur Regelung der Erwerbsarbeit der Kinder," quoted in Allen, *Feminism and Motherhood,* p. 147.

18. Of course, particularly in Catholic thought, Christian principles were already being interpreted quite aggressively in the 1930s as an alternative to "Bolshevism," capitalism, *and* fascism, all of which were denounced (sometimes almost in the same breath) as expressions either of the tyranny of the masses over the individual, or of an exaggerated spirit of individualism. See, for example, Hans Wollasch, "Erschütterung und Bestand der Familie," *Jugendwohl* 20 (1931): 106; W., "Kollektivismus," *Jugendwohl* 20 (1931): 295–296; Anna Zillken, "Staatsbürgerliche Erziehung," *Jugendwohl* 22 (1933): 229–234.

19. Heinz Sünker, "Soziale Arbeit im Nationalsozialismus: 'Endlösung der sozialen Frage'?," *Neue Praxis* 20 (1990): 356.

20. Detlev J. K. Peukert, "The Genesis of the 'Final Solution' from the Spirit of Science," in *Nazism and German Society, 1933–1945,* ed. David F. Crew (London: Routledge, 1994).

Index